Margaret Morris

ITALY

FROM THE RISORGIMENTO TO FASCISM

ITALY

FROM THE RISORGIMENTO TO FASCISM

AN INQUIRY INTO THE ORIGINS OF THE TOTALITARIAN STATE

EDITED WITH

AN INTRODUCTION BY

A. WILLIAM SALOMONE

DAVID & CHARLES NEWTON ABBOT

ISBN 0 7153 5249 0

First published 1970 in the United States of America
by Anchor Books, Doubleday & Company Inc

First published 1971 in Great Britain
by David & Charles (Publishers) Limited

Printed in Great Britain
by Redwood Press Limited Trowbridge Wilts
for David & Charles (Publishers) Limited
South Devon House Newton Abbot
Devon

To those young Italians
who fought and died
in the struggle against Fascism
to reopen all the possibilities
of the Risorgimento

CONTENTS

THE CONFLICT OF HISTORICAL OPINION

"Italian life after 1900 had overcome the chief obstacles in its course, and, confining itself within the channels imposed upon it, flowed on for the next ten years and more, rich both in achievement and in hope. It was not that Italy entered upon a period of felicity, or 'golden age,' for such times are known neither to philosophy nor history, and perhaps not even to poetry. But, as in the life of the individual there are years when a man reaps the fruit of the pains which he has endured and the experiences which he has gathered and suffered, and is able to work easily and freely without attaining to what is called felicity, or even thinking that he has attained it, so it is in the life of nations. He who has eyes for what is vital and characteristic . . . will discern, in the course of history certain definite times of refreshment and peace, cheerfulness and prosperity. Such were for Italy the years in which the ideal of a liberal regime was most fully realized. . . ."

BENEDETTO CROCE (1928)

"This is a stereotype, an artificial and, on the whole, a false picture: at any rate it is insufficient to give a genuine view of the Italy of that time. . . . The truth is that Croce is desperately fighting against today's [Fascist] Italy; and every one of his judgments upon the past, from 1871 to 1915, becomes colored by the reflections of this battle. . . ."

GIOACCHINO VOLPE (1928)

"If it were true that in Italy there has never been democracy, the Fascists would be in a strong position in maintaining that the Italian people is not made for democracy; to the historical experience which would be in favor of the Fascists, we would only oppose an act of faith which no one would be obliged to share, if that experience were true. Furthermore, no one would succeed any more in understanding what the Fascists have done in Italy, if they have not destroyed democracy . . ."

GAETANO SALVEMINI (1927)

"At the beginning of the twentieth century Italian politics necessarily culminated in *giolittismo,* after a reactionary parenthesis which was sufficient to corrupt the program and the spirit of the emerging socialist party and to demonstrate the danger to which liberty in Italy is always exposed. . . . Italy owes Giolitti ten years of social peace and honest administration. . . ."

PIERO GOBETTI (1924)

"The conquest of liberty was not bound in Italy with any mass movement capable of playing its role as myth and precursor. The masses were absent. The proletariat was not able to conquer its special freedoms of organization, the right to strike, the right to vote at the price of efforts and long-range sacrifices. Its apprenticeship around 1900 proved too brief. . . ."

CARLO ROSSELLI (1929)

"'Concession'? Even for this word everything depends upon the meaning we give it. If 'to concede' means to stop a resistance which has become very dangerous, we can say that Giolitti 'conceded' freedom to organize and to strike to the workers. . . . Giolitti had the good sense to understand that it was necessary to change ways or to change route and not to continue—given the new social and psychological conditions of the Italian people [after 1900]—the policy of the blindered mule. It would be foolish to deny him that good sense. But it should be made clear that when Giolitti undertook to make that 'concession' the Italian workers had already taken that concession for themselves, thanks to their sacrifices and to their determination."

GAETANO SALVEMINI (1952)

". . . I am not sure, but I do not believe that one can define those regimes which we had before Fascism as having been democratic . . ."

FERRUCCIO PARRI (1945)

"On the eve of the War of 1914–18, Giolitti was the most powerful man in Parliament, but the most unpopular man in the country. Italian democracy was in the making. Italian democracy would have needed still another generation of trial and error before becoming not a 'perfect democracy' but a 'less imperfect democracy.' The crisis that followed the First World War, however, was fatal to that democratic process. . . ."

GAETANO SALVEMINI (1945)

"It is absurd to pretend that Giovanni Giolitti, a political man emerged from the old bourgeois and conservative class, should have been the harbinger of a renovation of Italian society. However, it cannot be denied that among the politicians of his epoch he appears today the one who more than others had understood what the direction was toward which Italian society should have moved in order to overcome the contrasts of his times. . . . But that democracy, as we now know, could not progress, and when it is impossible to progress one must go back or be overwhelmed. History has given us proof of this, and the study of the man and his times reveals the reason to us. There is no progress possible for democracy in the modern world until the working class shall have asserted itself as a participant in the direction of the life of the country and a protagonist in it. . . ."

PALMIRO TOGLIATTI (1950)

"Mussolini was not completely inaccurate in saying that his movement was an extension or development of the national revolution of the 19th century. One can think this and still stop a long way short of believing that Fascism was an inevitable consequence of the risorgimento. . . . The megalomaniac folly of one man and his friends could not by itself have caused such a gigantic tragedy if it had not fitted into some larger process. Mussolini was a plagiarist and an eclectic in both his doctrine and his tactics. His movement can hardly be presented in any convincing perspective until its ancestry has been traced back into Italian and European history. And by thus delving back into the past one may incidentally learn something that might be of political value to the present."

DENIS MACK SMITH (1949)

"If Mussolini was continually being called *duce,* even in the early stages of his socialist period, this fact did not necessarily predestine him to be the 'Duce of Fascism.' The fact that from childhood on he possessed the temperament of a *condottiere* is a precondition for his later life, but it is not sufficient to determine its direction. A second, equally important motivation in his life is the fact that from his earliest days his father filled him with socialist ideas and introduced him to socialist literature. . . . The early possession of a political faith (*fede*) is no less decisive for Mussolini than the psychic disposition to be a *condottiere.*"

ERNST NOLTE (1963)

"The revisionist critique of the Risorgimento and the Liberal era . . . amounts to a series of variations on a single historiographical theme. This theme, it seems to me, is the recurring concept that at every critical stage, at every crucial moment, Italian history somehow failed to realize the promise intrinsic to the actual historical situation. Each moment of great crisis is then seen as resolving itself, obviously through the combination and predominant play of negative forces, into an essential, an organic 'failure.' In this manner, the whole of Italian history becomes subsumed under the negative concept of *rivoluzione mancata.*"

A. WILLIAM SALOMONE (1962)

". . . Today all the possibilities of the Risorgimento have been reopened for Italians: no gesture is useless if it is not an end unto itself."

GIAIME PINTOR (1943)

INTRODUCTION

In name and pristine character the twentieth-century historical phenomenon known as Fascism was an original Italian product. During the days of its triumph it claimed many European "mothers," but only one Italian "father"—Benito Mussolini. After two decades of that triumph, at what was to prove the beginning of its end in Italy, during the first years of the Second World War (1940–43), no less an authority than Sir Winston Churchill (who had not always been so certain either about Mussolini's "evil" character nor about the "immorality" of Fascism) stated that "one man and one man alone," Mussolini, was to be held responsible for Italian Fascism and for the disasters which his decision to fight against the Allied Powers would bring to his country.[1] In thus characterizing the relationship between Mussolini and Fascism, Churchill had made a portentous statement with very important political, ethical, and historical implications. Was he speaking as a leader of a coalition of military forces arrayed against the Nazi-Fascist bid for mastery over Europe, as a Conservative British politician, or as a student of Italian, European, and world history, or as all three at the same time—and what did his words really mean?

If "one man alone," Mussolini, was responsible

[1] See Churchill's speech of December 23, 1940, in The New York *Times,* December 24, 1940. For interpretations of Churchill's speech and his later pronouncements on Mussolini and Fascism, see Norman Kogan, *Italy and the Allies* (Cambridge, Mass., 1956), 190–91; Gaetano Salvemini, *Prelude to World War II* (Garden City, N. Y., 1954), 7–8.

for the rule of Fascism in Italy and for the ruin it would bring to his people through ultimate defeat, what would be the juridical, moral, and historical "case" against his regime and his country once this "one man" had fallen from power? This is in fact what occurred during a night and a day on July 24–25, 1943, when Mussolini received a vote of no confidence in his own Fascist Grand Council and later was dropped by the King, Victor Emmanuel III, who, on a fateful day in October 1922, had appointed him Premier of Italy without parliamentary consultation, had soon seen him turn into an absolute dictator over his people.[2] Now, in July 1943, Mussolini was dismissed and arrested. Would any "war-guilt" claims against Italy be foregone and forgotten now that this "one man alone" had been "caught" and could be held accountable for *his* international actions? Would the "case" against his regime, the Fascist ruling class, the hierarchs, the party members, the fellow-travelers, and the victimized bulk of the Italian people be automatically dropped for lack of relevance if not of evidence? No such thing, of course, happened at the end of the war in 1945, nor was the matter quite so simple. The question of Mussolini's personal guilt and of the collective responsibility that devolved upon his regime, found a way of becoming fused and confused on all sides—this, despite the fact that Churchill himself finally modified though not fully did retrace his steps in his verdict on the Duce.

[2] On the fall of Mussolini, see Ruggero Zangrandi, *1943: 25 luglio–8 settembre* (Milan, 1964), 38–119; Gianfranco Bianchi, *25 luglio: crollo di un regime* (Milan, 1964), is a voluminous study of that night and a day of July 24–25, 1943.

No less important was the question of whether a number of Italians themselves would accept Churchill's preventive pronouncement on Mussolini and Fascism. For had they done so outright they would have no political or moral "case" against anyone from their own midst who had flagrantly shared, enjoyed, or profited by the Duce's dictatorship at the expense of the helpless masses of the people. This aspect of the verdict could not be accepted by all those persons, parties, and Italian political personalities who, whether in Italy or in exile, had for many years suffered persecutions, privations, and imprisonment—and seen their anti-Fascist comrades die —not only, and often not so much, as a result of the implacable hostility of "one man alone," but through the iron laws of the Fascist regime as a system of government and as a ferociously exclusive ruling establishment that had brooked no dissent and no opposition. During the last bitter period of the War (1943–45), the Italian anti-Fascist Resistance movement, which had risen at the very moment of the assertion and triumph of Fascism itself in Italy and had for long fought against it underground or from exile, courageously struggled less against "one man alone," who, in a real sense, had become impotent after July 1943, than against the remnants of his system, against the fearful "Black Brigades" which, especially in North Italy, continued to co-operate with the German SS toward insuring the Nazi-Fascist military and political power in Italy.[3] Could

[3] On the armed phase of the Italian Resistance, see Charles F. Delzell, *Mussolini's Enemies. The Italian Anti-Fascist Resistance* (Princeton, 1961), Part II. An almost classic work on the Italian Resistance movement is that of

or would the anti-Fascist Resistance, of which that irreconcilable foe of Fascism, Ferruccio Parri, was to become the recognized leader, accept either the sort of "Fascism without Mussolini" that gripped North Italy until the Liberation in April 1945, or the prospect of a "return to the normalcy" of the pre-Fascist period in which such "accomplices" of Fascism as the Monarchy would be retained as the central national institution? Generous as it sounded, Churchill's simple phrase, "one man alone," proved misguided in this respect, too. Thus neither the practical-political nor the ethical-institutional implications of the Churchillian dictum seemed to correspond to acceptable realities, where either the external or the internal enemies of Fascism were concerned.

But was Churchill's famous apothegm perhaps closer to the truth in another sense, in a kind of third dimension? In other words, does it possibly crystallize an acceptable historical judgment in spite of its defects for practical and ethical purposes? It is, as a matter of fact, when this pronouncement—and similar ones—are transposed from the sphere of practical and ethical considerations to that of historical judgment that the question of invalidity or accuracy, much less historical error or truth, becomes even more paradoxical and complicated, and truly problematical. This anthology on modern Italy seeks, among other things, to provide some materials which may aid the attentive reader in formulating an appraisal of his own, based on a variety of evidence and a diversity of approaches to the prob-

---

Roberto Battaglia, *Storia della Resistenza italiana: 8 settembre 1943–25 aprile 1945* (new ed. Turin, 1964).

lem of the origins, nature, and meaning of Fascism seen against the perspective of Italian history since the Risorgimento.

Since in the very first section of this collection of readings I have included a large part of an article which critically discusses the context and major expressions of the historiographical problem that has had as its implicit or explicit backdrop within its post-1945 Italian framework the question of the origins of Fascism in Italy (H. Stuart Hughes's piece immediately following it further illustrates other terms of the problem), I will not elaborate at this point upon certain substantive particulars of the question. On the other hand, for a better understanding of the rationale I have adopted for the selection and the presentation of the readings, a minimum of factual elucidation seems necessary in this context.

That there is an almost inescapable element of subjective selectivity in any such collection of readings as this need hardly be stressed. In history, no one has as yet constructed sets of indisputable mathematical-geometrical formulas through which past or present reality may be approached with any modicum of certainty. In selecting from a vast body of contradictory historical materials, I have been very conscious of the subjective element at work. Wherever possible or desirable, therefore, I have sought to "balance" subjectivity by including selections with whose message or method I personally or professionally disagree, fully cognizant as I have tried to be of the possibility that my disagreement may matter only to me. More important, since the historical problem that is the focus of this anthology may itself seem either too obscure or too remote from the immediate intellectual or cultural concerns of those whose encounters with modern Italian history may have been for some reason casual, marginal, or somehow diluted within larger treatments of European or world history, I have given special emphasis to three factors: (a) the presentation of the readings in such a way as not only to obviate too much dependence upon other references but also to give them coherence through topical arrangement and prefatory explication; (b) an analytical chronological summary of a century of Italian history compiled in such a way as to facilitate comprehension of events, facts, and developments which are referred to in the selections themselves; and (c) a topical-critical series of "suggestions for additional reading" which, I trust, within the limitations imposed by space and linguistic requirements, may prove a working bibliography for those who may wish to pursue in greater depth or breadth problems raised by their exposure to modern Italian history in this anthology.

Though there are many categorical historical assertions throughout most of the readings I have selected for this anthology, there is little "pure history" in the mathematical-geometric sense. A variety of interpretations and points of views are presented, and some are more or less important than others. Taken together, they may spell not "pure" but "live" history. Under the guise of successive historical or historiographical "debates," members of at least two generations of Italians, as well as non-Italians—young and old, philosophers and historians, ideologues and intellectuals, moralists and polemicists, thinkers and activists—are seen grappling with a momentous historical problem. On one level this problem concerns the question of how, from the bosom of a liberal, democratic, or even socialist society, such as the Risorgimento and its aftermath strove to create in Italy, there could spring such an organic denial of that society's sacred values as Fascism represented. Connected with this question is the theoretically more fundamental problem concerning the role of continuity and contingency, of normal development and accident, of evolution, revolution, and counter-revolution in history. Is there "logic" in history, or does caprice or fortuitousness rule it? How does liberalism generate reaction, and democracy lead to dictatorship? What part does force play in creating or destroying a state, what function does active or passive consent exercize in the transformation of a nation? What is the relationship between the masses of the people and the ruling political classes? How much, and exactly how, can "one man alone" act in history? In what ways, through what means, with what consequences does the tragic element in life and history tend to emerge again and again brutally to dispel the grand illusions that vivify rational, idyllic, or Arcadian visions of the world? These are some of the questions that, it is to be hoped, will be directly or indirectly raised by parts or the whole of this anthology.

In its basic organization, substance, and purpose, this collection of readings addresses itself to a concrete historical problem. However theoretical and abstract, personal and political, or ideological and philosophical the forms in which the problem may appear to be couched by some of the "witnesses" themselves, its essence refers to a tangible historical cluster of events that, at a certain moment during the first quarter of the twentieth century, constituted the passage of Italy from a liberal order of politics to a dictatorial government and then to a totalitarian regime. There were elements in that "passage" that obviously transcended the purely Italian-national confines. In 1922 Italy was an integral part and function of a larger European context of society and culture that could not be escaped. Indeed, some significant factors in the Italian problem concerning Fascism and its antecedents were aspects of a vaster crisis in European life and politics, in events and values that lay beyond the making or control of any single nation or people. In a profound sense, the First World War and its aftermath had shaken to their very foundations the way of life and the sustaining principles of Europe's liberal civilization of the pre-1914 era. But the Italian experience of the post-war period that resulted in Fascism was also unique, and it is that uniqueness that must be kept in mind by the student of history. Historical understanding fundamentally consists of a continuous intellectual effort to separate and correlate, to see the whole, but only through a knowledge of the parts, and, in so far as possible, to do so without unchanging assumptions as to "causes" or inflexible preconceptions of patterns of process. To achieve such an understanding is not an easy task, but it is necessary if history is not to be confused with different, and often more facile, modes of knowledge.

Face to face with the Italian tragedy of the twentieth century, the victory of Fascism, it is infinitely easier to have recourse to pseudohistorical or metahistorical explanations than to labor systematically, intelligently and imaginatively, at ferreting out the sources of that tragedy. As a matter of fact, some careless pseudoscientists of "society," not the serious social scientists, witless fanatics of irrational intuition, not committed moralists, and sensation-mongering "historical" journalists, not serious observers of historical reality, tend to debase history into their own special "dismal science," senselessly formulating prejudiced abstractions in a vacuum of human values. By ignoring the concreteness of historical vicissitudes, they preclude men's responsibility for individual or collective action; and by forgetting that ever-present decisive margin of choice that, within whatever cycles of necessity, every generation possesses toward the making of its own history, they merely use and abuse history until they convert it into a kind of sophisticated palmistry that pretends to read the "destiny" of peoples, of nations, and of civilizations from the presumed configurations they discover in their "eternal character."

The major assumption underlying this collection of readings in modern Italian history is—despite occasional assertions to the contrary made by some of the "witnesses" themselves—that Fascism was not "predestined" in Italy by some such abstraction as the "Italian character" nor by some "providential" or demoniacal force built into Italian history. No historical era is ever completely beyond the control of the generation that lives, acts or suffers through its unfolding. The structure of this presentation, in fact, has been designed with a view toward facilitating comprehension not merely of a theoretical conflict of opinion but also—and even more—of a concentric dialectic between historical time and human action, between men and ideas, between leaders and movements, and between active political forces in search of power and passive social forces in quest of security, justice, or peace. It was the outcome of *this* conflict that, after all, spelled the transformation of modern Italy from a liberal-democratic country into a totalitarian dictatorship under the command of Benito Mussolini. It is perhaps only when it is placed within some such context, within such dimensions, that the rise of Fascism through the fateful Italian national crisis of 1919–22 can be intelligibly reconstructed as well from the other two perspectives of pre-Fascism and post-Fascism in Italy. The complex *background* of Italian *historical* problems after the Risorgimento and the controversial *foreground* of Italian *historiographical* questions after the fall of the dictatorship thus become linked to a concrete historical situation. Within the limitations of space and selectivity, this anthology seeks to help the student toward a serious study of Fascism by suggesting and, wherever possible, presenting a triple angle of vision of Fascism—that is, as the victor in the post-1919 Italian struggle for power, as a "function" of its Italian past, and as the subject of reappraisals in the light of its present during its hegemonic rule and subsequently, after its downfall, of Italy's future. Complex as this approach and procedure may seem, it is perhaps the only one that may render Italian Fascism an object of historical understanding.

Though they can be read as separate units, each having a special interest of its own, the major sections of this anthology are so arranged and presented as to offer a collective portrait of the historical problem whose larger "logic" of meaning transcends the focus of the separate parts. A brief summary of the order adopted in the presentation and of the most important substantive questions treated may perhaps obviate some of the formal difficulties that might otherwise arise in pursuing the readings.

Of the three parts into which this volume is divided, the first and the third seek to present sets of complementary points of view which converge upon the substance of the briefer but crucial second part. Part I attempts to present the pre-Fascist period—that is, the Risorgimento and the liberal era to the eve of the Great War of 1914 and, implicitly, to 1922—as it moved *forward* in terms of its historical problems. Part III seeks to capture the projection of the post-Fascist vision *backward* upon the pre-Fascist period in terms of historiographical questions. The biographical and historical "close-up" of Mussolini and Fascism in Part II constitutes the testing ground for the two converging perspectives preceding and following it.

In Part I, following the "statements" of the problem by two American students of modern Italian history, the first of whom focuses attention upon controversial reinterpretations of the Risorgimento and the second of whom (H. Stuart Hughes) reviews critically reappraisals of the aftermath, a series of contrasting views are presented which, with one exception (A. C. Jemolo's discussion of Cavour's ideas on freedom), offer recent reconsiderations by three "younger" American historians (Raymond Grew, John Cammett, and John A. Thayer) of important special aspects of the legacy of the Italian national revolution of the nineteenth century. These are followed by three diverse, but, in a sense, complementary revaluations of that legacy pursued through larger summations by a British (Denis Mack Smith), an American (A. William Salomone), and a German (Ernst Nolte) historian. At that point, the essence of the grave historical problem itself should be fairly well delineated in the reader's mind.

As its title attempts to suggest, Part II deals with Italian Fascism and its leader not in their full period of actual rule (1922–43)–for this would require other and more particularized materials–but in their moments of "rise and fall," that is, at the beginning, and then at the denouement, of their mastery over Italy. This procedure, it seems to me, is consistent with the fundamental purport of this volume, which is less to afford a direct study of Fascism itself as a dictatorial regime and totalitarian movement than to aid toward the understanding of how Fascism came into being and what its impact was upon the political conscience and the historical consciousness of Italians both during its domination and after its fall. Thus while G. A. Borgese and Gaudens Megaro sketch portraits of Mussolini as both socialist and Fascist activist, Emil Ludwig directly and Christopher Hibbert indirectly help us see the Duce engaged in self-portraiture at the height of power before 1933 and after his fall in 1943–45. On the other hand, Federico Chabod and Luigi Sturzo show us Fascism on the road to and at the moment of victory, while Sturzo and Angelo Tasca, both of whom were eminently, if from almost diametrically opposed positions, direct observers and victims of that Fascist victory, assess the meaning of Fascism as an Italian and European historical phenomenon.

Part III seeks, essentially, to "re-project" Italian historical vicissitudes from the Risorgimento to Fascism upon an historiographical "screen" from three connected but quite different perspectives: those of historical and ideological reassessments made during the Fascist period itself and that of post-Fascist historiographical reappraisals. Some crucial elements that traverse all three require at least a minimum of elucidation here.

At the very moment when Fascism was consolidating itself in power and the one-man rule of Mussolini was transforming the dictatorship into a full-fledged totalitarian regime, the world-renowned Italian philosopher Benedetto Croce struck an indirect but formidable blow against the self-claimed "spiritual" foundations of Fascism with a force in some ways greater than an act of physical violence. In 1928, on the morrow of the apparently total defeat of all anti-Fascist opposition and on the eve of the "reconciliation" between Church and state in Italy, Benedetto Croce published his *History of Italy from 1871 to 1915*. It amounted to a veritable milestone in the political and historical controversy on the origins of Fascism. Ironically, there was not a single direct reference to, not even a bare mention of, Fascism in Croce's work. And yet, as both historians sympathetic to Fascism like Gioacchino Volpe and anti-Fascist historians like Gaetano Salvemini, to say nothing of thousands of other eminent or obscure Italian and foreign readers of that work, immediately understood, Croce's *History of Italy* represented an exquisitely subtle attack upon Fascism and its pretenses to being the "culmination" of Italian history, by the most respected and famous thinker produced by modern Italy. For Croce was not only the philosopher of modern European Idealism but also the supreme master of Italian intellectual and cultural life, an extraordinary figure and exceptional moral personality who, during the twentieth century, had attained the status and stature which, in their times, only Erasmus, Voltaire, and Hegel had differently enjoyed. At this crucial juncture Croce had openly chosen to become the symbol of "internal" intellectual, moral, and spiritual resistance against Fascism. Mussolini was never to forgive this elusive defiance of his claims to be the "incarnation" of the Italian people and its historical aspirations.

Strangely enough, Croce had come "late" to assume the position of moral leader of the anti-Fascist opposition. Both before and after his book was published there had been groups of other eminent Italians—among them, Gaetano Salvemini, Don Luigi Sturzo, Piero Gobetti, Giovanni Amendola, and Giacomo Matteotti—who had thrown in their lot and, in the case of the last three, their very lives, in the fight against Fascism. Until the Fascist assassination of the courageous socialist parliamentary leader Giacomo Matteotti in 1924 and the proclamiation of the dictatorship at the beginning of 1925, Croce had not been altogether openly hostile to the "clinical" operations of Fascist "realism," in the delusion, which many lesser men harbored, that it might restore forms of "law and order" in distraught postwar Italy. It took Mussolini's own fierce and unrestrained unmasking of his anti-liberal and anti-socialist postures to reveal the naked face of

Fascism in all its brutal anti-historical features. Croce was not the first to understand this—other men had died because they had known it from the very start—but he was the first of his illustrious stature to give the "discovery" a "respectable" and highly authoritative historical structure. In his *History of Italy* he implied rather than directly stated that Mussolini was at the same time anti-Cavour and anti-Giolitti and, therefore, a dangerous adventurer without scruples or aims. Fascism, rather than being a "fulfillment," was an historic negation of the entire course, realities, and ideals of the Risorgimento and of Liberal Italy. For Croce, Fascism was a venomous growth sprung from the soil of the post-war Italian and European crisis, the anti-Risorgimento incarnate, a symptom of the internal barbarism that was enveloping liberal civilization in the name of "anti-Europe." More than a work of "pure" history, his *History* became a challenge to the entire scheme of politics, history, and "culture" that Fascism represented, a banner of resistance in the name of civilized values, and, during the period of the armed Resistance, a spiritual weapon, a sort of secret book of inspiration for all Italian liberal anti-Fascist forces at home and abroad.

The anger and acid ironies that pervade the pro-Fascist historian Gioacchino Volpe's almost officious retort to Croce in the Preface to the third edition of *L'Italia in cammino* (1932), from which we present a large segment, can only be understood in the light of the unique moral victory scored by Croce's *History*. Volpe, who was himself an eminent historian originally from the nationalist camp, was at the same time subtle and violent in his attempt to turn Croce against himself. Volpe suggested that Croce had been one of the philosophical "fathers" of the "idealistic" revolt against the pettiness and mortifications of Liberal Italy which Fascism had "at long last" come to bury. It is intriguing to note, among other things, the extent to which the extremes of criticism against Croce from the Fascist right and the Communist left occasionally have met. For the moment it is important to note how during both the Fascist and the post-Fascist periods such different "extremes" as are found in Gaetano Salvemini's democratic radicalism and Arturo Carlo Jemolo's liberal Catholicism are in strange historiographical agreement concerning the fundamental character of pre-Fascist Italy. Salvemini and Jemolo are not Croceans by any means and yet, each in his fashion, find one another in accord on the post-1914 origins of Fascism and its destructive "mission" against the freedoms–political, civil, religious, and intellectual–that Italians had arduously gained by the end of the Giolittian era.

The five representative spokesmen from the younger anti-Fascist generation, whose historical visions of the origins of Fascism are presented in the next to the last section of this collection of readings, were all literally victims of the totalitarian dictatorship. The radical liberal intellectual Piero Gobetti, the Marxist theoretician and activist Antonio Gramsci, the liberal socialist actionist Carlo Rosselli, the poet and liberal monarchist Lauro de Bosis, and the young "unpolitical" critic Giaime Pintor were all directly or indirectly destroyed by Fascism. Each of them bravely crossed the dangerous line dividing theoretical historical thought and anti-Fascist political action, and each died for having made that fateful passage. In my attempt to recapture the essence of their moral attitudes and of their spiritual personalities in brief excerpts from their writings, I have presented them in their moments of reflection—before, on the threshold, or immediately after their moments of action. All of them in some way at some time confronted the core-question of modern Italian history: How and for what reasons had the Italy created by the Risorgimento and molded by liberalism ended in the establishment of Mussolini's totalitarian dictatorship? I feel that what Gobetti, Gramsci, Rosselli, de Bosis, and Pintor wrote concerning this question is at the same time least known outside Italy and one of the most highly significant collective responses offered by the younger generation of Italian anti-Fascists. These men together, albeit with contrasting motivations and finalities, constitute an ideal bond between the unfinished business of the "first" Risorgimento and the new business of the "second" Risorgimento after the fall of Fascism in Italy. It is well to remember, in reading their impressions, that each of them regarded Fascism as something to be resisted and destroyed, not merely interpreted. For all of them, Fascism was not merely an object of historical contemplation and philosophical analysis, but a corrupter of the life of a people, a perverter of the ideals and values that give meaning to human history and to men's fate in it. This section of the readings, I believe, may be seen as both intimately related to the central historical problem in this anthology and yet significantly transcendent of that problem in so far as it touches upon the larger question of the connections between thought and action in recurring situations of vital choices. Caught in the vise of totalitarian tyranny and spiritual nihilism, these men did not seek escape either in self-destructive despair or in purposeless activism.

In the final section, the "heroes" are essentially two: the historical "ghost" of the great liberal statesman Giovanni Giolitti (1842–1928), and his irreconcilable opponent of the pre-1914 period, the incorrigible polemicist and democratic historian Gaetano Salvemini. In the second part of the second edition (1960) of an historical study of the Giolittian era which was originally published late in 1945, I have discussed in some detail the special historiographical problems concerning pre-Fascist democracy that arose after the fall of Fascism.[4] I will not, therefore, elaborate upon those problems here and merely refer the interested reader to that work—not only for this purpose, but also because in its own small way, given the Italian historic circumstances during which it first appeared in 1945 and four years later in an Italian translation, it perhaps had a kind of special if not catalytic function in the political and historiographical controversy on the Giolittian era. Worthy of particular emphasis, it now seems to me, at least for purposes of the present collection of readings, is an exposition of a few aspects and dimensions of the great post-Fascist "debate" on Giolittian Italy and pre-Fascist democracy that are not self-evident from a perusal of the selections themselves.

A mere first glance at those selections will quickly

[4] A. William Salomone, *Italy in the Giolittian Era. Italian Democracy in the Making, 1900–1914.* Introductory Essay by Gaetano Salvemini (new ed. Philadelphia, 1960), Section Two.

reveal the polemical overtones and political undertones that characterize most of them. A superficial view of them would therefore seem to justify the impression that what occurred after the fall of Fascism, and particularly after 1945, concerning the question of pre-Fascist democracy in Italy was a mere reprise, a sort of new round, in an old theoretical battle that had already been fought and was finished with since its first "Crocean" phase in the late 1920s and early 1930s. Not only would such an impression be distorted, but the judgment it might lead to would be both precipitous and almost absolutely wrong. Although the "idiom," the form and tonalities, of the post-1945 "great debate" was almost by necessity ideological, political and polemical at the same time, its substance was historical and vital. In 1945 and after, Italy and the rest of Europe were emerging from a monstrous "total war." Among other things, that total war had been one of the cruelest and fiercest wars of secular religions, a struggle of ideas and ideologies, a mortal conflict of values and beliefs concerning not merely power and political systems but the very principles of human life and death. When that conflict was over, those who survived, both victors and defeated alike, had to reappraise both the material basis of their civil existence and the ethical and spiritual *raison d'être* of their historic life. Finding themselves, like the Germans, among the defeated, if on a lesser scale, Italians, for the first time in their national life, had to confront a vast array of organic problems that touched upon their present, their historical past, and their future as a people and as a nation.

The fall of Fascism in Italy had occurred in the

midst of a gigantic struggle among world powers. The victors of the struggle would and did have the power of granting survival or annihilation to the defeated unless these, and Italy in particular, could expeditiously give proof of their willingness and capacity to be constructively reintegrated within the comity of the victorious coalition. But, during its closing phase, Mussolini's Fascist war had also unleashed an at first subtle and hidden, and then open and bitter, "civil war" among Italians, not only between Fascists and the anti-Fascist Resistance but also among the varieties of anti-Fascism itself (liberal, democratic, socialist, Catholic, and Communist). So long as they were actively bound together in the fight against a common enemy—the Nazi-Fascist forces desperately seeking to keep their hold upon North Central Italy—the Italian anti-Fascist currents, movements, parties, and leaders had had to de-emphasize their conflicting political and ideological interests and objectives. But once the struggle against the common enemy had relented or virtually ended, the partisan strife for primacy or supremacy among the varieties of anti-Fascism broke out in full force. At stake was the immiment question of leadership and initiative in the reconstruction of the Italian state and of Italian society. The more fundamental questions therefore became: In what form, upon what model, under whose leadership, with what immediate goals and historical directives, and through what means would or should a new Italian state be rebuilt out of the ruins of the Fascist regime and the crumbling edifice of the Savoy Monarchy? Would Italy return to the old pre-Fascist structure or would it be possible and desirable to create a new structure of state and society having no links with the past? Were the dangers of picking up the threads of continuity where Fascism had cut them in 1922–25 greater or lesser than an attempt at total innovation, at a revolutionary change, that would repudiate not only Fascism but all that had preceded it, since—as the extremist radicals and actionists argued—the pre-Fascist past had "led" inevitably, through the working of "iron historical laws," to the totalitarian involution? Was Italian post-Risorgimento history to be regarded as a useless burden that had to be totally rejected, or could it serve as a guide-line toward a more secure, if novel, political life in Italy? Seen in the light of such portentous questions as these and similar ones, the "great debate" on pre-Fascist democracy, its achievements and defects, its promise and its illusions, its grandeur and its misery, was not an "academic" problem! Underlying the polemical sound and the controversial fury of the "great debate" on Giolittian democracy were some of the most stupendously complex and crucial historic problems ever faced by the Italian people, and its spokesmen and leaders, as they emerged from the ashes of defeat and ruin brought upon Italy by Mussolini's Fascism.

If all this is clearly kept in mind, the conflict of personal opinion and historical judgment concerning pre-Fascist democracy that occurred in the Consulta (the Italian Consultative Assembly) in September 1945 between the leader of the anti-Fascist Resistance movement and at that moment Premier of Italy, Ferruccio Parri, and the venerable philosopher, Benedetto Croce, assumes a new, vital, significance.

Having begun in 1928–32 as an historiographical duel between Crocc the liberal philosopher and Volpe the official historian of Fascism, in 1945 the problem of Italian pre-Fascist democracy had momentarily become a source of disagreement between Croce's *positive* liberal view and Parri's *negative* radical democratic and socialist judgment. Soon, however, the centers of the historical controversy shifted to two different but related levels, whose common denominator was the Italian Marxist, neo-Gramscian ideological offensive against both the liberal and the democratic interpretations of Giolittian Italy. Thus, particularly from 1947 to 1952–when Antonio Gramsci's *Prison Notebooks* were being published and were providing Italian Marxists with an original and indigenous base of philosophical, historical, and ideological operations against their bourgeois, liberal and democratic, antagonists–the "great debate" on pre-Fascist democracy became obsessively acute. In their attempt to steal the thunder of historical reinterpretation from both bourgeois "camps," the liberal and the democratic, the Italian Marxists fixed their polemical sights upon two special personal targets: Benedetto Croce and his old adversary, Gaetano Salvemini. While the "young lions" of Italian Marxism–as the very first reading in this anthology seeks to point out–worked ceaselessly at demolishing the philosophical basis of Crocean idealism and liberalism, in 1950 no less a high personage in the Italian Communist Party than its astute leader, Palmiro Togliatti, tackled personally and directly the democratic basis of a Salveminian reappraisal of Giolittian Italy. It is a matter of no small wonder that by 1950 the apparently so abstract and theoretical historical problem of whether, during the Giolittian era (1900–14), Italian democracy had been "in the making" or had sown the seeds of Fascist totalitarianism, had become the practical concern of the leader of the largest European Communist Party outside Soviet Russia—Palmiro Togliatti! For Italian Marxists at least, in almost complete contradiction to the famous "thesis" of Karl Marx himself, the world of history was not merely something to be changed but to be interpreted!

In his Introduction to my work on *Italian Democracy in the Making* (1945; 1960), of which an Italian translation appeared in 1949 under the title of *L'Età giolittiana,* Gaetano Salvemini reassessed in positive terms his former castigations of Giolitti even as he reaffirmed his belief that during 1900–14 Italian democracy was strenuously but definitely "in the making." At the end of April 1950—the sequence of dates is quite revealing—Palmiro Togliatti delivered his "Discourse on Giolitti" before a large and distinguished Marxist and non-Marxist audience in Turin. As is evident even in the excerpts I have translated here and have included in the last section, Togliatti was in his "Discourse" ironically commenting upon Salvemini's afterthoughts and "misjudgments" concerning the liberal Piedmontese statesman Giovanni Giolitti. In point of fact, Togliatti delivered a kind of subtle eulogy of Giolitti, whom he presented almost as a forerunner of an Italian "progressive democracy." But, at the same time, he castigated the "bourgeois democracy" of the Giolittian era for its having become imperialistic and, therefore, a precursor of Italian Fascism. By disassociating Giolitti from the "democracy" of his era, Togliatti shrewdly administered ideological blows equally against the "bourgeois" Crocean "right" for its having exalted Giolitti without condemning his "democracy," and the Salveminian "left" for its positive reappraisal of Giolitti and its acceptance of his "democracy in the making."

This kind of ideological jugglery of Giolittian "personal" sympathies and Marxist historical dialectics on Togliatti's part exacerbated the old historian Salvemini's fury to such a point that he once again launched a polemical attack against Giolitti—now become Togliatti's idol. In the violence of his new wrath, Salvemini went to the extreme of calling Giolitti the precursor of Mussolini. In his 1952 piece, which appeared in the Florentine periodical *Il Ponte* and from which I have presented the central parts, Salvemini seemed to have become his old polemical self—but only up to a point. For what some people have missed in their judgment upon this last Salveminian burst of historical anger is the fact that, in spite of the exaggerations, distortions, and reversions it contains against Giolitti, whom Togliatti had practically sanctified as a liberal-bourgeois idol in the Italian Marxist ideological Pantheon, Salvemini remained essentially true to his long-held views on an "Italian democracy in the making" before the coming of the First World War. Against Togliatti's Marxist exegesis, but also against Croce's liberal interpretation, Salvemini in his 1952 article reiterated that during the Giolittian era Italian democracy had been precariously but palpably "in the making," but *not* because of Giolitti's initiative and efforts but rather *in spite of* his "corrupting" influence. Paradoxically, therefore, for Salvemini, while Giolitti was now seen as a precursor of Mussolini, Italian democracy during the Giolittian era had not been a seedtime of Fascism.

Thus a cycle of political and polemical debate was closed in Italy. As Nino Valeri perceptively suggests in the piece I have chosen as a "conclusion" to this collection of readings, a new cycle of calmer historiographical reconstruction of Italy's history from the Risorgimento to the Fascist dictatorship was opening. Interestingly, during the very years when the debate on pre-Fascist Italy was raging most furiously in post-Fascist Italy, a first new work of "pure" historiographical reconstruction, an undisputed masterpiece on the post-Risorgimento was published in Italy: Federico Chabod's *Storia della politica estera italiana dal 1871 al 1896. Le premesse* (Bari, 1951) [*History of Italian Foreign Policy from 1871 to 1896. The Premises*]—a unique fusion of diplomatic and intellectual, of political and cultural, history. Unfortunately, Chabod's work is not yet available in translation; tragically, it will remain forever "unfinished" since, in 1960, a mortal malady struck down one of contemporary Europe's greatest historians.

I wish to thank Miss Nancy Popoff and her staff in the Office of the Dean, College of Arts and Sciences, of the University of Rochester for their patience and courtesy in typing and retyping the translations included in this collection of readings. Dr. Reuben Garner has been most generous with his time and aid in reproducing many of the materials in this volume, and I am most grateful to him. I wish to express a special debt of gratitude to Miss Lisa Johnson of Anchor Books for her indispensable editorial care and wise suggestions toward the improvement of the structure and, I am certain, the quality of this book.

In order to conserve space, all of the footnotes in the original articles have been omitted, except those which were considered essential to the clarification and accuracy of the author's text. Editorial notes are so indicated.

PART ONE

THE LEGACY OF THE RISORGIMENTO: FROM LIBERALISM TO FASCISM

I. THE HISTORICAL PROBLEM OF THE RISORGIMENTO AND ITS AFTERMATH

In the history *of all modern nations moments have occurred, usually following great historic crises brought on by wars, revolutions, civil conflicts, grave social problems, or moral catastrophes, when not merely official search for immediate "causes" but vast-ranging reappraisals of historic developments have been undertaken. Crises of politics have thus tended to become crises of the national conscience, and these have led to re-examinations of the structural foundations and of the course of a people's collective life: three times in the history of modern France (following the two "falls" of France in 1870–71 and in 1940, with the great crisis precipitated by the Dreyfus Affair, 1896–1904, between them), at least twice in the case of Germany (following defeats in two World Wars), twice in American history (after the Civil War and following Pearl Harbor), even in post-Stalinist Soviet Russia at least once (with the XX Congress of the Communist Party and early stages of the Khrushchev era in 1956), and three times in the history of modern Italy—following the period of reaction at the turn of the twentieth century, after the defeat of Caporetto in 1917, and after the fall of Fascism and the end of the Second World War. Given the large-scale and profound character of the Italian crisis engendered by two decades of Fascist totalitarian tyranny and the ruin brought upon*

Italy by a lost war waged on the side of her friends' enemy, Italians in general and their political and moral leaders in particular after 1945 were confronted with a series of agonizing questions: Why and how had it happened? Who specifically and what historically was to be held responsible for the catastrophe brought by the mastery of Fascism over Italy? What were the uses of the past, the "lessons" of history toward the understanding of the sources for a national tragedy? And, finally, what recasting of political thought and the national conscience would be necessary in order to accelerate the process of recovery or renovation?

The two selections given below constitute an attempt, each in its fashion, made by two American students of modern Italian history to review these fundamental problems and to describe the forms and context they assumed in Italy after 1945. The author of the first selection has studied the pre-Fascist period in a work on Italian Democracy in the Making *(1945; 1960) and other writings and is professor of European and Italian history at the University of Rochester. H. Stuart Hughes, professor of European history at Harvard University, has contributed original studies on modern European intellectual and social history as the author of* Consciousness and Society *(1958) and an enlightening introduction to Italian contemporary history with his* United States and Italy *(1953; 1965).*

The Risorgimento and the Political Myth of "The Revolution that Failed"*

A. WILLIAM SALOMONE

THE CLOSE of centenary evocations marking the unification of Italy may well go down in the annals of Italian historical writing as the conclusion of the last battle of the Risorgimento. It is true that in 1970 there will be the twentieth of September and Rome to remember. But it seems relatively safe to say that the historians' battles over these tactical objectives have already been fought rather fiercely on other fields with other arms than those of the battle over Italy. As it is, therefore, the commemorative spell that ended in 1961 may have registered a turning point in a crucial battle of ideas. There are, at any rate, clear signs that the waning has begun of the most recent conflict between a "classic" tradition and a multiform critique in the interpretation of the Risorgimento and, a posteriori, of the Liberal aftermath to the crisis of a historic experiment and the dreary agony of an Italian era. Whatever the shadings and the emphases of particulars on each side, the heart of the great historiographical debate, the central question at issue, can now be clearly identified as having involved opposing views on the problem

* This article is from "The *Risorgimento* between Ideology and History: The Political Myth of *rivoluzione mancata,*" which originally appeared in *The American Historical Review,* LXVIII, No. 1, 38–53.

of freedom in the Risorgimento and in the development of the Italian unitary state from Cavour to Giolitti and thence to the coming of Fascism.

I have no intention of presenting here a full-fledged, formal review of recent Italian historical writing on the Risorgimento and the Liberal state. In fact, some of the most constructive contributions of that historiography are hardly mentioned because many belong to a "purer" scholarly and professional sphere outside and frequently above the terms of reference of the essential problem treated here. This essay is an attempt to call attention to the ideological aspects of a historiographical problem which, at least by implication, assumed significant political dimensions and moral overtones. Brief and sketchy as it must be, this preliminary study may possibly suggest an approach to some very subtle vicissitudes in the intellectual history of contemporary Italy. The study of the use and abuse of history at a time of grave political crises and ideological dissension, which Italians and other Europeans of this generation have undergone, may at least help toward a further understanding of the historian's perennial dilemma. A dilemma that springs, among other things, from the unique opportunity of reconstructing or manipulating the past thus involves the necessity of fidelity to his craft and the demands of commitment to a cause, a faith, an idea he cannot disown.

The Crocean vision of a century of Italian history as a heroic chapter in modern Europe's epic "story of liberty" has been challenged and subjected to a deadly cross fire of opposing "realist" critiques—nationalist, Fascist, democratic, Marxist—for so long and to such an extent as to make it appear, in the eyes of its critics, an anachronism, the faded document of a *Weltanschauung* that is no more. A massive revisionist trend, with essentially anti-Crocean emphasis, has characterized the most recent historical writing on the construction of the Italian national state, on the unitary movement, on the entire post-Risorgimento until it seemed for a time as if Cavour, the hero of Croce's *Storia d'Europa,* and Giolitti, the hero of his *Storia d'Italia,* and all their work would have to be considered among the greatest calamities in modern Italian history. Modishly subdued in tone and studiedly sophisticated in approach and style, a seductive quasi-historical literature assailed the citadel of classic orthodoxies on the Risorgimento, gained the field, and won promiscuous and often vociferous applause.

The wave of reinterpretation, whose crest, as will be further pointed out, was ridden by neo-Marxist historians and intellectuals, at once helped create and merged with an even wider vogue of cultural and professional iconoclasm that had, almost self-evidently, more practical sources and immediate aims than the arduous search for "pure" historical truth. That, in an important sense, what was involved among certain sectors of the Italian intelligentsia amounted to a genuine, for some an acute, crisis of conscience can hardly be denied. The personal and direct experiences, through peace and war, of a number of Italian intellectuals who had recoiled from the immorality of the doctrines of Fascism and had resisted and fought against the totalitarian corruption of history, impelled some of the best among them toward a restoration of elementary human and historical values. During the immediate postwar period, from within the most sensitive intellectual quarters in Italy, came excellent examples of a renewed dedication to "uncommitted" historiographical endeavor, to a quest for newer approaches to traditional problems, frequently through practical refinements of the theory and methodology of historical study beyond the beaten paths of the "classic models" of the nineteenth and twentieth centuries. Nevertheless, certain cadres of the Italian intelligentsia, operating upon premises that often seemed obscure in origin, but were quite patent in motivation, set the predominant tone and style of revisionist historical literature. Thus attachment to a partisan cause, political self-interest, journalistic opportunism, and, if infrequently, plain ingenuousness led to mercurial oscillations in intellectual commitment and ideological temper, depending occasionally on the rise and fall of the political temperature registered in Italy and in Europe by the vicissitudes of the contemporary struggle for power.

And yet, a careful analysis of the complicated Italian situation after 1945 reveals other, in a sense deeper, elements at work within the vogue of historical reinterpretation. As a matter of fact, the Crocean Liberal vision was swept by a more powerful force behind the revisionist trend. Fundamentally, this trend stemmed from the impact of identifiably large historic events that have overtaken Italy and Europe since 1914.

In modern Italian history an "avalanche of events" —the Great War, the crisis of the Liberal state, the rise, rule, and ruin of Fascism, the Second World War, the resistance, the glimpses of revolutionary change, the establishment of a democratic republic, the new political struggle, the sway of Christian Democracy, the rise of Communism, the European unity movement, the cold war, and, withal, the protean persistence of big historic problems—has at once resulted in and been refracted through a "world view" basically compounded of moral disenchantment and new intellectual and moral ferment. The new view seemed historiographically aimed at best to revisit calmly and at worst to refashion *ex novo* Italy's past in the light of that "avalanche of events" and of the old and new vital Italian problems. Thus, again, at best, a fruitful great debate was reopened, and, at worst, a sort of grim trial was mounted in connection with the Risorgimento and the history of the Italian unitary state, which was its most palpable political creature. At least momentarily, the revisionist critique appeared to dominate the field in the guise of an indivisible and irreversible "wave of the future" in historical thought and writing on modern Italy. Nevertheless, the Italian historiographical critique of the Risorgimento and the Liberal state was far from being a single bloc either in origin or in significance.

Reduced to its barest and possibly to its crudest essentials, that massive revisionist literature seems to have addressed itself to a subtle mixture of valid, half-authentic, and false historical problems which, for practical purposes, might be schematically summarized in the following questions: Could the traditional idea of the Risorgimento as a genuine liberation movement still be accepted historically? Was not a sort of original sin stamped upon the spirit of Italian liberalism at the cradle of the Risorgimento, which properly damned that liberalism to perverse growth and deserved perdition? Were there no real alternatives to the Cavourian solution of the Italian national problem? Was not the Italian liberals' claim to have made Italy in the likeness and image of European concepts of freedom merely the *sacro egoismo* of an authoritarian, class-conscious elite of landed magnates, upper-bourgeois "rich men," and the influential professional and intellectual classes? Had not the lower classes been simply used and exploited and then forgotten or excluded in the wake of a national spoils system that had been instituted under the pretext of the independence, unity, and liberty of Italy? Had not the Liberal state been enveloped in a pseudoparliamentary regime aimed merely at perpetuating the rule of an essentially illiberal oligarchy which occasionally changed the guard at the castle gate as a choreographical disguise for its retention of the inner citadel of Italian political power? Had there not been a dark thread of corruption and self-seeking that held the Italian ruling class together through the perversion of legitimate party alliances—a thread running straight from the Cavourian *connubio* and the Right's *consorteria* through the Left's *trasformismo* and *giolittismo* to Fascism itself? Had an Italian democratic society ever broken through the incorrigibly miasmic immorality of Italian political life during the entire Liberal era? Did not an "organic solution" to the chronicle of economic and social troubles represented by the history of modern Italy, particularly since the Risorgimento, actually exist both in theory and in practice? Could the expectation be plausibly entertained that a "real," a "hot," revolution would be achieved in Italy to break at long last the black magic spell of the monotonous series of "cold" revolutions that had characterized the history of Italy?

To document fully or to comment properly, to try to confute or to elaborate upon any or all parts of this schematic summation of the Italian, and partly non-Italian, revisionist critique would obviously require a counter-critique of exceedingly large dimensions certainly beyond present requirements or even necessity. Certain common features characterize a large, self-evident part of this historiographical "bill of indictment" of the Risorgimento and of the liberal efforts at reconstruction. A mood of obvious presentism runs with an exquisitely anti-Crocean irony through most of it, an exaggerated and exaggerating propensity to read the Italian past backward in order to project the present forward to an expected or desired future break in historical continuity. A legitimate curiosity as to how and why certain things did not happen in nineteenth-century Italy lies at the base of some of these questions, while some others derive from pure and simple sensation-mongering and a morbid "private-eye" mentality. Occasionally, one glimpses inquisitorial fanaticism behind the mask of objective inquisitiveness. A "hanging judge" lurked somewhere in the wings as the Risorgimento was put on trial. At any rate, some of these revisionist critiques, whether designedly or implicitly, tended to leave the Risorgimento and the Liberal state suspended somewhere between the pole of nostalgia for a pseudo-Arcadian *ancien régime* and that of the myth of a revolutionary "heavenly city."

The revisionist critique of the Risorgimento and the Liberal era, however separated in origins or even antithetical in purposes some of its parts may have been, amounts to a series of variations on a single historiographical theme. This theme, it seems to me, is the recurring concept that at every critical stage, at every crucial moment, Italian history somehow failed to realize the promise intrinsic to the actual historical situation. Each moment of great crisis is then seen as resolving itself, obviously through the combination and predominant play of negative forces, into an essential, an organic "failure." In this manner, the whole of Italian history becomes subsumed under the negative concept of *rivoluzione mancata.* A pessimistic vision of Italy's historic development is thus adopted as a historical and philosophical category and, often unwittingly, is turned into fatalism or secular providentialism. At the very least, the concept is utilized as a guide toward illustrating the fundamental assumption that Italian history has been characterized by a sort of "one-step-forward-two-steps-backward" procedure. The links with the past are seen as recurrently bent but not broken, the channels to the future obscurely but mathematically obstructed.

In quasi-Toynbeean fashion, a process of "challenge and response" is adduced to account for the repetitious disparity in Italian history between retardation and progress, the grip of tradition and the spurs to innovation, the successes of reaction and the defeats of revolution—an infernal cycle of dark secular victories of power over freedom in Italy. Thus it was, allegedly, with the great crisis of Renaissance Italy, the Italian Reformation, the Jacobin revolution, the national revolution, the democratic revolution, the liberal revolution, the Industrial Revolution, the socialist revolution, the anti-Fascist revolution—and, overlogically if incredibly, thus it was with the "Fascist Revolution" itself! A fantastic succession of historic disasters has haunted the genius of Italy through the modern age, or so it would seem. A hopeless series of failures, defeats, betrayals, the iron chain of *rivoluzioni mancate* has been raised into an exquisitely Italian specialization, the exclusive paradigm of one people's fate.

The normative transference or at least the tentative application of some such criteria to the historical development of other European nations and peoples would undoubtedly prove of immense interest to the searchers of overarching historical hypotheses and the theorists of comparative social science. An illuminating test, for instance, of the "scientific" validity of the principle of *rivoluzione mancata* could be made by adopting it to "explain" the course and consequences of the English revolutions of the seventeenth century, of the American and the French Revolutions, of the German revolution of the nineteenth century, of the Central European revolutions, and of the Russian Revolution itself in the twentieth century! The anatomy of revolution performed with such an Italian methodological "scalpel" might perchance result in the formulation of a new universal law of history or perhaps in the reduction into brittle absurdity of such an operation for Italy as well. At any rate, the performance of such an operation might make it clear to some students of Italian history that, beyond a certain empiric point, the concept of *rivoluzione mancata* involves either a new form of historical determinism or a pseudomystical function of historicist philosophy. Beyond those two extremes there would be no saving escape for the historian except in a *ritorno alla ragione* or in an existentialist plunge, an activistic surrender of historical intelligence to the pulverizing grip of *antistoria.*

A special comment must be reserved for a truly exceptional moving force behind the strongest revisionist influence in contemporary Italian historiography. The publication of Antonio Gramsci's *Quaderni dal Carcere* in 1947–1951 constituted one of the major cultural events of the postwar period, and, of course, proved to be a "political" and ideological event in itself. Gramsci's prison meditations on Italian history and society brought a strong gust of fresh historiographical winds but also controversy, polemics, and new ideological conflicts. Gramsci's original, vast-ranging, acute prison reflections and his Marxist critique on Italian culture and politics, from the Renaissance to the Risorgimento and from the inception of the unitary state to Fascism, acted as a catalyst upon the historical conscience of the younger Italian intelligentsia even as it fascinated and then roused contrasting reactions from the midst of the older intellectual and professional classes. In theory and practice, the Gramscian notebooks contributed greatly in redrawing the Risorgimento and the Liberal state once again within the greyish zones that stretch between politics and history.

Apparently the most genial and certainly the most seductive of Gramsci's historical meditations was that which led him to see the Risorgimento as "a complex and contradictory movement which results as an integral whole despite all its antithetical elements." In its final "integral" aspect, however, the

Risorgimento amounted to a new, perhaps decisive, historic deflection of a revolution *in potentia.* Thus a *rivoluzione passiva* occurred when the agrarian masses of Italy, particularly in the South, were left at the mercy of Moderate-Liberal ruling classes by the defects and defections from their cause of the Italian "Jacobin" radical movement and by the democratic Action party's lack of real cohesion, leadership, and a realistic sense of a concrete political direction toward the fulfillment of a tangible historic mission. For Gramsci the Risorgimento was essentially an agrarian-populist revolution that had a brief chance and then failed. Gramsci dissected the causes and sources of that failure with pitiless Marxist logic, but his historicist Crocean "education" and his exposure to the elitist theories of the political class led him to mete out "historical justice" equally, if naturally on different levels, to both victors and defeated. In essence, he seemed to feel that an Italian "Jacobin"-democratic-agrarian revolution could have and should have been pushed through, but that, in fact, ostensibly seeking too much with too little, that revolution remained unfulfilled and got nothing. Indeed, still worse, it got less than nothing because it had served no real purpose but that of the Italian and European antirevolutionary political classes.

Gramsci's analysis of the final phase of the Italian Liberal national revolution was crucial to his entire interpretation of the Risorgimento. Throughout the climactic struggle between democratic radicalism and liberal moderatism in 1859–1860, the Piedmontese dynasty, the monarch himself, according to Gramsci, had acted upon the assumption that Garibaldi, the "general of the popular revolution," was unswervingly captive in his loyalty to the King. In the fall of 1860, moderate Liberalism and Cavourian statecraft subtly turned the decisive historic trick: they succeeded in converting Garibaldi's populist-democratic "liberation of the South" into a sort of "royal conquest." Thus Cavour had proved equal to his task and to that of his social and political class by transforming a revolutionary-military movement, which, for the first time in the course of the national revolution, had aroused the active interest and participation of the masses of the South, into a function of hegemonic conservative-Liberal politics. Combining realism and audacity, the dynasty, the Liberal classes, and Cavour had kept themselves concretely attuned to the finalities of a genuine political class. No less important, the Cavourian elite had apparently known and fruitfully exploited the secret of operating always within—not against or outside, as the revolutionary Mazzinian Action party almost necessarily had to act —the boundaries of the permissible, if not quite the desirable, international novelties in the European balance of power.

Among other things, Gramsci's prison reflections on Italian history were essentially a function of his long, silent "dialogue" with Croce. To read Gramsci's notes on the Risorgimento and then to reread Croce's pages on the Italian national revolution in his *Storia d'Europa* is to shift between two contrasting but related historical worlds. In both, the "dialectic of freedom" operates constantly through the analysis and reconstruction of events and the great conflict of men and ideas. But whereas in the Crocean world of the Risorgimento, liberty stirs and breathes almost as a transcendent spirit, a secular faith, an idea larger than the men who are its instruments, in the Gramscian world freedom has no real identity outside of the "protagonists" and "antagonists" of the historic conflict. For Croce, Cavour lives and works in a Rankean sphere, as if on a providential mission beyond error and beyond judgment, while for Gramsci the entire Risorgimento is in the grip of an inescapable historic antinomy, and all its heroes are rebels and prisoners at the same time, victims and victors of a giant struggle, itself a "complex and contradictory" development of "active and latent forces."

Thus, in a Fascist prison cell, an ideal battle of the Risorgimento was fought again. Gramsci's Marxist "theory of praxis" grappled desperately with the Crocean philosophy of absolute historicism. The Sardinian ideologue's dialectics of power were pitted against the Neapolitan philosopher's "religion of liberty." Gramsci's ideological commitment, however, did not restrain him nor his singular intelligence from "acting" in freedom as he grappled with the deepest problems of modern Italian history. He knew the psychology of the defeated firsthand, but, as the self-confessed loser in a political struggle, he asked for no pity. The Fascist prison broke his body, but never constrained his spirit. Unfortunately, as his notebooks were issued, a strange constraint upon his spiritual legacy was imposed by his official and officious interpreters who, at least for a time, almost succeeded in converting into a system of doctrines with all the trappings of ideological orthodoxy what had been profound, but fragmentary, meditations on Italian history and on politics and culture. Among the first fruits of that conversion was a new Italian

Marxist variation on the theme of the *rivoluzione mancata,* whose earliest exponents Gramsci himself had castigated as intellectual dilettanti, "mercenaries of science."

The rising tide of the Marxist historiographical revisionism was reinforced at some crucial moments by other currents of interpretations of the Risorgimento and the Liberal aftermath. Though they cannot, obviously, be separately or extensively treated here, Italian and non-Italian radical democratic and "social" Catholic approaches, at least for a time, joined from different quarters in the wave of criticism and attack on the "classic" traditions. The Risorgimento was, for instance, reduced to "a civil war between the old and new ruling classes" in nineteenth-century Italy. It was stressed that the making of Italy had proved "a victory for the intellectuals, the liberals, the middle classes," but "not for the uneducated . . . ; not for the poor . . . ; not for those who lost a paternal, protective ordering of society . . . ; not for the Catholic masses . . ."–not, in a word, for "the ordinary people of Italy." If freedom had been at all involved as a moving force in the Risorgimento, it had been on the side of the Italian victims and antagonists of Cavour and of his Machiavellian system of politics and diplomacy. Cavourian statecraft had not merely appropriated Garibaldi's radical popular revolution; it had rather perverted it through chicanery and deceit into a function of a consummately self-seeking dynastic conservative liberalism.

Suggestive and sometimes enlightening as such assessments of victory and defeat in the Risorgimento may be, they are at best a legitimate "base of operations" for research into unexplored aspects of the Italian national revolution. At worst, generic, if attractive, value judgments, whether in exaltation or condemnation, tend, among other things, to amount to vicarious participation in the political and ideological passions of a historic drama in need of understanding. An actual contemporary, a true direct participant, must exercise to the full his human right to praise or to blame a turn of events; the elements that contributed to a success or a disaster were truly his to work with; the friends who helped toward a victory, for him to exalt; the enemy who brought him down to defeat, for him to curse. Mazzini, Cattaneo, and Garibaldi could, and did, legitimately defy, curse, and damn the agents of their failure, the forces and men whom they held responsible for their defeat. The historian, on the other hand, may and often must grant them and their brothers in defeat sympathy and compassion, but he cannot raise these into categories of understanding; he cannot reduce the Italian national revolution merely into a function of the unrealized potentialities of the Risorgimento. History is not a ledger of assets and liabilities, a scoreboard of defeats and triumphs.

Occurring within a particular context of European politics and involving a special set of realities and possibilities, the Risorgimento was not a bloc. Ends and means were ever at cross-purposes in its development; desirable results, conscious efforts, unpredictable consequences, accidents and contingencies, and the clash of human wills were at the heart of its historicity as of all great collective deeds. Unquestionably, concrete economic, social, and ideological forces operated in its dynamics much below the surface of chronology and choreography. But from the bedrock of its self-conscious purposes the idea and the reality of the Risorgimento as a struggle for freedom, however restrictively on purely theoretical bases it may be interpreted, cannot be excluded a priori. Unless, that is, one prefers, whether unconsciously or against all reason, to subsume the historicity of the Risorgimento under some concept of metahistory. In that case, the vicious circle would again be closed, and the Risorgimento would be uniquely reduced to the data of historical metaphysics or, perhaps more likely, to a function of historiographical politics. The pall of this spurious dilemma has, unfortunately, been an obscurer part of its fate during the recent revisionist vogue. But the Risorgimento perhaps need not suffer such fate much longer. For a paraphrase of a great historian's exhortation to polemicists may at long last be taken to heart: "Risorgimentalists" and "Antirisorgimentalists," we beg of you, for pity's sake, please tell us simply what was the Risorgimento.

As a matter of fact, the end of the almost hopeless if not altogether sterile conflict of ideological faiths in interpretations of the Risorgimento seems now in sight. Carlo Antoni's great wish has begun to be answered: at long last a *ritorno alla ragione,* a return to historical reason self-consciously committed only to genuine historical problems, appears to be quietly, undramatically assumed as the basis for a new and fruitful historiographical era. Such a "return" should not involve a retrogression to the rationalistic and positivistic idols of the past nor should it lead to anachronistic reimmersions in the dead seas of intellectualism and dogmatism, shining and realistic as these may appear in some quarters. That "return" should rather be an advance based upon the fearless appraisal of the errors but also of the achievements of the preceding generations of Italian and European master historians. Perhaps only thus can the emergence of a new historiography without dogmas be ensured toward the writing of a modern Italian history beyond myths. In the possibility of such an advance lies the true promise of the present moment and the challenge to be faced by the postrevisionist generation of Italian historians.

Shorn of the ritualistic rhetoric of nationalism and mysticism and of the moralistic antirhetoric of the opposing Liberal and Marxist world views, those subtle instruments of a bitter Italian and European ideological conflict, the history of modern Italy may then be placed within its proper terms of reference. The old ones cannot be accepted so long as they insist on constraining that history either between the "idyll" of Italian liberalism in the nineteenth century and the historic "accident" of its twentieth-century downfall, or between the "failure" of the Risorgimento and the catastrophe which was Fascism. The Risorgimento may continue to be presented as a great struggle for unity and freedom, which was unredeemably condemned by its very nature and the "iron laws of history" to the role of another *rivoluzione mancata.* But that view would then be accepted in its true dimensions as a mere datum in the politics of contemporary Italy. The rich, complex developments of the Liberal period may still be reduced to a series of ineffectual efforts that episodically obscured even as they organically ensured the denouement to the "built-in disaster" of Fascism. But such a reduction would then clearly be subsumed under the category of a clinical analysis of so-called "causes" for the fall of a state. It will no longer be assumed as a historical basis for the reconstruction of the life of a people, of an Italian society that had worked and struggled for its freedoms and a dignified existence within the active circle of Europe's liberal civilization.

A century after the achievement of Italian political unity it may not be too rash to hope that agreement on the nature of the fundamental problems of the Risorgimento and the succeeding era of Italian reconstruction will leave sufficient liberty for the historical intelligence to be creative. For the moment at least, the basis for that concord perhaps need be no wider than a tacit commitment to restore the Risorgimento and the Liberal era as objects of genuine historical reflection.

Reinterpretations of the Aftermath of the Risorgimento*

H. STUART HUGHES

THE FOUR DECADES of Italian history 1861–1900 offer an almost too neat example of the fashion in which historical understanding proceeds by successive approximations. Each major interpretation of the period in question has represented a corrective or answer to a previous interpretation. The general account that has become standard for most non-specialists—Croce's *History of Italy, 1871–1915*—already represents an answer to a previously accepted view. And both the original view and the reply to it reflected the historical circumstances out of which they were formed. Once the political objective of the Risorgimento had been achieved, the attitude of most reflective Italians toward their recent past had been frankly critical. They had emphasized the weaknesses in the nation's development and more particularly the sense of disappointment and of a fall in moral level that had followed the ardors of the Risorgimento itself. As long as this view represented nothing more than a national examination of conscience and a spur to future action, it need have caused no particular misgivings. But when the Fas-

* This article is from "The Aftermath of the Risorgimento in Four Successive Interpretations," which originally appeared in *The American Historical Review*, LXI, No. 1, 70–76. Copyright © October 1955 by H. Stuart Hughes. Reprinted with the permission of H. Stuart Hughes.

cists began to exploit the general conviction of political degeneration and missed opportunities, in order to discredit the whole parliamentary tradition, and when in particular they denied the very real progress that had occurred after the turn of the century, it was time for a responsible historian to redress the balance.

It was at this point that Croce raised his voice. With his customary attitude of lofty serenity, the philosopher-historian searched out the positive elements in his country's parliamentary past and sought to link them together in a narrative that would be both intellectually coherent and aesthetically pleasing. In its strictly political aspects, Croce's account has undergone little subsequent correction. His reassessment of the fall of the old Right in terms of natural development rather than sudden catastrophe, his shift in emphasis from the juridical conflict between church and state to a consideration of the manner in which the *dissidio* gradually resolved itself into a practical series of working arrangements—interpretations such as these have continued to find general acceptance. When it came to economic and social questions, however, Croce's method proved less satisfactory. He viewed his subject matter from so rarefied an altitude, and with an air of such divine detachment, that what he said simply glided over the concrete data, gently enveloping them in an elegant phrase, rather than biting into them or even properly outlining their configurations. The result was to leave with his readers the impression that all was well in certain areas of the national development in which a little statistical investigation of the sort that Croce scorned would have revealed that all was definitely not well. The problem of the South, for example—despite the author's southern origin and proudly Neapolitan allegiance—figured only dimly in his historical account.

The next stage of reinterpretation, then, was quite naturally one of probing into those very economic and social problems that Croce had neglected. And the Second World War and the fall of Mussolini contributed mightily to this new assessment. For once the façade of Fascism was torn away, the bitter reality that even the anti-Fascist Croce had been unwilling to face stood revealed without protective rhetoric or palliation. In the general ruin of the years 1943 to 1946, Italians of all political faiths were obliged to recognize the unpalatable truth that neither Giolitti nor Mussolini, neither parliamentarism nor Fascism, had done very much to alter the basic character of Italian society—to close the tragic gap between North and South, rich and poor, peasant and city-dweller. It was upon such problems as these that the historical writing of the immediate post-Fascist period found its normal focus. And it was symptomatic of the time that the most inclusive reassessment of the era 1860–1900, Emilio Sereni's *Il capitalismo nelle campagne,*[1] should have been written by a Marxist historian.

This highly critical, sociologically oriented, and consciously pro-peasant-and-worker viewpoint remains the dominant historical attitude toward the decades in question. Nearly everyone who has written on internal Italian history in the past few years, myself included, has cast his work to a greater or lesser extent in this mold. We are all still fighting

[1] Turin, 1947.

our private wars of liberation from the overpowering intellectual influence of Croce. But rather more important, the obsessive memory of the struggle against Fascism and the searing experience of a knowledge of Italy at first hand during the war years have left their permanent mark. From this sort of early conditioning it seems difficult to make a satisfactory intellectual escape. It is largely a question of generation: the very young historian, whose first direct acquaintance with things Italian dates, say, from 1948, might well find himself writing even about the period before 1900 quite differently from someone only ten years his senior.

The elements, the faint beginnings of such a third stage of reinterpretation–twice post-Crocian–are now observable. So far this effort at reassessment has been restricted to hints thrown out in the course of historical analysis of a more conventional sort. It has occurred not so much in the writings of very young historians as in those of older and more established writers, of the first or second post-Crocian generation, who have been led by recent developments–and in general against their own political and intellectual inclinations–to make minor modifications in long- and tenaciously held attitudes toward Italy's parliamentary past. Faced with the collapse and failure of militant anti-Fascism and of the hope of sweeping political and social renovation under the leadership of a united Left, with the establishment of Christian Democratic rule, and with the emergence of intellectual and social conformism as the dominating feature of contemporary Italian life, these older historians, while retaining the main outlines of their earlier thinking, have reluctantly undertaken to modify it in certain detailed but significant respects.

As examples of this post-1948 historiography, I should like to consider in particular the following four recent publications: Arturo Carlo Jemolo's great *Chiesa e stato in Italia negli ultimi cento anni,*[2] Federico Chabod's prefatory volume to his projected history of Italian foreign policy from 1870 to 1896,[3] Mario delle Piane's study of Gaetano Mosca in the context of the late nineteenth-century tradition of antiparliamentary writing,[4] and the series of articles on Italian history from 1860 to 1922 published three years ago in *Il Ponte* by the youthful-spirited and irrepressible Gaetano Salvemini under the title "Fu l'Italia prefascista una democrazia?"[5] In this recent literature I should like to discuss in schematic outline the treatment accorded the three outstanding problems of the immediate post-Risorgimento era: the class character of the new regime; the relations between church and state; and the functioning of the parliamentary system.

In the post-1948 atmosphere of resurgent conservatism, in which the struggle against Communism has virtually superseded the previous obsession with Fascism, historians are beginning to lose their guilty conscience about the class character of the pre-1913 parliamentary state. The oligarchic nature of this re-

[2] Turin, 1949.

[3] *Storia della politica estera italiana dal 1870 al 1896,* I: *Le premesse* (Bari, 1951).

[4] *Gaetano Mosca: Classe politica e liberalismo* (Naples, 1952).

[5] I (January, 1952), 11–23; II (February, 1952), 166–81; III (March, 1952), 281–97.

gime—even after the extension of the suffrage in 1882—appears less troubling than it used to. Faced with a situation in which laical democracy has practically ceased to count as a force in Italian politics and in which the bulk of Italian Marxists have passed into the Communist or philo-Communist camp, historians are perhaps less inclined than they once were to describe anticlerical democracy and militant socialism as the necessarily progressive forces in the national life and invariably to take the side of the poor against the rich. They are quite willing to grant with the anti-Fascist post-Crocians that the consolidation of the new kingdom brought terrible social injustices in its wake: a crushing burden of taxation on the classes least able to pay and the nearly uniform sacrifice of southern to northern interests. In this sense the post-Crocian economic and socially conscious emphasis has proved to be a permanent historiographic acquisition. At the same time these more recent accounts suggest that a social conscience is all very well and a moral quality definitely to be cultivated, but that in certain periods in a nation's history such tender-mindedness ranks as a luxury that simply cannot be indulged. A sense of the state, of the overriding importance of ensuring law and order, must necessarily take precedence.

Is it too fanciful, then, to surmise that the living example of De Gasperi's struggle with subversion in the critical years 1946 to 1948 has had something to do with the recent tendency of historians to take a more favorable view of the government of the historic Right in the period from 1861 to 1876? In those latter years, as Chabod asserts again and again, the consideration that dominated men's minds was to prove to the outside world that the new state was viable, to ward off foreign intervention by demonstrating Italy's capacity to deal with subversion—whether Black or Red—and to put its own house in order. Writing as a diplomatic historian, Chabod has drawn attention to the obvious but too often neglected fact that in the immediate post-Risorgimento era considerations of foreign policy almost invariably took precedence over internal concerns. Everything the government did at home it did with one eye over its shoulder to catch the reactions of the great powers. Hence criticism of its policy as one dictated by class egoism may simply miss the main point. Under circumstances such as those in which Italy found itself in the 1860's and early 1870's, class interest and national interest ran parallel. High taxes, free trade, vast expenditures on public works, and the building of north-south railway lines, while they may have intensified the sufferings of the poor and widened the gap in economic level between North and South, were absolutely indispensable if the new state was to become a united nation in anything more than name. And Quintino Sella, in arguing that a balanced budget was the "categorical imperative" of national survival, like Luigi Einaudi three quarters of a century later, was only incidentally advocating a monetary and fiscal policy that favored the rich over the poor.[6]

Even Salvemini—doughty old Jacobin that he is—in accepting a definition of the Risorgimento as "the revolution of the rich" expresses his impatience with the sentimentalism of writers who talk of the foundation of the new state as a "revolution be-

[6] Chabod, pp. 497–500.

trayed." "What revolution was betrayed?" he queries. "The revolution of the rich? But it succeeded. The revolution of the poor? But no rich man promised it, and only a certain number of intellectuals and no [authentic] poor man demanded it."[7] The revolution that actually took place was the only revolution that could possibly have occurred. In 1860 the rich alone were politically conscious, and the state they founded was by very necessity a class state.

On the question of church-state relations, the influence of present-day political alignments in the reorientation of historical judgments is more direct and obvious. Christian Democratic rule and the reversal of the laical tradition of the Italian parliamentary state that it implies naturally offer the dramatic change that dominates retrospective thinking in this sphere. Jemolo suggests that in the course of the century 1848–1948 Italy went full circle from clericalism to the lay state and back again, and ascribes an "anti-Risorgimento" character to the present regime.[8] Only a minority of historians may go that far. But it is difficult to dissent from Chabod's more moderate account of the slow but cumulative restoration of papal prestige from Porta Pia to the Second World War that was to culminate in that anguished winter of 1943–1944, when, as in the time of the barbarian invasions, the inhabitants of Rome, abandoned by their royal ruler, turned to their bishop as their sole protector. And Chabod notes with ironic satisfaction the clairvoyance of those conservatives who early predicted that a change from monarchy to

[7] Salvemini, I, 16.
[8] Jemolo, pp. 715–16.

republic would immensely strengthen the papacy as the only remaining institution capable of stirring the popular imagination.[9]

Hence, in considering the period 1861–1900, these recent historical works have tended to devote less attention to the *dissidio* itself and to look rather at the early beginnings of church-state reconciliation in the thought and practice of far-seeing individuals. Such themes are legion and I shall simply suggest a few of them: the efforts of independent-minded churchmen like Monsignor Tosti and Bishop Bonomelli to bring the papacy and the Italian government closer together in the period of Crispi's first ministry; the activities of the *Opera dei congressi* and the beginnings of co-operation between clericals and lay-minded conservatives on the local electoral level; the first signs of nationalist pride in the church as a characteristically *Italian* institution; and finally—and perhaps most important—the gradually dawning conviction that it was "high time to lay aside distrust of the clergy and the papacy and instead to seek the alliance of these solid pillars of order against the red peril." As Chabod has suggested, "in Italy, rather more than in France, the anti-clericalism of the bourgeoisie" soon proved to be "not congenital but incidental, a question more of contingencies than of principles."[10] The eventual results of such a reorientation of sentiment are only too well known—from the Gentiloni Pact of 1913, through the Lateran accords of 1929, to the Christian Democratic electoral landslide of 1948. In judging this evolution, Chabod, far from a Marxist himself, has reached a

[9] Chabod, pp. 259–60, 338.
[10] *Ibid.*, pp. 283, 408.

position strikingly similar to that of a young Marxist historian, Paolo Alatri, who has argued that the loss of the pope's temporal power, coupled with the threat of socialism, was bound sooner or later to bring the church to drop its essentially feudal opposition to the liberal capitalist Italian state, and to join forces with it in a new conservative alliance.[11]

Finally, the crystallization of the post-Fascist republican regime–democratic in theory and in much of its practice but with certain features that are still frankly oligarchic–is leading historians to take a more charitable view of the functioning of the late nineteenth-century parliamentary monarchy. If this latter state was definitely not a democracy, at least it did not claim to be one. To the great majority of Italian statesmen of the period, even those who sat on the left of the Chamber of Deputies, the idea would have seemed preposterous. And Salvemini has echoed this note of wonderment in suggesting that historians stop upbraiding the pre-1900 parliamentary regime for not being something that it never intended to be. Similarly, Delle Piane has reminded us that the antiparliamentarianism of Mosca and his fellows was the very opposite of democratic in origin: far from demanding that the institutions of the Italian monarchy should function in a more popular fashion, these critics were primarily concerned with the damage they believed that the intrusion of the democratic principle was already causing.[12] As constitutionally minded oligarchs they were seeking at all

[11] Paolo Alatri, "Appunti per una storia del movimento cattolico in Italia," *Società*, 1949, no. 2, pp. 249–50.

[12] Delle Piane, pp. 40–41.

costs to preserve the leading position of the educated strata of society. And the very device they found so reprehensible—*trasformismo*—was itself, as Chabod has so penetratingly observed, in part a reaction of conservative self-defense after the suffrage extension of 1882.[13]

All of which is only to repeat the old maxim that every country at every period of its history gets the political regime it deserves. In the last four decades of the nineteenth century Italy was obviously unready for political democracy. More than half a century later, it is still not wholly ready. A consideration of the difficulties that post-Fascist Italy has experienced in establishing political democracy as a living reality may lead us to be less doctrinaire in judging the malfunctioning of the pre-Fascist constitutional monarchy. As Salvemini has well stated, the trouble with this earlier regime was not that it was "more or less oligarchical, or more or less democratic, but that it was supported by a weak juridical and moral conscience both in the rulers and in the ruled."[14] And the same is the case today. May we not conclude that a mildly corrupt parliamentary regime, in which constitutional procedures are honored nearly as often in the breach as in the observance, can be considered the norm for contemporary Italy?

Hence I suggest that historians are beginning to believe that they have been too high-minded and Mazzinian in writing about the Italian parliamentary monarchy. They have tended to think in terms of an Italy that never existed and does not yet exist—an Italy in which civic rectitude would be as wide-

[13] Chabod, pp. 385–86.
[14] Salvemini, I, 23.

spread as it is in Britain or Scandinavia and in which economic plenty would have reduced class egoism to the vanishing point. If we begin to think more in terms of the continuing realities of Italian society and public life, we may undertake to rewrite the history of the decades 1861–1900 not as measured against some impossible ideal regime but with a proper regard for the desperately difficult problems that the country's rulers actually faced. If the solutions they devised were mostly rather mediocre, so was the physical and political material with which they had to work.

II. HISTORIOGRAPHICAL CONTRASTS ON THE MAKING OF ITALIAN UNITY

AFTER THE WANING *of the Italian Renaissance during the sixteenth century Italy suffered a decline in her political and social life and a profound transformation of her cultural, artistic, and intellectual creative powers. Whatever else may be disagreed upon in interpretations of the seventeenth and eighteenth centuries in Italy, there exists a kind of historiographical consensus that Italian society and political life became alienated from the predominant developments of the Western European nations, particularly in so far as the organization and currents of national unitary life were concerned. By the eve of the French Revolution the leaders of Italian culture and intelligence were agreed that, however it might have to be accomplished, whether by reform or enlightened despotism, by gradualism or revolution, by purely "indigenous" methods or by learning from the "example" of other societies and nations of Western Europe, Italy must change, which meant essentially a "return to Europe," to the mainstream of Western social, political, and cultural life. This, in essence, represented the ideal motivation of what thoughtful Italians came to consider the "resurgence" of Italy as a nation, as a people, as a culture—the Risorgimento. Thus, though political renovation was one of its indispensable prerequisites—particularly in the light of the historic fact that the crisis of Renais-*

sance politics had brought almost hegemonic foreign domination to North and South Italy—the Risorgimento was from the start, in the late-eighteenth and early nineteenth centuries, envisaged as something larger than an experiment in successful state-making. It was, rather, the extent to which the solution of the Italian "national question," both before and after the Revolutions of 1848–49, would be accompanied by and constructively related to the resolution of other problems—economic, social, religious, cultural, and "moral"—that the organic success of the Risorgimento during its classic era (1815–70) would have to be judged. If, therefore, the Risorgimento was a "revolution that failed" (rivoluzione mancata) *that "failure" would have to be measured against the whole vast range of problems it confronted and sought to resolve. It is against some such vaster background that the two contrasting readings in the first part of this section might be judged.*

Cavour, Statecraft, and Freedom

Raymond Grew, who is one of the younger American scholars of the politics of the Risorgimento, argues that limitations of time and circumstances are in themselves not sufficient to explain the early failings of the Cavour phase of the Risorgimento, particularly during one of its most crucial years—1859. A whole combination of other factors, he points out, among which the unfounded social fears, the institutional timidity, the elitist psychology, and the political hauteur *of the liberal classes that were "helping" Cavour "make" Italy, conspired to lead them to a kind of premature success, and it was such a success that spoiled the Risorgimento. The thesis that Grew advanced in the article from which the reading below is taken was further elaborated in a fullfledged work entitled* A Sterner Plan for Italian Unity *(1963), which is a detailed study of the Italian "National Society," an organ of Cavourian policy during the second half of the 1850s.*

As a contrast to the relatively negative thesis of the American historian, the second piece in this section emphasizes a positive aspect of Cavourian politics: the origins and significance of the famous formula for religious freedom in Italy—"a free Church in a free State." Until the Lateran Pact of 1929, this Cavourian formula was the dominant principle in Italy for the relations between Church and State. The selection on Cavour's religious policy gains interest and significance if it is kept in mind that its author, Arturo Carlo Jemolo, is perhaps the most prominent Italian Catholic scholar whose historical views fall under the category of "liberal." Jemolo's book Chiesa e Stato in Italia durante gli ultimi cento anni *(1948) (the selection is drawn from an abridged version of it) was immediately hailed as one of the truly great new works published after 1945 in Italy.*

How Success Spoiled the Risorgimento*

RAYMOND GREW

THE MAKING OF a united Italy is one of the magnificent stories of the nineteenth century, and hundreds of historians have been tempted to test their prose in the telling of it. For all of them the events of 1859 and 1860 are the climax. Here the ideas of at least half a century, painted in broad, bold strokes, reach fulfilment in a series of particular events, best depicted in neat and colorful miniatures. The ideas developed during the Napoleonic experience lead to the vague yearnings of the Carbonari, the mysticism of Mazzini, and the practical program of Cavour; they are then expressed in the clash of armies, the clamor in the *piazzas* of a score of cities, Garibaldi leading his redshirts, and Cavour excitedly rubbing his hands. Perhaps it is because the story is so good that the relationship between those ideas and the particular climactic events of 1859 has been so little explored. A close analysis of their connection suggests something of crucial significance for all of modern Italian history: no one intended Italy to achieve her unification in the way she did; no one consciously wanted the political system of united Italy to be what it became. In those very months of

* From Raymond Grew, "How Success Spoiled the Risorgimento," *The Journal of Modern History*, XXXI, No. 3 (September 1962), 239–45, 246–49, 250–53. Reprinted by permission of the University of Chicago Press and Raymond Grew.

triumph, from April to December 1859, the Risorgimento itself came to be conceived in new and narrower limits.

It is too easy to see the events of 1859 marching in perfect order to the rhythmic needs of a narrative. The volunteers streaming across the Ticino show the growing enthusiasm for unification and provoke Austria into rash hostility. After an agonizing moment of uncertainty, war is declared; and the French prove true to their word. Revolutions then sweep across the Duchies and into the Romagna, extending the war and displaying a unanimity of popular sentiment that is itself the climax of years of propaganda and daring. In contrast to those of 1848, however, these revolutions are bloodless, and they succeed. The provisional governments which replace the departed dukes then do the work of destiny by subordinating themselves to the agents of Cavour. Suddenly, hopes are dashed as the Truce of Villafranca ends the war, providing merely for the addition of Lombardy to the Piedmontese domains, but Italy's nationalists remain steadfast. The provisional regimes in Tuscany, the Duchies, and the Romagna maintain order and earnestly adopt Piedmontese coinage and tariffs. They hold assemblies where, with happy unanimity, the demand is made for their annexation by Piedmont. In effect, Europe is presented with a *fait accompli,* the accomplishment of rare restraint. The dark hour of Cavour's resignation has proved to be a new dawn. Northern Italy, save Venice, becomes one country. Cavour's policy has triumphed after all.

Seen in this light, the political events in Italy from the outbreak of the war to the end of 1859 are a mere supplement to the drama of the war itself and a logical extension of Cavour's general policy. Such a view is not wrong, although it tends inevitably to a somewhat unhistorical tone, but it is inadequate. It treats the Risorgimento as the contagion of a common sentiment rather than as a multiform political movement concerned with real and important issues. It misses the point that while skilfully conducting this campaign Italy's leaders were, without meaning to and certainly without facing the fact, doing much to determine what the politics of united Italy would be like. It was during this period of fulfilment that the Risorgimento became a movement which largely eliminated the masses from participation in politics. So conceived, it discouraged the discussion of those political questions which had been its substance. It restricted to a minimum those political and social changes which had been its promise. Administrative fiat and dictatorship became the means for making decisions.

The narrowing of popular participation in the movement to unify Italy began before the war. The volunteers who made their way to Piedmont that spring provided the greatest demonstration of Italian political consciousness in ten years. Nearly 20,000 had arrived by March; yet the leaders of Piedmont were never comfortable with this exciting sign of the success of their policies. They had suggested that those men being conscripted into Austrian or local Italian armies come to serve in Piedmont instead, thinking, with somewhat exaggerated realism, that these would be the only ones likely to come. There was, however, a graver reason for that suggestion: those avoiding conscription would be soldiers first and political demonstrators second. Volunteers, in contrast, were notoriously susceptible to infectious ideologies and were likely to be more loyal to Garibaldi than to formal military discipline. Thus the government remained ambivalent in its attitude toward these men, mostly students and not such a motley crew after all, who in increasing numbers slipped across the borders to prove, through the risks they took, their personal courage and their confidence in Piedmont. These and the other reasons, domestic and diplomatic, for the government's hesitance are easily understood. This was a movement that created an atmosphere of chaos. It was one that might easily get out of hand and begin to define its own political goals. It might even produce an unfortunate revolt across the Ticino or in the Duchies. The hesitance those reasons produced meant that the leading state in Italy could not support the demonstration of widespread belief in its leadership, that the opportunity to make a more popular movement of its policy had to be missed, that the war of Italian liberation would be a battle of professional armies, that neither the popularity of Garibaldi nor the political and military potentialities of the thousands ready to rally to him could be effectively used.

The same sort of fear prevented the moderates from advocating local insurrections in the spring of 1859. The war plans of the previous year had included local revolts both as the war's justification and as a device for extending it outside Lombardy. Yet these plans, so precise in 1858, became increasingly vague as the time came to use them. The National Society, which still thought of itself as the agent of revolution, shared all of Cavour's concern that revolt might break out too soon, either fail or spread too far, endanger the diplomatic security of Piedmont or allow more radical forces to triumph locally and then use their position to modify Piedmont's. When at last the National Society issued the call to revolt, it was muffled and faint. The moderates had turned from revolution; they preferred to have Italy's fortunes decided with the more limited risks of battle.

No real revolution occurred in Italy in 1859, no popular participation in government as in 1848. The revolt in Milan was a calm transference of powers, directed in part by an agent of Cavour immediately after the departure of the Austrians. A revolution might have taken place in Tuscany if the grand duke had not left before anything more serious than a demonstration was necessary. Again an ambassador of Cavour, Carlo Boncompagni, and the Tuscan moderates kept things well in hand so that the complications of unneeded enthusiasm were avoided. In Modena and the Romagna, too, the nationalists rose only as the Austrians left. Marco Minghetti, who was one of those closest to Cavour, had seen such cautious waiting as a means whereby the Romagna could avoid the "political question," a strange goal for a revolution. These were rather *coups d'état,* and, in contrast to the National Society's premature attempt in Parma, they relied on the proximity of Piedmontese troops. Minghetti was relieved that his country's future would now be "the necessary consequence of great happenings" and "no longer the work of any party." Politics as the public discussion of the form and methods of government was to be avoided.

In each town a faint legality was maintained, as the existing city council appointed a provisional government of moderate nationalists. The provisional governments tended to see their function as an extension of diplomacy. They were to do what Piedmont alone dared not, replace the previous government and then hand their authority to Victor Emmanuel. Thus any opposition, diplomatic or domestic, was faced with that surest of political weapons, the accomplished fact. Wherever possible the treaties of 1848 were re-invoked, and with little concern for the legality of their mandate the provisional governments then handed the full powers they claimed to a commissioner of Piedmont. Usually within a week an agent of Cavour exercised the full political power of the province. And Cavour's followers, in or out of office, tended to accept in the name of freedom the gravest restrictions on its practice. They could, like a group about to found a newspaper in Tuscany, volunteer for censorship believing that there would come "a time of free discussions"; and they expected a similar "sacrifice" from their more radical opponents. It is not surprising that under the new dispensation radicals and Mazzinians found they had no more rights in theory and perhaps fewer in practice, partly because the efficient men of the new government knew so well who the Mazzinians were.

But when the talk of the political and social changes which the Risorgimento must bring about had lessened, so did the pressure for reform. After their patriotic addresses to Victor Emmanuel and their somewhat fawning ones to Napoleon III, the provisional governments had made it a point to make few changes. The exigencies of war supported their own political desire to avoid controversy, and the provisional government of Tuscany spoke for them all when it declared that any reordering of institutions should be postponed until the "great enterprise is completed." Such postponement ran the risk, of course, of becoming permanent; but to men determined to avoid the errors of 1848 it appeared a "sacred duty" to avoid "untimely innovations." The provisional government in Milan had shown its doctrinal liberalism by abolishing the death penalty, declaring the civil equality of Jews, and allowing political exiles to return. The *giunta* in Bologna did these things, too, and even reduced tariffs and adopted the Napoleonic Code while demonstrating its reliable hardheadedness by prohibiting all newspapers and political writings from its first day in power. Yet the old bureaucracy was maintained, and the police little altered. Indeed, it had to be explained to the public by proclamation that these institutions of former repression had, with few changes even in personnel, now become trustworthy. Except for such brief flurries of activity, the Piedmontese commissioners found themselves presented with full powers essentially unlimited by the preceding acts of the provisional governments; and Cavour's men, Boncompagni, Luigi Carlo Farini, Diodato Pallieri, and Massimo d'Azeglio, made appointments to major administrative posts and picked their own advisers with surprisingly little regard for those who had so happily handed the reins to them. When the provisional governments dissolved, the moderates of daring quickly gave way to still milder moderates of greater respectability.

The changes they tended to institute were not those evoked by visions of a better society but those which resulted from administrative need. The extensive authority given the commissioners had a precedent in the granting of dictatorship to Victor Emmanuel, a step which had on all sides been regarded as essential, so much so that to suggest constitutional guarantees in the interim seemed an affront to the *Re Galantuomo.* This authority came to be wielded by others who, in his name and with doubtful constitutionality, limited the freedom of the press, applied the penal code, prorogued parliament, levied tariffs and taxes. It is a tribute to the probity of these provincial dictators that this power was not more seriously misused. But the constitutional precedents were dangerous, and the procedures used were often unfortunate. Piedmontese laws were extended by fiat without either theoretical concern for their merits or careful study of local conditions. It was in Lombardy that the processes of bureaucracy first began to deal (as they would later in the rest of Italy) with some of the crucial issues no assembly had discussed. The Piedmontese court system was extended there by decree; the new penal code, with its dangerously complex clauses on religious liberty, was announced, and the limited local government to be allowed in Lombardy was defined. Even these laws were often violated in practice, and the new Italian state experienced from the first some of the censorship and arbitrary imprisonment that had been familiar under other regimes. But the pattern for Italy's administration was set. It would be highly centralized and ruled by Piedmontese codes which protected liberty with few fundamental guarantees.

After the truce at Villafranca, these regimes were no longer directly supported by the power of Piedmont, and the commissioners turned their authority over to the local leaders with whom they had been working. These provincial governments then had to secure a popular sanction, and soon each of them followed Farini's lead from Modena in calling for elections to provincial "national assemblies." The suffrage, which varied in the different provinces, was announced by decree. With some pride it was usually added that the elections would in fact be free, although Baron Bettino Ricasoli included the warning that those who dared disturb the concord of Tuscans would be punished. Prefects were instructed to take a "beneficent initiative" in the naming of candidates in order that the election would not be "preempted by parties," and to encourage the political dominance of reliable citizens. Still, the prefects were expected to act at least with decorum; and the voting appears not to have been outrageously rigged.

II

The manner and tone of the politics of a united Italy were being determined, but the followers of Cavour who dominated those politics in 1859 took pride in being pragmatists. If in a sequence of crises their practices whittled away at their own liberal vision of the Risorgimento, they were scarcely aware of it. The interaction of ideas and events is always subtle, but the effect of that subtlety in this case is easily overlooked because the methods employed by Cavour's followers and the political system they created are, when seen with hindsight, so easily explained by calling these men "moderates." In this period the term was usually reserved for those like Cavour, Minghetti, Farina, Ricasoli, or perhaps D'Azeglio, who by the 1850's had come to dominate Italian politics—for those who were politically influential, decently nationalist, and loyally monarchist.

Often members of the aristocracy or at least men who could move with ease in such circles, these followers of Cavour had become reformers in the Enlightenment tradition of scientific societies and agricultural associations. They had discovered, like Cavour, that successful pig farming required political reform. Often they had, like Minghetti with Pius IX, tried to work within the old regimes. Finding themselves stifled there, and touched by the Mazzinian dream, they came to think in more than provincial terms. Yet they felt a deep distaste for revolution, and it was easy for them to lead Italians in learning from the failures of 1848. They found a pattern for reform without revolution in the contemporary history of England and France, models made natural for them by their own international connections. Thus the moderates tended to advocate representative institutions while remaining suspicious of politics and contemptuous of parties, for they had learned from Antonio Rosmini that parties are "worms which devour the fabric of society." They adopted liberal economic theory and believed in the importance and inevitability of economic growth. Here they most directly appealed to Italy's small middle class of merchants and lawyers. Combining a respect for the traditional institutions of power (such as the monarchy and the military) with demands for change, they easily adopted the tone of realism and naturally shared the fears of a Lord Malmesbury.

Finally, they were compromisers who were keenly aware of the weakness of their position; for compromise, as a principle, makes the dullest of political programs. Mazzini could fail and maintain a following. The moderates were certain they must succeed in winning much of what the nationalists wanted whenever they had the chance or lose their dominance. That conviction both stimulated their courage and increased their caution. It explains Cavour's panic that the war might not begin in April and his famous loss of temper on learning the news of Villafranca. These displays of emotion were not, as often interpreted, merely signs of an uncharacteristic flaw or uncontrolled patriotism. For the moment Cavour's policy had failed, and out of Mazzini's steady flow of prognostications, dire and utopian, the warnings against an alliance with France stood out as apparently proved. Yet the Cavourian policy did not collapse, and the Risorgimento contains no greater testimonial to the sagacity of the Moderates than their conduct of Italian affairs in the months following Villafranca.

The Moderates thought of themselves as liberal as well as nationalist, but the methods they employed in 1859 had done much to make a liberal state less likely. Like their ideological cousins elsewhere in Europe, Italian moderates had run too far from the failures of 1848. Determined to avoid fatal political divisions, they had sought unanimity less through agreement than by postponing all "lesser" issues, all questions but unification. Postponement in practice proved to be decision without discussion. Determined this time to succeed, they had stressed the military virtues of discipline and order. The very concepts of unification and liberty had been vigorously and deliberately separated as distinct issues unnecessarily cumbersome when taken together.

Only a program which took advantage of the ambitions of Piedmont, the aims of the lower middle class, and the discontents of the lower middle and artisan classes could have won widespread support. Only one with which Louis Napoleon could associate himself and which Great Britain could accept was likely to succeed. The moderates, with only occasional slips, provided that program. To do so, however, they expressed ideas which were the critique of the policies they pursued. They sounded like Gladstone but performed like Guizot. Confident there was a law of progress, the moderates believed they had opened Italy to its beneficial effects. They could rely on time to correct their omissions.

The moderates' policies in these exciting months of 1859 are important to historical understanding, then, for a number of reasons. Those policies succeeded, and they established the kind of political system under which united Italy operated: a highly centralized state dominated by the bureaucracy with effective power limited to a small group of men with similar backgrounds and interests. Those policies are important, too, precisely because what the moderates did was not what they had advocated. To begin with, a great deal about the kind of Risorgimento they would direct had not been determined by the spring of 1859. The moderates themselves did not know whether the war would extend to the Papal States,

Sicily, or even to Tuscany; there was little deliberation about the role revolutions might play. Even the old hope for something like a constituent assembly to follow a successful war had not been clearly rejected. As enemies of Mazzini, the moderates had denounced his tactics and condemned his means; but they had not, even in their own thinking, altogether divorced themselves from his vision of the future. In August Farini could still insist that a united Italy would not be centralized *alla francese,* and Minghetti years later would not understand the impossibility of fulfilling that promise.

More important, the moderates were both deeply nationalist and devoted to the concept of parliamentarism. The very assemblies which so avoided debate had medals struck for the men who had volunteered and monuments built to commemorate the actions of the populace. Perhaps it was the implications of social unity within nationalism which the moderates understood best, but they did not shun the suggestion of domestic freedom which was part of the meaning of independence. The moderates were fond of the word "liberty," and they had freely promised it as the fruit of their labors. For them a national parliament was the very symbol of unification; justice through law was the highest achievement of the state. In the chamber of deputies or in the various assemblies they expected their representative institutions to be treated with respect, and they took delight in parliamentary procedures. They espoused liberal economic theories which implied social changes that, in the Italy of the 1850's, were in fact revolutionary. Their deviations from such programs they saw only as the result of practical necessity. But their very practicality made it difficult for them to see how far they had strayed from such abstract standards and made it impossible for them to understand the charge that they had moved always in the direction of their immediate class interests. . . .

Finally, taken all together, these policies the moderates so practically pursued during the triumphant months of 1859 played their part in much of subsequent Italian history. The way in which Italy was united left a dull, persistent ache in the Italian body politic. The exclusion from politics of most Italians was part of that legacy. Garibaldi came to represent the participation through direct action of those who had been left out. It was this which made him seem a threat to Cavour in 1860 and caused the prime minister to view the general with such harsh fear. The tendency to substitute men proved in Piedmont for local leaders (including even those who had been active in the National Society), the split with Garibaldi, the intolerance toward the parliamentary Left (and the habit of seeing in it all the dangers of the Parisian proletariat) led to the narrowing of the political base of the new Italy. This was a moment, however, at which the urban lower middle class and some leading artisans were gaining a new political self-consciousness. When years later they were admitted to effective political life, they tended first to fight the battle of their past deprivation. Italy's political base was not broad enough to support a system of two parties, while the exclusion of democrats and Catholics left an increasingly isolated ruling caste. And the beleaguered, earnest moderates could not forget the moments of unanimity they had claimed in 1859; for them, disagreement would always smack of a selfish partisanship, a decline from the greatness of Cavour's age.

"Unconditional unitarianism" one of the moderates' opponents labeled this attitude, in arguing that inherently it led to the sacrifice of liberty. But that tendency was the more dangerous because united Italy suffered from the lack of traditions of legality and precedents of restraint. These shortcomings, too, were part of the legacy of moderate policy. One could not effectively cite the authority of constitution and laws when they were the product neither of some dominant ideology nor of a publicly welded compromise. They had been expedients, so tightly tied to the needs of the moment that they lost dignity as circumstances changed. They had been weakened from the first by the reliance on dictatorship in Piedmont and in the provinces. It would remain a temptation, as in the plebiscites of 1860, to use the instruments of representative government primarily for safe demonstrations which left a slight sense of sham. Urbano Rattazzi was only the first of a long line of lesser successors to be tempted by Cavour's gaudier successes. Well before Aspromonte or the days of Agostino Depretis, he had done his part in 1859 to make corridor intrigue and the extraconstitutional support of the King an important part of Italian politics. Too often diplomatic triumphs would seem, as they had in 1859 but with more reason, the only way of overcoming domestic division. And in the decade after 1860 parliament was plagued, in addition to its regular burdens, by the need to serve as the constituent assembly which had not been held. It is no wonder that the new legal codes were exceedingly cautious and inappropriately close to their

French models. They, too, became a source of disappointment and dissatisfaction.

Disappointment was deepened by the fact that, in the process of achieving national union, nationalism itself had been somewhat tainted. Caution and realism had led, in 1859, to that regional self-interest which made Tuscany hesitant to join with the Duchies and both of them reluctant to associate their claims to the diplomatically dangerous ones of the Romagna. The Perugian patriots had been abandoned; and if, in a few bloody days, they had displayed the weakness of revolution, they had established, too, the unheroic limits of Piedmontese realism. The cession of Nice was another of those bitter blows to the sanguine nationalist, a list of which could easily be extended to 1866. Many of these disappointments are a measure of how weak the forces were which worked for Italy's union. Indeed, an assessment of the difficulties the moderates faced suggests that unification was neither so inevitable nor so imminent as most contemporaries thought. In this sense, the moderates accomplished more than they could claim. But the discovery of what unification did not achieve led to the recognition of what narrow aims moderates had. When coupled with the assumption that Italian unification was a nineteenth-century necessity, it led to the feeling that the moderates had been guilty of some subtle treachery, of having stolen something.

But by far the most important legacy of the moderate policy was the disappointment in the Risorgimento, in Italy itself, which grew to haunt Italian politics. The discontent with Piedmontese laws, the sense of having been cheated out of the old dream of a constituent assembly arose even before the new state was established and spread as a criticism of the foundation of the regime. Inevitably the Left lamented the fall from its ideals, but even the conservative Alfonso La Marmora confessed a decade later that the means by which Italy had been made embarrassed those who later governed. Much of the caution of 1859 had been meant to reassure Europe, but even this could be self-defeating. With self-righteous perceptiveness the *Westminster Review* complained at the time that the Italians had shown "more sagacity than energy," that their freedom had been won "by a fortunate deficiency of vehemence and excitement." Italy's dependence on other countries had been made too clear; and these things, like the limited role granted the provisional governments, deprived the successful Risorgimento of 1859 of the heroic tradition of its predecessor. The famous post-unification political apathy was more than a letdown once the one great goal was achieved. It expressed a sense of disappointment with the past as well as the present. The feeling of the revolution *manquée* was born with the successes of 1859, and Boncompagni confessed more than he meant when, in 1871, he noticed that Italy was "more fortunate than great."

While the attention of all concerned was concentrated on the skill and luck with which political unification was at last being achieved in Italy, the meaning of that unification was being determined with far less attention. The moderates were almost pathetically eager to establish that Italians could behave with the popular restraint and political responsibility of Englishmen and Frenchmen. And that rather limited aim they attained. But in doing so they bore the burden not only of Italy's history but of their neighbors' as well. They could have been more generous to the classes beneath them if they had not confused them with the more demanding masses of the industrialized countries. They could have won a wider following if their opponents had not had ready at hand all the arguments against Whiggish limitations developed in the different context of Britain and France. What was done in 1859 is explicable in terms of the needs then felt and understandable in terms of the values the moderates held; and by so assessing it, one can escape the traditional polemics. The crucial months of 1859 stand, then, as something of a turning point; but their historical importance lies more deeply in the opportunity they afford for studying the ideals and realities of the Risorgimento. What was then done, when every act was a political decision, teaches something about the balance of forces in Italy as well as the weaknesses of that practical liberalism so common to the nineteenth century. As for the deeds themselves, one need only ponder them to recognize within the exciting story the importance of the precedents then set and of the pride Italian patriots could not feel in a country so compromisingly formed.

Cavour and Religious Freedom in Thought and Practice*

ARTURO CARLO JEMOLO

THE RISORGIMENTO GAVE to the world the man to whom Paléologue dedicated a volume subtitled *Un grand réaliste,* the man who was the true artificer of national unification: Camillo di Cavour. And Cavour, who had become set in his ideas well before 1848 as a result of his frequent contacts with political circles in Geneva, England and the France of Louis Philippe,[1] was devoted to the ideal of liberty. In his philosophy, true liberty is compounded of a number of individual freedoms, all of which are interdependent, so that if one is violated all the others suffer in consequence. It is worthy of note that among these freedoms he accorded a by-no-means insignificant place to freedom of trade.

We do not know a great deal about Cavour's religious beliefs. When he was little more than eighteen years of age he passed through a spiritual crisis which prompted him to embrace a crude rationalism.[2] Did he later revert to the faith of his fathers? On numerous occasions he declared himself to be

* From A. C. Jemolo, *Church and State in Italy, 1850–1950.* Translated by David Moore (Oxford: Basil Blackwell, 1960), 16–26. Reprinted by permission of Basil Blackwell, Publisher.

[1] F. Ruffini, *La giovinezza di Cavour,* 2nd ed. (two vols., Turin, 1937–38).

[2] F. Ruffini, *Ultimi studi sul conte di Cavour* (Bari, 1936).

a Catholic, and we know that on his death-bed he was at pains to obtain the consolations of religion. But it is doubtful whether his Catholicism signified an acceptance of the Church's dogmas and a belief in its sacraments–whether, in fact, it signified anything more than a belief in a personal God and an adhesion to the Church regarded as an organized institution with a high civilizing mission. And we may well ponder whether his anxiety not to die a reprobate was not merely the anxiety of a statesman, unwilling that his death should confirm in the eyes of the many the impossibility of remaining in the Church while disobeying the Pope in the political field.

What we do know is that it was Cavour's sincere belief in freedom that inspired his plan for the regularization of relations between Church and State–a plan which finds its epitome in the formula 'a Free Church in a Free State'.

In 1842 the Protestant pastor Alexandre Vinet had published his *Essai sur la manifestation des convictions religieuses et sur la séparation de l'Église et de l'État,* based on the concept that the acquisition of a religious faith is a spontaneous act, from which it follows that a State religion is inadmissible. From this source, as well as from his passionate belief in freedom, Cavour derived the idea that the State should renounce all control over the Church, which in its turn should not lay claim to any special privileges, but should be subject to the law of the land. Accordingly, all the fundamental institutions of civil life should be secularized, although the Church should be left free to expand, to win souls, to persuade an ever-increasing number of people to submit of their own free will to its discipline. But even an overwhelming majority of believers must never be allowed to impose its will on a minority or otherwise to embarrass it, just as a majority of unbelievers must never transform the State into an instrument of atheistic propaganda or in any way weaken the position of the Faithful.

Here is the essence of Cavour's thought. In effect, he always offers an equally stout opposition to clericals and Jacobins, to attempts on the part of the Church to interfere in the life of the State, and to measures aimed at the persecution of Catholics and clergy.

Utterly absorbed as he was in political life, Cavour wrote no books. Anyone who wishes to make a closer study of the separatist doctrine which inspired his policies should consult *La Chiesa e lo Stato in Piemonte* (1854–55), written by one of his most faithful followers, Pier Carlo Boggio. The author bases himself on the assumption that the State has jurisdiction only over the external acts of the individual and then only in so far as they affect the security and well-being of the community; whereas the Church has jurisdiction only over men's consciences, with special reference to the health of the individual soul. It follows that Church and State ought to exist side by side, each being independent of the other within its own sphere. Later, we read: 'The religious spirit seeks to make the individual perfect. The translation of this principle into the realm of politics invariably provokes a whole series of measures which are more or less vexatious and oppressive according to the intensity of their sponsor's conviction that he is acting in the interests of those against whom they are directed . . . there is no more inflexible and pertinacious tyrant than he who believes that he has a mandate from God to seek to promote by his rule the spiritual welfare of his subjects . . . as a general rule, the fruits of hieratical government are not freedom of thought, the advance of learning, industrial progress and commercial prosperity, but prostration, ignorance, poverty and enfeeblement.'

The student would also do well to read Marco Minghetti's twelve letters *Della libertà religiosa* (1855). Minghetti had represented Bologna in Pius IX's Council of State (to which reference has already been made), and in 1848 he had been a Papal minister. Subsequently he collaborated closely with Cavour in the negotiations which the great minister conducted with Rome during the last months of his life, and after Italy's unification he was twice Prime Minister of the Kingdom.

Minghetti denies that the spirit of Christianity is incompatible with religious freedom. The Gospel, he says, makes no reference to civil government nor to relations between Church and State. And he adds that nothing emerges more clearly from the Christian doctrine than the primacy of spiritual freedom. 'When Church and State forged their alliance and temporal punishments were combined with spiritual ones, or at least the exercise of civil rights was made conditional upon the profession of a State religion, then violence was countered by deception, to which even governments were party.' Like Cavour, Minghetti affirms the interdependence of all the freedoms. The separation of Church and State does not make a conflict between the two inevitable, rather does it establish between them a harmony no longer inspired by self-interest, fear and passion, but 'resulting from the fundamental unity of the spiritual and temporal orders, and indeed of all orders, whether of thought or life, speculation or action.'

If their theoretical concepts and basic principles are crystal-clear, the same cannot be said of the manner in which Cavour and his followers set about putting them into practice. They do not advocate the separation of Church and State, as exemplified in the U.S.A., where the idea of government legislation in the realm of ecclesiastical affairs is unknown. Nor, for that matter, do they express themselves in favour of the Belgian system. Indeed, they often point to it as an illustration of the axiom that the granting of freedom to the Church is the first step to a clerical dictatorship. Cavour was a man of action, and he was not deaf to the voices of those who sought to remind him that what might be done with impunity by a great State, a State not torn by internal dissensions, whose citizens were of one mind on all fundamental questions–on the need for the renunciation of any form of State supervision of ecclesiastical activities–could not be done by a State like Sardinia. For in the Kingdom there was still a deep division of opinion between those who wistfully recalled the peaceful days of the absolute monarchy and those who yearned for the gradual introduction of liberal measures, between those who desired the preservation of the *status quo* and looked askance at the political exiles from other Italian States to whom the Government had offered hospitality and in many cases employment–a considerable part of the Kingdom, to wit Savoy, made no secret of the fact that it felt completely extraneous to the rest of the peninsula–and those who would have liked to see the Kingdom of Sardinia absorbed into a united Italy.

All Catholics instinctively realized that separation would be more injurious to the principles to which they were pledged than the most rigorous jurisdictional measures, inasmuch as it would give the State complete control of the law and of the external life of the people, leaving the Church to keep watch over men's consciences and denying it any authority other than that voluntarily conceded to it by the Faithful. And old jurisdictionalists and Jacobins were equally dismayed by the idea of a disarmed State, powerless to punish bishops, to protect priests who were faithful to national ideals–'patriot' priests–from the wrath of their superiors, to prevent the formation of countless new religious associations, to prohibit the latter from giving instruction, and to prevent ecclesiastical bodies from receiving legacies. And, as always in politics, there were the prudent ones, those who accepted the idea in principle, but who felt that they must needs await a suitable moment to translate it into action, and who would willingly have left it to their successors to work out the practical details.

But there came a time when it seemed to Cavour that the moment was ripe to carry the idea into effect. It came on the morrow of Italy's unification, when he felt he would be justified in offering the Church her freedom–which he sincerely believed would be as beneficial to the Church as to the State –in exchange for the renunciation of her temporal power.

In 1859 the French Army crossed the Alps. The battles of Magenta, Solferino and San Martino were followed by the armistice of Villafranca. It seemed that Piedmont must surely annex Lombardy, that all Italy must revert to the *status quo* of 1814. But on the proclamation of war the States of Parma, Modena, Tuscany and Romagna had risen in revolt, and in order to restore their lawful governments it would have been necessary to use force. Austria was in the throes of a crisis; France announced that she did not propose to intervene. On May 5th, 1860, Garibaldi left Quarto with a thousand volunteers. First Sicily, then the continental part of the Kingdom collapsed. To the accompaniment of the rallying-cry of 'Italy for Victor Emmanuel' preparations were made to annex the territories in question. Finally, the regular army occupied Umbria and the Marches. France accepted the situation, claiming as the price of her acquiescence the surrender of Savoy, cradle of the dynasty, and Nice.

Napoleon III would have liked to help Italy and to avoid giving too much offence not merely to Catholic opinion throughout the world, but to almost all shades of French opinion, which regarded the unification of Italy as contrary to France's interests.

On December 22nd, 1859, there was published in Paris a pamphlet entitled *Le Pape et le Congrès*. Although unsigned, it was known to reflect the views of the Emperor. The author declared that the Pope must be allowed to retain his sovereignty, but that an authority which derived from God Himself could not be imposed on the peoples by force. The smaller the Pope's domain, and the more his position resembled that of the father of a family, the less likelihood would there be of any trouble in the future. The Pope should be content to keep Rome and a very small piece of the surrounding territory. All the Catholic Powers would combine to ensure the permanence of the Holy See. It was highly desirable that a meeting of those Powers should be held in Paris before the end of 1860 to guarantee the integrity of Rome and the Papal territory, as well as their economic security.

The pamphlet caused much indignation among French Catholics. Veuillot likened it to the kiss of Judas. Mgr. Dupanloup, Mgr. Pie and other French bishops, various eminent laymen, Catholics, Orleanists and even Protestants seized their pens and rushed to the attack. De Broglie, Falloux, Cochin, Corcelles, Guizot, Thiers, Cousin, Villemain and Montalembert all expressed themselves in vehement terms. After a campaign which bore the appearance of a protest against the Emperor's policy, Father Lacordaire was elected a member of the Academy. (In spite of this, the old champion of Catholic liberalism also took up his pen in defence not only of the temporal authority of the Pope, but of the recent reforms and of the idea of an Italian Confederation.)

In Paris there was much talk of establishing an Italian Confederation under the honorary presidency of the Pope. But Pius IX made his agreement to such a proposal conditional upon his recovery of Romagna; and at the same time he made it clear that he was opposed to the idea of appointing Victor Emmanuel to be vicar apostolic of the territory. For their part, neither the Government of Turin nor the liberals would hear of the suggestion that Umbria and the Marches should be restored to their former ruler. In February, 1861, another pamphlet entitled *La France, Rome et l'Italie* made its appearance. It was written ostensibly by the Vicomte de la Gueronnière, but in fact by Persigny, who extolled Napoleon III's work on behalf of the Church and laid emphasis on the Roman Curia's numerous manifestations of intransigence, and even of hostility to the Emperor. Peace, he declared, must be established between Italy and the Pope, for the bonds that united them were indissoluble. The Emperor, 'fidèle à son double devoir de souverain élu par la volonté national et de fils aîné de l'Église, ne peut sacrifier l'Italie à la cour de Rome ni livrer la Papauté à la révolution.' The publication provoked a fresh flood of polemics and pastoral letters.

Naturally, the period of transition to Italian unity, characterized by the military occupation of vast areas of the peninsula and the setting up of various provisional governments, was not devoid of incident. The ecclesiastical legislation adopted by Piedmont was wholly or in part extended to those regions of Italy which had been annexed or were in the process of being annexed. In the provinces that had risen against their lawful rulers the episcopate declined to recognize the new governments, and in face of this intransigence the latter reacted violently. For refusing to allow his clergy to take part in the nation-wide celebrations Cardinal Corsi, Archbishop of Pisa, was arrested and banished to Turin, where he was confined to a monastery. So corrupting are the effects of inflamed passions coupled with the empty pretence of *salus populi* that even so great a champion and exponent of the ideals of liberty as Cavour approved this measure, although he was aware of its doubtful legality. In addition, Mgr. Ratta, vicar capitular of Bologna, was arrested and tried.

The immediate preoccupation of Cavour and the Piedmontese Government was to remain outside the conflict; to ensure the elimination from the 1859 peace treaty of those clauses which provided that the banished rulers should return to their lands and that, apart from the incorporation of Lombardy in the State of Piedmont, there should be no change in the country's political structure; to induce the Powers to recognize the fact of Italy's unification (the Government's fears on this score grew daily less, for the situation was undoubtedly favourable to the cause of Italian nationalism); and–since a permanent state of conflict was not without its disadvantages–to arrive at a *modus vivendi* with the Pope. In the meantime, however, another problem had arisen–the problem of selecting a capital for the new Kingdom of Italy, which had been proclaimed on March 17th, 1861. Now that Savoy had been ceded to France, Turin was almost a frontier town. Cavour, who was tortured by the memory of the dissension that had arisen between Milan and Turin in 1848, feared that the new Kingdom might be plunged into a serious, possibly a fatal crisis over this question of a capital. Neither Naples nor Florence would be willing to play second fiddle to Turin, while deputies hailing from Sicily and Calabria would not take kindly to the idea of having to travel the whole length of Italy in order to sit in a Parliament whose headquarters were situated at the foot of the Alps.

It seemed to Cavour that the only possible solution to the problem was to make Rome the capital. Before the splendour of that name, with all its great associations, the claims of all other Italian cities paled into insignificance. Realist that he was, Cavour was acutely conscious of the problems of his time, and he was by temperament utterly disinclined to glorify the memory of a greatness that had ended more than fifteen centuries before. A true European, he was completely absorbed in the events that were unfolding in the north of the Continent, and he had never in his life had any desire to visit the city of the Caesars. It is therefore all the more remarkable that, by a strange combination of circumstances, he should have come to regard the question of Rome's future as the most important of all the problems that beset Italy at the moment of her unification, and that he should have associated the question of the annexation of Rome by Italy, and hence the question of the Church's loss of her temporal power, with the question of the relations between Italy and the Holy See. The consequences of this linking of two seemingly unrelated problems were alike incalculable and enduring; and it is not without interest that the great statesman's contemporaries, save for a few shrewd spirits who regarded it as a mistake on his part, completely failed to appreciate its significance.

In the parliamentary debate of March, 1861, Boncompagni, a loyal supporter of Cavour, declared that the Pope could no longer be allowed to retain his temporal power and that Rome must now become the capital of Italy. In his reply Cavour rammed home this point, adding that the Government hoped 'to solve the Roman problem by convincing the more responsible section of the Catholic community that the reunion of Rome with Italy would be in no way prejudicial to the independence of the Church'. And he went on to quote part of the message which the Government intended to address to the Pope: 'Holy Father, for you the possession of temporal power is no longer a guarantee of independence. Renounce it, and we will give you that freedom which you have sought in vain for three centuries from all the great Catholic Powers. You have endeavoured to secure a part of this freedom by means of concordats, in consideration of which you, Holy Father, have been forced to concede privileges–nay, worse than that, you have been compelled to surrender your spiritual weapons–to those temporal Powers which have accorded you some small degree of freedom. But now we come to offer you in full measure something that you have never been able to obtain from those Powers which boasted that they were your allies and your devoted children. We are ready to proclaim throughout Italy this great principle: A Free Church in a Free State.' He then proceeded to remind his audience that the programme of the Government, of the political party in whose name he spoke, was 'to imbue all sections of society, both civil and religious, with the ideal of liberty. We desire economic liberty, we desire administrative liberty, we desire full and absolute liberty of conscience. We desire all the political liberties that are compatible with the maintenance of public order. And therefore, as a necessary consequence of this order of things, we deem it essential to the harmony of the edifice which we seek to raise that the principle of liberty should be applied to the relations between Church and State'.

Enemies of Cavour declared at the time, and more especially later on, that he had worked a clever parliamentary trick, that the expression 'a Free

Church in a Free State' was one of those resounding but empty phrases which political parties often insert in their programmes, but that in the mind of the statesman it carried no precise significance. It seems certain that these allegations do not correspond to the truth. There can be little doubt that Cavour sincerely believed in the possibility of establishing a dual régime, calculated to benefit the Church as much as the State, and indeed that he believed such a system must surely prevail in the future. It is necessary to add, however, not only that he had to have a basic plan, if not a detailed programme, but that here too the politician, the man of action, he who was confronted with the task of solving day-to-day problems, took precedence both of the theorist and of thc visionary, who, alike as an Italian and as a citizen of the world, had his eyes constantly fixed on a dim and distant future.

During the winter of 1860–61 Cavour secretly opened negotiations with the Roman Curia through the medium of two trusted liegemen, Father Carlo Passaglia and the Professor of Medicine in the University of Rome, Diomede Pantaleoni, who for his part was convinced that the Pope must be persuaded to renounce every particle of his temporal power, retaining only the trappings of sovereignty, together with absolute jurisdiction over the Church.

Both Passaglia and Pantaleoni had influential contacts in Rome, and both enjoyed the acquaintance or friendship of a number of cardinals (Pantaleoni was medical adviser to Cardinal Wiseman). Slowly and painfully the negotiations got under way. What Cavour offered was to all intents and purposes a Concordat: in return for the Pope's renunciation of his temporal power the State would renounce all its jurisdictional weapons. The Pope would retain all the outward and visible signs of sovereignty, and the administrative offices of the Church would enjoy a privileged position. In Italy no official recognition would be accorded to religious organizations, but the State would allocate property, both movable and immovable, for the maintenance of the episcopate, of ecclesiastical chapters and seminaries, and of those members of the clergy having the cure of souls. The number of the dioceses would be reduced to eighty, and bishops would be appointed by means of an electoral system to be decided upon at some time in the future, the State renouncing all rights in the matter, save that it would be entitled to exercise a veto in controversial cases.

The news of the conference spread to Paris, where it was received with suspicion and scepticism. It was also revealed to the Austrian ambassador by Cardinal Antonelli. Suddenly, however, the negotiations were broken off. On March 18th, 1861, Pius IX in his consistorial address reminded the assembled prelates of all the wrongs which the Church had suffered at the hands of the Piedmontese liberals, and declared that he could never permit 'the unjust aggressor to remain peacefully and honourably in possession of that which he had wrongfully seized'; for to do so would be to 'establish the false principle that wrongdoing is justified by success'. The Pope 'can in no wise consent to such a vandalic act of piracy without violating the basis of that moral discipline of which he is recognized to be, as it were, the prototype and exemplar'. The emissaries were accordingly obliged to leave Rome.

It is probable that in any event the negotiations would have had an unfavourable outcome. Pius IX would never willingly have assumed the enormous responsibility of renouncing his temporal power; while his mistrust of liberalism, of Piedmont, and even of Napoleon III, whom he regarded as a treacherous ally, would have made him even less inclined to take such a step. It must, however, be added that the veiled reproaches which the two emissaries, Pantaleoni and Father Passaglia, cast upon Cavour in their letters were not without justification. The actions of the Government, as well as of the governors of the annexed provinces, who abrogated the old concordats, extended Piedmont's anti-Catholic legislation, and seized numerous monasteries, could not but diminish still further the Holy See's already scant enthusiasm for an agreement.

Cavour, the great architect of Italian unity, died less than three months after the proclamation of the Kingdom. Napoleon III, who had such a great regard for the Piedmontese minister, even though he was at times embarrassed by his policies, and who appreciated his greatness better than did King Victor Emmanuel,[3] generously availed himself of the opportunity to recognize the new Kingdom unconditionally. Nevertheless, in a letter to the King, written on July 12th, 1861, he declared that France could not evacuate Rome so long as the Holy See remained at odds with the Kingdom, and the Pope ran the risk

[3] The King had a kind of inferiority complex towards Cavour. The relationship between the two men was not unlike that which later existed between the German Emperor Wilhelm I and Bismarck.

of seeing what was left of his State invaded by regular or irregular forces.

Economic and Institutional Problems of the Liberal State

None of the great political revolutions of the modern era–the English revolutions of the seventeenth century, the American and French revolutions of the late-eighteenth century, even the Russian Revolution of the twentieth century–succeeded in immediately realizing or fulfilling the larger complex of expectations or hopes they aroused while they were still in the making. In one way or another, all of them somehow attained the status of permanent revolutions, that is, of model moments whose ideal motives, political ideas, and social objectives, whatever they may have been, could or might become integrated with the very historic evolution of their respective peoples or nations. As a unique modern Italian national revolution the Risorgimento may have acted as the catalyst of political and institutional change whose loosening of other forces could in fact or in potentia *lead to an organic historic mutation affecting the fundamental bases of Italian life, society, and culture. Whatever the defects or "failures" of Cavourian unitary politics and statecraft, only an utterly fatalistic or deterministic view of history could, in the immediate aftermath or later, gauge them as irremovable fixtures of the entire future scheme of things in Italy. Even assuming the worst concerning the "failure" of the Risorgimento as an organic revolution, one can judge that "failure" to be perhaps a very high-interest "mortgage" upon the future of*

Italy but not necessarily "unredeemable" given any circumstance or effort at implementation or fulfillment. After Cavour, therefore, the new questions were: Did the post-Risorgimento find itself a prisoner of the legacy of unresolved problems, or was it at least relatively free to modify, to implement, to transmute that legacy toward a further realization of the highest ideals and objectives of the Risorgimento? Was post-Risorgimento Italy as if condemned to bear the new burden of a recent promising "past" whose hopes were only partially realized, or could it mold its own destiny toward whatever liberal, democratic, or truly "revolutionary" goals might seem historically possible as well as desirable?

The following two selections, each in its way, touch upon these fundamental problems of post-Risorgimento Italian history. John Cammett, professor of history at the City University of New York, has for many years devoted his scholarly attention to European revolutionary history and is the author of the first biography in the English language of Antonio Gramsci, the Italian Marxist theoretician and founder of the Italian Communist Party. Cammett's article is the Appendix of that biography, and essentially it argues that the critique on Risorgimento and post-Risorgimento that the Italian historian, Rosario Romeo, made in a well-known series of articles and then in a book called Risorgimento e capitalismo (*1959*) *which attacked the neo-Marxist negative views of them, cannot be accepted without serious modification. Against Romeo, Cammett maintains that the "Jacobin," if not a "socialist," solution for Risorgimento social problems envisaged by Gramsci would have served* both *the fuller uses of the productive forces of capitalistic development in Italy and the acute demands for distributive justice among the vast masses of the Italian peasantry and, therefore, at least by implication, have created a solid basis of social resistance against the erosion of the Liberal State and its destruction by Fascism.*

John A. Thayer, the author of a solid and exceedingly well-documented study on modern Italy, Italy and the Great War: Politics and Culture, 1870–1915 *(1964), teaches at the University of Minnesota. The selection from that work focuses attention upon the distinction between what the Risorgimento had actually achieved in institutional and administrative Italian life and the way the post-Risorgimento faced or could face the problems. Among these, one of the most crucial was the question of the centralism of political institutions created by the unitary phase and administrative decentralization on a regional or other basis. Carlo Cattaneo, the great Risorgimento federalist thinker, had envisaged a democratic federation of Italian states and even members of the Cavourian liberal party had glimpsed the validity and urgency of the problem posed by the creation of the unitary national state minus popular participation by the masses of Italians, and some of them had at least theoretically grappled with the question of administrative and, if less frequently, regional decentralization. In a sense, what Thayer suggests in this selection returns from a different angle of historical vision to the problems raised, again from divergent positions, by Raymond Grew and John Cammett.*

Risorgimento, Jacobinism, and Capitalism*

JOHN CAMMETT

GRAMSCI'S THOUGHT ON the political party and the historical role of intellectuals profoundly influenced his interpretation of the Risorgimento. This interpretation has occasioned an interesting controversy between liberal and Marxist historians. Rosario Romeo, author of an important book on the Risorgimento in Sicily, began the polemic by publishing two articles in *Nord e Sud* in 1956 and 1958. Although the first article was supposedly a general survey of Italian Marxist historiography, its main purpose–and the sole purpose of the second article–was to refute Gramsci's interpretation of the Risorgimento. Romeo justifies this emphasis by asserting that Italian Marxists almost "universally accept Gramsci's theses on the Risorgimento." An examination of these theses and the opinions of Romeo and others regarding them will provide an excellent example of Gramsci's impact on present-day Italian culture.

Considering Gramsci's views on political parties and intellectuals, it is not surprising that his interpretation of the Risorgimento centered on the political leadership of its "revolutionary" social classes and groups. This leadership was supplied by only

* Reprinted from *Antonio Gramsci and the Origins of Italian Communism* by John M. Cammett, 213–22, with the permission of the publishers, Stanford University Press, © 1967 by the Board of Leland Stanford Junior University.

two parties: the "moderates," led by men like Cavour, D'Azeglio, and Balbo, were a relatively homogeneous group made up of the bourgeoisie, those members of the nobility whose economic activities were capitalistic, and most of the "upper" intelligentsia; the "Party of Action," led by men like Mazzini, Garibaldi, and Pisacane, was a more diverse group supported by the radical petty bourgeoisie (artisans, small entrepreneurs, and many professional intellectuals) and the exiguous urban proletariat.

The moderates managed to establish a hegemony over the Party of Action by a "gradual but continual absorption" of actionist elements. This process made the Risorgimento a movement "without 'terror,' a 'revolution' without a 'revolution.'" While the moderates were "organically" related to the bourgeois-aristocratic forces–indeed, they were the "organic intellectuals" of this group–the actionist leaders had no close connection with the heterogeneous classes they supposedly represented. Consequently, the actionists never established a "concrete program of government." To effectively counter the moderate program, they had to create an alternative program that would attract the rural masses, almost four-fifths of the people. Only an economic and social program of the "Jacobin" type would have offered a viable alternative to moderate politics. Gramsci's analysis of the Risorgimento aimed at showing why the Party of Action did not develop a "Jacobin" program—that is, why the Italian Revolution of 1859 was not the French Revolution of 1789.

To begin with, the petty-bourgeois social base of the actionists retained a semi-agrarian character that limited its autonomy vis-à-vis the older landowning class and also made it fear the possible economic demands of the peasantry. The political interests of the European and Italian bourgeoisie in 1859 were very different from those of 1789. The "specter of Communism" had made them cautious: it seemed that a "proletarian" alternative to bourgeois rule was at least possible. In addition, the political weakness of Italy, its lack of national "autonomy," limited effective action by the Italian bourgeoisie. The audacity of the Jacobin spirit was "certainly related to the hegemony so long exercised by France in Europe." Finally, the "national" character of the Risorgimento—its goal of expelling the Austrians and forming an Italian State—made it easy for the moderates, and even some actionists, to neglect the social character of the revolution in the interests of achieving the largest possible unity of action. Gramsci did not believe that these conditions necessarily and absolutely paralyzed the actionists. He insisted that in spite of these difficulties "an alliance with the peasants was certainly always possible." Still, historical complications are a major reason for the limited, moderate character of the Risorgimento and the inherent weaknesses of the more democratic groups participating in the movement.

According to Romeo, the core of Gramsci's thought on the Risorgimento is a criticism of its leaders, both moderate and democratic, for failing to promote agrarian revolution (pp. 19–21).* Working on this assumption, Romeo then attempts to demonstrate: (1) that Gramsci's conclusions resulted from his political position, and not from "serene" histori-

* Page numbers in parentheses refer to Romeo's book *Risorgimento e capitalismo.*

cal examination; (2) that his work was vitiated by using the French Revolution as a model to demonstrate the inadequacy of the Italian Revolution; (3) that his belief in the possibility of an agrarian revolution in the nineteenth century was mistaken; (4) that in any case a revolution would have seriously delayed the development of capitalism in Italy, a situation that Gramsci, as a Marxist, should have deplored.

Romeo believes that almost all Italian Marxist historical writing–not just Gramsci's–exhibits unhistorical political attitudes. "Quite a few Italian historians," he writes, came to Marxism from complex motives, "among which politically contingent passion and attitudes played a predominant role" (p. 94). Italian Marxist historiography shows political bias with its lack of interest in periods preceding the French Revolution and the Risorgimento. Gramsci's work is merely part of a "revisionist" tendency in Italian historiography, stressing what the Risorgimento did *not* do rather than what it did. Romeo follows Benedetto Croce, Carlo Antoni, and Federico Chabod (pp. 20, 46) in charging that Gramsci "anachronistically" reflected the twentieth-century interests of the PCI* in stressing the importance of the peasant movement and the Southern Question during the Risorgimento, in underestimating the influence of the European powers on the Risorgimento, and even in using terms like "national-popular," supposedly derived from the Russian term *narodnost* (p. 25, n. 12).

* PCI = *Partito Comunista Italiano,* Italian Communist Party, founded in 1921 under the leadership of Gramsci and a group of his friends, all dissidents from the official Italian Socialist Party. (*Editor's note*)

Romeo has a special dislike for Gramsci's alleged tendency to use the French Revolution as a "model" for analyzing Italian history; the much greater industrial development of France invalidates the comparison (p. 26). Romeo does not object to the comparative method for studying revolutionary processes, though he tends to regard it as "arbitrary and incomplete"; he does object strongly to the "assumption that French historical development is an 'exemplary' model for a modern bourgeois and capitalist country" (p. 44): from the economic and social points of view, the "Prussian way" is "far more energetic and expansive." Romeo follows Lenin in defining the "Prussian way" as a "compromise of the capitalistic bourgeoisie with feudal elements" (p. 39), and recognizes that it is undoubtedly less "democratic" (p. 40) than the French way. Romeo attributes the tendency of Italian Marxists to exalt French history to a "certain Francophilia of our democratic thought" (p. 44). He even asserts that Italy was fortunate in not following the pattern of the French Revolution, especially among the peasants, since French industrial and agricultural development had been hindered by the Revolution's changes in the relations of production in the countryside.

Romeo flatly denies the possibility of an Italian agrarian revolution in the nineteenth century (or indeed of any "alternative to the Risorgimento as it was concretely realized"). Despite innumerable peasant insurrections and the admitted existence of grinding rural poverty, an agrarian revolution would not have been tolerated by the great powers (p. 22). Although Romeo admits that Gramsci recognized this problem, he finds it contradictory that Gramsci could still assert the possibility of "alliance with the peasants."

Finally, Romeo thinks it fortunate that an "agrarian revolution" did not occur in Italy. Employing the Marxist concept of "primitive capital accumulation" and modern theories of economic development, he attempts to show that an agrarian revolution would have increased the consumption of the peasants, then more than eighty per cent of Italy's population, and therefore would have severely retarded capital accumulation. Italian agricultural production increased greatly in the period 1861–80, but the surplus was not absorbed by the rural masses; instead, it took the form of rents and profits, providing capital for investment, especially in the "infrastructure" of society (public utilities, transportation, communication). True, high taxes and foreign investment also built up Italian capital, but the bulk of it came from low rural consumption accompanied by higher production. If agrarian reforms had been carried out, the peasants would themselves have consumed any meager surplus they might have gained from the inherently inefficient small holdings that a revolution would have created.

The agricultural crisis of the 1880's ended the flow of capital from country to city. By then, however, investments were derived mainly from the profits of commerce and industry (p. 174). Romeo optimistically concludes that Italian industrial development in the 1880's was "probably the most rapid in the history of the Italian industrial economy" before the twentieth century (p. 188). "Because of the sacrifice imposed for so many decades on the countryside and the South, Italy, poor in territory and natural resources, was the only country in the Mediterranean area to create a great industrial complex and a highly developed urban civilization" (p. 197).

The tone of Romeo's work is often harsh and condescending, which explains the none-too-gentle response of Italian Marxists. Although the dispute is not yet over, it is now possible to summarize the principal Marxist criticisms of Romeo's theses, as well as some observations made by other scholars.

Gramsci himself was strongly opposed to "immediate and ideological, non-historical" interpretations of the Risorgimento. It is nonetheless true that any history of the Risorgimento immediately excites political interests. Giorgio Candeloro, writing of the conflict between tendencies to exalt and to denigrate the Risorgimento, urges the avoidance of either extreme, but further explains that these positions

> have an ideological foundation that goes back to the Risorgimento itself, and to the politico-social situation deriving from the events of a hundred years ago. Those events have preserved an immediacy that continues to stimulate discussion of them in substantially political terms . . . chiefly because they gave birth to new problems (or a new face to old problems) central to the later history of Italy–problems that still exist today, albeit partly changed in some respects.

Candeloro concludes that any discussion of the Risorgimento must keep in mind the fundamental characteristics of both the Risorgimento and "united Italy and its social and economic development."

Romeo's case for the "non-historical" character of Gramsci's work on the Risorgimento rests on the assertion that Gramsci's concern with the "agrarian question" reflects a political problem of twentieth-century Communism, and is an "anachronism" when applied to the "concrete reality" (p. 20) of the Risorgimento. Was agrarian revolution only Gramsci's problem or also a problem in 1848 and 1860?

Awareness of the need for agrarian reform, however vaguely expressed, was certainly widespread among radicals before the Risorgimento. For example, the left wing of the Carbonari (c. 1820) required its more advanced members to swear to "favor with all my forces and at the cost of my life the promulgation and execution of the agrarian law–without which there is no liberty, since private property is an offense against the rights of humanity." There was also the social program of Carlo Bianco di St. Jorioz, who urged that at the successful conclusion of the "national war of insurrection" the combatants receive "the lands and private possessions of the princes and the enemies of liberty."

Although these statements may be dismissed as the expression of an insignificant lunatic fringe, two recent works by Italian Marxists have shown how important the question of agrarian revolution was by 1860. Indeed, a principal reason for the support given Garibaldi by the Sicilian peasantry was his promise to "divide up the large estates and distribute the land." Very little came of this promise, it is true; the point is merely that the question of "agrarian revolution" originated in the Risorgimento, and not in the twentieth century. Almost immediately after the completion of national unity, the agricultural question became a major issue for both democrats and moderates—as the famous parliamentary inquiry into agriculture demonstrated.* Gramsci's concern with the agrarian question (which is inseparable from the question of the South) is the culmination of a specifically Italian tradition going back through Gaetano Salvemini and Antonio Labriola to Carlo Cattaneo. Even the idea of allying southern peasantry and northern workers is not "Bolshevik" in origin: this very alliance had been demanded by Salvemini in 1900. The tradition culminates in Gramsci because only after World War I did it seem "concretely possible to overcome the social contradictions inherited from the Risorgimento."

According to Romeo, the French Revolution unduly influenced Gramsci's view of the Risorgimento; but since social and economic conditions were entirely different in the two countries, any comparison of their respective historical developments would have been gratuitous. Indeed, Gramsci did emphasize the failure of Italian revolutionists to develop a Jacobin-like program during the Risorgimento, involving an alliance of urban bourgeoisie and peasantry.† He believed that the absence of Jacobinism greatly influenced the outcome of the Risorgimento, and he gave many reasons for the underdevelop-

* Ironically, Romeo himself, in another work, makes a judgment on the importance of the agrarian question that is almost identical with Gramsci's. Discussing why the thirteenth-century Della Torre lords of Milan did not attack feudalism in the rural areas, Romeo concludes that the "lack of concrete support in the countryside, which they were unable or unwilling to find in the peasants, made effective control of the realm much more difficult for the powerful city." As quoted in *Studi Gramsciani,* p. 383, n. 1.

† See pp. 209–10.

ment of Italian Jacobinism. The success of the moderates and the failure of the actionists to develop a Jacobin program established the fundamental character of the united Italian State: a compromise of the old (the landed aristocracy) with the new (the commercial and industrial bourgeoisie). Gramsci wished to prove that under the limitations imposed on the Italian bourgeoisie, where essentially *political* problems like national independence and unity prevail, a limited bourgeois revolution is possible without an alliance with the peasants and masses but through an alliance with the previous ruling class.

Is Gramsci's use of the Jacobin idea as a tool for analysis valid? Certainly not, if he meant to establish the French Revolution as an abstract model for all other bourgeois revolutions. That Gramsci never intended this is shown by his disapproval of Giuseppe Ferrari (1811–76), a federalist republican who tried to apply "French schemes" to Italian questions. But Gramsci reasoned that to know what the Risorgimento was, it was also necessary to know what it was *not.* The "comparative method" could show why Italian developments were different from French. As a matter of fact, the comparison itself was an old tradition in Europe. In 1801 Vincenzo Cuoco had developed the idea of "passive revolution"—i.e., revolution from above, or because of external pressures —as contrasted with the "active revolution" that occurred in France. In the 1860's Alessandro Manzoni wrote *La Rivoluzione francese del 1789 e la rivoluzione italiana del 1859,* defending the Risorgimento as "legal" and attacking the French Revolution for its violence. The comparison is even more valid today, as is shown by Albert Soboul's recent essay on "Risorgimento et révolution bourgeoise." Giuseppe Talamo seems equally unable to avoid a Gramscian interpretation in discussing the Risorgimento. With regard to the first constitutional ministry in Naples during the revolution of 1848, he says:

> In the rural areas, and in all the provinces in general, the position of the constitutional ministry was very weak. The age-old question of assigning the common domains, arbitrarily occupied by the landowners, was not even discussed. This was undeniably to the advantage of the king, who (as Spellanzon has written) would later be able to take advantage of widespread discontent among the agricultural masses in his opposition to the political aspirations of the bourgeoisie.

Thus Italian political leaders of every camp, from the Risorgimento to the present, have deplored the lack of change in the agrarian economy. But Romeo charges that Gramsci asserts the *possibility* of an agrarian revolution and makes it central to his "indictment" of the Risorgimento. Actually, the main point of Gramsci's work is to show why such a revolution *did not* occur in Italy: he outlines the reasons for the failure of the Party of Action and the success of the moderates. Perhaps Gramsci's only concrete reference to a real possibility of enrolling peasants in the national movement comes when he accuses the actionists of not effecting an "alliance with the peasants, [which] was certainly always possible." But this vague charge follows a discussion of that very party's weakness. Elsewhere Gramsci explains very clearly why such a movement was not historically possible: "Did any of the conditions exist in Italy for a movement like that of the French Jacobins? For many centuries France was a hegemonic nation: its international autonomy was extensive. Italy had nothing of the kind: it had no international autonomy." Agrarian revolution was impossible because of the strength of the moderates: Cavour and his party "represented the only correct politics of the era, since they had no strong, politically intelligent competitors." An undistorted view of Gramsci's historiography forbids the arbitrary removal of any one idea from its context, be it the absence of Jacobinism or of agrarian revolution. In his own words,

> The Risorgimento is a complex and contradictory historical movement, which achieves wholeness from all its antithetical elements: its protagonists and antagonists, its struggles and the reciprocal modifications those struggles brought about, the action of latent and passive forces like the great agricultural masses, and the preeminent consideration of international relations.

His historical justification of the moderates does not prevent Gramsci from pointing out the unfortunate results of their victory in the long run. The moderates

> said they proposed to build a modern State in Italy, and they produced a kind of bastard; they proposed to develop a numerous and energetic ruling class, and they did not succeed; [they proposed] to include the people in the

life of the State, and they did not succeed. The consequences of this deficiency were the poverty-stricken political life of 1870–1900, the basic and endemic unrest of the lower classes, and the crude, petty existence of a cynical and idle ruling class. Another consequence was the international position of the new State, deprived of effective autonomy because it was undermined by the Papacy and the stubborn passivity of the great masses. Hence, the right-wingers of the Risorgimento were really great demagogues. They made an instrument and an object of the democratic nation by degrading it, and therein lies the greatest and most contemptible demagoguery.

Aldo Berselli, a liberal, recognized that Gramsci's views cannot be included in the "general category of 'Risorgimental revisionism.'" Similarly, A. W. Salomone recently attacked revisionist tendencies in the historiography of the Risorgimento, but treated Gramsci's work with considerable respect. Romeo's charge of "present-mindedness" in Gramsci might better be applied to himself. He attempts to "idealize" the past, to demonstrate that what "really" happened was for the best and, indeed, could only have happened as it did. This is a far from disinterested examination of the past. As Aurelio Macchioro has said, it may be dangerous to hypothesize alternative possibilities in history, but it is more dangerous "to make what happened in the past not only the real history—which it is—but also the ideal history."

Gaetano Salvemini's discussion of his own apparently contradictory evaluation of Cavour expresses the Gramscian view:

> We must distinguish "historical" judgment from "political" judgment. One can recognize "historically" that the Italian democratic parties produced an excessive number of inconclusive windbags; and that, granted their incapacity and the objective conditions under which they worked, their defeats were not only inevitable, but deserved—however, one is not therefore obliged to condemn their ideals for all times and all places. One can recognize the superior political capacities of the conservatives compared with the democrats, and still not pass over bag and baggage to the official historians of the conservative parties. . . . As a "historian," I must see men as they were; as a "man of politics"—which is not the same thing as a "politician"—or as a "moralist" (to add a note of Croceian contempt), I do not remove my hat before accomplished facts, and, if necessary, shall even take a stand for the defeated.

But for Romeo the actual course of Italian history was "the quickest and shortest historic road for Italy to the structure and characteristics of a modern country." True, he cannot ignore the continued ailments of the South, but these he regards as an aspect of "potentializing the city at the expense of the country." And southern backwardness is a "temporary condition (even if protracted for many decades), destined to be corrected by the internal development of northern industrialism." Capitalism must continue because it will eventually provide for all, and any violence committed along the way is justified once the pieces have been picked up. But recent statistics show that the regional contrast in Italy is increasing rather than decreasing. Romeo seems to be the one imposing "abstract schemes" on historical development. Gramsci's approach is much more sensible—and ultimately more "historical":

> The hegemony of the North would have been "normal" and historically beneficial if industrialization had been able to widen its confines rapidly to incorporate new economic zones. Then this hegemony would have been the expression of a struggle between the old and the new, between the more productive and the less productive. . . . [However,] it was not so. The hegemony was presented as permanent: the contrast was presented as a historical condition necessary for an indeterminate time—and therefore apparently "perpetual"—to the existence of northern industry.

Romeo's last point, that development of a modern capitalistic Italy came about chiefly because there was no agrarian revolution, has received as much attention from scholars as his critique of other aspects of Gramscian historiography. In sum, criticism of the thesis has been on four grounds: (1) Romeo's version of "primitive accumulation" of capital is mistaken; (2) his assumption of a direct relationship between the growth of small peasant property and increased consumption is unwarranted; (3) his belief that large landholdings are necessarily more progressive than small peasant holdings is, for the nineteenth century, often untrue; and (4) his data on the reasons for and extent of economic growth in Italy compared with other countries are often misleading and exaggerated.

The whole controversy has generally demonstrated the inadequacy of Romeo's critique of Gramscian historiography and his view of capital formation in Italy. Nevertheless, he has unintentionally rendered great service to Italian Marxist scholars by forcing them to avoid unhistorical condemnations of the past and apply Gramsci's method to a more concrete and creative study of Italian history.

Risorgimento Achievement and Post-Risorgimento Problems*

JOHN A. THAYER

THERE IS ONE more fundamental theme pertinent to the era of the Postrisorgimento that must be touched upon before proceeding to an analysis of Italian political thought. It, too, grew out of the Regional Question. Among those who regarded the unification of Italy as a "royal conquest" by the Piedmontese it was fashionable to add that the true Risorgimento had not been fulfilled—it was, indeed, still going on. Italy, Giovanni Bovio declaimed in the Chamber, was made by "gentlemen wearing white gloves." The people were absent. The whole

* From John A. Thayer, *Italy and the Great War: Politics and Culture, 1870–1915* (Madison and Milwaukee: the University of Wisconsin Press, copyright © 1964 by the Regents of the University of Wisconsin), 33–39. Reprinted by the permission of the University of Wisconsin Press.

edifice after 1870, therefore, was false, lacking its proper roots. The period of the Postrisorgimento, for those who shared this feeling, was an age of waiting, waiting until the moment rolled around again at which the popular element could be fused with the nation as it existed in theory. In this theme of the "revolution that failed," moreover, one may discern the beginnings of a merging of extreme positions that were largely the outgrowth of the material problems thus far discussed, and which were to become the source of future political ambiguities.

The contrast between the "real" Italy, a product of history with its provincial characteristics and virtues, and the administrative system, a product of political expediency that had been put together in the 1860's, was a reflection of the more fundamental distinction between Risorgimento and Postrisorgimento. That basic cleavage was also to be reflected in a debate closely related to the Regional Question: that of Italy's diplomatic rather than revolutionary birth. Those Piedmontese administrative practices which were looked upon as a mechanistic humiliation of vital local forces could also be portrayed as a great net in which the nation's revolutionary flight and impetus were trapped and brought down to earth. Garibaldi's savage attack on Cavour in 1861 was not forgotten. The "Hero of Two Worlds" had charged the statesman with diplomaticizing the revolution. In the Chamber at Turin the Premier was accused of provoking fraticidal war. In the final moments of the Risorgimento the "nation in arms" was absent. Garibaldi spoke with bitterness of his legions being "put at the tail end." As if to discredit by personal valor the government's lack of dynamic action, he went to fight for France in 1870, thus keeping alive the fire of action and revolution then symbolized by the Commune. At the same time, the Italian government was moving with diplomatic caution, taking Rome when France was beaten.

In truth, there had been little mass support for the national revolution. Of Garibaldi's volunteers, most were northern. In effect they were an elite, there being no contadini among the Thousand, and only twenty-eight Sicilians. No attempt had been made to capture the peasantry for the Risorgimento. Mazzini neglected them prior to 1860. After that date he was reluctant to condone revolutionary action which would be aimed, now that unity had been achieved, at economic and social ends. In the years to come the Italian socialists also neglected the great bulk of southern agrarian workers. It was this lack of a popular base for Italian political institutions that Count Sforza considered one of the country's fundamental weaknesses.

It would have been unrealistic to expect anything other than a middle-class revolution. To lament the absence of the "people" in the creation of national unity, Salvemini and Chabod wrote in 1952, was unhistorical; for in no nineteenth-century nation did the people, if this includes the lower classes, participate in public affairs. Salvemini insists, however, that if the Risorgimento was a revolution, it was essentially a conservative victory in which the illegal, truly revolutionary impulse acted as a spur to legal, diplomatic action. The politicians and diplomats triumphed, and in so doing produced a vast change in the pre-existing situation. Hence, Salvemini would not accept the view that the Risorgimento was a revolutionary failure.

But in the decades of the Postrisorgimento, this historical perspective was not likely to satisfy the longing to repair what many–including a younger Salvemini–believed to have been a defect of national unity. In time, a literature devoted to the question of whether the Risorgimento had been a royal war or a people's war took shape. Garibaldi became the symbol of the voluntaristic element in the nation's birth. His being placed at the tail end by the Piedmontese suggested a betrayal of the revolutionary spirit. Carlo Pisacane was to become another precursor of the populist concept of the nation. For Pisacane, national independence without liberty, and without the active participation of the masses, was useless. Better to remain under Bourbon rule than to achieve unity under the House of Savoy. At least the Bourbon reactionaries aroused men's passions; the rule of the Piedmontese would only deaden them. In his *Guerra combattuta in Italia negli anni 1848–49* (1850), the romantic patriot extolled the virtues of the people who had sparked the revolutions of 1848. He charged the Republicans with having prevented the spread of revolutionary socialist ideas among the masses. Charles Albert, invincible when backed by his humble subjects, had turned on them in fear. The monarchy at that point passed from "poetry to commerce."

Pisacane's thoughts, imprecise as they were, changed significantly after 1850. The Bonapartist *coup d'état* in France, followed by the abortive Milan uprising of February 6, 1853, caused him to lose faith in the revolutionary virtues of the people. And yet, what was the nation to become without the masses? Pisacane turned to the ideas of Rousseau, proposing a *patto sociale* in which the immutable constitution would be established in accordance with the laws of nature. The creator of this eternal bond was to be the "genius legislator." Pisacane insisted that this was not to be a dictatorship. The role of the masses, however, had become that of a spontaneously revolutionary force, moved not by the love of liberty, much less democracy, but by purely physical wants. It was because of this that he placed his hopes in the peasants of the Mezzogiorno. In 1857, his quixotic revolutionary expedition came to a tragic end when the contadini, as well as the Bourbon troops, turned on him. His death marked another failure for a people's war of national redemption. The collapse of the federalist solution to Italian unification, in which Pisacane also believed, came a few years later. In time the lonely hero of Sapri was to take his place in the ranks of the martyred prophets of a revolution that had failed.

After 1860 regional resentment of Piedmont served to perpetuate the idea of an unfulfilled nationhood. Local sentiments as well as economic hardships were behind the Palermo uprising in 1866. Romagna too became a center of resistance to central authority. Despite the fact that Republican strength was waning, it became a badge of honor in Romagna to be placed on the police surveillance lists. It was recognized by anarchist leaders that much revolutionary activity in the Postrisorgimento was more than a reflection of increased economic burdens. One of these leaders, Francesco Merlino, writing in 1889, noted that the popularity of anarchism in Romagna was the result not so much of greater financial drain as of regionalist hatred for Piedmont. The Government, he wrote, treated Romagna like a conquered province. It and Sicily were Italy's two Irelands.

The Republican party continued to call for action, for the "second revolution." Popular revolutionary ferment, however, was for the Mazzinians too often tied to regionalism. Their unitarian tradition made it difficult for them to capture a great following after 1870. The decline of the Republicans as a party would be due in part to the appeal which the anarchists, with their opposition to the "State," were able to make to this anticentralist feeling, particularly in the Mezzogiorno.

The myth of revolution as an essential of national status remained a source of dissatisfaction with the Postrisorgimento. What was meant by revolution was clearly not the profound change in the political structure which had been effected under northern leadership, prodded by the daring of Garibaldi. What had taken place was an undeniable reality; for many, however, it was only a bureaucratic readjustment. What was lacking was the popular element. Because of this it was possible for dissatisfied spirits to seek means of utilizing the people, for the sake of the unfulfilled nation, which were not necessarily democratic, nor even political. Pisacane's pessimism after 1851, his ill-defined concept of the "genius legislator," and the permanent social contract that harnesses the masses to the nation are illustrative of one alternative. It was also possible to convert militant populism into war, which, like revolution, could be conceived as a mass undertaking for the consecration of the nation. The revolutionary failure, in the minds of some, and the wish to rub out the memory of Lissa and Custozza, could become interchangeable.

It is interesting to note that this equating of war and revolution was appreciated by foreign observers. In 1888 a dispatch from Baron Karl Bruck, ambassador at Rome, to Count Gustav Kálnoky, the Austro-Hungarian Minister of Foreign Affairs, contains a shrewd analysis of this problem, with a suggestion as to how the revolutionary impetus might be channeled into acceptable conservative paths. Vienna recognized Italy's need for a military victory. It was possible to fulfill this need and at the same time satisfy the revolutionary past of Italy's Premier, Francesco Crispi, by encouraging Italy to seek her outlet in Africa. What was to be avoided was anti-Austrian irredentism, in itself a part of the revolutionary drive of the Risorgimento. Crispi's radical past could be harmonized with the conservative nature of the Triple Alliance through war.

Implicit in this policy is the recognition that war could be a substitute for political radicalism. In Crispi, an ex-Garibaldian, Vienna perceived the agent of a conservative siphoning off of revolutionary and irredentist energies. This was a very astute evaluation of Crispi's character. In fact, the revolutionary had embraced the monarchy as early as 1865, writing to Mazzini that the republic would divide Italy, the monarchy unite it. By 1888, he had already made his celebrated visit to Bismarck at Friedrichsruh. And in later years, looking back on Bismarck's policy, he would criticize the Chancellor for not having tried to promote a monarchical restoration in France. But it was also true that Crispi had told Mazzini that Garibaldi's war was a popular triumph over the Bourbons—that in the South the people alone had overthrown an ancient dynasty. While insisting on a unitarian rather than federalist solution, the Sicilian patriot spoke of his resentment of the plebiscite, which seemed to imply a supine yielding to Piedmontese annexation. "Our country must not *give* herself to another, must not *annex* herself, which verb savors overmuch of servitude." He advocated the use of Bourbon administrative and legal instruments as the basis for the united nation, rather than those of Piedmont which, despite the greater liberty of the North, were archaic. For all of Crispi's conservatism, the strain of the southern regionalist remained, and with it the concept of a people's war which Garibaldi's expedition symbolized.

Crispi was to become ministerial, parliamentarian of necessity, and a defender of the monarchy. But, as will be seen, his vision of the military possibilities of the Triple Alliance betrayed his revolutionary, popular past. His role in the Postrisorgimento might be described as that of uniting the nation through mass military rather than political action. This urge for action which Crispi converted from revolutionary to diplomatic methods had its fascination as well for men who refused to abandon popular radicalism. Felice Cavallotti was to become Crispi's most outspoken critic. His democratic faith refused to bend to the cause of monarchy. Yet Cavallotti could speak in 1881 in terms no less illustrative of the conversion of revolution into war. Italy after fifteen years of unity still paid the bitter price of military failure. Until success in war came to her through some "bloody baptism," she would not have that place among nations worthy of her new destiny. Crispi had said much the same thing, and D'Annunzio would later add his poetic touch.

It is worthy of note that the baptism of blood theme was present long before D'Annunzio and his cultural offspring in the art of irrational politics made their appearance. In the age of prose, the decades of Lanza, Sella, Depretis, and Giolitti, such phrases were not yet the common stock of the "humanistic petty bourgeoisie." The prevailing mood was one of material achievements, seeking the good and comfortable life. There was not that myth of action which had been described as one of the most dangerous aspects of Italian political life. A thirst for action and violence was present, but only as a minor note. It remained for a new generation, born too late for the real revolution, to seize upon all the deficiencies of the age of commerce and clerks as fuel for the journalistic fires of national redemption.

What is apparent in the theme of a *rivoluzione mancata* is that the nation as legally constituted did not represent the country as embodied in the people. How deep this sense of incompleteness went may be seen by turning from revolutionary to conservative spokesmen. Moderate voices of discontent were also to function as purveyors of dissident opinion. While rejecting the revolutionary or militaristic solution to Italy's ills, men like D'Azeglio and Jacini coined phrases that could be put to decidedly subversive use. D'Azeglio's oft-quoted remark–now that Italy was made, the job was to make Italians–could be turned to radical purposes. If the process of infusing the people of the Peninsula with a sense of the *patria* were to be one of war or revolution, or both, rather than progressive reforms, that epigram could become the motto of popularism as well. That it was not merely a rhetorical figure of speech, moreover, was clear. The Palermo revolts of 1866, Merlino's reference to Sicily and Romagna as Italy's two Irelands, the high incidence of desertion among the military, the apolitical discontent of the southern contadini—these realities gave substance to the statement.

The same may be said for another stock expression that became a catchword of the disillusioned. As in the case of D'Azeglio, the author was a conservative. Jacini was certainly not given to Crispian diplomatic melodramatics. We have seen that he opposed the transfer of the capital to Rome, as did D'Azeglio, and hoped to see federalism rather than administrative centralization win out in Italy. Later, when Crispi was Premier and Foreign Minister, Jacini wrote one of the principal attacks on the policy of seeking redemption through war, accusing Crispi of megalomania in politics and diplomacy, as well as with excessive anticlericalism. But in an earlier book, describing Italian political and social conditions after 1866, Jacini found that the nation rested on a false foundation. Despite economic advances, despite the fact that Italian unity was accepted by the powers, Italy, he wrote, was afflicted with "an indefinable, terrible sickness." Its cause was not to be sought in brigandage, in sporadic popular demonstrations. Italy was not in a state of rebellion, as some thought. Nor did Jacini subscribe to D'Azeglio's views about the necessity of creating Italians. The problem lay, he felt, in the excessive centrality of Italy's administrative and parliamentary systems.

"There is," he wrote, "a *real* Italy which is not the *legal* Italy."

Incompleteness was felt by both radicals and conservatives. It was also a factor, as will be seen, in the ultraconservative doctrines that were later taken up by the Nationalist party in the Giolittian age. Jacini's catchword would be carried over into the new generation, where its function would be anything but conservative. A "real" and a "legal" Italy—or "official" Italy, as it would later be called—seemed to exist side by side. For those who shared the mentality of the continuing sense of revolution, who burned with a desire to return to Italy's origins (to borrow a phrase from Giovanni Gentile), the job was to put the two together by some act of fusion that would fulfill the promise of the past.

The question was, what agency would effect this desired drawing of the people closer to the constitutional framework of government? Speculation on this subject was to produce political theories on both the right and the left which claimed to solve what their authors considered to be the great historical problem of modern Italy. Before turning to these theories, however, it is essential to look at the role of the Parliament itself, both as it existed in fact and as it was often seen by men who were dissatisfied with the results of the wars for Italian unity. Here was the constitutional mechanism which was the proper and legal vehicle for the growth of greater mass participation in Italian politics after 1870. However it, too, was to feel the effects of the dialogue between culture and society and the corresponding Italian clash between the memory of the Risorgimento and the existing climate of the present.

III. THREE VIEWS ON THE POST-RISORGIMENTO AND ORIGINS OF FASCISM

WITHOUT DOUBT, THE *single most important question that can be and has been asked by historiographers concerning the post-Risorgimento seen as the "long era" from the Italian Monarchy's occupation of Rome in September 1870 to Italian Fascism's march on Rome in October 1922, may be formulated as follows: Was the Italian historical road leading from the one event to the other, or from Cavour to Mussolini, an inescapable one-way route of which the Liberal period may have occasionally given the impression of being a detour merely leading to the no-exit of Fascism—or was that road marked by a series of efforts and struggles to avoid exactly such a destination which, however, only uncalculated errors, misjudgments, misreadings of road-signs marked "danger," and, after 1914, terrible accidents (the Great War itself and the crisis that followed it) ultimately made unavoidable? The three selections that follow may perhaps help one to visualize more clearly and to judge for one's self this historic "either-or." The readings represent the views of three modern historians—British, American, and German—as each seeks, within different conceptual frameworks, to grapple with important aspects of that question.*

Denis Mack Smith, professor of European and Italian history formerly at Cambridge, now at Oxford

University, is the most outstanding contemporary British historian of modern Italy. His works on Cavour and Garibaldi: 1860 (*1954*) *and* Italy, A Modern History (*1959*) *have elicited at the same time admiration and controversy, but few serious students of modern Italy have denied the originality of his approach and the excellence of his treatment. The reading on the prehistory of Fascism constitutes a relatively brief compendium of Mack Smith's tantalizing historical anti-traditionalism, if not quite a full-fledged revisionism, and the article, which is reprinted in full, deserves careful attention in reference to both its methodology and its conclusions. The reading on freedom and power in Liberal Italy is predicated on the assumption that between 1870 and 1914 a sort of dialectical conflict tended continually to pit authoritarian versus libertarian tendencies within Italian society, politics, and culture. The arduous quests for liberty within Italian society, the author suggests, collided again and again with elements in which authority–that is a combination of social fears, institutional inertia, political ambitions, and spiritual malaise–frustrated complete or solid realization of ideal goals of civil life. Discontinuity, therefore, rather than any kind of historical coherence, let alone inevitability, is seen as characterizing the eventual road to Fascism. In the reading on "How the European Knot Was Tied in Italy," the contemporary German historian Ernst Nolte comes to grips with the uniqueness of the historic problems with which the Risorgimento and,* a posteriori, *the post-Risorgimento had had to deal in contrast to the other Western nations. Nolte, whose book on Fascism as a European phenomenon entitled* Three

Faces of Fascism (*1965*) *amounts to one of the most challenging efforts at comparative history in reference to the origins and nature of Fascist totalitarianism, was born in 1923 in Witten in the Ruhr. Before devoting himself to history he studied philology and philosophy. In 1964 he was appointed professor of modern history at Marburg University. What Nolte suggests on the connections between Fascism as an historical phenomenon and as a function of the biography of Mussolini is worthy of careful appraisal.*

A Prehistory of Fascism*

DENIS MACK SMITH

ANY STUDY OF Mussolini's rise to power must inevitably concentrate for the most part on the immediate historical context of the troubled years 1919–22. In so far as there was a real revolution, this is the time when it took place, favoured by all the economic, social, political and psychological conditions brought on in the aftermath of a crippling war. The temptation is even to concentrate on this period entirely, and to see convincing and sufficient reasons in such a short space of time for the so-called march on Rome and its consequences. This concentration on the short-term aspect has the attraction of making the subject more dramatic. It also

* From Denis Mack Smith, "The Prehistory of Fascism," *Occidente. Rivista Anglo-Italiana di Studi Politici* (Turin; 1954), 509–21. Reprinted through the courtesy and by permission of Denis Mack Smith and Ernesto DeMarchi, former editor of *Occidente.*

helps to exonerate in part many prominent Italians whom the anti-fascists have tried to hold responsible. For if the main causes of fascism were so immediate and catastrophic, no one can be blamed for not seeing what was happening and not acting to stop it while there was still time. In other words, just as the fascists sometimes had an interest in stressing the sharp break in history which they said took place in *anno primo,* so did some of the liberals for the opposite reason. The fascists wanted to exaggerate the difference between *Italietta* and their new order. The liberals needed to show that they were not forerunners of what was to come. It was important for them to exaggerate the liberalism of Giolittian Italy in order that they might excuse themselves and deplore and castigate what came after. On a theoretical plane, it was expedient that liberalism and fascism should be sharply set off against one another.

This clear demarcation is by no means simply untrue; but it is not the whole truth. One of the functions of the historical process is to show how nothing ever happens out of nothing, how there is no revolution but has its place in a larger evolutionary continuum. Neither theoretically nor historically was Giolittian liberalism quite distinct from fascism. Croce at the time was more concerned to show that this liberalism was distinct from, indeed was almost the opposite of, democracy; and Salandra publicly maintained in 1924 that Mussolini was but carrying on the main quasi-liberal traditions deriving from Cavour. We may also remember that Mussolini did not exactly conquer power in an altogether revolutionary manner. He was invited by the king to assume office. Strictly speaking there was no constitutional impropriety about such an invitation. Nor was parliament technically overridden. On the contrary, the overwhelming majority of liberal deputies and senators agreed in giving dictatorial powers to Mussolini by far more substantial majorities than they had accorded to Nitti, Giolitti, and Bonomi, the liberals who had preceded him. Both liberals and Christian democrats were glad to join his cabinet. One may even guess—for what such a guess is worth—that most of the old liberal ruling class in Italy continued to support Mussolini, at least until after the Ethiopian war. In other words, 1922 was not a great revolutionary date, not nearly so much at least as both the fascists and the liberals for various reasons tried to make out. The *Storia del Fascismo* of Salvatorelli and Mira does not leave the impression that the dictator was a great revolutionary, heroically evil, stained with many murders; but rather that he became someone almost futile, swept along often without realising what was happening, a man of vast illusions that would be comic if they were not tragic. Other and deeper forces were at work than the will of what Churchill called *One man alone.* A fruitful line of study therefore takes us back in time to try and discover the deeper roots beneath the soil. It is not that Italy lacks any liberal tradition at all. Far from it, Cavour and Giolitti were both in their various ways great liberals, and innovators in the field of liberalism. It is rather that Italy has too many and too diverse such traditions, and that they sometimes cancelled each other out. There were too many tendencies working against one another, many of them inside the broad field of liberalism, and the result of this was sometimes a political anarchy which in moments like 1893, 1915 and 1922 showed up dangerous inherent weaknesses in the constitution. Giolitti, Salandra, Nitti, Orlando, Amendola, all these called themselves liberals, and yet their various factions could not form a coalition even under extreme pressure. The explanation of this fact is no simple matter, but a large part of the explanation must be looked for much earlier than the years 1919–22.

One must remember that the Risorgimento was not only a story of national liberation against the foreigner. It was also a series of terrible civil wars, none the less painful for sometimes being bloodless; and in these civil wars many Italians were on the defeated side, and carried over their suppressed resentments into the new period of national unification. The Bourbonists, the Mazzinians, the Papalists, all the court circles of the various *anciens régimes,* the federalists, the autonomists in Sicily and Naples, the peasants who rose in dozens of minor revolts against the policy typified by Sella's grist tax, those industrialists who were hit by free trade—these were people who paid a heavy price for unification. Ferrari likened the Piedmontese invaders to the barbarous Goths, and Ricasoli himself even declared on one occasion that Piedmontese rule was "more antipathetic to him than the Austrian". Important fissures and tensions continued to appear, between the north and the south, between centralisers and regionalists, between the rich and the poor. The tragic inability of Italy to produce a strong conservative party was partly due to the fact that even the leading members of Cavour's party were divided over important points. Sella and Minghetti could never sit in the same cabinet. Lanza went his own way on Church policy. Spaventa shocked some of his older colleagues by trying to nationalise the railways. Others learned from Germany to thwart Cavour's free trade tradition, and to ignore his injunctions against administrative centralisation. When the Right fell in 1876 it was primarily because of its internal disunity.

Sometimes, indeed, one is forced to pose the almost sacrilegious question of how far Italians at the time really wanted the national revolution which fate and human heroism were combining to produce in the Risorgimento. The plebiscitary majorities, for all their apparent unanimity, look differently in the light of the Palermo rebellion of 1866, of the long-drawn-out civil war of the sixties in the Napoletano, and of the fact that even government officials could write home from the south that barely a dozen people wanted a continuation of the union. The very apostle of unity, Mazzini, found little joy in what he had done so much to create. "I had thought to evoke the soul of Italy," he lamented, "but all I find before me is its corpse." The historian, watching Mazzini's successive attempts at revolution, is continually puzzled by his utopian belief in popular initiative and the readiness of Italians to rebel. Again and again he had to humble his pride and beg from foreigners the monetary contributions that his countrymen would not provide for the revolution. Again and again it was rather the moderates who were proved right. He had maintained that Italy was one great powder magazine, ready to explode at the slightest detonation, and that one small rising in Genoa or the Lunigiana would 'inevitably' be followed by others until the whole peninsula was in flames. The moderates ridiculed this notion, and the facts seemed to justify their criticism. The truth is that his message was grossly oversimplified, and perhaps, if it was partially efficacious, this was precisely in so far as it *was* oversimplified. The idea that Italians collectively were burning to make a united republic was apparently quite false in fact. It was, nevertheless, one of those myths which, true or false, are a cause of heroic and superhuman action.

Probably everyone would agree that not only idealism but also hard calculation and even some underhand dealing were necessary for the unification of Italy. In this respect the Risorgimento did not differ much from other revolutions everywhere. As Cavour told parliament, "non so se i mezzi adoperati per compiere questo grande atto siano perfettamente regolari, ma so che lo scopo è santo, e che lo scopo forse giustificherà quello che vi può essere d'irregolare nei mezzi. (*Segni di approvazione*)".[1] Apart from this, the will of the people would also have been useless without a singularly favourable situation in Europe for Cavour to exploit, without the rivalry between France and Germany, or the irremediable weakness of the Austrian empire. Cavour, true enough, found it expedient at least to claim the right of popular sovereignty as justification for his revolution, and to invoke (against his own principles) the doctrine of universal suffrage. But even in his own mind this was but a convenient fiction. He, and his

[1] "I do not know whether the means adopted for this great act are perfectly regular, but I do know that the aim is sacred, and that the aim perhaps will justify whatever may be irregular in the means (*signs of approval*)." Editor's note.

followers paid little attention to similar liberal ideas when they did not suit him so well. Mazzini's election to parliament was repeatedly quashed; Cavour sometimes felt impelled to manipulate elections against what he called the *tirannia dei dottoruzzi di villaggio*;[2] and occasionally he suppressed the free publication of opposition views by methods which he himself confessed to be illegal. To state all this is not, of course, to challenge or attempt to invalidate either what happened or Cavour's unique genius in the conduct of affairs. But it does suggest that the Risorgimento, like every other movement in history, was based on conflicting motives, some more worthy than others, and also that the direction it took was much less than one might at first suppose the result of conscious planning, let alone the conscious wish of 'the Italian people'. To some this statement will be a truism. To others it will be altogether unacceptable. Yet it is worth looking to see the connection between it and the subject now under discussion.

It is a plausible hypothesis that far more influential in the Risorgimento than national feeling was the diffused sense of rebellion against governmental oppression. In retrospect people too easily assumed a necessary connection between nationalism and liberalism. They were thus led to several manifestly false and damaging conclusions, first of all that nationalism in Italy was always by definition something liberal, and secondly that no liberalism was justifiable that was so little national as (for instance) Cattaneo's. This association of concepts was made, of course, in order to justify the particular amalgam

[2] "The tyranny of these little country doctors." Editor's note.

of these two notions that emerged victorious in 1861. But, in the process, it helped to blind the eyes of both contemporaries and subsequent observers to something of what was going on all the time.

To take the former conclusion first, one must appreciate how important it was for Cavour and his successors to seal the success of their revolution, and to do this by stressing, even exaggerating, the fact of a unified and centralised monarchy. Probably this was done far more than such people as Cavour, Farini and Minghetti would purely on its own merits have liked. The much-discussed question of regional devolution is too complex for discussion here. Cavour at least proclaimed himself in favour of it, though the effect of his policy was to act in the other direction. Well into the twentieth century some keen observers really went on fearing that the kingdom might split up again, and Giustino Fortunato for one welcomed the Libyan war precisely because it would help the necessary work of fostering national solidarity. Here was one genuine liberal who did not perhaps fully understand that nationalism was not necessarily liberal. It was even a fact that some people were nationalists as a method of destroying liberalism.

The second conclusion was equally dangerous. Thus the way in which Cattaneo, Ferrari and Mazzini were so to speak driven underground was far from being altogether a wholesome influence in Italian politics. It cut off and frustrated some of the most interesting minds in the country; it deprived Italy of a healthy challenge to Cavourian orthodoxy, and of some of her most lively and longest-lived political traditions; and also, by the manner of its effecting, it coarsened those of her other liberal traditions that still remained on the political scene.

If we leave self-conscious national feeling on one side as (though important) a by no means decisive influence on the creation of a united kingdom, we are confronted with the fact that the pivotal rebellions of the Risorgimento were local risings against oppressive government, in fact that the key motives at first were more liberal than national. For instance, it might be a protest by Milanese citizens against the Austrian tax-gatherers; and the important point here was that they were tax collectors, not that they were Austrians, for similar risings took place elsewhere in Italy. At another time it was a protest by laymen against the overweening pretensions and privileges of the Church. Very often one town was protesting against dependence on another which was monopolising the perquisites of a capital city in a particular province or region. The resentment of Messina against Palermo, of Pisa against Florence, of Potenza against Naples, Genoa against Turin, Ancona against Rome, all these resentments were—paradoxically perhaps—powerful agents in kindling the sparks from which developed a national revolution. In 1860, perhaps the most compelling motive of all in joining the two halves of the kingdom was Sicily's mounting dislike of its dependence on Naples, that is to say it was an almost anti-national feeling in origin. Again, a whole book could be written on the blind but often irresistible force of peasants rising against the landlords and their agents, and this was an indispensable part of most political movements at the time. More self-conscious than the peasants, if less incendiary, were the lawyers and professional classes fighting for recognition against an effete court aristocracy. It was out of such local and partial movements as these, many of them non-political, most of them non-national, that grew the events of 1831, 1848, and 1860. It can be shown in detail how the coalescence of basically incompatible components—for instance, peasants and bourgeois combining against the Neapolitan Bourbons—changed the whole nature of the revolution and brought about results which were quite other than had been intended.

Turning now to the post-Risorgimento period, we see that this same argument can be taken a step further in quite a different context. All this various insubordination against authority, learnt under centuries of despotism and foreign rule, did not at all work itself out by victory over the *ancien régime,* but was merely transferred to disobedience against the new régime which succeeded it. One suspects that the original protests which made up the driving force of the early Risorgimento were not so much against any particular kind of state, as against the state itself, against government just because it was government. And this attitude did not suddenly cease in 1861. The weakness of national sentiment, despite all that was done by its devotees to demonstrate the opposite, left citizens of the newly formed nation without sufficient conviction that they shared things in common. Personal sacrifices were not always made gladly to help distant provinces, but a sense of rivalry with other regions continued. The national government was frequently regarded rather as something alien, to be cheated and disobeyed with impunity, and even with an *omertà* that made disobedience seem positively virtuous.

To take a conspicuous example, one can see clearly enough how Mazzini, protesting against the new as he had done against the old, was not the man to set an example of humble cooperation in realising a second-best solution once his ideal state had failed of achievement. Neither he nor others were ready to sacrifice their partial disagreements so that the nation might be strengthened during the prosaic and disillusioning years now that the time for poetry and heroism was over. Mazzini was a great nationalist, but he left behind him a legacy of rebellion against authority, of hatred, of conspiracy, and even memories of political assassination. His failure to see that half a loaf was better than no bread could not help but spread disillusion with the imperfect results which had emerged. His resentment against not only the monarchy, but against parliament and the judiciary, could not help but bring the whole constitution into dislike and contempt. The effects of this were not long in becoming apparent. Perhaps it is a small instance, but anyone seeking for the origins of fascism will discover sooner or later that the continued conflict between monarchists and republicans was not altogether irrelevant to the revolution of 1922. At any rate it is interesting to see how one of the chief motives in the Risorgimento soon became one reason why united Italy remained insufficiently strong.

Mazzini's was only one of the protests that continued after 1861. The *non expedit* represents another of a quite different order. Cavour had justified his own aggressive policy by citing the inequity of Papal rule towards the seculars. But was his own altogether equitable towards the Pope? And did not his own actions provoke and justify a Catholic counterrevolution quite as much as Papal impercipience had earlier provoked his own revolution? The arbitrary dissolution of the monasteries, his exclusion of the Catholic extremists from parliament when they won too many seats for his liking, and the wholesale nationalisation of church property by his successors, were all at least injudicious if not unjust, and left a scar that would not easily heal. What it meant to Italy for the Catholics to abstain from politics can only be conjectured. But the absolute majority for a Catholic party in 1948 is impressive testimony to the fact that the political situation after 1861 must have been highly unreal and unrepresentative. Moreover, the existence of a strong conservative party in the early years might have helped in another way to make politics more real and more healthy. And whether or not the Vatican actively encouraged the fascists in 1922, it is probably correct to assume that Don Sturzo's differences with the moderate anticlerical Giolitti played quite an important part in the suicide of Italian liberalism.

If we admit the justice of Italian claims against Austria and the Pope in 1859–60, we may also admit that there were more or less justifiable grounds for the papal campaign against united Italy which did so much harm. Again, if we allow the justice of the "five days of Milan," we may also allow that of the Sicilian "fasci" who rebelled against Crispi—the protest of peasants who had had bread and circuses under the old régime, but who now were deprived of agricultural protection, and taxed far more heavily by a more grasping and more efficient government. If we admit Garibaldi at Marsala, can we censure D'Annunzio at Fiume without changing our standards? In any event, were the students and idealists who joined Garibaldi so very much different from those who first rallied to Mussolini? In each case they were enthusiasts, ignorant if you like, but not all of them working out of malice and wickedness. Garibaldi and D'Annunzio were both factious outlaws, whose nationalism did not prevent their rebellion against the Italian government, and both of whom had to be fired upon by the national army. What happened before went on happening afterwards, and the essential characteristics of Italy do not change with unification as much as one might have expected. The more one looks at it, the more does it seem that both the strength and the weakness of Italy were in her factions and her factiousness. It was from all these multitudinous local and partial movements that the Risorgimento derived its initial vigour. But as they weakened loyalty to Ferdinand of Bourbon and Francis of Modena, so later they also weakened loyalty to Victor Emmanuel and his successors.

One of Cavour's chief difficulties was the lack of loyalty and public spirit. People were not used to governing themselves, even in the localities. They had never received any political training in responsibility, or in compromise. Local government continued all too often to be exploited by cliques who created jobs for their relatives, and managed the communal lands and charities in their own interests; who exempted themselves as far as possible from taxation, yet built roads at public cost for their own benefit. Classes, provinces, individuals are found too frequently to be trying to profit at the expense of the community. It is more than possible that there is a close connection between all this and the breakdown of government in pre-1922 Italy. Rich and poor were alike involved. Turin in 1864 showed herself as selfish and rebellious as did Sicily in 1866. One cannot just single out the landowners or the bankers for responsibility over the early success of fascism, because the strikers, the red leagues, and the absurdly unrealistic and fissiparous factions of the socialist party were equally selfish and myopic. The communists too, preferring dogma to realism, chose to make socialist cooperation against Mussolini even more impossible. Probably they hoped to create a revolutionary situation from which the extreme Left could profit. In fact they were without knowing it playing Mussolini's game, and they too reaped their just reward. Fascism could hardly have come to power if the individual classes and factions inside Italy had not feared and disliked each other more than they were collectively loyal to the nation. The excesses of Italian nationalism were not a sign of strength but of weakness. A genuine nationalism is too sure of itself to need the posturing of a Corradini or a D'Annunzio.

The ineffectiveness of parliament in Italy had been well attested long before Giolitti, Bonomi, De Gasperi, Orlando, Salandra and the other liberal and Christian democrat leaders so unthinkingly gave Mussolini the exceptional powers he required and virtually voted themselves out of useful existence. After Mussolini's threatening speech in November 1922, Matteotti rose to his feet and cried 'long live parliament'. To which the communists and most of the socialists called out in reply, 'down with parliament'; and if they meant what they said, they must have been pleased with the way things were going. At the other extreme, ever since the time of Bonghi and Sonnino, there had been leaders of the Right who wanted to reverse the constitution in a more authoritarian direction. It was frequently said that a foreign political system had been too precipitately installed in a country which lacked parliamentary traditions.

In particular the practice of transformism had never succeeded in working out a way of properly focussing organised criticism on the government, and of providing an alternative government with an alternative programme for consideration by the electorate or the king. Neither Giolitti, Crispi, nor even Cavour had ever bothered much to organise opposition when out of office, but had tended to preoccupy themselves with their own private affairs. A succession of vague coalition governments had worked to suppress proper consideration of dangerous issues like social reform, colonialism, the Roman question, or fascism; because people who belonged to, or hoped to join, a coalition realised that their future depended on the tacit suppression of some highly controversial questions. A factious individualism and an inability to compromise left the constitutional groups quite unable to form a liberal-democratic bloc in 1919–22 and so prevent Mussolini with his 35 deputies from assuming power. Each group leader, himself finding the reality of power elusive, just made it hard for other liberal groups to succeed where he had failed, and each of them was reluctant to antagonise Mussolini with whom they all might soon wish to form another coalition.

The growth of a nationalist party in the early years of the twentieth century was another alarming symptom, and reflected certain deficiencies in both the nationalism and the liberalism of the Risorgimento. Crispi's Ethiopian war, with its tremendous psychological disaster at Adowa, was in one sense a penalty for giving power to a single man who treated all criticism of himself as unpatriotic. It was another apt commentary on a parliamentary system which allowed for no well-constituted opposition party with an alternative policy. But it was followed by a rapid growth in the belief that further wars were needed to blot out this particular memory, to strengthen moral fibre and restore national self confidence. Mussolini thus found plenty of people before 1914 on both Right and Left from whom to learn the creed of violence, of power for the sake of power. Crispi and Salandra showed him how to rule without recourse to parliament. Crispi at least raised taxes by decree. And history seemed to show that there was a close connection between authoritarianism at home and a policy of expansion abroad. Mazzini had assumed that the completion of national unity would make Italy a satisfied power; but, on the contrary, in the event it seemed only to enlarge her appetite just as it also enlarged her capacity for expansion. It was decreed that her dignity as a nation state forced her to maintain naval parity with Austria, and to indulge in an arms race which she had neither the raw materials nor the money to afford. The further result of this was to create a dangerously strong faction of industrialists who had an interest in war. John Bright in 1866 had looked on the unification of Italy and Germany as 'two great causes of disturbance got out of the way'. Lord John Russell, however, while he gave a qualified but sometimes enthusiastic approval to what was going on, had seen certain dangers in the unification of north and south: it might "make a despotism instead of a free government, an unwieldy power instead of a compact one." Cattaneo and D'Azeglio would have seen his point.

If Cattaneo had been able to look back over the results of unification, he might well have remarked that nationalism had in the end overcome or perverted liberalism. In origin, the Risorgimento had been essentially a liberal or liberating movement, or rather a series of many liberating movements; but the sorcerer's apprentice had liberated at least one force that he could not entirely control. Mazzini had formerly assumed by definition that all European nationalisms had an interest in common, that they would aid each other, and subsequently be able to live happily together in mutual sympathy and encouragement. But his own idea of helping to liberate the Slavs did not make the same appeal to his successors. Italian nationalism even came to derive a sometimes artificial strength and compactness out of stimulated rivalry with the inhabitants of Istria and Dalmatia. Nationalisms essentially have to feed on animosity, and it was perhaps absurd of Mazzini to have expected that, once the Austrians were out of the way, Italians would settle down to a saccharine feeling of love and forbearance for their immediate neighbours. Legitimate feelings of patriotism soon shaded off imperceptibly into a desire of conquest, as people began to say that the new frontiers needed protection and that the new nation had to show her mettle alongside and in rivalry with the other imperialist powers. It would not be particularly difficult to justify this process. But here and now it is merely important to note it as a fact, to recognise for instance how even the passive Giolitti was led into African adventures from which he himself expected little positive good. One must also note that this was another aspect of the connection between imperialism and the decline of parliamentarianism. Hostilities in 1911 were deliberately commenced in the middle of a seven and a half months' parliamentary recess. Parliament was not called upon to sanction the war, nor to debate the annexation of Libya by royal decree. When the House eventually met in February 1912, Turati was shouted down, and San Giuliano announced that the deputies should debate only administrative matters, not political or military. In the flush of victory a vote of indemnity was secured for the taxes already raised by decree, and there was hardly a voice so bold as to object.

This association of nationalism with what one might call illiberalism was repeated again in 1914–15. . . . On both occasions D'Annunzio, as might be expected, full of the joy of conquest, burst out into streams of bad poetry which did much to drown or etherealise the saner objections which could be advanced. On both occasions the nationalists were in their element, and began to assault their less warlike opponents in the open street. For some reason at which one can only guess, the same deputies who had shown in early May, 1915, that they were in a majority for a profitable neutralism changed their minds almost overnight and voted enthusiastically for war; and the leader of the parliamentary opposition did not dare to promote a public discussion of this critical issue, but sulked in his tent hundreds of miles away from Rome. This was not only undignified but–with an eye to 1922–frightening. The old ruling class of Italy was losing control. It was giving way before the nationalists and the socialists, and later before the *popolari* and fascism–all parties which based themselves on new elements in society. The liberals were losing their comfortable monopoly of politics. New layers of society were appearing, with visions of national and imperial greatness, and with new principles of violence and authoritarianism as their justification. They were to prove much more intractable than the other social forces which Giolitti had hitherto managed to control or corrupt, and were shortly to overthrow the whole Giolittian system of government. Having failed to stop the wars of 1911 and 1915, the liberals then failed to profit from them adequately. By 1919–22, the whole political situation was out of balance and out of control.

Once again, it is interesting to see, the King was forced into a position where he was a decisive, indeed the decisive element in the constitution. One may believe that he was reluctant to be so, and that he would have preferred to remain offstage in happy preoccupation with his other less political interests. But the King, who had large residual powers under the constitution, had at certain important moments in the past been forced into the open to take decisions on his own, and then the results had often been unfortunate. Over entry into the Crimean war, over the Calabiana episode, over Villafranca, over Victor Emmanuel's attitude to Garibaldi in 1860, over Aspromonte and Mentana, over the conquest of Rome in 1870, over Umberto's association with Tanlongo, one could multiply the occasions when the monarchy in all appearance took Italy into dangerous waters. The continued secrecy of the royal archives makes the precise story always difficult to unravel, and it is fair to say that one has to rely a good deal on unsatisfactory guesswork. But again in 1915 it seems that, either for reasons of his own, or else more likely through a clever intrigue of Salandra to cover himself in an unprincipled manoeuvre, Victor Emmanuel III sealed the fate of Italy by his sovereign fiat, and the royal involvement effectively kept Giolitti from bringing his disagreements into the open. In 1922 things were done more openly. Possibly with the fear of losing his throne, the King then took it upon himself to reject the advice of his prime minister, and invited Mussolini to form a cabinet. The downfall of the constitution and of the monarchy itself thus went almost hand in hand.

There is no simple conclusion to this story. History and politics are alike too complicated for simple conclusions. But perhaps enough has been said in this short and inadequate essay to show how difficult it is to maintain that fascism was the complete negation of previous history. It is hard to deny that certain trends existed connecting the two. Mussolini was not completely inaccurate in saying that his movement was an extension or development of the national revolution in the 19th century. One can think this and still stop a long way short of believing that fascism was an inevitable consequence of the Risorgimento.

Furthermore, it might be added that the alternative view of a sharp antithesis between these two movements is not only untrue historically, it also could be dangerous in present-day politics. If the liberals played so lamentable a part in 1922, this was due to a precisely similar failure in self-analysis, not believing that these horrors could happen to them, but convinced that Italians were too intelligent, too liberal, even too Machiavellian, to fall victim to such a shallow and ignoble poseur as Mussolini. Surely no one in this twentieth-century world can afford to be so sure of himself. The megalomaniac folly of one man and his friends could not by itself have caused such a gigantic tragedy if it had not fitted into some larger process. Mussolini was a plagiarist and an eclectic in both his doctrine and his tactics. His movement can hardly be presented in any convincing perspective until its ancestry has been traced back into Italian and European history. And by thus delving back into the past one may incidentally learn something that might be of political value to the present.

Freedom and Power in Liberal Italy*

A. WILLIAM SALOMONE

THE ITALIAN INTELLECTUAL atmosphere has been pregnant with questionings and revaluations since 1945. Frustration and disenchantment with the rule and ruin of Fascism brought in their train a profound crisis of the Italian political and moral conscience. A great battle of ideas was fought in postwar Italy over the immediate issues relating to the historical foundations of the political and ideological sources of Fascism. But in that atmosphere a vaster movement of historical revisionism soon gained the force and momentum of an apparently irresistible wave of the future. Before long, the entire range of problems involved in the interpretation of modern Italian history, particularly since the Risorgimento, was revisited and revised. The Risorgimento and its aftermath were put on trial together with the great historian and defender of Liberal Italy—Benedetto Croce.

The publication of Antonio Gramsci's *Quaderni dal Carcere* during 1947–51 at first acted as an ideological catalyst. Gramsci's reflections soon were practically converted into a new system of secular dogmas toward the reinterpretation of Italian history.

* From A. William Salomone, "Problems of Freedom in the Post-Risorgimento," *The Cesare Barbieri Courier* (Trinity College), IV, No. 2 (Spring 1962), 3–10. Reprinted through the courtesy of Michael R. Campo, Editor of *The Cesare Barbieri Courier.*

Gramsci's neo-Marxist "philosophy of praxis" was rigidly pitted against Croce's "religion of liberty" as the basis for analysis and understanding of the historical significance of the Risorgimento and the developments of Liberal Italy from Cavour to Giolitti and then to D'Annunzio and Mussolini. The fury of a vast-ranging storm of "historical revisionism," led by the Italian neo-Marxist revolt against Croce and his Liberal philosophy of history, re-enveloped the Risorgimento and the Liberal era in the grey zones between ideology and history. Theory and practice, metahistory and moralism were subtly fused and confused in the organic Marxist critique of Crocean historicism. Crocean idealism, which in the philosopher's *Storia d'Europa* and *Storia d'Italia* had made an implicit exaltation of the "progress of liberty" before the Great War of 1914 and the coming of Fascism, was subjected to the castigations of Italian Marxist realism and accused of intellectual and moral complicity in the involution of Italian political life. The Marxist intelligentsia sought to reduce the history of Italy from the Risorgimento to the end of the Liberal period to the dust and ashes of a dreary *rivoluzione mancata.* Against the Crocean idea of Italian history in the nineteenth century as a great stage in an essentially irreversible "progress of liberty" Marxist historiography raised the myth of an indivisible "process of authority." On the eve of centenary celebrations of the Risorgimento and the making of Italian political unity, interpretative norms seemed hopelessly polarized between those that predicated liberty and those that subsumed authority as keys to the history of modern Italy.

A *ritorno alla ragione* seems now necessary and

possible–a return to historical reason uncommitted to either ideology or dogma can bring a fresh understanding of modern Italian history. This essay represents the sketch for an approach that, while not repudiating the concepts of liberty and authority as valid historical criteria in the study of Italian history, seeks to disengage "liberty" from its historicist-philosophical mooring and "authority" from its metahistorical-ideological mold. A thread is then experimentally isolated from the complex vicissitudes of modern Italian history and empirically adopted for purposes of historical understanding. That thread is seen in the great, continuous conflict between authority and liberty in the history of modern Italy.

European as it was in essential historic character, the conflict between force and freedom assumed a special Italian form exactly because the Risorgimento itself, through the great expectations it aroused among vast zones of the Italian people in its course and the disproportionately modest practical results it seemed to have achieved at its conclusion, impressed upon it the urgency of a fruitful resolution. Inescapable as it became, the conflict was not inevitable in the dimensions it acquired in post-Risorgimento Italy. Tragic and fertile at the same time, the great conflict began with the disparity between the immense authority of the new Italian unitary State and the precarious liberty of Italy's national civil society. During the post-Risorgimento, the conflict led to profound cleavages but also to strenuous conciliations between the State and Italian society. It was only in the twentieth century that two great, if different, experiments at deeper and wider reconciliations were undertaken, with the tyranny and breakdown of Fascism between them: the experiment at an Italian democracy during the Giolittian era before the First World War and the great promise of democracy's fruition after the Second World War. It is with Italy's historic road to that first experiment that this essay is substantively concerned.

The conflict between liberty and authority was implicit in the character of the Risorgimento itself. The Liberal leadership and the actual outcome of the Italian national revolution in 1859–61 contributed in making it almost irrepressible. Cavour himself had had to fix his unique political genius upon the creation and survival of a State within the European system of States. During his Piedmontese "apprenticeship" he had had time and opportunity to turn freedom into a function of constructive statecraft. In 1861, his Italian hour of triumph, fate gave him no time to begin a fundamental reconstruction of the new Italian national community. The tragedy of his premature death became part of the emerging tragic conflict between the State he had made and the Italian society he was not able to mold. Rightly proud as he was of his exceptional achievement, he died in the full knowledge that his larger task was unfinished, his magnificent victory only half-won. But he was also conscious that the new history of Italy had begun with the assertion "in the face of the world" of an essential act of freedom—the right of a nation to the determination of its own destiny. On March 17, 1861, the very day which saw the official crowning of his unparalleled work toward the making of a State,

Cavour wrote in a confidential dispatch to the minister plenipotentiary in London:

> . . . Constitutional legality has consecrated the labor of justice and reparation which has restored Italy to herself. From this day forward Italy proudly asserts her existence in the face of the world. She solemnly proclaims today the right which is hers to be independent and free and which she has sustained on battlefields and in the Councils [of Europe]. . . .

A long "labor of justice and reparation" was now indeed at an end for Italy. But it also left a legacy of a new labor of conciliation and reconstruction. In the course of the national revolution, an audacious, an almost arbitrary, commitment had been made of the entire Italian national community to a new way of life. But that community was as yet only half-consciously aware of its new national identity nor had it been forewarned of the tremendous price, of the further strains and sacrifices, required for its passage from the quasi-archaic Italian world to the new civil order of nineteenth-century Europe. It was in that strenuous passage, after 1861, that Italians painfully learned for themselves of the immensity of the price to be paid for immersion into the mainstream of national and liberal civilization. Perhaps only Cavour, among his contemporaries, had fully understood the monumental proportions that "price" would attain while the leaders of the political class which inherited his succession had to grapple desperately with them. The "labor of justice and reparation" had given birth to the new Italy but infancy was fraught with dangers and uncertainties. Below the surface of the Risorgimento triumphant stirred a dark conflict between the new Italian national *ragion di Stato* and the "reasons" of liberty, the requirements of peace and justice, of Italy's civil society.

Cavourian statemaking had been the practical resultant, perhaps not the ideal one but certainly the most positive, among a variety of objectives envisaged during the course of the Italian Risorgimento. The democratic "alternatives" to the solution of the "Italian Question" and the success of the national revolution had continually projected and impelled the Risorgimento onto ever-widening spheres of thought and action, of possibilities and hopes of fulfillment. For Mazzini and Cattaneo, in particular, the politics of the Risorgimento had been seen, albeit for different reasons and in different ways, as the premise of a larger ethic of liberation, the Italian prelude to a vast European movement of freedom and justice. The failure of their Promethean vision left a deep scar in the Italian political and moral conscience. The vision vanished, but the victorious Liberal élites inherited the legacy of its failure. For, once the vital, historic commitment was made by the leaders of the Liberal classes toward the fulfillment of a great change only in the Italian political order, there could be no turning back or forward to dangerous experiments with the structure of Italy's civil society. But neither was there a real chance that, given their ancient social and spiritual condition, the larger masses of the Italian people would actively re-participate in or quickly accept the results of an Italian political revolution founded upon the secular faiths of liberalism and nationalism. Indeed, in the new Italian and European atmosphere of the age of realism and socialism, which dawned in 1870–71 with the Franco-Prussian War and the Paris Commune, only hard-headed liberalism and cautious nationalism could be the true riders of that "fiery steed of liberty" which the liberal political classes had found so dangerous to ride at all during their first exposure to war and revolution in 1848–49.

And yet, the boldest members of the post-Cavourian Italian political class did not cease to invoke a concord between liberty and authority in Italy. The day after the "breach at Porta Pia," on September 21, 1870, Emilio Visconti Venosta, too, confidentially restated the aim of Italian polity. That aim, he wrote, did not consist in the acquisition of territory nor in the occupation of a city, however illustrious it may be:

> . . . We are inspired by a greater ambition. The complete separation of Church and State, the harmonious development of social and religious forces in order to moralize the popular classes, the accord between liberty and authority: these are the maxims which we propose to proclaim in Rome.

Visconti Venosta's historic "ambition" and the liberal "maxims" in which it was couched were, of course, the moving forces and ideal of the victors of the Italian national revolution. But they were exactly those upon which the larger movement of the Risorgimento had broken and then had been fragmented into contrasting currents of thought and action. Their reassertion, at that crucial moment, as the master-ideas, the guiding-principles of liberal politics, meant keeping faith with the Cavourian spiritual legacy. But it could, in fact it was, also interpreted as a restatement of liberal aims in a continuing war of ideologies, a reawakening of political passions, the renewal of a conflict of interests and loyalties and purposes that might break asunder the tenuous fabric of Italy's new national life. It was, indeed, upon the interpretation of the practical nature of that "accord between liberty and authority"—the liberty of Italian civil society and the authority of the Italian unitary State—that the most acute and dangerous aspects of the great conflict arose in post-Risorgimento Italy.

The immediacy of the political question during the climactic years of the Risorgimento had, in some cases understandably, led to precipitous solutions of very grave Italian problems. In 1859–60, threats of "European" intervention, rumors of preventive international action under the auspices of the "Concert of Powers," and the dangers of social revolution led to recourse to civil dictatorships and the adoption of plebiscitary policy. But the exigencies of war in 1859 having passed, the problems posed by the unexpected peace of Villafranca proved a blessing in disguise, as Cavour himself in due time admitted. Again, the alarm roused in both Italian liberal and European conservative quarters by Garibaldi's revolutionary-military movement of liberation of the South in 1860 was rather quickly matched and surpassed by the enthusiasm and applause of European liberal opinion as well as by the crucial non-interventionism of Palmerston and Russell and the enigmatic neutralism of Napoleon III. And, not least, visions of the possible perils the Italian cause would fall prey to through the loss of the "national initiative" either to a resurgent democratic radicalism of the Mazzinian Party of Action or to a neo-*sanfedista* clerical reaction were dispersed in the murky atmosphere of Garibaldi's generous "surrender" at Teano.

In the winter of 1860–61, there seems to have been still some time to revaluate and possibly revise, or at least to review, in the light of the liberal victory assured and peace restored, the policy of expediency dictated by war and revolution. At any rate, the results of that policy and the implications of retaining it beyond and outside the immediate circumstances in which it had been adopted seemed in fundamental need of reappraisal. Much of that policy and its practical consequences–the annexations, the real and symbolic significance of the plebiscites as expressions of national self-determination, the political and moral implications of the downfall of the Austrian, Papal, and Bourbon *anciens régimes*–could not but persist. But some of the rest, involving vital questions of institutional organization, economic and social policy, and the delay in nurturing an atmosphere of "peace without victory" in the internal Italian sphere, might realistically have been reviewed. At any rate, there is some reason to feel that what was retained of the policy of expediency could have been accepted, not as a permanent basis for the irreversible solution of Italian national problems, but rather as the empiric and preliminary groundwork, which it indeed had really been, toward the consolidation of the unitary State and toward a patient "labor of justice and reparation" for Italy's new civil society. For this now was a time of decision when the politics of the national revolution might have been re-tested and possibly transmuted into a more substantial, a palpable, function of that ethic of freedom that had been the propelling force, the ideal bedrock of the Risorgimento.

In the crucial aftermath of 1861 there was urgent need of a fearless and fruitful reconstruction of Italy. This reconstruction would itself have required a heroic act of imagination and audacity: genuine Cavourian political genius. Such an act would have involved the realization that there was need to do more than to create the structure of the State and the image of authority as if Italy's newly-won national freedom automatically secured and insured the liberty of Italians. The liberal conscience of the nineteenth century, in Italy as elsewhere in Europe, generously harbored the illusion of that equation in theory even as liberal politics tended to deny it in practice. After 1861 the political foundations of the State were, in fact, strenuously made firm in Italy almost as if Italian society were another antagonist to be subdued rather than the necessary agent and collaborator in its own reconstruction. Thus it happened that, despite their selfless and courageous dedication to a gigantic task, the Cavourian successors of the Historical Right (1861–76) appeared to have converted what were absolute necessities of reconstructive statecraft into functions, sometimes into actual instruments, of an erosive "social war." Administrative centralization, the iron grip of ubiquitous fiscalism, the expansion and capillary consolidation of the bureaucracy, the wanton, profitless disposal of confiscated ecclesiastical property, the establishment and maintenance of a large military apparatus, the evanescent remoteness of the State as a source of justice and its inescapable proximity as a new fountainhead of ancient tyrannies—these and more were soon matched by sullen suspicion and moral rejection and then by a mixture of active and passive resistance among large sectors of the Italian people for whom they seemed only newer and more efficient weapons of old oppressions.

The Left's *trasformismo,* after the fall of the Right in 1876, seemed momentarily pregnant with great possibilities of renovation of Italian life. The potential range of its alternatives of polity appeared to stretch all the way between the "democratic" politics of retrenchment enunciated by Agostino Depretis and the "authoritarian" politics of expansion later adopted by Francesco Crispi. *Trasformismo,* however, hardly touched the fringe of Italian political and social realities. Even as it sponsored a Draconian beginning in the economic transformation of post-Risorgimento Italy into a capitalistic and industrializing nation, *trasformismo* became a dark-grey screen upon which the realities of Italian politics and life were faintly reflected. Italians recoiled equally from the sterile shadow-politics of *trasformismo* and the stern requirements of its incipient economic revolution. They sought refuge in antiparliamentary critiques, in political invective, in ideological dissent. Resentment and tumults against the notorious *macinato* taxes imposed by the Right were converted into social conspiracies and moral abstentionism under the rule of the Left. After exposure to the terroristic and messianic message of Bakunin's anarchism, an Italian working-class movement slowly laid the foundations for the rise of Socialism. The founding of the Italian Socialist Party in 1892 marked the beginning of a new era in post-Risorgimento politics. In practice, Italian Socialism brought the promise of conciliation not the sword of conflict. Thus for almost a quarter century (1876–1900), Italian civil life was astir even as it resisted the politics of futility. Italian society developed and grew but as if at the same time *outside* and *against* the sterile and constrictive circle of official Italian politics.

Concord and liberty, freedom and power, conciliation and conflict were thus subtly, if unevenly, woven in the texture of Italian life during the era of *trasformismo*. The separation of Church and State consecrated the conflict between Italian liberalism and the Papacy. Pius IX appeared to have become a reed caught in the winds of two romanticisms: the political romanticism of engagement of his vertiginous "Italian" moment of 1846–48 and the organic romanticism of alienation and rejection of all the secular creeds of the nineteenth century. The Decrees of the Vatican Council of 1869–70 had sealed the repudiations of the "Syllabus of Modern Errors" of 1864. The Church's duel with the Italian Liberal State, which Pio Nono regarded a creature of the "moral, civil, and religious oppression" of the "so-called Risorgimento," the "triumph of disorder and the victory of the most wicked revolution," continued apparently unabated beyond the turn of the twentieth century. But fears common to both Church and State of the coming of even worse "revolutions" and the splendid common sense of the Italian people led to no open religious war in Italy, to no outbreak of sterile *Kulturkampf,* despite the fanaticism of restricted clerical and anticlerical circles. In the meantime, however, regardless of the transcendent importance ascribed to the religious *dissidio* in sensitive Italian quarters, Italian civil society found itself faced and had to deal with other *dissidi* which affected the large or the petty pace of their daily existence.

The "discovery" of the fantastically grave, the almost monumental "Questione del Mezzogiorno" in the post-Risorgimento roused at first unbelief in its reality and then skepticism over its true proportions. An intrepid group of enlightened reformers and conservative intellectuals, led by Pasquale Villari, Sidney Sonnino, Leopoldo Franchetti, and then by Giustino Fortunato, fused technical knowledge and political sense, intelligence and compassion, in laying bare in their gravest dimensions some of the most complex problems of the South. All too slowly these men were to succeed in impressing upon the conscience of other Italians the existence of a south Italian world oppressed by the tyranny of geography, unredeemed by the politics of the new Italy. That Italian conscience wasted precious time in hopeless indifference and pseudo-scientific rationalizations before it extended its solidarity with the obscure "labor of justice and reparation" undertaken by the *contadini* of the South themselves. During the post-Risorgimento, for many among the poorer masses of the peasants of the South the sole alternatives to freedom and elemental justice appeared to lie either in revolt or in escape, either in brigandage or in emigration. From the Palermo revolt of 1866 to the revolutionary explosion of the *Fasci Siciliani* of 1893–94, the history of the South resembled a chronicle of fearful *jacqueries*. But bridges to the North—moral, ideological, and political bonds of solidarity—were slowly being built.

The revolt against Crispi in 1896 was not partisan but national: it lay in the very logic of his policy of social repression and of the colonial adventurism which had led to the tragedy of Adowa. Now North and South seemed engaged in an unconscious search for their common Italian "soul," in a quest for a minimum of social justice and elementary civil freedoms. But the aftermath of Adowa was fraught with more times of trouble: the bloody "Fatti di Maggio" of 1898, the great Socialist parliamentary battle of obstructionism to restore a sense of dignity to constitutional and civil life, the downfall of the experiment at military dictatorship by General Pelloux, and then the assassination of the second King of United Italy in July 1900. These were the bitter fruits of the great quest for "the accord between liberty and authority" in post-Risorgimento Italy. If they contained also the seeds of a potential reconciliation between an Italian State converted into a citadel of reaction and an embattled Italian society eager for civil peace and social justice, the ground would have to be prepared anew for their fruition.

In 1900, at the crossroads of two European historic periods, in Italy only the culmination of a long, tragic dissension seemed apparent. Political loyalties to the unitary State were superficially intact. But neither the Monarchy nor the new ruling classes, neither the *notabili* of the Right nor the opportunists of the Left appeared to have made any consistent effort toward setting up dikes against the re-emergence, in vaster dimensions and more dangerous circumstances, of an historic Italian disenchantment with politics. True that a thousand years of bad and indifferent governments and recurring calamities had taken their toll upon the spiritual fabric of Italian life. Indeed, the heritage of physical and moral misery was too profound for even the combined genius of a gifted people to undo it in a short space. Nevertheless, in the post-Risorgimento another Italian generation was almost lost through persistent times of trouble and magnificent energies were wasted. Even as they were invoked as indispensable in the realm of national power, those great Italian energies and human resources were treated as if they were expendable in the realm of freedom. The Italian State had survived through those times of trouble, but Italian civil society was still in need of essential reconstruction.

A strong wind of fresh liberalism swept upon Italy and broke the evil spell imposed upon civil society by the half-misguided and half-blind despotism of a self-defeating oligarchy of conservative *notabili,* stolid bureaucrats, and "Napoleonic" political generals. The passage to the dawn of an Italian democratic era was somewhat obscurely but coherently opened in 1900–03 through the irresistible pressure exerted by the Italian masses *from below* and through the vision and courage and labor, *from above,* of a genuinely liberal *notabile,* a statesman of Cavourian stature: Giovanni Giolitti. Now, at that crucial moment which marked the beginning of an era to which he properly gave his name, Giolitti and his liberal politics became the link binding the mute Italian aspiration for a civil peace and the great hunger for a measure of social justice and real freedom among the masses of the people. For a brief time Giolitti let the leaders and the newer élites emerging from the ranks of the ideological and social opposition to the sterile reactionary politics of Crispi, Di Rudinì, and Pelloux enjoy their hour of triumph. Italian conservatism and the authoritarians of the extreme Right could blame no one but themselves if their policies had helped mold the dispersed forces of radicalism, republicanism, and Socialism into a cohesive political Opposition bound together as an Extreme Left—the *Estrema.* The extreme Right had thus made their liberal "enemy," Giolitti, the "free gift" of the potential vanguard of the *Estrema* as *his* political and parliamentary wedge toward the initiation and pursuit of a new democratic policy.

The "opening to the Left" of the crucial first phase of Giolittian politics had been forced by the extreme Right's stubborn willfulness in seeking only authoritarian "openings" to a dead Italian past. Conservatism and reaction under Crispi and Pelloux had brought Italy to the brink of social disaster and national catastrophe. Giolitti's cautious turn to the *Estrema* was a subtle tactical move in his larger strategy of democratic liberalism. In Parliament and throughout the country Giolitti called upon all the live forces of Italian social and political life for aid and active cooperation toward the hard work of fulfilling immediately the moderate desires for freedom and the elementary economic needs of the Italian people. Together, they helped tremendously in removing liberty from the stall of disembodied myths in the Italian market place of rhetoric and then in giving it substance and concrete functions and vitality in the new Italian struggle for a dignified political and social existence.

For the first time in modern Italian history, Giolitti prepared a tentative common ground between the Italian State and civil society. He called that common ground "the field of liberty." Upon it he was willing to risk battle equally with the reactionary Right, which hated and feared all he stood for, and the revolutionary Left, which suspected and understood only too well everything he worked for. Giolitti believed in and prosaically practised a "policy of liberty for all within the limits of the law." That policy worked wonders where violence and coercion had been of little use. With that policy of liberty Giolitti led Italy to take giant steps toward a solid conciliation, after dreadfully long years of unsplendid divorce, between the State and the Italian people. If at the end of his long, fertile rule in 1914, the miracle of a full-fledged "accord between liberty and authority" had not occurred, it was due as much to the immensity of that problem in Italy as to the limitations in his policy and the defects in his vision of Italian potentialities.

Giolitti's vision was circumscribed by many things which were the other side of his successful liberal politics: tradition, temperament, contempt for rhetoric, disregard for ideas, fidelity to the Monarchy, belief in the bureaucracy as the staunchest servant of the State, faith in the State as the chief guardian of civil order. There was much in the complicated and fervid world of his day that Giolitti could not, perhaps would not, understand. In many cases it made little difference that he was not stirred to give his attention to the multiform threads and nuances in the rich pattern of Italian life and culture. Cavour, too, in his day, had had to practise a division of labor to reserve his energies for concentration upon the economic, juridical, and diplomatic aspects of his politics. But in some cases, given the delicate balance of social and moral forces in *his* Italy, Giolitti neglected or pretended to forget aspects and developments of Italian life and culture that *malgré lui* were integral parts of his immediate success and then proved decisive elements in his ultimate failure.

The moods and symptoms of "moral" rebellion in activistic circles of the Italian intelligentsia of the Giolittian era grew and expanded. In the name of a "renovation of life and culture," a clamorous vanguard of the Italian intelligentsia became more and more as if inebriated with its own exaltation of war and violence, of unreason and authority, and of mysticism and force. Fed by other elements–reactionary or ultra-democratic, moralistic or revolutionary, militaristic or authoritarian–promiscuously thrown together by *common* hatred for the real or imagined defects and for the progressive or regressive character of Giolittian politics, the new ideologues of authority succeeded in wrapping their congenital opposition to the liberty restored by an "Italian democracy in the making" under the mystique of a revolt against *giolittismo.*

Tragically, less for his political fate than for Italy, Giolitti ignored the real dimensions of that smoldering revolt against his system of politics and never quite comprehended the true anti-democratic finalities of the authoritarian wing of his ideological and political opponents. That Enrico Corradini and Antonio Salandra, D'Annunzio and Mussolini, each in his fashion, should have been vociferous spokesmen of that wing is perhaps no cause for surprise. But that men who should have been Giolitti's friends, because they differently sought the same ends of Italian freedom he pursued, became his most implacable enemies does offer reason for historical meditation. Among the anti-Giolittians of genuine liberal faith or democratic stamp the figures of Luigi Albertini and Gaetano Salvemini towered above all others.

Albertini's *Corriere della Sera,* a journalistic institution *sui generis* in pre-1914 Italy and Europe, was turned into one of the most consistently aggressive anti-Giolittian organs throughout the entire period. The liberal Milanese and Lombard *bourgeoisie* and the professional *notables* of the North always found an echo of their anti-Giolittian animus in the pages of Albertini's great newspaper. It is, therefore, at once surprising, saddening, and ironical to read the following estimate of the origins of Fascism in Albertini's monumental memoirs:

> There is no reason to wonder if a nation-in-arms reveals a valor that corresponds to the degree of progress attained by its average citizen. What is my point? It is that for the moral crisis of Caporetto the entire responsibility must be borne by the Italian ruling class—that class which was first with Giolitti, then with Orlando and Nitti, and which judged as the height of ability their methods of license. That class later joined up, with Mussolini, supporting and approving even worse manumissions of our constitutional rights. It was at first neutralist and then sought to avoid the War with [Gio-

litti's] *parecchio*. When the War was over that class became intransigently patriotic. It only ceased to feel enthusiasm for Mussolini when he revalued the lira and created the Corporations, but it did not find the courage to express its opinion: it murmured but continued to applaud. At any rate, with a more worthy and more respectable ruling class, could what has been happening in Italy have happened at all? Would it have been possible for the dictator to find in the parties of the Left his most servile and satisfied supporters? . . . With few exceptions, our middle class was always with the Pope, with Giolitti, with Treves and Turati. . . . I write and bear witness of all this, not to give vent to my resentment against those who constituted the fulcrum of the Fascist regime, but to speak out the truth, to coordinate and furnish an explanation for the facts that have come to light, and in order to extract a lesson from our misfortunes. For, after all, what is this Italian ruling class if not my class, that to which my children belong, my relatives, my friends, my colleagues, and all those who form the backbone, the nerves, the brains of my Country, to which I have dedicated all of myself? Yet, despite all that I have said and all that I think, I do not despair of that class nor of the future . . .

The historian cannot but be perplexed when he reflects upon this page from Albertini's strange remembrances of things past in Italy. Truth and half-truth, historical fact and political bias are so mixed in that page, as in others of Albertini's huge *Venti anni di vita politica,* that it becomes difficult or impossible to say where history leaves off and politics begins. Albertini never forgave Giolitti for his stand against Italy's intervention into the War of 1914–18. Giolittian neutralism and the frightening prospect that Giolitti might have negotiated, through the notorious *"parecchio,"* Italy's peaceful abstention from the Great War became for Albertini the unforgivable mortal sin he gratuitously placed upon the conscience of the Piedmontese statesman. Around that "mortal sin" Albertini wove all the other sins of Giolitti before and after the War and beat the wrong *mea culpa* for his own and the Italian ruling class. For if that class had really been not only "with the Pope" but also "with Giolitti and Turati" perhaps *its* "misfortunes" under Fascism would not have been so great. As it was, the "misfortunes" of Albertini's own middle class were those of all classes of Italians who, after 1914, were dragged through the tragedy of war, social conflict, Fascism, and then war again in 1940–45.

Gaetano Salvemini's own revolt against Giolitti and *giolittismo* stemmed from other sources. This is not the place to recount once again Salvemini's anti-Giolittian *curriculum vitae.* But a famous page from his remembrances of Italian things past deserves to be meditated upon once again in the light of the historic conflict, here analyzed, between liberty and authority. Toward the close of the Second World War, with a fresh revaluation of the Giolittian era before him, Salvemini wrote as follows:

In the course of his researches [the author]

has come upon my name and he has devoted some space in his book to my activities in Italy during the years of Giolitti. It is not up to me to comment on what he has written about me. But to one point I feel duty-bound to call the reader's attention. While during those years I practised, as well as I could, my profession of historian (which has always been my true profession), I devoted my spare time to a political crusade. The reader will find in this book the crusader and not the historian.

Looking back at the work of the crusader after thirty years, I find that I have nothing to regret. I must acknowledge, however, that I would have been wiser had I been more moderate in my criticism of the Giolittian system. My knowledge of the men who came after Giolitti in Italy as well as of countries in which I have lived during the last twenty years has convinced me that if Giolitti was not better, neither was he worse than many non-Italian politicians, and he was certainly less reprehensible than the Italian politicians who followed him. For while we Italian crusaders attacked him from the Left accusing him of being—and he was—a corrupter of Italian democracy in the making, others assailed him from the Right because he was even too democratic for their taste. Our criticism thus did not help to direct the evolution of Italian public life toward less imperfect forms of democracy, but rather toward the victory of those militarist, nationalist, and reactionary groups who had found even Giolitti's democracy too perfect. . . . If it were possible

> for me to live again in Italy between 1900 and 1914 with that modicum of experience which I have gained during these successive thirty years, I would not omit any of my censures of the Giolittian system, but I would be more indulgent and I would regard with greater suspicion those who found pleasure in my criticism because they wanted to lead Italy in the opposite direction from that which I envisaged for her.

Salvemini's courageous reappraisal is its own best comment. If, in the last years of his long and laborious life, irked by the uses and abuse his calm Giolittian reappraisal had been subject to at the hands of the professionals of historical nostalgia and the adepts of political ideology, Salvemini angrily "retracted" a part of his positive judgment on Giolitti, but not on Giolittian democracy, it involved no retraction of his self-confession of paradoxical and unwitting "complicity" in the undermining of an "Italian democracy in making," to which he had dedicated all of himself. In the twentieth century, an ironic twist of historic fate not only in Italy but elsewhere in Europe, too, has often led the staunchest friends of liberty to give aid and comfort to its enemies and destroyers–the lovers of authority.

As for Giolitti and his politics during his great day, they, too, became part of a strange antinomy. The most perceptive and constructive statesman of Italy since Cavour, Giolitti never took serious notice of the historic irony of which he became at the same time sponsor, agent, and victim. He succeeded in making freedom a function of Italian politics, but ultimately only as an instrument of government. Liberty, for him, never became a passion nor an idea larger than even its most important practical expressions. He was satisfied that liberty was a useful lubricant for the mechanical balance of conflicting economic and social forces in Italy. Necessary and solid as this success was, it gradually turned into the other side of his final failure. Under the aegis of freedom Giolitti nursed to health and vigor an Italian body politic and economic, long torn by conflict and dissension. But he neglected the spirit and never roused the conscience of the Italian people to a moral solidarity with his own work toward the making of an Italian democracy. He underestimated the necessity in his Italy of laboring not only with empiric political means toward genuinely liberal ends but also toward the creation and persistence of a fundamental moral consensus that might truly have cemented and insured the new Italian national community and its hard-won liberties against disastrous reversions. Had Italy been rooted in such a foundation of moral consensus, neither war nor Fascism could have shaken and destroyed her freedom. Only in having failed to work harder toward the building of that foundation did Giolitti truly prove to be an incorruptible "corrupter" of a nascent Italian democracy.

Ultimately, Giolitti was overwhelmed by the very forces to which he had given sustenance and freedom under his over-consistent policy of "liberty for all within the limits of the law." The worst of those forces eventually took diabolical advantage of that liberty in order to subvert those liberal "limits of the law." Thus Giolitti proved to have been the last Italian representative figure of a classic but vanishing race of great European liberal statesmen. At the end, Giolitti stood alone, in honorable obscurity, the Mephistophelian keeper of a secret of Italian politics which was becoming inconsequential as the long night of Fascism descended upon Italy. Only then did liberty truly perish in Italy, the victim of a new conflict with an authoritarian State that made the "authority" invoked and practised by conservative liberals of the post-Risorgimento pale into a form of political moderation. Fascism was not the "culmination" of the Risorgimento but rather the dark victory of Italy's Antirisorgimento.

How the European Knot Was Tied in Italy*

ERNST NOLTE

IN ITALY THE relationship between national state and antifeudal revolution, which was basic to the internal constitution of all European states, had been quite different from that in France. In France the revolution followed the national state; in a sense, the revolution endangered the state by destroying its solid foundation through the elimination of its state-forming power, the monarchy, and by jeopardizing its outward supremacy by proclaiming the principle of nationality. In Italy the national state was the re-

* From *Three Faces of Fascism* by Ernst Nolte, 145–152. Translated by Leila Vennewitz. Copyright © 1965 by R. Piper & Co., Verlag, Munich. Reprinted by permission of Holt, Rinehart and Winston, Inc. and George Weidenfeld & Nicolson Ltd.

sult of the revolution, and in spite of all internal tension, the motivating factors of this revolution never disintegrated as they had in France. Gioberti as Sardinian prime minister in 1848 was no Mirabeau, and Mazzini as triumvir of the Republic of Rome was far from being a Robespierre. The people as a whole were never really aroused, and what were called *moti popolari* were directed against the foreigners who for centuries had obstructed Italy's path to unity. No royal assassination struck terror and discord into men's souls, yet the triumph of Cavour and Victor Emmanuel opened up a freer path for the future than the French revolution had been able to do. The prerevolutionary leading class did not, as in France, continue to play a prominent role in spite of its defeat. Papal administration in the church state disappeared forever, as did that of the Bourbons in Naples. No bond of continuity linked the officers' corps of the new state to that of the old, although for decades the "black aristocracy" of Rome continued to regard the House of Savoy as infamous brigands. With his *non expedit* the pope had removed himself and his followers more thoroughly from political life than the bloodiest work of the guillotine could ever have done; on the other hand, the state was astute enough not to jeopardize the authority of the church in the life of the people.

In France the *ancien régime* and the various revolutionary factions split up in hatred and yet remained associated in an inconclusive battle, whereas in Italy they lived side by side as more or less good neighbors, either no longer associated or not yet separated. Admittedly Mazzini and Garibaldi had wanted to fight not for the Savoy monarchy but for a democratic republic; but they put up with the fact that their victories and defeats benefited the opponent, who was nevertheless fighting on their side, and they did not die as outcasts in irreconcilable hatred like most of the German revolutionaries. On the other hand the liberal Count Cavour and the semibourgeois royal house did not need to outlaw the bourgeois revolutionary party, as happened in Germany: the creation of the national state by a double-headed revolution gave the nation a unity and spiritual consistency which neither France nor Germany possessed.

Thus the Italian Risorgimento was the last successful spiritual and political trend in Western Europe to have a continuous and positive link with the great emancipatory movement. Both Mazzini and Gioberti agreed that the law of life is progress, that this progress is to be regarded primarily as the trend toward the equality of all people in liberty, that it is only within this trend that the principle of nationality can find justification. And however much the two most outstanding thinkers of the Risorgimento diverged from each other in the metaphysical substantiation of these principles, they approached each other again in the criticism of certain manifestations of the French revolution: its individualism, its hedonism, its emphasis on rights instead of duties. In this sense the Risorgimento is the first and only political victory of critical liberalism in Europe.

But it was a highly precarious victory. Had not Gioberti himself written a book in 1843 on the *primato morale e civile degli italiani,* basing his proof largely on the existence of the church? Yet can primacy be compatible with equality, and might not pride in the church override service to the church? Do we not find in Mazzini the concept of *mare nostro,* as well as a very dubious reference to natural boundaries when he deals with border disputes? Does not this theory that Austria must be destroyed by the liberation of its oppressed peoples bear the unmistakable mark of duplicity? If Taine and Renan bowed and turned before the pressure of new realities, we also find in Gioberti and Mazzini a few rudimentary indications of new trends.

Another point to be considered is that, if the politically active bourgeoisie revealed such an unbroken relationship to liberalism, it was only because it was conscious of being the undisputed protagonist of the change-over and because there was no imminent popular rebellion threatening its position. The Commune was not, as it was in France and Germany, experienced as a deep divide: if there were riots in Rome in 1870, their aim was to demand the new monarchy's annexation of the leonine city.

For Italy as for all Europe, the entry of the masses into politics and the testing of liberal ideas was to be the problem of the coming decades. The sons of the heroes of the Risorgimento solved it skillfully but unspectacularly, with a slowness of pace that could only have been called wisdom if it had been able to preclude the unforeseen. The franchise was expanded very gradually, and it was a long time before Italy entered into rivalry with the great powers over colonial territories. The defeat at Adowa in 1896 represented the first serious injury to youthful national pride as well as the moral defeat of one of the last survivors of the Risorgimento, Francesco Crispi.

At the same time it kindled the beginnings of nationalism, even if at first this occurred more in the minds of individual men (notably Enrico Corradini) than in the visible form of publications or organizations. But its significance cannot be even remotely compared to what the defeat of 1871 meant for France.

At roughly the same time, socialist and anarchist agitation met with their first successes. Severe repressive measures availed little, and the general strike of 1904 generated such alarm among the bourgeoisie that Pius X virtually revoked the *non expedit,* thus opening up the way for the formation of a Catholic mass party whose ideological attitude toward the Risorgimento was bound to be more negative than that of the socialists. However, it was precisely the association of socialism with liberalism that led the first nationalists to look askance at their party of origin and consider the possibility of an alliance with the Catholics. Although this unrest was far milder than that caused by the Dreyfus affair in France, it had greater prospects inasmuch as it was directed primarily against the socialists and only secondarily against democrats and liberals.

But by this time socialism had already become a card in Prime Minister Giovanni Giolitti's political game. His aim was to strengthen the reformist wing of the Socialist party and then draw the PSI into the government as bourgeois democracy's left wing. In 1910 he seemed to be on the verge of success. The revolutionary faction surrounding Costantino Lazzari had sunk to insignificance, the only remaining point of dispute between Filippo Turati and Leonida Bissolati was the timing of collaboration. Moreover, the prime minister had made such excellent diplomatic preparations for the planned colonial campaign in Libya that, as far as could be judged, it would be possible to conduct it without seriously impairing the political and intellectual stability of the country. Hence the intended introduction of universal suffrage did not appear to entail any danger.

If Giolitti's plan had succeeded, he would have brought Italy in one leap to the forefront of political developments in all of Europe and simultaneously completed the great task inherited from the Risorgimento. In looking back, observers might have found no more convincing example of historical determinism.

But the war roused more resistance in the Socialist party than Giolitti had envisaged, and at the party conference at Reggio Emilia in 1912 the hitherto totally unknown party secretary of Forlì, Benito Mussolini, succeeded in having the right-wing reformists led by Bissolati and Bonomi expelled from the party, thus creating a definite ascendancy for the revolutionary faction. Shortly afterward he became managing editor of *Avanti!,* and it was mainly due to him that the Socialist party, now again unquestionably antigovernment, emerged as the chief gainer from the first general elections in 1913. Thus Giolitti, although he won the war, had lost the real, the political, battle. He had actually set the course that was to lead him and Italian liberalism to their downfall, because the victory of the intransigent Socialists had resulted, on the opposing side, in the strengthening of the nationalists and conservatives led by Salandra, and because the first disturbance to the peace of Europe had proved impossible to control and therefore became one of the prime causes of World War I. But this whole development, at least in its early stages, was by no means inevitable. It was to a marked degree the result of a "temperament" and would presumably have taken a different course had this temperament been absent.

However, why it should have taken this direction and no other, why it was able to arouse emotions and to convince, will become clearer from a number of contingent circumstances, and not least from a study of the intellectual climate as a whole. Here, too, the unforeseeable has an important place. The fact that the survivors and descendants of the Risorgimento employed bitter words of reproach during the colorless period of transformation and the Giolitti era, that in the face of the triumph of a hard-hearted positivism they turned nostalgically to former times and antiquity, is as readily understandable as that this criticism was not directed in principle against the liberal character of the century.

It is true that Alfredo Oriani, whom Mussolini saw with doubtful reasoning as Italian fascism's sole precursor, sang the praises of the heroes and warriors of old, but he never went so far as to condone war per se, nor did he ever forget that Garibaldi was "a warrior who did not like war." It is also true that Giosuè Carducci condemned the wretchedness of the times and attributed its beginnings to that day when "a red-haired Galilean mounted the steps of the Capitol," yet the old republican was far from using the theory of the revolt of the slaves to place his paganism in a polemical and reactionary relation to the social movements of his time.

But it was impossible to foresee that a man with

almost no associations with the Risorgimento, Gabriele D'Annunzio, should achieve a position of the utmost influence over Italy's intellectual youth. For Italy's younger generation he was Nietzsche and Barrès rolled into one. He eluded the difficulties inherent in his concepts through the captivating melody of words, of which he was a master like Baudelaire or Rilke. He was far removed from the philosophy and the agony of Nietzsche, but, like him, he praised "the terrible energies, the sense of power, the instinct for battle and domination, the abundance of productive and fructifying forces, all the virtues of Dionysian man, the victor, the destroyer, the creator." Like Barrès he proclaimed the fatherland as far back as the early eighteen nineties; but all he ever saw in the nation was the most desirable scope for his own personality, whereas the objective aggregate of experience such as underlay the work of the Frenchman, who had looked at the defeat of 1870, was foreign to D'Annunzio.

D'Annunzio was in fact a Dionysian man of modern and highly original stamp, more so than almost any other man in Europe. His influence in Italy was incalculable. If the common European endeavor around the turn of the century toward rejuvenation often took on a more markedly irrational character in Italy—in spite of contrary native traditions—than in France and Germany, this was in great part attributable to D'Annunzio.

The oldest of the Florentine avant-garde publications, *Leonardo,* founded early in 1903 by Giuseppe Prezzolini and Giovanni Papini, devoted most of its attention to this change in the intellectual climate: the defeat of positivism, the rebirth of spiritualism, the reawakening of faith and mysticism. Its program was the formulation of a vague pressure, and finally it opened up its columns to magical idealism and the occult. The young contributors to *Hermes,* led by Giuseppe Antonio Borgese, paid homage to an esthetic imperialism; while in *Regno* (in which Pareto often appeared), expansion of life was the watchword of Corradini's nationalism, not the defense of traditional values as in the *Action Française.*

Clarified and matured, but not abandoned, all these beginnings appear in *La Voce,* Prezzolini's and Papini's second and more important publication founded in 1908. The chief thing to be clarified is nationalism: it is detached from Corradini's Roman imperial rhetoric, removed from its sharply antisocialist objective, and led to a more mature understanding of social phenomena. It is not surprising, therefore, that the journal opposes the Tripolitanian war. The philosophical basis is also clarified in detail, although not formally defined, by Benedetto Croce and Giovanni Gentile, who at the time scarcely suspected their future antagonism and closely cooperated to make their journal *Critica* a subtle organ of intellectual rejuvenation. Also clarified is the relationship to futurism and syndicalism, to Giolitti and Bergson, to Barrès and Maurras.

Nevertheless when world war broke out, the desire for the "new," for "action," was for *La Voce* and most of its contributors more powerful than considerations of expediency or obligation. In combination with all "young" forces, it worked toward that decision which set Italy apart from all other European nations: the decision to enter the war voluntarily. And Prezzolini went to Rome as political correspondent of the only daily newspaper which was founded for the specific purpose of bringing about intervention: the *Popolo d'Italia* of Benito Mussolini.

The "rejuvenation movement" as such was not the source of fascism but merely its precondition, and it also produced some of its principal opponents: Giovanni Amendola, leader of the Aventine opposition; Gaetano Salvemini, the first of the antifascist historians; Giuseppe Antonio Borgese, the outstanding poet, literary historian, and political writer. The springs of fascism were: the nationalists led by Enrico Corradini, the legionaries led by the D'Annunzio of the Fiume enterprise, and the former Marxists who had split off from the Socialist party and were led by Mussolini. These three groups gave Italian fascism the leaders, the ethos, and the ideas. Hence it is impossible to understand fascism without a look at the nature of Italian nationalism, the events in Fiume, and Mussolini's socialist period. Of these three elements, Mussolini's development is at one and the same time the least familiar and the most important. Thus, for this period, and even more so for later times, Mussolini's intellectual biography must be our principal guideline. It also offers the inestimable advantage of presenting us with that very Marxism which as the cause of middle-class alarm became the main precondition for fascism.

This does not mean that fascism is identical with "Mussolinism." Yet even when Mussolini appeared to be excluded from the fascist movement for a few months between 1920 and 1921, nothing could be settled in the party which did not in the end obtain

—or compel—his consent. This applies, of course, still more to the period of his rule.

We should not ignore the objection that there can be no "intellectual biography" of Mussolini, that with his superficial education and what was at best a journalistic flair, he sometimes sought to cover up his strivings for power with a veneer of incoherent thoughts, while in actual fact he was merely led by arbitrary contingencies.

But it would be manifestly unfair to judge Mussolini by the standards of Benedetto Croce or even of university scholarship. It is true that his love of Greek philosophy always turns out to be an unhappy one when he displays it in any form other than the wholly abstract, but the oft-repeated claim that the only work of Marx he had read was the *Communist Manifesto* is as false as the argument that he knew scarcely anything of Nietzsche beyond his "Live dangerously." His command of contemporary philosophy and political literature was at least as great as that of any other contemporary European political leader. So it would seem best not to cast doubts on Mussolini's sincerity without good reason, and not to be skeptical in our approach to his self-interpretation.

The great difficulty remains of containing a widely ramified historical phenomenon within the narrow circle of a single life. Interpolations and hindsight will be unavoidable, and the serious problem of periodization permits no completely satisfactory solution. There were no such difficulties in the case of the Action Française, because political history and the significance of the doctrine could be separated relatively easily and Maurras did not experience any notable personal development. But Italian fascism *is* its history, and this history is indissolubly linked to the biography of Mussolini.

To call Mussolini a Marxist is to evoke surprise, even today. Friends and foes alike have generally credited him with a mere vague revolutionism, a feeling which had been widespread in the Romagna since papal times and which after 1870, due to the activity of Bakunin's emissaries (with whom Mussolini's father Alessandro soon established contact) had assumed an anarchist character. The determining factor for Mussolini, it was said, was his lower middle-class origin; to this he owed his legacy of protest which, because it was ambitious, was of a purely personal nature. His father was a small property owner and a farrier (*fabbro ferraio*) and his mother a schoolteacher. But if the family were badly off, this was due mainly to the father's political ardor, which too often kept him from his work. But then, where in all Italy at that time were there, in the strict Marxist sense of the word, proletarians; where in all Europe did a socialist leader emerge from this class? At the time his son was born (1883) Alessandro was no more an anarchist than his revered model Andrea Costa who, although Bakunin's secretary in former years, had meanwhile come a great deal closer to the German Social Democrats and to Marxism.

Reliable reports, and reminiscences of Mussolini himself, depict the sturdy lad as a kind of gang leader disporting himself on the slopes around Forlimpopoli and in the gorges of the nearby river. At the age of ten he was separated from the other schoolboys at mealtime in the Salesian College at Faenza and made to eat with a few others of his kind at the "poor table." There is no reason why rage at injustice should not become a legitimate starting point for lasting socialistic feelings.

If Mussolini was continually being called *duce,* even in the early stages of his socialist period, this fact did not necessarily predestine him to be the "Duce of fascism." The fact that from childhood on he possessed the temperament of a *condottiere* is a precondition for his later life, but it is not sufficient to determine its direction. A second, equally important motivation in his life is the fact that from his earliest days his father filled him with socialist ideas and introduced him to socialist literature. It is not the tales of heroic deeds or imperialist dreams, invented or adapted by fascist biographers, that reflect the spiritual atmosphere of Mussolini's youthful years, but a simple report such as the following, originating from Mussolini himself in 1912: "We acknowledge our heresy. We cannot conceive of a patriotic socialism. Socialism is truly of a panhuman and universal nature. Ever since our earliest years, when socialist manuals large and small passed through our hands, we have known that there are only two fatherlands in the world, that of the exploited and that of the exploiters." The early possession of a political faith (*fede*) is no less decisive for Mussolini than the psychic disposition to be a *condottiere.*

Throughout his life Mussolini was a *condottiere* in possession of a faith or in search of a faith. The relationship between the two basic elements is what constitutes his history. The only time they were wholly united was during the first and longest period of his political activity, dedicated entirely to service in the Socialist party.

PART TWO

THE RISE AND FALL OF ITALIAN FASCISM: THE LEADER AND THE MOVEMENT

IV. ALIENATION AND REBELLION: THE NIHILIST IN SEARCH OF POWER

WAS BENITO MUSSOLINI (*1883–1945*), *both as frustrated revolutionary socialist before 1914 and as successful counterrevolutionary Fascist after 1919, the greatest single "accident" that occurred* to *modern Italy—or was he, either because or in spite of the continuous contradictions he revealed in his historical and moral personality, merely such a product, expression, or representative figure of the problematics of twentieth-century Italian life as to have become the crucial central link between the unresolved antinomies of post-Risorgimento and their resolution through the Fascist victory? Did Mussolini cut the historic "knot" of which Ernst Nolte writes, or was he only reinsuring its inextricable complexity? What was the connection between Mussolini the socialist revolutionary and Mussolini the Fascist, or, in a different way, in terms of the historical problems of the post-Risorgimento, how did currents of "classic" socialism come to be converted through Mussolini into the new subversive force of a Fascist totalitarian ideology? Upon what political, social, or spiritual soil can the uprooted revolutionary intellectual be submerged; in what milieu can he thrive and reach the heights of power? These and other similar questions must be posed, hurled, so to speak, within the stream of rational or intelligible historical problems such as the aftermath of the Ri-*

sorgimento and the Liberal era in Italy had or may be seen to have confronted. For, in a complex historical sense, Mussolini, no less than Hitler or Lenin, represented literally a unique innovation thrown into the whirlpool of pre- and post-1914 Italian social life. The selections in this and the following two sections seek to shed light upon the part and function exerted by "one man alone," a single individual seeking to find expression and a vehicle unsuccessfully through socialism and then victoriously through Fascism, upon the life of a nation and a people.

G. A. Borgese (1882–1952) was an eminent Italian literary critic, novelist, poet, political intellectual, and anti-nationalist who had opposed Mussolini and Fascism almost from the very beginning after 1919. But it was only in 1931, when he refused to take the oath of loyalty to the Fascist regime demanded by Mussolini of all "state employees"—and Borgese was a professor in an Italian state university—that he, among thirteen other professors, became an enemy of the Fascist State and took the road to exile in the United States. He taught Italian literature at the University of Chicago after 1936 and was one of the most active exponents of anti-Fascism in exile. His Goliath: The March of Fascism *(1938) was published at the height of the Nazi-Fascist diplomatic and psychological onslaught against the West, on the eve of the outbreak of the military conflict. For its interpretation of Fascism in the light of Italian history, for its literary style, and for its commitment, Borgese's book was hailed as a unique piece of political literature in the United States.*

Federico Chabod (1901–60) was the most illus-

trious Italian historian of the post-Fascist period. His reputation was deservedly so high that in 1955 he was elected President of the International Committee of Historical Sciences and the following year was honored with membership in the Italian National Academy of the Lincei. Chabod's historical interests and work had been vast and varied, ranging from the Renaissance and Machiavelli to a unique history of the city of Milan during the early modern period to modern history. The publication in 1951 of his masterly volume La politica estera italiana dal 1870 al 1896. Le premesse *amounted to an event all its own in Italian historiographical achievement. In 1952 Chabod delivered a series of lectures at the Sorbonne dealing with contemporary Italy, and they became the basis for his* History of Italian Fascism *from which the reading is derived.*

Don Luigi Sturzo (1871–1959) was one of the most significant figures in the history of Italian social and political Catholicism from the beginning of the century until his exile (1924) under Fascism. A Sicilian by birth and early activity, Don Sturzo dedicated himself at first not to the massive national problems connected with the status of Catholics in the Liberal State but rather to problems at the base of Italian social life—in the communes, in the provinces, in the regions of Italy—in search for that decentralization that might insure autonomy and liberty to the larger masses of Italians. In 1919 he founded the Partito Popolare Italiano *(PPI), the first Catholic mass-party in Italian history, and therefore a direct ancestor of his disciple, follower, and successor Alcide De Gasperi's Christian Democratic Party after 1945. In the early 1920s, as Fascism was rising in Italy, Don Sturzo opposed it with all his personal and intellectual resources, but, for reasons that may have ranged from temperamental to officious (that is, his obedience to the wishes of the Vatican), Don Sturzo found himself unable or unwilling to co-operate with either other mass-parties (chiefly the centrist socialists) or with the Giolittians in creating a parliamentary or political united front against the Fascists in 1921–22. Don Sturzo's integrity, his dedication to Italian social problems, his uncompromising stand against Fascism only gained him in 1924 the road to exile, first to England and later, until the fall of Fascism in Italy, to the United States. His knowledge of how Mussolini, the Monarchy, and the so-called established classes in Italy brought about the* coup de main *that resulted in the dark maneuver of October 1922, derived from direct exposure to what had occurred. Don Sturzo's book on* Italy and Fascism *(1926) was one of the first authoritative and courageous accounts of how "the Fascist revolution" had imposed a tyranny on all Italians–Catholics, Liberals, Socialists, and nonpartisans.*

Mussolini the Revolutionary: The Intellectual in Flux*

G. A. BORGESE

THIS IS THE mind of the man whom so many—more or less compulsorily in Italy, but quite freely abroad—have called a genius. An intermediate place between Italian and foreign applauders was held by an American Muse, named Ezra Pound, cackling: genius! genius! from an orchard in Rapallo.

A striking feature in the intellectual career of Mussolini is that no progress is noticeable in it. He starts with the atheistic pamphlet in which, mentioning Plato among the forerunners of modern atheism, he does not neglect to explain that Plato was "a Greek philosopher, a disciple of Socrates." He reaches the peak with the *Encyclopædia in nuce* of the *Talks* with Ludwig, and the peak is at the same level as the start. In the middle of his course, when the name of Einstein suddenly became popular, he wrote an article in which he assumed that Einstein's relativity means that everything is relative, nothing absolute, and therefore all incongruities are allowed to the politician.

Theoretically, although only theoretically, it is admissible that a mind totally devoid of philosoph-

* From *Goliath: The March of Fascism* by G. A. Borgese, 187–94, 196–203.

ical, æsthetic, and religious interests can yet be the mind of a great statesman. It is absurd to suppose that in a soul, or brain, where such futility and inconsistency can thrive as Mussolini, the artist and philosopher, has evidenced for thirty years, there may be place left for earnestness and greatness of any objective kind.

Anywhere, but especially in the Italian and Dantean tradition, the supreme ideal of human ambition consists in the hope of being a poet or a statesman or both. Young Mussolini, like so many youngsters, wanted to be both. This is in itself no blame.

But poetry and thought are difficult, whereas the life of action seems facile. The subjective greatness, or better said, the origin of Mussolini's luck, lay in the resoluteness with which—aside from a number of desultory fits—he submitted whatever remained of his literary and philosophical ambitions to the political purpose.

Often, a poet who has failed becomes a journalist, a philosopher who has failed becomes an orator. This happened to Mussolini too. He is renowned the world over as a great journalist and orator.

The management of the newspapers, small and large, of which he was the editor-in-chief never exceeded the standard of the yellow or tabloid press. His editorials, utterly unscrupulous in logic and information, attained not seldom a raw efficacy in sarcasm and threats. The same is valid about his oratory, whose most substantial secret, as well as of his writing, is the eradication of words like *perhaps* or any other that might express or infuse a feeling, however slight, of honest doubt. An improvised dogmatism, in hammering rhythm, is the kernel and pulp of his word, written or spoken. Whatever he thought or said yesterday, even if, especially if it was the contrary of what he thinks or says today, seems to be deleted from his consciousness and must be deleted from the memory of those who read or listen. No one, in the Italian libraries, is allowed to consult the articles of Mussolini's socialistic or anarchistic time, and one of his courtiers worded fittingly the master's fondest desire when he imposed upon all Italy the slogan: "Mussolini is always right."

The visible image of that kind of mentality may be contemplated in such motion pictures as *Mussolini Speaks.* With grimaces and contortions, which the audience beneath the lofty balcony does not see and which only the close-ups of the camera can record, he literally squeezes himself into words that find no response in either his heart or his mind.

This barbaric culture and art—far worse than no culture or art at all—certainly is one of the weightiest constituents of his personality. It is meaningless to regret that his poverty prevented him from having a university education, and that his intellectual preparation, that of an elementary schoolteacher, remained always of the mongrel sort; since the historical experiences of our age are far from proving that a high scientific training necessarily fosters good will and real knowledge: much of the most hateful nationalism and war-mongering, in Germany as well as in France and elsewhere, has been and is a specific product of those hothouses of specialized learning. At any rate Mussolini personally felt, although carefully hiding his feeling, that there was inferiority not only in his social origins but also in the quality of scholastic training that was allotted to him. This latter kind of inferiority he tried to counterbalance with a screaming dogmatism; which was to him an emergency expedient to pass his examinations.

The repressed scholar and the disappointed poet worked on in the surviving politician. He used those impulses, perverting their aims.

The little man was an anarchist and an artist.

He said once, with a whimsical exaggeration, that every anarchist is a dictator who failed.

His road to greatness consisted in making, of the anarchist who failed in him, the dictator who won.

But this very word would have been, in his youth, incomprehensible to him. He was no artist in the real meaning, neither was he an inventor of ideas. He could not be an announcer or forerunner, not even of himself. His low-class, belated culture did not yet put him in contact with the reactionary literature of France or Germany. D'Annunzio could hardly be to him anything else than a despicable bourgeois minstrel.

For many years his eagerness, led or misled by an almost aching and neurotic sense of smell, went after opportunities, always deceiving.

Whoever knows his personality, as he himself described it in the few words we have chosen among the many he has uttered—an atavistic avatar of the Renaissance man, a retrograde *homunculus* wanting to enlarge himself into a reality of today and tomorrow—may safely overlook the details of his career. His life was altogether inside, as several of his interlocutors guessed from the aloofness of his starved eyes, staring at the other man but never mingling with his personality. Whatever events he made or underwent were feathers, caducous, on the immutable shape of his soul; whatever objective ideas he seemed to adopt were the protective shades of the chameleon.

Since he too, Mussolini too, is a human being and our brother, there was a human moment in his early youth.

That he, instead of carryimg on as an elementary schoolteacher and a noodle-eater, an Albana-drinker, in his native Romagna, wandered to Switzerland, there to earn a scant bread as a manual worker by the sweat of his brow and to take part in debates where he, while denying God and ridiculing Christ, proclaimed the gospel of universal brotherhood and universal peace; that the real purpose of his hegira was the desire of escaping military servitude and of embracing his freedom; that he was jailed and fingerprinted; that he sometimes slept or hid under the arches of a railway-bridge; that on one occasion he snatched food from two Englishwomen picnicking in a park: these were and are his real glories. The blame for the transgressions against the written and common law does not affect a higher feeling of sympathy toward the solitary struggler who sought his life at his own risk. Charlie Chaplin would have liked what he did and endured; at first he would also have liked him who endured and did.

Then came the momentous decision, hastened by the police of Geneva, of his return to Italy and to Romagna. He had proved inadequate to the solitary effort, to the ascetic challenge of the real anarchist, as he had been inferior to the tortured self-sufficiency of the real artist. He found contact again with his stock and ground.

The years between 1909 and 1914, from the

twenty-sixth to the thirty-first years of his age, contain all his career as a Socialist editor and organizer. For a short time he was in Trento, the Italian city at that time still under Austrian rule. That, during those months, he seemed sensitive to the national irredentism of the city where he happened to live, is a legend invented by a lady friend of his, many years later. Even were it true, it would prove nothing except his already well-proved promptitude of adjustment to the environment. Ideas had never for him a worth in themselves.

Immediately after, at any rate, he totally forgot about whatever his experience in Trento might have been. His five years in Forlì and later in Milan were all one fight against fatherland and nation.

The dates and details of this period are irrelevant. What happened to him and what he happened to do were only an allegory of his solipsistic soul. No less irrelevant are the financial and sexual gossip.

. . .

Persons and events as well as ideas were shadows of his inner self, insubstantial in themselves. This is what makes inconclusive and wearisome any detailed biography of Mussolini, whose events and deeds, intimately arbitrary, are merely determined by the pressure of a changing environment upon his eagerness, which, never changing, remains indifferent to the directions and qualities and is sensitive only to the degrees of intensity, or to the amount and speed of its own satisfaction. This also is what makes meaningless any discussion about his socialism and about his so-called conversion to something different.

Socialism, as he preached and practised it between 1909 and 1914, was a ready-made product, handed to him by his social surroundings. The pillars of Marxian orthodoxy were already shaken by scientific criticism, inside and outside the party; at the same time, the vogue of socialism among the intellectual élite seemed to be fading. His mind, untrained in the search for truth and therefore slow and passive, hardly noticed either fact. He clung to the tenets of social revolution as he had received them from his father or from his Russian friend, in Predappio or in Switzerland, without carrying any personal contribution whatsoever to the development of socialist and economic theory. Capitalism and the capitalist state, or, unqualifiedly, the State–namely, the might and wealth of the privileged groups–were the targets of his envy; universal brotherhood and world peace in the classless society were, quite orthodoxly, his alleged hopes.

Four elements of Italian and European culture touched tangentially the surface of his personality without affecting its permanent core.

It seems that in Switzerland he had somehow come in contact with Vilfredo Pareto, professor at Lausanne–whose *Mind and Society* did not appear, however, until 1916. The importance of this contact was later fabulously magnified, until in 1937 the Faculty of Lausanne unblushingly conferred an honorary degree on the visitor of former days. At any rate there was in Pareto's theory of history a pessimistic sarcasm, nay, a sneer, and a restless bitterness which fitted Mussolini's temper. There was, besides, a much-promising moral indifference toward any kind of political doctrine and practice, all of them being considered as issuing from a social determinism no less inflexible than the mechanism of nature.

That indifference, like any kind of moral indifference, unavoidably inclined toward the side of evil. There was, rather unaccountably, in Pareto's mechanism a large place left for the individual's arbitrariness and a sub-species of aristocratic anarchism. The tendency of the system, however confused, was toward reaction and antidemocratic involution. Mussolini stored this latter implication for the future.

When he came back to Italy he found d'Annunzio's reputation well established, no longer only in small intellectual groups but also in larger masses of the population, and the poet's personality towering over all the other writers. He did not come in contact with d'Annunzio, who stood too far above him, but he extracted from the work of the poet and dramatist some quintessences of violence and revolt. Moreover, he found in d'Annunzio a further stimulus to his worship of Nietzsche, whom he had read at least partially a few years before, learning from him only what was apt to his mind—the idea or word of the Superman, or wild blond beast—with the understood correction that the Superman to come might also be of southern and dark complexion. However, it took several years before he came under the actual influence of d'Annunzio's whole personality and teaching. One day finally he changed even his script, which had been so far an ordinary cursive one, into the stiff ambitious style, with commanding capitals and angles as sharp as bayonets, which the world at large knows now as his own but which really is an imitation of the megalomaniac penmanship that d'Annunzio's goose quill has displayed for over forty years on his magnificently hand-made and watermarked sheets of paper.

The first decade of the century saw also the sweeping success, in a larger audience than is usually concerned with philosophy, of Croce's philosophy. It was called idealism, or neo-idealism. From idealism also Mussolini could in his own way draw vital nourishment for his mind. Philosophic idealism was to him the doctrine teaching that mind and will, nay, the individual mind and will, make the world, and that the world in itself has no existence at all.

Fourth and last: he came in desultory contact with a group of young people in Florence who published weeklies and magazines, where they had a laboratory for insufficient intellectual experiences and for masterpieces to come, and where nothing was continuous except the belief that youth is supreme and that it was the task of a smart juvenile gang like theirs to sap the edifice of academicism and conservatism and to build a new one on an ever-changing design, for life, dream, poetry, and the fine arts. Marinetti and Futurism were at several moments connected with the so-called Florentine movement.

All these tendencies, parallel to the disintegration of contemporary culture in France and elsewhere, were more or less obviously tinged with a reactionary dye. Democracy, of a sort, and the bourgeoisie held the power; Italian socialism, fairly meek and sentimental, seemed a by-product of the democratic bourgeoisie. It was a rule in the smart set to scoff at democracy, bourgeoisie, liberalism, and socialism.

Croce himself, who in many respects was superior to all the rest, had dismissed the socialism of his early years, turning to something that was not quite identical with the economic and political toryism, or conservative liberalism, which would have been natural to him as a landowner and scholar. In his *Philosophy of the Practical,* published in 1909, he upheld the Machiavellian theory of power and state, and inserted also a theoretical apology for the Holy Inquisition—which was *really holy,* as he, though not at all a Catholic, emphasized—considering it an instance of the unavoidable and philosophically legitimate use of violence in politics. At about the same time he published an Italian translation of Sorel's *Reflections on Violence,* accompanying it with a very flattering preface and pushing its diffusion with all the power of publicity at his disposal. The little book, a classic of intellectual and moral disorder, obliterated altogether from socialism whatever features of humanitarian feeling and rational finalism it had shown even in its fiery German-Jewish prophets, disfiguring it into a Ragnarök or Wagnerian twilight: a gleeful dream of universal subversion and destruction, which he called religious upheaval, or renovation, or Syndicalism, or creative myth of the general strike. Croce delighted in Sorel because of the moral value he supposed in the latter's opposition to optimism, pacifism, humanitarianism, and all the other trashy ideals of the "eighteenth-century mentality," which he ever and wholeheartedly abhorred. But the effect of the book by far exceeded his expectations. It united in one scum all the intellectual hysterias of twentieth-century Italy. Now even the meanest scribes in d'Annunzio's herd felt entitled to claim a philosophic, nay, a mystic, justification for their heroic-erotic daydreams.

Mussolini, however, slow-paced, did not yet follow the black suggestions that were implied more or less directly in those blackish tendencies. He still clung to the assumption that socialism, a revolutionary socialism, was his opportunity. To be sure, he drew from Pareto or Sorel, d'Annunzio or Croce alike, whatever encouragement he needed or wanted in his fight against the soft-boiled socialism of the official party and in his hatred for compromising, Freemasonic, half-bourgeois methods of Socialist politics. All of them, including also his occasional Florentine acquaintances, were interpreted by him as teachers of a radical Machiavellism in a political school whose coat of arms had more room for the lion than for the fox, and no room at all for the dove. But the direct, subversive action which he coveted was still one-hundred-percent red; at the end of the struggle he still visioned, or thought he visioned, a classless, pacified, scientific, international society. Nietzsche himself, the prophet whom he later was to exploit as a herald of tyranny and of war for war's sake, and whom he formerly had cherished as an inspirer of individual anarchism, was at that time an ambivalent or plurivalent oracle to him; and he did not hesitate to complete in his own way a famous Nietzschean sentence, bestowing on it the halo of a socialist anticipation, precursory of the Millennium. Herman Finer, one of Mussolini's biographers, quotes him as writing, "almost in Nietzsche's words": "The bridge between man as animal and man as human, the bridge between pre-history and history, the bridge which will lead humanity from the struggle for life to an agreement for the sake of life, will be built."[1] Here the Nietzschean metaphor of man-

[1] Herman Finer, *Mussolini's Italy,* New York, Henry Holt & Company, 1935.

kind as an evolutionary bridge was utilized for something good and true—for the idea that such a bridge leads to Man as to the complete fulfilment of a human ideal and hope and not to the atavistic reversal of the frenzied Superman. It is not surprising, however, that Mussolini's mind, capable of retaining only what fitted his practical opportunity of the day, quickly cancelled that ephemeral truth, the inspiration of an instant.

His action in the years of the immediate pre-war time scarcely needs an explanation for those who have watched his action in the years of dictatorship. From 1923 onward he has steadily tried to set the world afire, using his conquered Italy as an incendiary torch. From 1909, and especially from 1911 to 1914, he tried in a smaller setting to kindle Italy, waving as a flame his subversive Romagna.

At first he thought that the Libyan war, in 1911, and whatever proletarian discontent was thereto connected might become the opportunity he sought. He wrote articles and delivered speeches condemning that "miserable war of conquest" which the government propaganda masqueraded as a Roman glory, and he brought about, at least in his provincial section, a united front of the anti-war parties. "Socialists and Republicans were united. A strike was engineered. Barricades were put up. For two days there were turbulence, cavalry charges, and many casualties. Mussolini proceeded from argument to violent harangues, and thence to incitements to open resistance to the Government. When the cavalry charged, the crowd left him in the *piazza*. He was arrested. . . . Condemned to five years' imprisonment, he appealed, and actually served only five months. . . .

The obvious thing was to expect little of cowards and to hope a great deal to have the cavalry under his own command. Yet the evidence . . . seems to show that Mussolini himself had a fit of nerves when the action was commenced against him. He tried to put the blame on his fellow-culprits and the crowd, and suspected his counsel."

This is the summary of events as outlined by Herman Finer, an opponent of Fascism but an admirer of Mussolini's genius: probably a better authority on Sociology and Government than on spiritual appreciation of individuals, in which latter field he does not seem to have freed himself from the aftermath of romantic hero-worship and the idolatry of success.

It would be arbitrary, however, to suppose that Mussolini had at that time already consciously started to drift from Socialism to Reactionism, and that he had conceived as early as 1911 the ambition of having the king's cavalry under his command. On the contrary, he persisted in his extreme-leftist attempts, the most noted of which was the so-called "red week" of June 1914.

It was undoubtedly an advancement to pass from the two days of 1911 to the week of 1914; but it was a slight one. The plan was very ambitious. Mussolini and his close associate, the anarchist Malatesta, wanted to spread riot and revolution in all Central Italy, thereby breaking the backbone of the state—the railway between Rome and Milan—and snatching the disrupted nation. The plan collapsed almost farcically, without even the halo of "quasi-martyrdom" which, three years earlier, had accompanied Mussolini into the short seclusion in the prisons of liberal Italy. Republics, carnival-like imitations of medieval communal life, were proclaimed in several small cities and towns, where Socialism and Communism found a surprising expression in a kind of Cockaigne, favoured by the epicurean suggestions of the balmy season. The supplies of food were given away or sold at nominal prices; a chicken could be had for five cents. Hence the popular name of "chicken-republics." At last the *jeunesse dorée* and the nationalists, among them some editors and reporters of the conservative *Giornale d'Italia,* paraded in the streets of Rome, showing with a kind of jolly grimness that they felt ready, if need be, to use violence against violence. That mobilization, although still Platonic, provided the first evidence—in Italy and in the world at large—that the methods of class warfare suggested by Socialist and Syndicalist propaganda to the insurgent workers might occasionally be adopted, in the opposite direction, by the ruling classes, if these at last were able to whip up their courage.

The red week ended in a colourless Sunday. Its Lord, rather ingloriously, reposed.

Finer, the impartial, thus summarizes the tragicomedy, whose comic elements were the only catharsis: "For days the towns were in the hands of the people, the troops besieged in their barracks, people needed Socialist or Republican passports to be allowed to pass through the streets. It was expected that the republic would be proclaimed in Rome. . . . Mussolini believed that the Revolution had come. Yet Mussolini did not go into the *piazza* to lead the insurrection. After a week the Reformist wing called a truce."

After a few days the crown prince of Austria was assassinated in Sarajevo. After a few weeks the Great War broke out.

There was not even time for the remembrance of the red week to become ludicrous. Its flush—of wine and speeches—was thoroughly engulfed in the real blood-red of the starting catastrophe.

"Little man, what next?" Mussolini was utterly a failure.

Paddling in his canoe towards the invisible shore of a world-revolution, he found himself instead amidst the hurricane of the World War.

Fascism on the Road to Rome*

FEDERICO CHABOD

Causes of the Fascist Success

WHAT WERE THE causes of this rapid advance which six months earlier had seemed unthinkable? I described just now the various interests which were involved in the political struggle and induced Fascism to take action: the industrialists, the big landowners, especially in the region between Bologna and Ferrara, where Grandi and Balbo were active. That region constituted what might henceforth be called the 'agrarian' centre of Fascism. It lies on the borders of Tuscany; and between the end of 1920 and the beginning of 1921 Tuscan Fascism lent its support

* From *A History of Italian Fascism,* by Federico Chabod, translated by Muriel Grindrod, 51–61. Copyright © 1963 by George Weidenfeld & Nicolson, Ltd. Reprinted by permission of Random House, Inc. and George Weidenfeld & Nicolson, Ltd.

to the already strong Fascist organization in Emilia-Romagna, thus producing an experienced combat group which at a certain point adopted an attitude of opposition even towards Mussolini himself.

But the interests working in favour of Fascism are by no means the whole story: they played an important part, but there were other factors as well. We must now consider, in particular, the situation of the small *bourgeoisie*—clerks, small tradespeople, and professional men.

The Fascists also included some workers among their numbers. At the Rome congress of 1921 there were 310,000 registered party members. A sort of census carried out over about half that number showed 22,418 industrial workers and 36,847 peasants. Nevertheless the percentage of Fascist workers was very low in relation to the total numbers of the working classes. What is important, moreover, is not so much the number of those registered in a party as the attitude of the countless non-registered towards the various political trends. This is particularly true of the *bourgeoisie,* always—and especially so at that time—somewhat unwilling to accept party discipline, but nevertheless prepared to give the support of their vote: this is what is known as public opinion, in the long run a formidably important source of support. Now among the working classes the prevalent opinions and ideals were Socialist or Communist, sometimes Catholic, but always anti-Fascist; and the small percentage of workers adhering to Fascism in no way altered the general orientation of the working masses.

What was the attitude of the lesser *bourgeoisie?* It will be recalled that Fascism had found its earliest adherents among this class, in the ex-officers and students who had followed Mussolini largely because of wounded national pride–wounded because of the long-drawn-out delays of the peace conference and the discussions on the eastern frontiers, or because a part of the population had failed to recognize the sacrifices made in the war. Fascism had found its first recruits among such people. But it was soon to find others. What did the small *bourgeoisie* really want? They too, feared revolution above everything else. As I said earlier, the occupation of the factories in September 1920 and its failure made it clear to any intelligent observer that the hopes of a revolution in Italy had now vanished. But, I added, the perspicacious observer is rare: the great mass of the small and medium *bourgeoisie* had remained strongly under the impression of those events, which appeared to them not as a climax prefacing a decline but rather as the first act in a tragedy destined to end in total revolution. Viewed in this light Giolitti's tactics–his policy of letting the workers have their head and not shooting them but allowing them to occupy the factories so that they could discover for themselves their own inability to run them –may have been wise from a political point of view, but they were destined to produce highly negative effects on *bourgeois* mentalities and feelings. Clerks and professional men asked themselves how the State was reacting towards this serious situation: the State which, according to all the time-honoured principles, had the duty to ensure the protection of the life and property of its citizens. But what did the State do? It appeared impotent; if the Government took no action against the workers, it must be because it lacked the strength to act. Thus the prudence which was an element of strength in Giolitti's action was transformed in the mind of the masses into an element of weakness: for them the important fact was the State's failure to intervene.

After September 1920, although revolutionary fervour was now on the decline, strikes continued and there were also other manifestations of disorder, unrest, and violence on the part of the Reds. People asked themselves how it would all end. They complained of the number of working days lost and the inconveniences of the strikes, often called, it must be confessed, for trivial or unjustifiable reasons. (I have already spoken of the mistakes made by the Socialists, of their revolutionary hankerings and how, though unable to reach the point of revolution themselves, they refused to share power with the *bourgeoisie*. The same mistake can be seen with the workers: they administered too many pinpricks which irritated their opponents without influencing them.) The clerk or lawyer who had to go to his office and found all the buses and trams off asked himself why the State did not intervene to put an end to this perpetual state of disorder.

Thus a general state of fear, discontent, and disorder prevailed. And in addition to all this there was another strong feeling among the educated *bourgeoisie,* people who read D'Annunzio and recalled the 'patriotic' poet Carducci and looked upon the Risorgimento and the unification of Italy as the outstanding achievement of their forefathers: this was the feeling of patriotism. Who, they asked, were these masses who inveighed against the tricolour and the fatherland, who even said the 'patria' did not exist? It was their patriotic sentiment that was wounded.

All these considerations explain how it was that Fascism obtained fresh followers among the *bourgeoisie*. Fascism is a highly complex phenomenon which cannot be explained by any rigid formula. There is certainly an element of 'class struggle' in it; but there are also other elements which cannot be reduced to pure and simple terms of class struggle. Above all, Fascism cannot be explained simply as an emanation of big industry and landownership. Even after the March on Rome, when it had the government of the country in its hands, and throughout its subsequent evolution up to the Second World War, even then Fascism could not be characterized solely on a basis of class considerations. That it defended certain class interests is obvious, and some of its earliest decrees show it. Giolitti had made compulsory (by a law of 24 September 1920) the registration of shares in the holder's name. The aim of this measure was fiscal, and the result was to hit the wealthy man's income. By another law, also of 24 September 1920, Giolitti, with the same aim of countering the Budget deficit by imposing taxes on the well-to-do classes, had established death duties so heavy as to amount to total confiscation in the case of large inheritances and distant heirs. On 10 November 1922, thirteen days after the March on Rome, the Fascist Government abolished the compulsory registration of shares in the holder's name, a measure which had met with considerable opposition ever since Giolitti introduced it; and on 20 August 1923 another law abolished the law on inheritance. Thus the decisions of Giolitti's Government were annulled, and the taxes on inheritance were not only reduced but in the case of direct heirs (sons, wives, brothers, etc.) were completely suppressed. These measures were obviously intended to pacify certain sections of society—it is superfluous to point out which.

But there was more to Fascism than this. Some of its manifestations can only be explained by what I call a super-emphasis on the idea of the *bourgeoisie,* or rather the small *bourgeoisie,* from a spiritual and sentimental as well as an economic angle. The *bourgeoisie* was no longer thought of merely as a social class or an economic phenomenon but was regarded also as representing, so to speak, a state of mind. Consider, for instance, one of the epoch-making events of the régime, the conclusion of the Lateran Pacts with the Holy See on 11 February 1929. These agreements were received with enthusiasm by a large part of the Italian population: at last peace had been made with the Church. It is true that in 1929 the Roman Question was no longer what it was in 1882; there was no danger that the Pope might leave Rome, as Leo XIII had more than once threatened to do; the question had, in fact, with time become much less acute. The fact that a prominent Catholic such as Meda had taken part in the Italian Government during the war was in itself an indication of considerable progress. After 23 March 1920, the date of Benedict XV's Encyclical *Pacem Dei munus,* Catholic Heads of State could visit the King in the Quirinal, a thing hitherto not permitted by the Vatican. But the knowledge that the Church was not yet formally reconciled with the royal government and continued to maintain reserve on matters of principle left a feeling of discomfort in the minds of the Italian *bourgeoisie*. These were for the most part Catholics whom the anti-clerical propaganda of the years between 1860 and 1914 had affected only superficially even when it touched them at all. They loved their country, united Italy, and its capital Rome; but they were believers in their faith. An Italy at peace with the Papacy would guarantee for ever their spiritual quiet and interior tranquillity. Why is it that the image of Pius IX in 1847, the 'Italian' Pius IX, has always traditionally been so popular and survived to appear in all the school text-books? The reason is because for a short time it seemed that he might realize this dream.

Mussolini, naturally, had another and more immediate aim: the Concordat was signed in February 1929, and in March elections were due to take place. But the mere tactical aims of the moment do not suffice to explain the attitude adopted by the Fascist régime in reviving and putting into effect Orlando's earlier attempts of 1919 at conciliation, while at the same time making concessions to the Church which could never have been contemplated by a Liberal Government. Mussolini, who, at least up to 1935–6, showed an undeniable flair for what would appeal to the masses, fastened on to this deeply rooted sentiment in the Italian *bourgeois* mind. This characteristic of Fascism also shows itself in other forms: it can be seen, in particular, in relation to the patriotic lesser *bourgeoisie* who wanted to see the country respected and liked the idea of enjoying a certain prestige in the world, and who, therefore, could be influenced by nationalistic press campaigns and speeches. Nevertheless this *bour-*

geoisie, devoted as it was to peace, order and respectability, would never go beyond certain limits.

This explains how it was that in the last years of Fascism a breach developed between the régime and the *bourgeois* masses. It began even before the war; and in this connection a single fact will suffice to explain a great many things. The racial laws enacted against the Jews in 1938 took the nation completely unawares. There was a profound difference here between the Fascist and the Nazi régimes, between Italy and Germany. The laws were indeed applied in Italy, but most of the population did their best to help the Jews under persecution. The violent passion of anti-semitism was something unknown in Italy that went against the grain. This time no one followed Mussolini's lead.

Thus it is clear that in the rise of Fascism a complex variety of interests and passions played their part. They included some clearly defined class interests on the part of the big landowners, who hoped to break the resistance of the farm workers, and on the part of the industrialists. But such interests were also intermingled with simple considerations of passion and sentiment: wounded patriotism, the fear of revolution after September 1920, the dread of disorder and anarchy—all of them motives that were no less strongly felt by those who would have had little to lose by a change of social structure.

Deeper Reasons for Fascism's Rise to Power

Such, in brief, were the causes behind the hold obtained by Fascism between the end of 1920 and the beginning of 1921.

How are we to interpret the events of the years leading up to the March on Rome of 28 October 1922, and Fascism's advent to power? What did its supporters want? Was it dictatorship? A big industrialist has said: 'We did not want dictatorship; all we wanted was simply that Mussolini, when he took over the government, should bring back order and tranquillity to the country. After that, we would have gone back to the old system.'

That may well be true. But there is also another and more important factor. Very few of the leading politicians realized that they were on the threshold of a highly dangerous venture into which Italy was to be drawn for twenty years, culminating in catastrophe. The example of Giolitti is typical. No one can doubt that Giolitti was wholly and profoundly liberal at heart. When he perceived that Fascism was taking a very different course from that envisaged, he adopted a highly dignified attitude. He never left the Chamber of Deputies, and on some occasions he confronted Mussolini practically alone. Four months before his death, in March 1928, on the occasion of the vote on the new electoral law which in effect put an end to the *Statuto* (it introduced the single list of candidates, drawn up by the Fascist Grand Council), the veteran Piedmontese statesman, then aged eighty-six, rose to declare his formal opposition to this draft law, which represented the definite break of the Fascist régime with the old order based on the *Statuto* of 1848. His words were aimed beyond Mussolini, at the King. In fact, Giolitti, once he had realized his error, failed neither in courage nor in dignity. But in the early stages he too had been mistaken. What was it that he hoped for? There has recently been published a letter of his, dated 1 January 1923, to his journalist friend Luigi Ambrosini, in which he said: 'You are astonished that a "Fifth Estate" should arise with such extraordinary speed; but this is really one of the most common phenomena in history. After violent agitations (and what could be more violent than the last war?) there comes a wave of youthful Saint-Justs, Napoleons, Hoches, and thousands of unknowns. But the really significant people make themselves felt and remain in the forefront, the others disappear, and then the world resumes its normal rhythm.' Here is the explanation of his attitude. Giolitti believed that he could do the same with Fascism as he had partly succeeded in doing with the Socialists before the war: breaking their revolutionary impetus.

The whole of Giolitti's post-1919 policy is but a repetition of his earlier political methods. In this connection a speech he made in the Chamber on 2 February 1921 is indicative. In it he recalled the line he had adopted after he became Prime Minister at the beginning of the century, when strikes were looked upon as something monstrous: 'In 1904 there was a strike movement which I viewed with distrust. It was the first General Strike of a political character. I remember very well that I telegraphed to the prefects saying: "This strike does not arise from any vital cause or deep-rooted feeling among the masses; therefore, don't worry–it will only last a few days."' This harking back of the eighty-year-old statesman to his way of dealing with an earlier crisis shows clearly how his mind was working twenty years after. He believed that he could still overcome the present difficulties by the same methods as in the past–that Fascism could be lulled, canalized, and absorbed. He argued roughly like this: 'I'll give them two or three ministries, but the Ministry of the Interior I'll keep in my own hands; in that way I shall control the police, and the prefects will have to obey me. After a time the revolutionary impetus of the movement will be spent and the crisis will be resolved.'

In short, the country was faced with a profound crisis which the old political leaders were incapable of understanding or appreciating in its essential terms: they were therefore incapable of dominating it. In May 1921 Giolitti even helped the Fascists to enter the Chamber as deputies. He believed that he could make use of them against the Socialists or the Partito Popolare–against, in other words, the two parties who were making it impossible for him to govern according to the old methods. Indeed, in the letter to Ambrosini just quoted, Giolitti goes on to say: 'Political and above all parliamentary affairs could not continue in this way without bringing the country to ruin. That wretched electoral law (i.e. the law introducing proportional representation, which worked in favour of well-organized parties and reduced the scope for the old Giolittian tactics of manoeuvring with individuals) had split the Chamber in such a way as to make it impossible to have a strong Government with a definite programme. The point had been reached when an intriguing little priest (i.e. Don Sturzo) with no superior qualities dominated the whole Italian political scene.' These words were written after the March on Rome. And Giolitti was certainly not an isolated case; there were scores of others among the old Liberals who thought the same.

Thus the policy was, in case of need, to make use of Fascism, for its potentially subversive qualities were still discounted. Fascism was measured and evaluated according to the same antiquated criteria that had been used in estimating parties and political forces in the past. And indeed, viewed from this angle, it seemed unlikely that Fascism, even after its successes of 1921, could come to power unaided. It was a minority, a considerable one it is true, but still a minority; and a minority–it must be remembered–it was to remain, even at the time of the March on Rome. I spoke earlier of the adherents to Fascism among the small *bourgeoisie,* but this class was a long way from joining Fascism *en bloc.* Some university students certainly became Fascists, but in 1922 and even after most of them still remained firmly anchored to the idea of liberty and hostile to Fascism, violence and armed struggle. In the elections of May 1921, even after the advances made in the winter of 1920–1, Fascist deputies numbered only 35 out of a total of 535. Even in the elections of 1924, carried out after Fascism had come to power and in a climate of violence, the Fascist list fell considerably short of obtaining 'plebiscitary' adherence; it registered 4,635,488 votes, or 64.9 per cent out of a total of 7,165,502 voters–and by that time the Fascist régime was already an accomplished fact.

Thus in 1921–2 anyone evaluating Fascism on the basis of the old formulae of political and parliamentary struggle could still believe in the possibility of blandishing it, making use of it, and giving it the role of a subordinate assistant to be dispensed with later on.

But it was just here that the basic error in evaluation lay. Fascism was not a political force of the old stamp. Its leaders—granting that it had any—had nothing in common with the men who had guided politics hitherto. Legality did not concern them; liberty, the preservation of Parliament, all the old principles of the liberal State were foreign to them. They might talk about them for simple reasons of opportunism or tactics, but in reality they cared not a jot for them. At the beginning, the movement amounted merely to action without any definite objective; but as it gradually developed and gained strength and weight in the country's life, its leaders began to aim at something more than action for its own sake. The conquest of the State, the March on Rome? These would come later, as the final goal; but already the desire could be detected to occupy a place in the forefront of public life, a place not transient but permanent. This was a far cry from the simple reaction against 'anti-patriotism'—the longing to conquer power had entered in. As early as 1921 some leaders, mindful of D'Annunzio's expedition to Fiume, were thinking of a 'march on Rome'. Always, and in any case, the belief was that 'force' would succeed in gaining the upper hand—and, if need be, armed force.

The Fascist party (transformed from 'movement' to 'party' at the Rome Congress of November 1921) represented, from the point of view of organization and technique, something new by comparison with the traditional parties. It possessed a military organization whose moving spirits, in the early stages, were

Balbo, De Vecchi, and De Bono, an Italian Army General who had gone over to Fascism. The feeling for military and revolutionary technique can be clearly discerned from the importance attached to securing the control of the main railway junctions (Bologna, Verona, Alessandria), a measure which was to prove its value in October 1922.

To sum up, Fascism, alike from the standpoint of principles and of organization, represented a novelty which could not be absorbed into the liberal and constitutional system. Failure to perceive this dangerous novelty in time was the cardinal mistake of the majority of those who till then had been at the head of Italian political life. In this lies the main cause of what happened in October 1922: the conquest of power by Fascism required no real revolution, no basic overthrow: in fact, when the news of the March on Rome reached the capital, the King refused to sign the proclamation of a state of siege and decided to entrust the task of forming a new Government first to Salandra and then, immediately after, to Mussolini. When the Blackshirts reached the capital their victory was already an accomplished fact; their entry was a parade, not a battle. The King was by no means the only person responsible. According to the *Memoirs* of Soleri[1], Minister of War in 1922, it would seem that the Prime Minister himself, Facta, advised the King not to sign the decree proposed by the Cabinet proclaiming a state of siege, on the ground that it would have provoked the intervention of the army against the Fascists. Facta had started negotiations with one of the Blackshirt leaders, Michele Bianchi, with a view to ar-

[1] Einaudi, 1949.

ranging the entry of the Fascists into his Government; and perhaps he hoped to the last that he would succeed, thus avoiding bloodshed and chaos and 'absorbing' the Fascists. Once again the same mistake . . . Giolitti, too, had embarked on negotiations with Mussolini, through the prefect of Milan. The plan was the same: to form a Government with the inclusion of the Fascists (Mussolini had demanded five ministries) and so to canalize the movement and bring it on to the legal and parliamentary plane of liberal practice.

Mussolini was quite ready to negotiate, for he did not want to exclude a parliamentary solution in the old style if that seemed necessary. He was the kind of man who would never slam any door against himself. But, at the same time, he was a man full of doubts and uncertainties. During these first years, at least, he was not always the one who made the daring gestures. The 'duri', the toughs of those days who believed in fighting to the limit, were Farinacci, Balbo, Grandi, and the like. In the summer and autumn of 1924, after the murder of the Socialist deputy Matteotti, when Italian public opinion woke up with a start and even the Fascists themselves were in a state of alarm, the party's man with the iron fist was Farinacci. Besides, Mussolini had the gift of recovering from his crises at the right moment and regaining the upper hand.

After all, he would argue, negotiations served only to lull his adversaries into a sense of security. It would never be his real line to accept normal parliamentary tactics. Moreover, side by side with Mussolini were Fascists who would never hear of anything of the kind, and who had always in mind that example which I mentioned earlier: D'Annunzio's expedition to Fiume. And that was a serious matter, not only because D'Annunzio's followers provided the first instance of insubordination in the Italian army, but also because Fascist leaders such as Balbo looked on the expedition as a sort of dress rehearsal for what was to come.

The Government lacked resolution and daring. The impression of weakness which it gave, and which, as I said earlier, alarmed the small and medium *bourgeoisie,* corresponded only too nearly to reality. Now it was from among the *bourgeoisie* that the prefects, senior police officials and generals came, and Fascism undoubtedly aroused a certain sympathy among these high officials, who preferred to shut their eyes when they should have decided to act. There was also some sympathy for it in the army; for example, the name of General Giardino, one of the big army leaders in the 1915–18 war, was spoken of in that connection.

Yet another source of indulgence towards Fascism was to be found in the House of Savoy, if not actually in the person of the King himself, in a possibly even more dangerous figure, the Duke of Aosta, who enjoyed great popularity. So much so, in fact, that Victor Emmanuel III felt some apprehension about his cousin's ambitions towards the Crown. Fascism did not hide its hand here: it argued something like this: 'If the King doesn't want to help us, we shall get on very well with the monarchy without him: we'll turn out Victor Emmanuel III from the Quirinal and instal the Duke of Aosta in his place.'

Finally, there was the Queen Mother, Queen Margherita. The Queen Mother had had in the course of her life the great good fortune to encounter a poet of the stature of Carducci who extolled her grace and beauty. This is one of those cases when it is possible to gauge what an effect the words of a great poet and writer can have in transfiguring a personality by presenting it under guises that conceal the true reality. Beneath a very attractive outward appearance–for she possessed the art of pleasing, and knew it–the Queen was a woman of iron will and, from the political point of view (the only one that need concern us here), completely reactionary. Now the Queen Mother, too, cherished a great sympathy for Fascism.

Taking all these elements together, it is easy to understand why the old liberal state was on the verge of collapsing to make way for a dictatorship in which, nevertheless, many people could not yet believe.

How Counterrevolutions Are Made: The *Coup de Main* of October 1922*

LUIGI STURZO

IN A MODERN State it would seem inconceivable that a political party should form bands of armed Irregulars and move towards the Capital with the intention of capturing the governing power despite the prospect of having to fight against the regular army, and

* From Luigi Sturzo, *Italy and Fascism,* 115–20. Translated by Barbara Barclay Carter, with a Preface by Gilbert Murray. Reprinted by permission of Faber and Faber Ltd.

that this should be done in the name of patriotism. Mob riots and popular revolutions there have been; Spain has had experience of military *'pronunciamientos'*, but constitutional history does not record any event similar to that which occurred in Italy in October, 1922. If we had not shown in the first part of this book the remote causes and immediate premises of the rise of Fascism, it would appear absolutely inexplicable.

The position of the Facta Cabinet was not only insecure but had become untenable, and the Prime Minister was only awaiting the reopening of the Chamber to tender his resignation–at least, so rumour said. As Facta's successor there was talk of Giolitti and Salandra; the Liberal Democrats agitated for Giolitti, the Liberals of the Right and the Nationalists for Salandra. Both parties recognized that it would not be possible to form a new Cabinet without including the Fascisti, who dominated the forums and market-places from Perugia to Upper Italy. Facta secretly worked for the return of Giolitti, but his efforts bore no fruit. Signor Lusignoli, a Senator and, at that time, Prefect of Milan, maintained clandestine relations both with Giolitti and Mussolini, striving to bring about an understanding between them. Certain Fascisti in Rome led another ex-Prime Minister, Orlando, to believe that Mussolini was disposed to favour him–news not displeasing to Orlando, who would have welcomed the chance to retrieve what his uncertainty had lost him in July. Salandra, supported by the Nationalists, was much surer of returning as head of the Government.

These three ex-Premiers shared at that moment the state of mind of those who, while they judged the violent acts of the Fascisti to be excessive and disturbing, thought it would be wise to bring the Fascisti, and above all, Mussolini, into the Government, and to clip their wings by making them share in the responsibilities of power. All of which meant that they still believed themselves to be the rulers and representatives of a political class alive and master of itself, and showed clearly that they had understood neither the spirit of Fascism nor the inevitable psychological and moral effects of two years' unbridled lawlessness on the part of an armed faction.

I remember that, in those days, a certain politician asked me if the Popolari, in the event of Giolitti's returning to power, would again make stipulations and bring up the so-called *veto*.

'Is Giolitti disposed to form his Cabinet with the Fascisti?' I asked him.

'Yes', said he.

'And without the Fascisti?'

'I think it very unlikely.'

'And against the Fascisti?'

'Oh no! That is impossible!' was his answer.

'Then', I concluded, 'Giolitti will not form the Ministry, and thus it is useless for me to say what would be the attitude of the Popolari towards him.'

It must be noted that the Fascisti had then only thirty-five Deputies in the Chamber, and that the whole of the Right, including Nationalists and Fascisti, barely numbered seventy out of five hundred and thirty-five. But the Fascisti, by the extra-legal position they had assumed, dominated the situation, so that Liberals and Democrats were no longer sure of themselves.

A very serious obstacle to the participation of

the Fascisti in the government was Mussolini's declaration concerning the *Republican tendencies* of the movement; it was feared that there would be conflict between these new forces and the Monarchy, and there were even wild rumours that a new claimant to the throne, a surer exponent of Nationalist aims, might be put forward.

But, as Mussolini perceived that his position was growing stronger and that it would be quite possible for him to attempt a *coup de main,* he himself wished to remove this obstacle; so he cast away all his Republican leanings, changed his language, and let it be understood that he was disposed to support Monarchy and Monarch if he found no hindrance in that quarter. This new attitude was greeted with approbation and pæans of praise—not that all believed in this sudden conversion, but because it meant that support of Fascism was not incompatible with loyalty to the King.

Meanwhile people continued to discuss the name of the next Premier. Giolitti? Salandra? Orlando? No one, save Mussolini himself, thought of Mussolini as a possible Premier, least of all the Nationalists. When he saw the success of the Fascist Congress and the rally of his legions at Naples, on 24 October, with the ready consent of the Government and amid the applause of Conservatives and Liberals, he left the ingenuous congressists to their discussion and hastened to Milan to gather up the threads for his *coup.* All felt the gravity of the hour and the menace of so large a body of armed Irregulars—all except the head of the Government, Facta, who declared himself satisfied that no regrettable incident had occurred at Naples to disturb the peace.

But on 26 October Facta was challenged by certain Fascisti to hand in his resignation at once; and, that very evening, in an emergency Cabinet meeting, summoned in the hope of finding a middle course that would save appearances, all the Ministers decided to place their portfolios at the Premier's disposal. But on 27 October the Fascisti, in the name of their leader, declared themselves still unsatisfied, and, with threats of risings, insisted that Facta should agree to their demand, whereupon that excellent man that very evening tendered to the King the resignations of the entire Cabinet.

And that very night of 27–28 October, which saw the opening of the Ministerial crisis, saw the beginning of the Fascist revolt and the mobilization of the armed Irregulars, the attempts to occupy the Prefectures of Upper Italy, and the organization of the March on Rome. The Ministry of the Interior was in an uproar; an hour before dawn the Cabinet met and resolved upon resistance and the proclamation of martial law throughout the Kingdom. The decision was brought to the King, and telegraphed to the Prefects with orders to put it into force at noon (28 October). A proclamation to all citizens was printed. It bore the names of all the Ministers, and denounced the Fascist rebellion.

I was asked by an authoritative person if the Popolari would support the proclamation of Martial Law. My answer was that such a measure could not originate with a Ministry which had already resigned; that the Ministry should either withdraw its resignation or be immediately replaced by another, and that most certainly the Popolari would take a stand for constitutional order and against armed revolt.

Meanwhile Facta, always vacillating, not only did not withdraw the resignations of his Cabinet but, while he was deciding that martial law should be enforced at noon, still hoped to be able to negotiate with the rebels—to such an extent had he grown accustomed to consider his office as a continual and ineffectual mediation between lawful power and lawless faction.

At the same time various persons gave the King to understand that a fight between the Army and the Fascisti would be a most serious matter of which the consequences could not be foreseen; while, on the other hand, it would be possible to resume negotiations for a Salandra Cabinet in which the Fascisti should be well represented. The fear that worse might befall, the hope of a possible understanding, the weak and ambiguous position of the Cabinet which, having already resigned, found itself without authority, and the advice of certain Army chiefs decided the King to refuse his signature to the decree proclaiming Martial Law and to invite Salandra to take office.

Mussolini, who saw that his *coup* had succeeded beyond the wildest hopes either of himself or his followers, understood that his hour had struck, thanks to the position of inferiority in which all the lawful representatives of the country had placed themselves by their own action. Through his friends in Rome he made it known that he could not join a Salandra Ministry or any other; that power must be given to himself; that, unless it were conferred on him then and there, at Milan, and unless his armed followers were allowed to make a peaceful entry into the Capital in symbol of victory, he would not stay his march on Rome. All was granted, by the King, and by the Facta Government which looked on passively. The 31st October saw the triumphal entry into Rome of about thirty thousand Black Shirts, amid the applause of their friends and the pensive dismay of the greater number of citizens.

Mussolini immediately turned his attention to forming his Cabinet, more as an army chief choosing his Staff than as the head of a government nominating his colleagues. Having refused to treat with Parties so as not to tie himself in any way, he dealt only with individual politicians, many of whom were alien to the Fascist Party. He needed men experienced in public affairs, for both he and his followers were new to government and without administrative experience.

The non-Fascists whom he asked to join the Cabinet had to face a serious problem of conscience. If they decided to work with him, they would be taking responsibility for tendencies not their own nor in harmony with their convictions. If they refused, they ran the risk of inciting the man, who believed himself a victor, to return to a system of violence. Public opinion was divided. The fact that the King had commissioned Mussolini to form the Ministry, after a ministerial crisis previous to the march on Rome, lent to its formation an appearance of constitutionality, and might be construed as an attempt to bring a faction back to lawful methods. In these circumstances, a coalition ministry might seem an attempt at pacification, and, from this point of view, the collaboration of constitutionalists might counterbalance the triumph of the armed faction. Such, at least, was the opinion of the philo-Fascisti, of those who sought conciliation at all costs, and even of not a few anti-Fascisti. Others, on the contrary, thought that the state of mind of a faction triumphant in its seizure of the Capital of the Kingdom must have consequences beyond all measure, that the event in itself was a blow at the heart of the parliamentary *régime,* and that there was therefore no bridging the gulf between Fascisti and constitutionalists. Among those of this opinion was the present writer, who opposed any understandings with the new Government. However, among the Popolari, as among the Liberals and Social-Democrats, the opinion prevailed that they had better collaborate with Mussolini, in the hope that, having once attained power, albeit by methods of revolt, he and his friends would tread the path of law and order and respect for liberty, and in the belief that their presence would preserve continuity in the constitutional life of the Kingdom.

Thus constituted, the first Mussolini Cabinet faced the Chamber of Deputies and the Senate on 15 November.

V. SELF-PORTRAITS AND A SKETCH OF THE LEADER

TWO CLOSE VIEWS *of the Duce of Fascism are offered below to help deepen understanding of the dictator and the meaning he gave to his work and to his regime. In the first selection, Mussolini more or less states his own case at the height of power, on the eve of the rise of "one greater than he," Hitler and Nazism in Germany in 1933. In the second selection, the general setting is quite different. Fascism had fallen in Italy and the final agonizing phase of the Second World War was in process. In 1944–45 Mussolini had become the shadow-ruler of the spectral "Social Republic of Salò" which under the suzerainty of the entrenched and ever so slowly retreating German-Nazi forces in North Italy held sway chiefly in the Po Valley. During his talks with Emil Ludwig, Mussolini was the master of all that he surveyed from the Sala del Mappamondo in the Palazzo Venezia, beyond which loomed the Roman Capitol. In the interviews he granted to a number of journalists from the Palazzo Feltrinelli on Lake Garda, while he was "captive" of his German protectors from September 1943 to April 1945, he dominated a magnificent scenery but was in fact merely the "Mayor of Gargnano." It is well to keep in mind in the two readings that while the famous German journalist Emil Ludwig reports from direct personal interviews conducted through an extended series of dialogues with the Duce, the English journalist and biographer, Christopher Hibbert, writes from indirect sources, many of which are available in Italian, which he has skilfully "telescoped" for his portrait of the Duce after the fall.*

. . . At the Height of Power*

EMIL LUDWIG

The School of History

SOME ONE HAD made me a present of the edition *de luxe* of Machiavelli, which the Fascist State publishing organisation has somewhat too conspicuously dedicated to the Duce. All the same, it is doubtless better that a dictatorial government should acknowledge its obligations to this instructor of dictators than that, while secretly acting on his theories, it should use "Machiavellian" as a term of abuse. When Frederick the Great was yet only crown prince he wrote his moralising "Anti-Machiavel." In later days he became more straightforward, governing frankly in accordance with Machiavelli's principles.

"Did you make early acquaintance with Machiavelli's 'The Prince?' " I asked Mussolini.

"My father used to read the book aloud in the evenings, when we were warming ourselves beside the smithy fire and were drinking the *vin ordinaire* produced from our own vineyard. It made a deep

* From Emil Ludwig, *Talks with Mussolini.* Translated by Eden and Cedar Paul (Boston: Little, Brown and Company, 1933), 51–62, 66–71, 87–96. Reprinted by permission of Elga Ludwig.

impression on me. When, at the age of forty, I read Machiavelli once again, the effect was reinforced."

"It is strange," I said, "how such men as Machiavelli flourish for a time, pass into oblivion, and are then resuscitated. It seems as if there were seasonal variations."

"What you say is certainly true of nations. They have a spring and a winter, more than one. At length they perish."

"It is because there are recurring seasons in the national life that I have never been much alarmed that winter now prevails in Germany," said I. "A hundred years ago and more, when Germany had fallen on evil days, Goethe made fun of those who spoke of our 'decay.' Have you studied any of the notable figures of our political life?"

"Bismarck," he promptly answered. "From the outlook of political actualities, he was the greatest man of his century. I have never thought of him as merely the comic figure with three hairs on his bald head and a heavy footfall. Your book confirmed my impression as to how versatile and complex he was. In Germany, do people know much about our Cavour?"

"Very little," I answered. "They know much more about Mazzini. Recently I read a very fine letter of Mazzini's to Charles Albert, written, I think, in 1831 or 1832; the invocation of a poet to a prince. Do you approve of Charles Albert's having issued orders for Mazzini's imprisonment should he cross the frontier?"

"The letter," said Mussolini, "is one of the most splendid documents ever written. Charles Albert's figure has not yet become very clear to us Italians.

A little while ago his diary was published and this throws considerable light upon his psychology. At first, of course, he inclined to the side of the liberals. When, in 1832–no, in 1833–the Sardinian Government sentenced Mazzini to death *in contumaciam,* this happened in a peculiar political situation."

The answer seemed to me so guarded that, in my persistent but unavowed determination to compare the present to the past, I considered it necessary to speak more clearly.

"Those were the days when *Young Italy* was being published illegally. Don't you think that such periodicals appear under all censorships? Would you have imprisoned Mazzini?"

"Certainly not," he rejoined. "If a man has ideas in his head, let him come to me, and we will talk things over. But when Mazzini wrote that letter, he was guided more by his feelings than by his reason. Piedmont in those days had only four million inhabitants and could not possibly form front against powerful Austria with her thirty millions."

"Well, Mazzini was jailed," I resumed. "Soon afterwards, Garibaldi was sentenced to death. Two generations later, you were put in prison. Should we not infer that a ruler ought to think twice before punishing his political opponents?"

"I suppose you mean that we don't think twice here in Italy?" he inquired with some heat.

"But you have reintroduced capital punishment."

"There is capital punishment in all civilised countries; in Germany, no less than in France and in England."

"Yet it was in Italy," I insisted, "in the mind of

Beccaria, that the idea of abolishing capital punishment originated. Why have you revived it?"

"Because I have read Beccaria," replied Mussolini, simply and without irony. He went on, with the utmost gravity: "What Beccaria writes is contrary to what most people believe. Besides, after capital punishment was abolished in Italy, there was a terrible increase in serious crime. As compared with England, the tally in Italy was five to one. I am guided, in this matter, exclusively by social considerations. Was it not Saint Thomas who said that it would be better to cut off a gangrenous arm if thereby the whole body could be saved? Anyhow, I proceed with the utmost caution and circumspection. Only in cases of acknowledged and exceptionally brutal murders is the death punishment inflicted. Not very long ago, two rascals violated a youth and then murdered him. Both the offenders were sentenced to death. I had followed the trial with close attention. At the last moment doubt became insistent. One of the two offenders was a habitual criminal who had avowed his crime; the other, a much younger man, had pleaded not guilty, and there were no previous charges against him. Six hours before the execution I reprieved the younger of the two."

"You could put that in the chapter, 'Advantages of Dictatorship,'" I said.

His repartee was swift and couched in a tone of mockery:

"The alternative is a state machine which grinds on automatically without any one having the power to stop its working."

"Would you like to leave this contentious topic and talk about Napoleon?"

"Go ahead!"

"Despite our previous conversations, I am not clear whether you regard him as a model or as a warning."

He sat back in his chair, looked rather gloomy, and said in a restrained tone:

"As a warning. I have never taken Napoleon as an examplar, for in no respect am I comparable to him. His activities were of a very different kind from mine. He put a term to a revolution, whereas I have begun one. The record of his life has made me aware of errors which are by no means easy to avoid." Mussolini ticked them off on his fingers. "Nepotism. A contest with the papacy. A lack of understanding of finance and economic life. He saw nothing more than that after his victories there was a rise in securities."

"What laid him low? The professors declare that he was shipwrecked on the rock of England."

"That is nonsense," answered Mussolini. "Napoleon fell, as you yourself have shown, because of the contradictions in his own character. At long last, that is what always leads to a man's downfall. He wanted to wear the imperial crown! He wanted to found a dynasty! As First Consul he was at the climax of his greatness. The decline began with the foundation of the empire. Beethoven was perfectly right when he withdrew the dedication of the *Eroica.* It was the wearing of the crown which continually entangled the Corsican in fresh wars. Compare him with Cromwell. The latter had a splendid idea; supreme power in the State and no war!"

I had brought him to a point of outstanding importance.

"There can, then, be imperialism without an imperium?"

"There are half a dozen different kinds of imperialism. There is really no need for all the blazons of empire. Indeed, they are dangerous. The more widely empire is diffused, the more does it forfeit its organic energy. All the same, the tendency towards imperialism is one of the elementary trends of human nature, an expression of the will to power. Nowadays we see the imperialism of the dollar; there is also a religious imperialism, and an artistic imperialism as well. In any case, these are tokens of the human vital energy. So long as a man lives, he is an imperialist. When he is dead, for him imperialism is over."

At this moment Mussolini looked extraordinarily Napoleonic, reminding me of Lefèvre's engraving of 1815. But now the tension of his features relaxed and in a quieter tone he continued:

"Naturally every imperium has its zenith. Since it is always the creation of exceptional men, it carries within it the seeds of its own decay. Like everything exceptional, it contains ephemeral elements. It may last one or two centuries, or no more than ten years. The will to power."

"Is it to be kept going only by war?" I asked.

"Not only," he answered. "Of that there can be no question." He became a little didactic. "Thrones need wars for their maintenance, but dictatorships can sometimes get on without them. The power of a nation is the resultant of numerous elements and these are not exclusively military. Still, I must admit that hitherto, as far as the general opinion is concerned, the position of a nation has greatly depended upon its military strength. Down to the present time, people have regarded the capacity for war as the synthesis of all the national energies."

"Till yesterday," I interpolated. "But what about to-morrow?"

"To-morrow?" he reiterated sceptically. "It is true that capacity for war-making is no longer a dependable criterion of power. For to-morrow, therefore, there is need of some sort of international authority. At least, the unification of a continent. Now that the unity of States has been achieved, an attempt will be made to achieve the unity of continents. But as far as Europe is concerned, that will be damnably difficult, since each nation has its own peculiar countenance, its own language, its own customs, its own types. For each nation, a certain percentage of these characteristics (*x* per cent., let us say) remains completely original, and this induces resistance to any sort of fusion. In America, no doubt, things are easier. There eight-and-forty States, in which the same language is spoken everywhere and whose history is so short, can maintain their union."

"But surely," I put in, "each nation possesses *y* per cent. of characteristics which are purely European?"

"This lies outside the power of each nation. Napoleon wanted to establish unity in Europe. The unification of Europe was his leading ambition. To-day such a unification has perhaps become possible, but even then only on the ideal plane, as Charlemagne or Charles V tried to bring it about, from the Atlantic Ocean to the Urals."

"Or, maybe, only to the Vistula?"

"Yes, maybe, only to the Vistula."

"Is it your idea that such a Europe would be under Fascist leadership?"

"What is leadership?" he countered. "Here in Italy our Fascism is what it is. Perhaps it contains certain elements which other countries might adopt."

"I always find you more moderate than most Fascists," said I. "You would be amazed if you knew what a foreigner in Rome has to listen to. Perhaps it was the same thing under Napoleon at the climax of his career. Apropos, can you explain to me why the Emperor never became completely wedded to his capital, why he always remained *le fiancé de Paris?*"

Mussolini smiled and began his reply in French: "*Ses manières n'étaient pas très parisiennes.* Perhaps there was a brutal strain in him. Moreover, he had many opponents. The Jacobins were against him because he had crushed the revolution; the legitimates, because he was a usurper; the religious-minded, because of his contest with the papacy. It was only the common folk who loved him. They had plenty to eat under his régime, and they are more impressed by fame than are the educated classes. You must remember that fame is a matter not of logic, but of sentiment."

"You speak rather sympathetically of Napoleon! It would seem that your respect for him has not diminished during your own tenure of power, in which you have become enabled to understand his situation from personal experience."

"No, on the contrary, my respect for him has increased."

"When he was still a youthful general, he said

that an empty throne always tempted him to take his seat upon it. What do you think of that?"

Mussolini opened his eyes wide, as he does when in an ironical mood, but at the same time he smiled.

"Since the days when Napoleon was emperor," he said, "thrones have become much less alluring than they were."

"True enough," I replied. "Nobody wants to be a king nowadays. When, a little while ago, I said to King Fuad of Egypt, 'Kings must be loved, but dictators dreaded,' he exclaimed, 'How I should like to be a dictator!' Does history give any record of a usurper who was loved?"

Mussolini, whose changes of countenance always foreshadow his answers (unless he wants to conceal his thoughts) became earnest of mien once more. His expression of sustained energy relaxed, so that he looked younger than usual. After a pause, and even then hesitatingly, he rejoined:

"Julius Cæsar, perhaps. The assassination of Cæsar was a misfortune for mankind." He added softly, "I love Cæsar. He was unique in that he combined the will of the warrior with the genius of the sage. At bottom he was a philosopher who saw everything *sub specie eternitatis*. It is true that he had a passion for fame, but his ambition did not cut him off from human kind."

"After all, then, a dictator can be loved?"

"Yes," answered Mussolini with renewed decisiveness. "Provided that the masses fear him at the same time. The crowd loves strong men. The crowd is like a woman."

. . .

Socialism and Nationalism

He was silent but amused, while I went on:

"Is it possible that you do not believe in the magical power of a name? Do you not find it strange that a blacksmith should have named his two sons after two well-named disturbers of the peace?"

"It did not do my brother much good," answered Mussolini. "He lacked the passionate impetus of that Arnaldo after whom he was called. A revolutionist is born, not made."

"Do you think there is any notable difference between the composition of a modern revolutionist and that of one of earlier days?"

"The form has changed. One condition, however, has been requisite through all the ages–courage, physical as well as moral. For the rest, every revolution creates new forms, new myths and new rites; and the would-be revolutionist, while using old traditions, must refashion them. He must create new festivals, new gestures, new forms, which will themselves in turn become traditional. The airplane festival is new to-day. In half a century it will be encrusted with the patina of tradition."

"Don't you think that many young men are only anarchists because they have no chance of becoming rulers?"

"Of course," he replied; "every anarchist is a dictator who has missed fire."

"But since you feel that you yourself were educated by the revolutionary spirit of your youth, by rebelliousness and originality, why is it that to-day you enforce obedience and order upon the young and construct a new bureaucracy, you who made mock of the old one?"

"You are mistaken," he tranquilly objected. "In our fathers' days, governments had not a sufficient sense of the State. Besides, new times have brought new tasks for the nation; if there is to be a maximum of efficiency, there must be a maximum of order. Here in Italy we have realised as much as is realisable in the present phase of development. As regards bureaucracy, I admit the force of your criticism, but bureaucracy is inevitable. Concerning order, we have to do with historical necessities. We are living in the third act of the drama. There comes a moment when every revolutionist grows conservative."

"It ought to make you long-suffering when you remember your own imprisonment, and when those who used to be your friends have become your foes."

"Well, I have not troubled those of my comrades who have ceased to march in line with me."

"It must be difficult," I went on, "for a revolutionist, one who acts outside the law, to impose limits upon himself. In the year 1911, when you were being prosecuted, you said that sabotage must have a moral purpose; it was permissible to cut telegraph wires but not to derail a neutral train. That remark of yours made a great impression on me. How are we to draw the line between permissible and unpermissible revolution?"

"That is a moral question which each revolutionist must decide for himself."

I seized the opportunity of asking him about his plans in those pre-war days.

"If, in the year 1913, you had been successful

in the revolt at Milan, what would have been the upshot?"

"Then? The republic!" came the reply, short and sharp.

"But how do these ideas comport with a nationalism which was already a fully developed creed?"

"Surely a republican can just as well be a nationalist as a monarchist can be—perhaps better. Are there not plenty of examples?"

"But if nationalism be independent of forms of government, and also of questions of class, then it must also be independent of questions of race. Do you really believe, as some ethnologists contend, that there are still pure races in Europe? Do you believe that racial unity is a requisite guarantee for vigorous nationalist aspirations? Are you not exposed to the danger that the apologists of Fascism will (like Professor Blank) talk the same nonsense about the Latin races as northern pedants have talked about the 'noble blonds,' and thereby increase rival pugnacities?"

Mussolini grew animated, for this is a matter upon which, owing no doubt to the exaggeration of some of the Fascists, he feels that he is likely to be misunderstood.

"Of course there are no pure races left; not even the Jews have kept their blood unmingled. Successful crossings have often promoted the energy and the beauty of a nation. Race! It is a feeling, not a reality; ninety-five per cent., at least, is a feeling. Nothing will ever make me believe that biologically pure races can be shown to exist to-day. Amusingly enough, not one of those who have proclaimed the 'nobility' of the Teutonic race was himself a Teuton.

Gobineau was a Frenchman; Houston Chamberlain, an Englishman; Woltmann, a Jew; Lapogue, another Frenchman. Chamberlain actually declared that Rome was the capital of chaos. No such doctrine will ever find wide acceptance here in Italy. Professor Blank, whom you quoted just now, is a man with more poetic imagination than science in his composition. National pride has no need of the delirium of race."

"That is the best argument against anti-Semitism," said I.

"Anti-Semitism does not exist in Italy," answered Mussolini. "Italians of Jewish birth have shown themselves good citizens, and they fought bravely in the war. Many of them occupy leading positions in the universities, in the army, in the banks. Quite a number of them are generals; Modena, the commandant of Sardinia, is a general of the artillery."

"Nevertheless," I put in, "Italian refugees in Paris use it as an argument against you that you have forbidden the admission of Jews to the Academy."

"The accusation is absurd. Since my day, there has been no Jew suitable for admission. Now Della Seta is a candidate; a man of great learning, the leading authority on prehistoric Italy."

"If you are falsely accused in this matter, you suffer in good company. In Germany there is a preposterous fable that Bismarck and Goethe were prejudiced against Jews. Without any justification, the French speak of a certain anomaly as *'le vice allemand.'* The term might be more reasonably applied to anti-Semitism."

"How do you explain that?" asked Mussolini.

"Whenever things go awry in Germany, the Jews

are blamed for it. Just now we are in exceptionally bad case!"

"Ah, yes, the scapegoat!"

I returned to the wider question of race.

"If, then, neither race nor the form of government accounts for nationalism, are we to attribute it to community of speech? But ancient Rome, like other empires, was a State in which many tongues were spoken; and in modern history it has never seemed to me that multiplicity of languages was a source of weakness to a State. The Habsburg dominion fell, but Switzerland flourishes."

. . .

"Fate!" he cried mockingly. "Statesmen only talk of fate when they have blundered."

"A fourth reason for nationalism," I went on, continuing my analysis, "seems to me to exist universally in what are called 'the demands of history.' For instance, you once spoke of a colony which belonged to classical Rome."

"That was only a literary flourish," said Mussolini. "I was speaking of Libya, which was then unpeopled. If the government in modern Rome wanted to claim the territory colonised by classical Rome, it would have to demand the return of Portugal, Switzerland, Glasgow, Pannonia, and, indeed, all western, central, and southern Europe, to the Italian flag."

When making such statements, which in print seem obviously ironical, Mussolini remains perfectly serious, and because he therefore wishes to avoid any mannerisms which would give an abstract flavour to what he means to be concrete.

By a transition whose details I have forgotten, I passed on to discuss the physiognomical results of nationalist education.

"It seems to me that Fascism is changing the faces of the Italians. I am doubtful if this is a matter for congratulation. Goethe said that the finger of God was more plainly visible in an Italian countenance than in a German."

"There is a moral reason for the change," said Mussolini. "Our faces are becoming more tensed. The will to action modifies the features; even sports and physical exercise induce changes. That is why a handicraftsman looks so different from a factory worker."

"Your head," I rejoined, "has been compared with that of Colleoni. Like such comparisons in general, it is only applicable from time to time. You Italians know full well that the *condottieri* were not *condottieri* all the time. Montefeltre was a thinker!"

"Yes," replied Mussolini, "the *condottiere* is not a mere brute. Once in his life, perhaps, he may have been a savage beast. In general, however, these men were no more savage than their contemporaries. It was the times that were savage."

"Does the comparison to which I have just referred please you?" I asked.

Mussolini looked at me with a penetrating glance, thrust forward his lower jaw, and made no answer. At that moment he certainly did look like Colleoni.

. . .

On the Road to Power

Mussolini looked pale and out of humour in the lamplight. He ruffled the newspaper in his hand as I came to the end of the twenty yards' promenade from the door to his desk. This was not unencumbered as usual, for on it there lay a thick pile of documents. I knew that the two men who had left him a minute or two before my arrival were bank directors, so I said:

"You are tired this evening. Would you rather postpone our conversation?"

"I have had to study the balance sheet of the Banca di Roma," he said, resting his chin on his hand. "Never mind. Let's have our talk. It will be a relaxation."

The strain he had been undergoing was manifest in the curtness of his subsequent rejoinders. I inquired:

"Had you not many such moments of fatigue, of discouragement, during the war? In your articles, especially in the later ones, you write so bitterly about fraternity that I read into them disillusionment concerning all that happened, even the victory. In one of them you said that the germs of decay are hidden in a victorious nation. That remark is rather too philosophic for a man of action."

He pulled down the corners of his mouth and stared at me vacantly as he replied:

"Was it not enough to make a man weary when these symptoms of decay persisted for years after the victory? Every nation engaged in the war made heroic efforts; but it seemed to us here in Italy as if we were being deprived of the reward of victory."

"I can understand that you felt yourselves to have been cheated in Paris," said I. "But why did you and your adherents speak of a Fiume *'sacrificato,'* merely because your friends of yesterday, the Allies, continued to hold the place? A man who at that time was a prominent figure said to me that Fiume was only thrust into the foreground by the referendum, and that the sole reason why Orlando, the arch-parliamentarian, made such a to-do about it was that it had become a popular catchword. Why should Fiume have developed into a sort of holy of holies just after the war, as if it had played a great part in Italian history and civilisation like Florence or Bologna?"

He continued to gaze into vacancy and said:

"You are wrong in thinking that that was a mere matter of parliamentary finesse. Fiume was an Italian town, as dear to us as any other. In Fiume, just as in Trieste and Trent, there were Irredentists who wanted their native city to become part of Italy."

I alluded to the fact that the number of inhabitants of Fiume who had acclaimed D'Annunzio's raid had, after all, not been very large.

"He was idolised by the people! Naturally such a situation as arose there tends to become oppressive after twelve months or so. Still, there can be no doubt whatever that we owe Fiume to D'Annunzio."

He said this bluntly, without sign of emotion, as one who utters a historical truth about which there can be no question. I went on to speak of the peace, quoted some of the utterances of the delegates to Versailles, and proceeded to inquire:

"Do you blame Orlando for the losses of Italy at

the Peace Conference? Was his character flawed? According to certain Fascists, he was one of the most unsatisfactory of mortals."

"The diplomatic situation was unfavourable. Other men than he might have made a mess of things in Paris."

"Why, then, was the feeling in Italy so bitter? Considering the victors in the war objectively, it can certainly be maintained that Italy was the only one who not merely conquered her chief enemy, but annihilated that enemy."

"We know that."

Seeing that I could get no farther along this line, I returned to the question of the Socialist attitude during the war, hoping that that would provide a stimulus.

"Really your own case resembled that of your country," said I. "You were the only man who annihilated his own particular foe. But what does that prove against the system, if during the years from 1918 to 1921 the socialist leaders were weaklings? Were not some of your generals incompetent during the war, and yet your troops were victorious?"

"Some. But still there was a mass movement!"

"And was this mass movement to be fought only with its own means? The burning of Avanti, the destruction of the telegraphic apparatus—were not these Russian tactics?"

"Much the same. Our tactics were decidedly Russian."

This curt, military style of answering was unusual in him, but to-day it was a manifestation of fatigue, and perhaps in conformity with the military trend of his thoughts at the moment. I tried to give the conversation a new turn.

"Is it true that in the year 1921 you were inclined to renounce the leadership of your youthful party?"

"No," he snapped, as ungraciously as before. "I told them they must accept my ideas or I should quit. It was necessary to transform a mob into a party."

"Why did you hold back for a year when many of your followers wanted to take instant action?"

"It would have been a mistake."

"I have been told by a friend of mine that when, at that date, you visited the Wilhelmstrasse, you said: 'At this juncture there are only two parties in Italy, myself and the King!' "

"That's all right."

"And when subsequently, in the autumn of 1922, you sent your conditions to the Facta administration, were you confident that he would reject them?"

"Certainly. Wanted to gain time."

"What do you think of generals who break their oath of allegiance to an established government in order to make a revolution and set up a new one—like the four who participated in your March on Rome?"

"In certain historical crises that must happen."

"Your proclamation was printed before you set out. Hadn't you the feeling that you were forestalling things?"

"There wasn't a moment to lose."

"How do you account for the fact that there was no resistance to your March on Rome? It was just like what happened in Germany on November 9, 1918."

"Same reasons; obsolete system."

"I have been told that the King had already signed an ordinance declaring a state of siege."

"The ministers had decided on this course, but the King refused to sign, even when pressed to do so a second time."

"Suppose the King had agreed, and a state of siege had been declared, would you have felt sure of victory even in the case of resistance?"

"We held the valley of the Po and it is there that the fate of Italy has always been decided."

"How could you, a soldier, be content during those last weeks to stay so far from the centre of action?"

"I was in command at Milan."

"When you received the King's telegram asking you to take over the government, were you surprised or had you expected it?"

"Expected."

"When on your way to Rome, were you in the mood of an artist who is about to begin his work, or in that of a prophet who is fulfilling a mission?"

"Artist."

He was too laconic for my taste, and so, in the hope of bringing about a little relaxation, I had recourse to an anecdote.

"Do you remember what Napoleon said to his brother when they entered the Tuileries after the *coup d'état?* 'Well, here we are. Let's see to it that we stay here!' "

It was a palpable hit. Mussolini laughed. The spell the bank directors had laid upon his nerves was broken. His customary serenity had returned, so that he could speak once more in his usual voice and formulate his views at reasonable length. When I went on to question him about his personal, his mental preparation for the rôle of leadership, he thrust the thick balance sheet aside, laid his arms on the table in front of him, and then became reminiscent.

"I was prepared as far as broad lines were concerned, but not in matters of detail. To begin with, I was overburdened with work. Within forty-eight hours I had to get fifty-two thousand revolutionary soldiers out of the capital and to see to it that these excited young men were held in leash. During the first days the most important affair was to keep the machinery running. But I, who had to do this, lacked first-hand knowledge of the machinery of administration. I promptly dismissed some of the leading officials, but I left a great many of them where they were. It was incumbent upon me to convince the most important civil servants, during the very first weeks, that we were not to be trifled with. They were a danger to me but at the outset I had to trust them."

"That," I said, "was what took all the fire out of the German revolution. The old permanent officials were stronger than the new leaders and humbugged them. But how does one begin a new régime? Is it like setting up a monument, or building a house in the forest, when one begins by clearing a lot of trees to make room?"

"That is an interesting simile," he said alertly. "Most revolutions begin with a hundred per cent., but little by little the new spirit evaporates, becomes diluted with the old. Concessions are made, now here, now there; and before long your revolution has declined to fifty per cent., or less."

"That is what happened in Germany," I interjected.

"We did it the reverse way. I began with fifty per cent. Why? Because history had taught me that the courage of most revolutionists begins to fail after the first alarums and excursions. I started with a coalition and it was six months before I dismissed the Catholics. In other countries, revolutionists have by degrees become more complaisant; but here in Italy, year by year, we have grown more radical, more stubborn. Not until last year, for instance, did I insist upon the university professors swearing allegiance. I took the democrats as I found them and I gave the Socialists the opportunity of participating in the government. Turati, who died yesterday, would perhaps have agreed to this, but Baldesi and other men of his sort obstinately refused their chances. Since I had planned a complete renovation of my country, I had to accustom it gradually to the new order of things and to make use of the outstanding forces of the old order. The Russians were in a different position. The old order had utterly collapsed and they could clear the ground completely in order to build their house in the forest. But where should we have been to-day if I had set out by making a clean sweep?"

He was full of vivacity once more, all signs of fatigue having vanished.

"Your enemies gave you a helping hand," I said, "by marching out of parliament. I suppose that suited your book and that you had looked forward to it?"

"Of course!" he exclaimed. "They had withdrawn

to the Sacred Mount, and that is a hill which brings misfortune to all who climb it."

"In the army," I said, "in the course of the revolution you have made, did you find more good will and talent to begin with or later?"

"Later. To-day people have faith in it!"

"Did you anticipate this? Did you expect to sit ten years or longer at this table?"

He made a whimsical grimace, rolling his eyes as if to inspire fear, but laughing at the same time as if to counteract the impression. Then he said, in low tones, and assuming a playful air of mystery:

"I came here in order to stay as long as possible."

. . . After the Fall*

CHRISTOPHER HIBBERT

AFTER THE TRIAL at Verona the changes of mood which during the last few years had been an essential trait of an increasingly unstable temperament became more sudden and pronounced than ever. On the day after the executions Mussolini said to the Minister for Foreign Affairs, 'Now that we've started rolling heads in the dust we'll carry on to the end,' and he gave to Tamburini, his Chief of Police, a list of untrustworthy Fascists who were to be arrested. A few days later, however, he had changed his mind. He cancelled the instructions he had given Tamburini

* From Christopher Hibbert, *Benito Mussolini, A Biography*, 254–57, 260–63, 265–66, 276–81. Reprinted by permission of Little, Brown & Co. and Longmans Green & Co. Ltd.

and spoke instead of pardon and forgiveness. Indeed, he seemed, on occasions, to have lost altogether his wish to govern and wanted only to think of his past and of his place in history. Photographers and journalists who came to see him to prove that he was still alive tried to indicate also that he had lost nothing of his spiritual fire; but they admitted in private that he seemed listless and defeated. He looked in much better health than he had done at the time of his rescue from the Gran Sasso; he gave brave answers to their questions and stared with familiar force into the camera's lens, but when the photograph was taken and the notebook shut he seemed to sink into lethargy. One day he asked Colonel Dollmann if it were really true that no one in Rome had moved a finger to help him after his arrest, and when Dollmann had to admit that it was so, he said with a flash of anger that he could never forgive such ingratitude. 'No man has done more for Rome,' he went on, 'since Julius Caesar. I will never go to Palazzo Venezia again unless as a conqueror.' The next day his anger and claims were forgotten, and he was sunk again into lethargy.

He spent hours reading newspapers and looking eagerly for references to himself, cutting out those articles which directly concerned him, even those printed in Rome newspapers during his captivity which gave sensational and spurious descriptions of his private life and his supposed mistresses. He carefully numbered each item and annotated most of them with coloured pencils. He was constantly making excuses for his failure and the loss of the Empire. He blamed alternately the British and the Americans, the Germans and the Italians, the Freemasons, the *bourgeoisie,* the Jews, the conspirators of 25 July, above all the King. 'If the *colpo di Stato* had not taken place,' he once told a parade of Fascist soldiers in Guardia, 'I should not now be standing in a suburb of Brescia, but in a square in Cairo.'

'He thinks only of history,' his Minister for Popular Culture, Fernando Mezzasoma, wrote, 'and how he will appear in it.'

He spent hours too in lecturing and haranguing his Ministers and visitors on historical and political themes, using the grandiose gestures and phrases of his youth. Once at the Party headquarters at Villa Cavallero he got up from a conference which was boring him and walked round the room, abruptly stopping with his arms crossed on his chest to ask intently, 'What is Fascism?'

It was obviously a rhetorical question and he went on to answer it himself. 'It can be answered in only one way. Fascism is Mussolinism. Let us not delude ourselves. As a doctrine Fascism contains nothing new. It is a product of the modern crisis–the crisis of man who can no longer remain within the normal bounds of the existing laws. One could call it irrationalism.' He had not created Fascism, he maintained another day, he had merely exploited the Italians' latent and inborn Fascist tendencies. 'If this had not been so I would not have been followed for twenty years. The Italians are a most fickle people. When I am gone I am confident that the historians and the psychologists will ask how a man had the power to lead such a people for so long. If I had done nothing else this masterpiece would be enough to prevent me being swallowed up in oblivion. Others will conquer with sword and fire, perhaps, but certainly not with consent as I did. . . . When people say that we were the white guard of the *bourgeoisie* they lie shamelessly. I have promoted–and I say this with a clear conscience–the progress of the workers more than anyone. . . . I have made dictatorship noble. I have not, in fact, been a dictator, because my power was no more than the will of the Italian people.'

And on he went, becoming more convoluted, more obscure, until his hearers could not understand what he was talking about and doubted that he could himself. On another occasion, when the defence of Rome was being discussed, he gave a long dissertation upon the 'biological decadence of France'. At other times he would talk as he had done years before as a Socialist, dismissing the recent development of Fascism as a political calamity. 'We've lost completely,' he said to Nicola Bombacci, 'without the possibility of appeal. One day history will judge us and say that many buildings were built, that many bridges were thrown across many rivers; but it will be forced to conclude that as far as the spirit is concerned we were only common pawns in the recent crisis of human conscience, and that we remained pawns to the end.'

It was becoming a frequently voiced assessment. 'Hitler and I,' he admitted in one of these moments of self-analysis, 'have surrendered ourselves to our illusions like a couple of lunatics. We have only one hope left; to create a myth.' Others had not needed to do so; their work had survived. He often spoke of these men: of Frederick the Great, Napoleon, Washington, Bismarck, of his fellow-Italians–Garibaldi, Mazzini, Giolitti and particularly of Crispi, whose career offers so many parallels with his own. He spoke frequently too of his contemporaries: of Pietro Nenni, who 'when all was said and done remained a good Italian'; of Dino Grandi, who 'despite everything' was 'the finest man Fascism produced'; of Briand, 'perhaps the only statesman who wished to create a European federation without resorting to arms'; of Eden, whom he hated; of Roosevelt, whom he despised; of Lansbury, Hoare and Lloyd George, whom he had liked; of Stalin, whom he envied; and often of Churchill, whom he greatly admired. He was, however, sometimes unable to disguise his jealousy of Churchill's success. He 'does not have the European spirit' he once decided, 'and doesn't really understand anything except the necessity of those English. But he is the man of the moment because he hates the Germans.' Churchill's great merit, of course, was that he was not so much a politician as a buccaneer. 'He is an obdurate and obstinate old man,' he once told Mezzasoma with a respect which was almost affectionate. 'In some respects he is like my father.'

He did not always speak with so detached and tolerant an air, and occasionally the mere mention of a man's name would induce in him a sudden surge of fury. Farinacci was one of these names that he could not bear to hear discussed. 'Don't talk about him,' he once told Dollmann angrily. 'He wants to be my successor.' 'Don't mention his name,' he snapped on another occasion when the conversation turned to another Fascist whom he did not like; 'the very *sound* of it,' he added, scratching his fingers feverishly, 'makes me itch all over.' In an effort to bring Mussolini's mind to a favourite topic Mezzasoma asked him one day when he was plainly beside himself with irritation, 'And you, Duce? How about yourself?'

'I?' Mussolini said, smiling that consciously enigmatic smile which he was apt to use before delivering himself of one of his celebrated neologisms. 'I? I am not a statesman. I am more like a mad poet.'

He would have liked to have been one just as Hitler would have liked to have been a great painter —most dictators are, it seems, artists *manqués*. He would have liked to have had D'Annunzio's bizarre gifts, or Baudelaire's or Rimbaud's, and he spoke of these men with veneration, if not always with discrimination. But he was not a poet, not even in the sense that he thought he was. He wrote a great deal as he had always done. He formed a news agency, *Corrispondenza Repubblicana,* which issued reams of his polemical writings; he wrote a series of autobiographical articles for the *Corriere della Sera,* which were eventually expanded into a book; he translated an Italian version of *Walküre* back into German to see how it compared with the original; he even wrote for a schoolboys' magazine. But none of these writings was the work of a mad poet.

He felt nearer to this ideal, perhaps, when he played his violin. 'It leads me to a glimpse of eternity,' he said. 'And when I play the world slips away from me.' He played without grace but with a kind of emphatic power, sometimes with a wild hysteria that suggested the agony of a great mind distraught. 'He was dictatorial even where music was concerned,' Margherita Sarfatti says, 'and had no respect for style or form. He had expression and technique, but he played everything in his own way.' Often in the evenings at Villa Feltrinelli he would shut himself away to practise his favourite pieces by Beethoven, Wagner, Schubert and Verdi, and sometimes he would stand alone in the garden with the pink marble walls of the villa for a backcloth playing with an abandoned force that the German guards took for genius. Once in a bombed house after an air-raid he played parts of the Beethoven Violin Concerto to some German officers, and when he had finished and they applauded him he closed his eyes as if in ecstasy.

. . .

Although he spent so many hours at his desk, the questions which really concerned him were of a philosophical or personal nature rather than a practical one. Only occasionally did a problem of government occupy and absorb his mind, and even then it was usually one which did not appear to deserve the sudden interest which he took in it.

He was, for instance, passionate in his determination to obtain the formal recognition of the Vatican for his régime. He could not carry on, he once exclaimed in exasperation, without this recognition, although his Government's functioning was not likely to be any the more successful with it. It was a matter of personal pride, and he began to feel himself insulted by the Pope's reluctance, which became so much an obsession with him that he declared that his patience was exhausted and he would denounce the Lateran Pacts and set up a schismatic Church. He went so far as to consider the qualifications of certain politically sound priests for new bishoprics and was only dissuaded from his reckless course by the Germans, who did not want their bad relations with the Papacy made any worse than they already were.

The only other matter which excited in him, at this time, a comparable interest was his recognition of himself as a man who had never in his heart lost the Socialist principles of his youth. Although most of his Ministers privately condemned this renewed belief in authoritative Socialism as a misguided one, they could not doubt the sincerity with which he held it. It was certainly not a passing enthusiasm, but remained with him to the end. 'Socialism', he was fond of saying, 'is the cornerstone of the Republic.' Such pronouncements were heard with alarm by the Germans and by the new *élite* of Fascism and in particular by men such as Farinacci, Pavolini and Buffarini-Guidi, who viewed with profound misgivings Mussolini's endeavours to widen the appeal of the *Partito Fascista Repubblicano* by making what they took to be servile concessions to the Left: concessions amounting almost to the abrogation of the Fascist ideal and—even more tragic to some of them—the rejection of the myth of the Duce as Superman.

The ideological pattern for the Social Republic had been set at Verona on 14 November, when the first congress of the Republican Fascist Party met to define the principles upon which it would govern. The proceedings were opened by the reading of a letter from the Duce in which the importance of returning to 'the original intentions of the Fascist revolution' was stressed. Indeed the *Manifesto di Verona* which was ultimately issued was largely a recapitulation of the aspirations of 1919 with the added reference, which had become almost obligatory in Fascist circles, to the 'decadence of the monarchy'.

So far as Mussolini himself was concerned its most important points were those dealing with the welfare of the workers; and he refused to accept the suggestion that this aspect of Socialism was a newly discovered interest.

Any accusation, particularly in the newspapers which he still read so avidly, that Fascism had not in the past been seriously concerned with the good of the working-class and that it had been maintained in power by bourgeois capitalists, aroused in Mussolini an anger and contempt that seemed otherwise reserved for Roosevelt, the King and Anthony Eden. Having read one day a report of a meeting of the General Confederation of Workers in Naples where a delegate had alleged that the social laws of the Fascist régime had proved of no benefit to the workers, he immediately wrote a passionate reply for the *Corrispondenza Repubblicana* in which he listed the laws he had enacted on their behalf, the number of hospitals he had built for them, the pensions he had provided, the scales of minimum wages he had introduced. 'These charges,' he insisted, were made by 'Communists and other enemies of our country who use the workers as pawns in their devilish games.' But the 'workers themselves knew them to be false'.

'It is impossible,' he said during a subsequent discussion on the same subject, 'to corrupt the proletariat. The workers are not capable of the sort of betrayal that the bourgeois are. The bourgeois with their materialistic mentality and greed are the ruin of Italy. I am an old Socialist at heart.'

Certainly it was true that while other aspects of his Government's business received scant attention, he was determined to show that with what little power and funds it possessed the Social Republic should live up to its name. In the last month of his life, when the Gothic Line was broken and the complete overthrow of the shattered Axis and of his Government seemed certain, he was still giving his attention to such, by then irrelevant, matters as the possibility of introducing collective farming as a means of saving the small peasant and the reorganization of hospitals for impoverished victims of tuberculosis. Möllhausen told Rahn that even at this hour Mussolini—despite his detachment and his attitudinizing protestations that he and his work were already a part of history—was dominated by an ingenuous concern to leave behind him some sort of framework on which a Welfare State could be built.

But few problems concerned him as deeply as this, and for most of the time he seemed content to sit quietly reading or writing in his office, to be left alone and to become less and less the dictator and more and more the 'university professor' which the admiring Doctor Zachariae had decided he so much resembled. His office was a small stuffy room with a majolica stove disproportionately large and a desk set across the corner, and he sat there by himself for hours on end reading and writing and looking out of the window into the garden. When a secretary entered the room he would look up slowly, not troubling to remove the spectacles the necessity for which he would have strongly denied a year before; but he had no pride of that sort now. His eyelids were often swollen and inflamed and he admitted without compunction that his sight was getting worse and worse every day.

He did not trouble either to foster the impression of a great mind at work as he had done at Palazzo Venezia, where his enormous desk had sometimes been completely bare to show how his mind contained all that he needed to know and sometimes littered with documents to show how busy he was. At Villa delle Orsoline it was merely untidy. Newspaper cuttings, papers and books, jars of coloured pencils and photographs, were piled higgledy-piggledy upon it without regard to order or, more unusually, effect. A journalist once looked at the spines of the books to see what the Duce was reading. They were a characteristically disparate selection–Dostoevsky, Tolstoy, Hemingway, Plato, Sappho, Kant, Sholokov's *Quiet Flows the Don,* Nietzsche, Emil Ludwig's *Napoleon,* Sorel's *Réflexions sur la Violence,* Goethe, Schopenhauer, books about Christ, about Frederick the Great, about Beethoven–and they all had bits of paper stuck between the pages to mark a significant passage or pencilled notes scribbled in the margins. So engrossed did he become on occasions that visitors and officials, particularly German ones, were dismissed with an impatient order to go and see Graziani or the Minister of Popular Culture or his Principal Private Secretary. 'Mussolini tends to withdraw from all questions of Government,' the young German officer Fürst Urach wrote home. 'If a German General comes to him with some request he says, "Oh, do talk to Graziani." If Leyers or some economic expert comes he says, "Oh, do see my Economics Minister, won't you?"' When one visitor, more importunate than the rest, insisted that the Duce's decision was vital, Mussolini replied that if the decision really were a vital one he could not possibly make it. The Germans must: he himself was merely Mayor of Gargnano.

But however vindictively he spoke against the Germans, those 'criminals by birth', as he referred to them on one occasion, those 'barbaric vandals, cruel, unjust, violent and rapacious', as he called them on another, he could not escape from the spell of their leader.

• • •

The meeting between the two men [Hitler–Mussolini, July 20, 1944] had been valueless. Mussolini had repeated none of the protests he had found the courage to mention in April and he returned to Italy gloomy and silent. People had become used to his coming back from Germany infused by Hitler's confidence and spirit, but this time if there was a change in him it was for the worse. He had been given some statistics by an Embassy official concerning the Italians in Germany and they had appalled him.[1]

He returned to the inconsequential routine of his work with even less energy and enthusiasm than before. Earlier in that summer he had played an occasional game of tennis, but his opponents always let him win and he became bored with the game and confined his exercise to riding a bicycle round the shores of the lake, and to walking in the woods either alone or with Romano, but followed always by his German guards. He also gave up the German lessons which he had previously been having three times a week; he could always make himself under-

[1] Salvatorelli and Mira say that in all 700,000 Italian soldiers were sent to Germany during the war for various noncombatant duties and that 30,000 of them died.

stood, and the expert fluency which he had hoped to achieve seemed no longer necessary. He left for the office earlier than ever now, sometimes before eight o'clock, in order to escape from the squabbling household, and returned home late to spend the evening, whenever he could, reading alone in his room or sitting outside in a garden chair with his hands clasped behind his head staring out over the lake until the sun went down.

He hated the twilight. As soon as it grew dark, he went indoors and switched on the light in his room. One evening the current had failed and Quinto Navarra, who had returned to Mussolini's service, brought in a candle. 'But he couldn't stand its low light,' Navarra said, 'so he went out into the garden until the electric light came on again, and stood by the lake throwing stones into the water.'

Either his Italian physician or Professor Zachariae called on him every morning to satisfy themselves that the diet they had recommended him to follow was having the required effect. He was excessively pale, Zachariae noticed, and his dark eyes were on occasions almost feverish as they gazed out of a head that seemed curiously gaunt. He had no more than a cup of tea for breakfast, a very light lunch and dinner. He never drank milk although in the past he had had as many as six pints a day. The plain uniform of the Fascist Militia, which he wore habitually, though usually well pressed seemed to hang about him, and the black collars of his shirts were much too big, revealing his formerly massive neck as lined and wrinkled like the neck of a tortoise. He took care to see that his skull was always well shaved and twice a month a girl came from Gardone to manicure his nails, but these were his only concessions to a personal vanity which had once been compulsive. 'Only rarely,' Navarra said, 'was he in a good humour, and these rare moments were always followed by long, black hours of sadness.'

The month after his visit to Hitler in Prussia he decided to make a tour of inspection of the front. Encouraged by the regimented cheers that greeted him he spent five days touring the lines, giving advice to the generals which they did not take and suggesting counter-offensives which were obviously impractical. Kesselring listened politely, but to Mussolini's annoyance made it clear that his suggestions were not considered of undue importance. 'That Kesselring,' Mussolini had already decided crossly, 'is not worth a fig.'

The cheers which had greeted him, however, from both Italian and German troops, had an invigoratingly restorative effect. He returned to Gargnano with new confidence and hope and told Rachele over and over again how the soldiers had displayed their spontaneous affection. The Germans in particular, he said, had 'gone wild with excitement and'—a seemingly incompatible reaction—'stiffened to attention in the cramped space of their dug-outs'. But the mood did not last. Within a week he had relapsed into his former despondency.

• • •

He seemed drained of all hope. He had no illusions left. Previously he had been able to retain them by succumbing to his own propaganda that the Germans' secret weapons and their new secret army would soon turn the fortunes of war, that the Allies' losses were more than they could bear, that the discord between the Russians and Americans would result in war between them, or at least make it possible for him to make a separate peace with one or other of them, preferring if it came to that, so he told both his Finance Minister and Preziosi that Italy should become a Soviet Republic rather than an Anglo-American colony. But now he derived comfort only from the reflection that even if the British did win the war they would lose their Empire after it, just as he had done. When his Ministers tried to give him encouragement, he smiled at them ironically. When Graziani told him of his latest quarrel with Kesselring he shrugged his shoulders with indifference. One day after Mezzasoma had burst into his office to announce that 'wonderful news' had just come in of a successful German counterattack on the Meuse, Mussolini remarked, without interest, as if indeed he had not understood what the excitable young man had said, 'That's good.' And he made a gesture of dismissal, not troubling to ask for any details.

On the anniversary of D'Annunzio's death he went to the Vittoriale and, standing beside the poet's tomb, he made a sad, almost despairing speech which one of his audience described as being 'short and mysterious, grave with a sense of tragedy'. His face was pale and sad and 'looked like stone', and the sky was grey and the atmosphere oppressive. 'You are not dead, my friend,' he said, 'and you will not die so long as there remains, standing in the Mediterranean, an island called Italy. You are not dead and you will not die so long as in the centre of Italy there is a city to which we shall return–a city called Rome.'

'He lives by dreams, in dreams and through dreams,' Mezzasoma said. 'He does not have the least contact with reality. He lives and functions in a world which he builds for himself, a completely fantastic world. He lives outside time. His reactions, his enthusiasms, his breakdowns, never have any relation to life. They come at any moment and without any definite reason.'

Sometimes, indeed, he talked and behaved as if he had in fact become the mad poet which the year before he had claimed to be.

The journalist Ivanoe Fossani has described a revealing interview which Mussolini gave him at this time. It took place in the middle of Lake Garda on the island of Trimellone under a night sky brilliant with stars. A ferocious police dog was barking savagely, and Mussolini went up to it and took its lower jaw in one hand so that he could stroke it with the other. He gazed into its eyes, Fossani said, as he told it to be quiet, and after a few moments it stopped barking and lay down at his feet and went to sleep, and Mussolini began talking to Fossani. He spoke so fast and at such length that when he had finished and went back to Gargnano in his motor-boat, Fossani wrote furiously for three hours without stopping, in an effort to record everything that Mussolini had said. Fossani himself during the whole interview only spoke one word–'Tell'–the name of the police dog. 'I suspected from the beginning,' he said, 'that the sound of my voice would have dammed the flow of talk of a man who had decided to confess to the stars.'

Away from the guards, and the Germans and the arguments of his Ministers, the tantrums of his wife and the tears of his mistress, Mussolini felt a sudden liberation which was close to delirium. 'If it were a summer's day,' he said, 'I would take off my coat and roll in the grass like a wildly happy child.' He spoke of the stars, and the mysterious power of the soil, of his dead son and his brother Arnaldo, of the inconsequence of human life and of the life of the soul. He spoke like a feverish prophet, spinning a web of argument and fantasy and unrelated fact, catching a thread in one train of thought to leap away to another, suddenly breaking through the muddle of contradiction, extravagant metaphor and half-formed ideas to make an observation of striking truth and clarity, or a prophecy of deep prescience. He tried to analyse the reasons for his successes and failures. He was not infallible, he said. He had made mistakes. He could see them now and recognize them. It had not been easy for he had been surrounded for years by idolators. 'I heard the word genius,' he said with a kind of bitter disgust, 'a hundred times a day.' But others had made greater mistakes, and all his own would have been forgotten if the war, forced upon him by the diabolical foreign policy of the English, had been conducted by the Germans with restraint. The attack on Russia had been made against his strong advice, and now Germany was almost destroyed and the Russians would soon be in a position in Central Europe from which it would be impossible to dislodge them. If the same mistakes were committed in the East, China too would help to strangle the world. 'How can England and America fail to see so enormous a danger?'

This reference to the English aroused in him a fresh burst of invective. He attacked them and the

French for failing to support him in his demands for a revision of the Treaty of Versailles, for the cancellation of war debts and reparations and in his stand against Germany in the early 1930s. He attacked the King and the reactionary Court which surrounded him, he attacked the *bourgeoisie* who had infused a false spirit into the faith of Fascism, he attacked the General Staff for betraying the soldiers, he attacked the sordid industrial and financial groups who had outrageously ill-treated the workers whom he himself had 'always loved and love still. They are good and indestructible,' he said, 'and infinitely superior to all the false prophets who pretend to represent them.' And the thought of them brought a new mood of sadness. 'I have been a prisoner ever since I was arrested in the King's villa,' he said, in a quieter voice. 'There is no longer any escape. To our enemies we are those who must surrender unconditionally, to the others we are traitors. . . . I have no illusions about my fate. Life is only a short span in eternity. After the struggle is over they will spit on me, but later perhaps they will come to wipe me clean. And then I shall smile because I shall be at peace with my people.'

He stood up at last and shook Fossani silently by the hand. And as he walked back to his boat, the journalist, deeply impressed by the calm dignity of this 'great, unfortunate man in his hour of tragedy', says that the police dog 'leapt on to a rock where it let out a long, shrill howl'.

But if it were possible to recognize the greatness of this tragic figure in a moment of ecstatic pity beneath the purity of the stars, it was more difficult to do so in the stuffy little room in Villa delle Orsoline where most journalists saw him. One of these, Madeleine Mollier, found a man she scarcely recognized, a man who looked like a convict with his white face and shaven head and black, lacklustre eyes. He was not so much resigned as humble. His resignation and calm acceptance of his fate had an almost apologetic, self-pitying air.

'What do you want to know?' he asked her. 'Seven years ago I remember you came to Rome. I was an interesting person then. Now I am defunct. But I am not afraid any more. Death is a thank-you to God who has suffered so much. This morning in my room a little swallow was trapped. It flew around desperately in the room until it fell exhausted on my bed. I picked it up with care so as not to frighten it, opened my window, then opened my hand. It did not understand at first and looked around, before opening its wings and flying, with a little cry of joy, out to freedom. I shall never forget that cry of joy. But for me, the window will never open except to let me out to death. And it is right. I have made mistakes and I shall pay for them, if my poor life is worth the payment. I have never made mistakes when I have followed my instincts, but often when I have obeyed my reason. . . .

'Yes, signora, I am finished. My star has set. I still work, but I know that everything is a farce. I await the end of the tragedy, strangely detached from it all. I don't feel well and for a year have eaten nothing but slops. I don't drink. I don't smoke. . . . Perhaps I was, after all, only destined to indicate the road to my people. But then have you ever heard of a prudent, calculating dictator?'

He only derived comfort now, he said, from his

books, the works of the great philosophers. He did not want to do anything except read and go on reading as he waited for the end.

'I have been dying,' he said when asked a question about Ciano, 'since that January morning when he too met his destiny. The agony is atrociously long. I am like the captain of a ship in a storm; the ship is broken up and I find myself in the furious ocean on a raft which it is impossible to guide or to govern. No one hears my voice any more. But one day perhaps the world will listen to me.'

To everyone who came to see him now he spoke in this way–consciously tragic, sometimes mystical, occasionally obscure, often lyrical. To the young French writer Pierre Pascal, who had translated his *Parlo con Bruno,* he said: 'Have you noticed on your way here this morning the violent colours of the lake? The deep blue? I look at it when it is red at sunset or grey in the wintriness of the dawn and I see it as if for the first time. The beauties of Italy are profound.' Then, changing the subject suddenly, not waiting for an answer, he asked Pascal if he believed in God. He was not certain, himself, and wished that he could be so. Darting from God to Napoleon, to Charles Maurras, to the Italian painters, to Dante, to D'Annunzio, he avoided any mention of politics until Pascal made an observation about the necessity of uniting Europe so that it could defend itself from the intervention of the English. 'That will be the task of your generation,' Mussolini said, dismissing the unwelcome thought of the English, who had contributed so much to his ruin, 'and of the next one.' He was not in the mood for a talk about politics, and after Pascal had made a few remarks about the partisans in Italy and the maquis in France the conversation came to an abrupt end.

Another writer, Pia Reggidori Corti, found him equally unwilling to discuss contemporary events. He preferred to talk of Mazzini, Garibaldi, of philosophy and of sexual love. Every love died, he said, sooner or later through the impossibility of lovers to understand each other; and when Corti replied that disillusion only came when simple infatuation was mistaken for love, Mussolini referred to Plato and ended the interview by saying that for his part he was convinced that to live was to suffer.

He would even interrupt an important conference with his Ministers or the Germans to talk of philosophy or history or religion. On 6 April when the last offensive of the Allies had already begun, when Massa had been occupied and the German armies were retreating fast through Tuscany, he shocked Colonel Dollmann, who was only concerned with the problems of withdrawal and surrender, by suddenly saying to him in the middle of an urgent discussion, 'Tell me, Colonel, do you believe in God? General Wolff does.'

Mussolini, Power, and Nihilism*

GAUDENS MEGARO

THERE ARE *and have been other ways of assessing the core of the character of Mussolini through his metamorphosis from revolutionary socialist agitator before 1914 to Duce of Italian Fascism after 1922 than those which Gaudens Megaro adopted. But Megaro was truly pioneering in his attempt to transcend the "official" sources for Mussolini's life before 1914. During a time of troubles and danger for anyone suspected of anti-Fascist intentions and motivation, Megaro ransacked Italian collections of materials on the socialist career of the Duce and produced the first full-bodied biographical study of him to have its emphasis on the murky days preceding his rise to power within the ranks of Italian socialism before the First World War. Megaro's* Mussolini in the Making *(1938) appeared at the same time as Borgese's* Goliath: *though from quite different approaches, methods, and styles, the two works did much to blast away the flood of hagiographical writings with which official or officious biographers—and often their ingenuous imitators outside Fascist Italy—had suffused the life of Mussolini, portraying him variously as an uprooted intellectual, social agitator, and ideological nihilist during the Giolittian*

* From Gaudens Megaro, *Mussolini in the Making* (London: George Allen and Unwin Ltd., 1938), 318–19, 323–28, 331–34. Reprinted by permission of George Allen and Unwin Ltd. and Houghton Mifflin Company.

era in Italy. The selection given below is taken from what amounted to an epilogue in Megaro's book in which the particularized monographic procedure gives way to an attempt to conclusively capture the essence of the Duce's character across the great divide between his agitationist phase and his hegemonic period in Italy. Megaro never believed that there were two sides to Fascism, and he felt that its dominant dark side was merely a dimension of its leader's thirst for totalitarian and essentially nihilist power.

MUSSOLINI'S EVENTUAL SHIFT from internationalism to nationalism, from socialism to fascism, is merely an external event in the career of a man who has always had a pre-eminently individualistic conception of life. He has individualized everything in his lifetime, including, of course, both socialism and fascism. Born in a family of miserably poor people, in a region where revolutionists, sincere and insincere, abound, this *révolté* by instinct, temperament, and upbringing aligned himself with the socialist movement because this movement was easily adapted to give full scope to his rebellious impulses. He followed in the wake of his father, Alessandro, a courageous and articulate socialist whose memory is being continually insulted by fascist authors who have written travesties on his life. Those who ramble about Mussolini's intellectual father, be he Nietzsche or Sorel, would do well to pause and consider the influence of his real father.

Mussolini's training as an elementary school teacher raised him above the condition of the average socialist party member. With his extraordinary and facile power of assimilation, he read extensively, especially in the field of periodical literature. A young man of uncommon intelligence and discernment, he had a predilection for the literature of revolt, which buttressed and lent an intellectual air to his refractory nature. He was receptive to that literature which harmonized with his temperament. He appropriated what he wanted. Never has he been interested in learning, research or ideas except in so far as he could use them for his self-advancement as a man of action. His sole preoccupation is himself. It would be unjust to the anarchist tradition established by such men as Bakunin, Kropotkin, Reclus, and Malatesta who emphasized the spirit of solidarity among men, to call Mussolini an anarchist. Mussolini has always been an authoritarian. If the term anarchist is to be applied to him at all, because of his emphasis on individualism, it must be interpreted as meaning an individualist who cares nothing for the masses, nothing for human solidarity. What Mussolini said in April 1920 thus becomes clear:

"I start with the individual and strike at the state. The number of individuals who are in potential revolt against the state, not this or that state, but against the state in itself, is a minority that is not unaware of is fate, but it exists.*** Down with the state in all its forms and incarnations: the state of yesterday, of to-day and of to-morrow; the bourgeois state and the socialist state. To us, who are the dying symbols of individualism, there remains, during the present gloom and the dark to-morrow, only the religion, at present absurd, but always consoling, of Anarchy!"

Mussolini gave his real personal estimate of the masses when he said in 1911 that they were cowardly. He did indeed speak in the name of the masses, of the need for their elevation, but this was a part of the conventional socialist technique. Mussolini was among them, not of them. He was an individualist in their midst, with that disdain or disregard for the masses, for the people, for humanity that has found its most complete literary expression in Max Stirner, the German author of *The Ego and His Own,* a book which appealed so strongly to him that in 1911, when he was twenty-seven years old, he enthusiastically described it as "the Gospel of individualism and the greatest poem that has ever been sung to the glory of man become god". Both as a socialist and as a fascist, Mussolini has been a rather lone, solitary figure. Sceptical of the efficacy of mass action, he placed his faith in the action of small, resolute, audacious *élites* to which he, of course, appointed himself, whether their object was socialism or fascism.

. . .

Mussolini has seen mankind at its worst, and this he gloats over. He has always had little respect for human life, defending assassination in the name of socialism, allowing it under his fascist regime. He disapproves of assassination not because he believes in the inviolability of human life, but because it so frequently is inexpedient for certain political ends. He was not in the least moved as a man when members of his party butchered Matteotti. He was furious over this murder not because it was a crime, but because he deemed it to be a political blunder which might cost him his power. As editor of the *Avanti!,* he yearned for a "bath of blood", the "historic day" of judgment in the battle between the proletariat and the bourgeoisie. As leader of the fascists, he has viewed more than one "bath of blood", more than one "historic day" of judgment in his effort to seize and maintain unlimited power for himself. Whatever his alleged social objective, socialism or fascism, he has always been certain that "it is blood which gives movement to the resounding wheel of history". Once entrenched in power, he translated into imperialist terms his former bellicose socialist exhortations and he told the world that "war alone brings up to its highest tension all human energy and puts the stamp of nobility upon the peoples who have the courage to meet it". The ex-Hervéiste was one of the most vociferous exponents of Italy's entrance into the Great War. After the war, he excited those passions in Italy that would lead to civil war. The contemporary event he has perhaps admired most, outside of the fascist movement which he regards as his personal creation, is the Bolshevik Revolution–particularly its achievement in violently overthrowing an old regime. He has not hatred, but contempt for the Italian communist leaders because they failed miserably to effect a revolution in Italy, because they talked too much about revolution without resorting to the weapon of violence with sufficient success. Mussolini has utilized to the full his masterful knowledge of revolutionary technique. Ideas do not count for him; power does–power achieved through violence, maintained by violence. Two legends adorned his newspaper *Il Popolo d'Italia,* the organ he founded in November 1914 in order to advocate Italy's intervention in the war: one, "Whoever has arms has bread–Blanqui"; the other, "Revolution is an idea that has found bayonets–Napoleon". Almost all the writers on Mussolini's life cite these mottoes as though Mussolini had been the first to make use of them, but I am quite sure that he had found them at random on the title page of *La Conquête de l'Armée,* a book written by Gustave Hervé and published in 1913.

Mussolini assimilated these mottoes for his own purpose, emphasizing arms and bayonets, not revolution, although with his abiding fascination for "revolution", he persists in calling the fascist seizure and exercise of power a revolution. He is a master in the manipulation and exploitation of sentiments. In this respect, he has displayed veritable political genius at certain times in his career, notably in the immediate post-war period when he was at the nadir of his political fortunes. He exalts nationalism in much the same way that he used to exalt internationalism. It makes little difference to him what the flag is, whether that of fascism or of socialism, so long as he is its standard-bearer. The innumerable changes in his fascist programme before and after the "March on Rome" did not disturb him, for his eye was set on one thing only: the seizure of power and its maintenance. For example, in 1919 and 1920, when "bolshevism" was supposed to have threatened Italy, Mussolini fomented the passions of discord and conflict in the peninsula. He championed an advanced radical programme. He favoured the occupation of the factories by Italian workers in September and October 1920, and he supported their economic grievances. Later, he was able to exploit the "horror" and "fear" engendered in vast strata of the Italian public by the occupation of the factories, which was represented as the high-water mark of Italian "bolshevism".

In July 1920, Mussolini wrote one of his many articles denouncing the Bolshevik regime and Lenin. We are not at present interested in the truth or falsity, the soundness or unsoundness of his observations. Rather, we are interested in noting that he later built up his fascist state in Italy along the lines he had condemned in the Bolshevik state. His attack on Lenin and Soviet Russia gives us an excellent description of the later fascist, totalitarian, Mussolinian state. Substitute the word Mussolini for Lenin, the word Italy for Russia, the words fascist party for communist or socialist party, and an accurate idea will be formed of the Italian fascist state. Mussolini really was fond of what he appeared to hate. According to him, the Bolshevik state was a "state in the most concrete meaning of this word: a state, that is, a government, composed of men who exercise power, imposing an iron discipline upon individuals and groups and practising 'reaction' whenever necessary ***. In the Russia of Lenin, there is only one authority: his authority. There is only one liberty: his liberty. There is only one opinion: his opinion. There is only one law: his law. One must either submit or perish.*** No crisis, therefore, of state authority in Russia, but a state, that is, a super-state ***, a state that swallows up and crushes the individual and governs his entire life. It is understood that the zealots of the 'strong', Prussian or iron-fisted state find that their ideal has been realized there. In order to maintain the authority of the state in full force, no speeches, manifestos or lachrymose invocations are wanted; armed force is wanted. The most powerfully armed state, for domestic and foreign purposes, that exists in the world to-day is precisely Russia. The army of the Soviets is formidable, and as for the 'police', it has nothing to envy in the Okrana of the time of the Romanoffs. Whoever says state necessarily says the army, the police, the judiciary and the bureaucracy. The Russian state is the state *par excellence,* and it is clear that having *statetized* economic life in its innumerable manifestations, a huge army of bureaucrats has been formed. At the base of this pyramid, on the summit of which stands a handful of men, there is the multitude; there is the proletariat which, as in the old bourgeois regimes, obeys, works, and eats little or allows itself to be massacred. Dictatorship of the proletariat? The members of the wine clubs in their 'drinking' meetings still believe in it. In Russia, there exists, indeed, a dictatorship of the proletariat, exercised not by the proletarians, but rather *** by the communist party which, if it has, as is said,*** scarcely 700,000 members, represents a very small minority of the total population. In reality, it is a few men of this party who govern Russia. Their republic, 'with absolute and unlimited power', is a genuine and veritable autocracy ***. The reality is this ***: In Russia, there does not exist anything that even distantly resembles socialism; in Russia, owing to a series of well-known historical circumstances, a small fraction of the socialist party has seized power.*** That of Lenin is a gigantic, terrible experience in *corpore vili.* Lenin is an artist who has worked men, as other artists have worked marble or metals. But men are stronger than stone and less malleable than iron. There is no masterpiece. The artist has failed. The task was superior to his capacities."

Whatever doubts Mussolini may have had about Lenin, he has certainly entertained none about his own capacity to work men, to subdue them to his own will and to cast them in any mould he wished. He is the prey of a boundless ambition which was whetted early in his life by the extraordinary power he wielded in the socialist movement and which is still far from being satisfied despite his enormous personal success in many fields. We find it easy to believe that apparently when he was only twenty-six years old, he told one of his close Romagnuole acquaintances, Torquato Nanni, that he had found few men in Italy who were his equals. Always in search of an ideological lever with which to move the masses and to assert the supremacy of his ego, he found it first in socialism and later in an extreme form of nationalism. During the Great War, as he quoted the saying "Give me a fulcrum for a lever and I will move the world", he thought of Buddha, Christ, and Mahomet as men who had found a point of support and had moved three worlds in different ideological directions. With his flair for whatever will impress the masses, Mussolini has been superlatively successful in identifying his person with such popular causes as socialism and nationalism, exploiting every opportunity and occasion that would advance his quest for personal power. He has had the singular good fortune to be the Duce both of extreme revolutionary socialism and extreme reactionary fascism. Is it any wonder that he has wished to make his own life his masterpiece? A little more than a year before the fascist "March on Rome", when certain fascists were recalcitrant to his will, he brusquely declared that if fascism, his child, would not follow him, no one could oblige him to follow fascism. "The man who has guided and led a movement and has given it the best of his energy has the right to go beyond the analysis of a thousand local elements in order to view in its synthesis the political and moral panorama *** which is not that of Bologna, of Venice or of Cuneo, but which is Italian, European, worldwide.*** I am a leader who leads, not a leader who follows. Besides and above all, I go against the current; I will never yield and I will always be on the watch, especially when the changing wind swells the sails of my destiny." After achieving power, he spoke to his coquettish and official biographer Signora Sarfatti about his desire to be *someone:* "Yes, I am possessed by this mania. It inflames, gnaws and consumes me, like a physical malady. I want to make a mark on history with my will, like a lion with his claws."

All Mussolini's doctrinal and moral somersaults and divagations, all his outward allegiance to varied and contradictory political theories become intelligible only if it is borne in mind that he cannot pay even lip-service to ideas unless he can utilize them as instruments of his ambition for power, unless he can convince himself of the identity between an idea and his will for power. With him, as with so many men of action, the utterance of an idea and the conviction that he alone can be its standard-bearer are inseparable. Since his dominant passion is the pursuit of personal power, his apostasy does not disconcert him in the least. A few years before the Great War, he castigated the corrupters of political principles by hurling at them the definition of conscience as a pair of breeches that can be lowered whenever necessary. In later years, he offered history his own person as one of the most shameless symbols of political hypocrisy, glorifying everything he once condemned, allying himself with his former political and personal enemies, and tearing to pieces whatever sense of solidarity he had at any time professed with the humble and the underprivileged. The same man who warned his socialist comrades against adopting the Nietzschean maxim "Nothing is true, everything is permitted" has made this maxim the cornerstone of his fascist philosophy of life. As a hater of the bourgeoisie, he saw no reason for becoming sentimental if a "bourgeois son of a bitch" were killed by a bomb. Why should he later become sentimental over the murder of an anti-fascist "son of a bitch"? Why get sentimental if someone should try to kill the King, asked Mussolini before the Great War? Since an attempt on the King's life is an accident to be expected in a King's profession, "why be moved and why weep for the King, 'only' for the King? Why this hysterical, excessive sensibility when it is a question of crowned heads?" After the war, Mussolini's fascist programme demanded a republic in Italy. But after the "March on Rome", a law was passed establishing the death penalty in cases involving the assassination of or the attempt to assassinate the King, the Queen, the Crown Prince, or the Head of the Government–Mussolini.

. . .

Amid all these contradictions, the one concern from which he has never swerved has been his search for power. Truly, he has given us the best definition of fascism by calling it a hierarchy culminating in a pin-point–the pin-point, of course, being himself. Both as a socialist and as a fascist, he has conceived of himself as the infallible leader who must be obeyed. By order, by discipline, by law, by duty, he means subservience to his own person. Perhaps the record of no statesman in history offers as many illogical, inconsistent, and contradictory elements and yet such inflexible faith in his own capacity for leadership as that of Mussolini. Whether at Forlì, as the Duce of a small band of socialists, or at Rome, as the Duce of a large army of fascists, the autocratic bent of his mind, the ex-cathedra character of his pronouncements and the brisk gestures of finality with which he clothes his decisions have always been in evidence. His demand for the conquest of Ethiopia offered him occasion to display in all its plenitude his arrogant sense of pride in his own leadership. With rare political subtlety combined with audacious truculence, he achieved the most resounding personal triumph of his entire career by suppressing the independence of Ethiopia. Little did the fate of his own people matter to him as long as his personal prestige was at stake. When the fall of Addis Ababa sealed the victory of his personal policy, he said to a group of Italian peasants: "I am with you because I know you are with me." And yet, great as his victory in Ethiopia has been, it has by no means appeased his thirst for personal glory. As long as Mussolini lives as the head of the Italian State, the world will know no peace, for this man's constant and restless search for power knows no bounds and no restraint. He has taken advantage and he will continue to take advantage of any situation that will help him to project his personality, so as to make it dominant not only in Italy but also in Europe and even the rest of the Western world. Having satisfied his ambition to become the undisputed master of forty million people, he has achieved success in crushing a free African state; he has aided and abetted in the establishment of clerical fascism in Austria, the Nazi victory in Germany, the breakdown of the League of Nations system, and the fascist attempt to control Spain. He will never stop fomenting disorder, arousing hatred, and threatening war as long as he envisages himself as the founder of a new world politic, as long as there lies before him the formidable temptation of seeing the fascist mentality, as incarnated in his own person, dominate the Western world.

Mussolini the socialist was as imperious, fiery, dictatorial, and disdainful as is Mussolini the fascist. He has always been refractory to any law, to any norm tending to restrict his personal will. Hence his aversion to liberalism, to democracy and to parliamentary institutions. The closer one studies his socialist career, the more one realizes how irregular he was as a party member. He thoroughly enjoyed being the Duce of the socialist party, but when it refused to embrace his views contemplating intervention in the Great War though he had for weeks insisted upon a policy of absolute neutrality, he resigned his post as editor of the *Avanti!* and advocated intervention. For several years, from 1914 until 1920, he played a minor rôle in national politics. The years of his greatest isolation were those immediately following the war; the socialists were too strong, but it must be said that he never despaired. Fighting for power with an extraordinary singleness of purpose, an astute political sense, and a complete disregard for scruples, he manœuvred himself into a strong position with the "March on Rome" in October 1922. By 1925, after ruthlessly destroying all traces of serious opposition, he found his way clear to establishing a totalitarian regime. Thereafter, the Duce of a political party and a well-organized militia became the Duce of a state.

Nationalism, patriotism, Italy, the interests of the Italian people are mere words to him, mere symbols of sentiments which he can and does use and exploit to his own advantage with superlative effectiveness. Italy, the nation, the national interest are shibboleths to him, just as socialism, the social revolution, human welfare were shibboleths to him. Few are the men in history who have seen their consuming ambition and love of power as effectually realized as Mussolini. He has had the satisfaction of becoming what he always wanted to be–a duce, a superman beyond good and evil, a "man become god". No one has more effectively described Mussolini than Mussolini himself, when in the year 1910, at the age of twenty-seven, he uttered the words: "Within me, I recognize no one superior to myself."

VI. IN QUEST OF MEANING: TWO VIEWS ON THE NATURE OF ITALIAN FASCISM

WHAT HAS FASCISM *been in the history of the twentieth century and why did it assume a primordial ideology, structure and power, in Italy? Many students have attempted to grapple with both aspects of this question and the answers have been as divergent as the historical, philosophical, ideological, or social-scientific points of view from which they stemmed. Social psychology and psychoanalysis, too, have been adopted as instruments of understanding, and eschatological and chiliastic doctrines have dealt with the depths of modern totalitarian phenomena. In its own way, this collection of readings as a whole has its* raison d'être *in the attempt to suggest alternative responses to the second part of that fundamental question. From among many diverse "witnesses" we could have called upon to "testify"* directly *in answer to that question, two have been selected here for a number of reasons, not least among them the fact that in political tradition, ideological background, and historical experience Don Luigi Sturzo and Angelo Tasca derived from almost diametrically opposed spiritual worlds. What they may be said to have had in common is the integrity of their moral personalities face to face with all forms of modern totalitarian dominations and their resistance against these dominations. Whether and to what extent Don*

Sturzo the Christian democrat and Tasca the former Marxist and socialist democrat are concordant in their fundamental views on the sources and nature of Italian Fascism must be judged on the basis of their lives and total work, but the selections from their different studies of Fascism in Italy may perhaps suggest the similarities and the divergences in their approach to the sources of the historic problem.

Luigi Sturzo, the exiled anti-Fascist Catholic leader of the Popolari, in his book on Italy and Fascism (1926) had focused attention upon the defections of the pre-Fascist political class but saw no logic in some commonly held opinions which viewed Fascism as the necessary or inevitable outcome of those defections. The realm of alternative choices toward the resolution of the post-1919 Italian political crisis remained open to the end, to the Royal and Fascist coup de main of October 1922. For Sturzo, what was missed and misjudged in the rise of Fascism to power was the profoundly deviationist, counterhistorical character it possessed, the extent to which the triumph of Fascism cut the ground from under the potentially democratic tradition of the Risorgimento and the essentially European character of modern Italian life, politics, and civilization.

Angelo Tasca (who adopted the pseudonym of Angelo Rossi), in a work which was published twelve years after Sturzo's book—The Rise of Italian Fascism (1938)—and which, almost immediately became a sort of classic in its own right, tackled many of the same problems relating to the Italian historic tradition and the European character of the post-war crisis. His approach, however, was not only mono-

graphic, particularized, localized in time practically only to the four years preceding the advent of Fascism; it also came from a different angle of vision. For Tasca, a great part of the problem must be sought not merely in the "defections" of the Italian liberal political classes but also in the sources of the socialist "revolution that failed" in Italy and in Europe in the post-war period. That Tasca should have called attention to this aspect of the question is not surprising since few surpassed him for his direct acquaintance with the rise and fall of the Italian pre-Fascist socialist movement. He had been a militant in the socialist movement since 1907, and in 1919–21 he was close to Antonio Gramsci. With Gramsci, Togliatti, Bordiga, Terracini, and a few others, Tasca became one of the founders of the Italian Communist Party in 1921. In 1926 he emigrated to Soviet Russia where, after Gramsci's arrest and imprisonment, he represented the PCI in the Third International. In 1929, after the full assertion of Stalin's dictatorship in Russia, Tasca became an exile again—against Communism as he had formerly been against Fascism. In France, Tasca worked with the Italian anti-Fascist emigré *groups and became foreign affairs editor of the socialist newspaper* Populaire. *After the fall of France in 1940 he became a member of the Resistance—as a French citizen. He died in 1960, leaving a rich legacy of personal and official documents indispensable for the study of Italian socialism and Communism. His book on the rise of Fascism was written at the height of his rejection of both Fascist and Communist totalitarianisms.*

Fascism as a Deviation of Italian History*

LUIGI STURZO

THE IRREMEDIABLE CONTRADICTION between the character and aims of Fascism and the natural and historical mission of the Kingdom of Italy, as it has evolved from the time of its formation to the present day, seems to the present writer self-evident. If, moreover, we consider Italian Fascism in the light of the general situation of post-war Europe, we can but affirm once again that it is an abnormal phenomenon which will disappear as Europe, recovering from the effects of the war, gradually attains the necessary conditions for peace, economic equilibrium and the prevalence of the democratic *régime*.

As an abnormal phenomenon Fascism is a war product which found in Italy circumstances propitious to the conquest of power; this was due principally to the decadence of the political class which not only failed to offer any resistance, but favoured the new movement to the point of surrendering all dignity and even the seats of government. Fascism owes its success to the attitude of the wealthy and conservative classes which, thanks to this new force, have maintained their hold on the powers of the State, overcoming the Socialists on the one hand and the Popolari on the other.

This revolutionary attitude on the part of the con-

* From Luigi Sturzo, *Italy and Fascism*, 286–95. Translated by Barbara Barclay Carter, with a Preface by Gilbert Murray. Reprinted by permission of Faber and Faber Ltd.

servatives merely continues the tactics they have constantly employed in order to preserve their hold on the policy of the country. Thus they were Liberal Conservatives during the predominance of the Left, and are Fascist Conservatives in the 'New Era'.

The persistence, under varying political forms, of a conservative domination in revolutionary guise, does not mean that power has ever been held by a real Conservative Party, responsible for its actions and with a programme to be defended against the other parties. Its predominance has been reached through the medium of the men, parties, and ideologies which, at a given moment, have met with success and risen to the top.

This was possible only through a species of dictatorship, masked or apparent; Italy's real dictators have been Cavour under the method of liberty, Depretis and Giolitti under the method of transformism, Mussolini under the method of reaction. Crispi was said to have a dictator's fist, but in spite of appearances he was less of a dictator than any of them, or was so only in so far as he failed to escape from the influence of the conservative classes.

At the centre or on the apex of the conservative classes stands the Dynasty, which has also known its phases of Liberalism, Transformism and Fascism. In Italy the Monarchy has always been known as constitutional and, from 1848 onwards, the Kings of the House of Savoy were constitutional in the accepted sense of the word–that is, reigning but not governing, personally nonresponsible, with responsible Ministers. The first King of Italy, Victor Emmanuel II, earned the title of *Il Re Galantuomo* because he kept faith to the Constitution, at a time when other Italian Kings and Princes went back on their word and repudiated it. But the manner of the 'Royal Conquest' by which the unity of Italy was achieved, the conception of Italy as a military State and the ally of the Central Empires, the exercise of political power for sixty-five years by an electorate restricted, under a property qualification, to a single class–universal suffrage was attained only in 1913–could result only in binding the Dynasty to the conservative classes. The Conservatives have been and are the mainstay of the Monarchy. Only on the day when Mussolini threw aside his republican leanings could he secure their unconditional support and thus his own triumph.

Had there been no war, Italy might still have had a disguised dictator in the person of Giolitti, or of others of his stamp, until the new forces, the parties with a following among the masses, came into their own. Even so, if the House of Savoy had linked its destinies with those of the conservative classes, the existence of the Monarchy might have been called in question.

This the Conservatives felt instinctively when the Socialists, on the one hand, and the Popolari, on the other, were bringing the working and middle classes, consciously organized, into economic and political life. Therefore, they did not hesitate to throw themselves into the arms of a revolution, confident that the Monarchy would uphold them in the hour of danger. The duel was not fought out, for the organized parties, the Socialists and the Popolari, did not give decisive battle. They were deceived as to the nature and bearings of the Fascist phenomenon, judging it only as something abnormal and therefore transitory, and failing to see that, in substance, it was the political agency of the conservative classes.

Thus three forces are united, the conservative classes, the Monarchy, and Fascism, the last armed with dictatorial power, acting as the political agency of the two former. It is only natural that Fascism should seek to assimilate all the forces of the nation, including the army, to which it has juxtaposed the National Militia—that is to say, a party militia—and the economic system, to which it has given a party form of corporate organization in order to subject it to a system of State paternalism.

Centralization, which has corroded the modern continental State, is thus carried to its logical extreme. The State is become Leviathan, assimilating every other force, the embodiment of an oppressive political pantheism. There is no longer any room for man, for the free individual, for the sake of whom State and Society exist. Instead, man exists for the sake of the State. The apotheosis of the State or, as it is now called, the Nation, is complete. In practice, and in the Fascist conception, the State is the Government. Hence the necessity of securing the power to the Dictator and his Party, and thus to the classes of which the Dictator and his Party are the political agents. The head of the Government is responsible to the King alone, but the King is no longer morally free to change the head of the Government since he no longer finds in the political edifice an element of counterthrust on which to lean in effecting the change. Here is an abnormal innovation no longer in conformity with the historical tradition of the Kingdom of Italy. It is the starting point for the Second Risorgimento. For the First Risorgimento ended with the abolition of the conservative Constitution of Charles Albert, and with the creation of a morally and politically irremovable head of the executive power.

When one reads the chorus of praise, the homage, the adulation rising to Mussolini from various bodies and from representative men of Italy, and even from a section of the world abroad which still approves of his methods, one has the impression that, in the mind of the people, certain figures and symbols are being subtly displaced by others. Mussolini is Dictator, though without the Crown. . . .

Against this historical development stands its opposite, the participation, with a certain degree of autonomy, of the middle and working classes in political power. During the Risorgimento the Mazzinians, Republicans, Federalists, and Neo-Guelfs who, in their different ways, expressed the antithesis to the conservative currents and to the Monarchical and unitary conception, and represented more closely popular tendencies, were mostly assimilated or destroyed in the attainment of Italian unity and independence by means of the Royal Conquest. The remainder formed the groups of the Left and the Opposition, and later on gave birth to the Radical and Workers' Parties.

On the fall of the Right in 1876, the transformist Left, acting on behalf of the middle classes, fulfilled a part of the social aspirations of the masses, but though they felt their pressure, took care to withhold political power from the masses themselves. This pressure became urgent through the Socialist Party which, however, did not attain real political efficiency until the grant of universal suffrage in 1913 and of

P.R. in 1919. The latter year saw the rise of the Popular Party, which competed with the Socialists and neutralized their strength. But this was the moment when the post-war economic and political difficulties reached their height. We have seen how the old political class had reached a crisis; how it feared the free and autonomous participation of the people in power, their growing political consciousness, their organization in parties and trade unions, and how it feared too their errors and vagaries. Having neither strength to resist this movement nor belief in its future, the old political class preferred the adventure of Fascism and the sacrifice of constitutional liberty.

The defeat of the Socialist parties and the Popular Party is the result not only of the Fascist reaction in 1925, but also, as we have seen, of their position in the period between 1919 and 1922. In brief, the Socialists by persisting in their refusal to share in the Government for fear of losing the confidence of the masses, and by proclaiming a revolution which they did not and could not carry out, forfeited the fruits of their thirty years of labour. The Popolari, on the other hand, caught in the toils of participation in the Government, to which they had assented in order to defend the country from the Bolshevist currents and to safeguard the existence of Parliament itself, were bound, in a certain measure, to share the fate of the decaying political class, bearing at one and the same time its responsibilities and its attacks.

But both Socialists and Popolari, from different and opposed standpoints, counted on the political maturity of the masses and on their power of resistance; but these proved unequal to the reactionary offensive.

Here is the knot of the present situation in Italy, making of the future a source of anxiety and of present events food for meditation. It would seem that the situation to-day is a repetition of the situation at the time of the Risorgimento, which was the work of the intellectual and wealthy classes rather than of the people. To-day, when the suppression of every dissenting force and every independent current of thought may be considered complete, the people of Italy look on, silent and timorous, while others form a chorus round the triumphal car of the victor. True, these seem an innumerable host only because the places where they assemble are small, and because their shouts divert attention from the silence of those who mutely stand by; but even so, they cannot be accounted few.

The Socialist Party is re-organizing; the Popular Party is re-organizing. Many have fallen by the way-side or have left the field. Others are abroad. Others have withdrawn from the struggle, considering the plight of their families. Such parties can no longer play an active part; they serve merely as signs of protest and as guide posts for the future. The same applies to the other ever dwindling Opposition and anti-Fascist groups which have taken the old names of Liberals and Democrats.

What remains of their past is a banner and a programme. Their aspiration is that the middle and working classes of Italy should regain their autonomy and personality and once more do battle for a share in political power and in the policy of their country.

The Fascisti seek the total elimination of these centres of resistance from the new national life; but these parties and groups seek to live on so as to renew the struggle when the moment comes. No matter whether in their present form or in others more suitable, the anti-Fascist groups and parties will persist, even if they are suppressed by decree, for they discharge a social function. The people, it is true, remains inert, but it feels the need to have about it a means of defence, an issue from crises and convulsions, a haven in time of storm.

Yet the people, which to-day seems to look on passively, finds no impulse to act or react in the names of the discomfited men and parties, for neither in their programmes nor in their tactics does it see anything that could be the starting point or goal of fresh action.

In fact, parliamentary action is over; the moral question has become confused with the system and *régime;* economic problems are pressing, but they are absorbed or neutralized by certain forms of prosperity; the question of constitutional liberty is keenly felt only by the political classes and parties, not by the masses who had never reached the point of sharing actively and positively in political life. Moreover, the novelty of Fascist enterprises, the large output of laws, the exalted tone of propaganda and the harangues on the Roman Empire, are bewildering, tending to create belief in an imaginary life and to foster a state of mind of messianic expectation.

This period calls for reflection, for the husbanding of strength, for the cautious avoidance of hazardous adventures, for the formation of reliable nuclei, for the elaboration of necessary reforms with a view to a democratic renaissance. Italy's *institutional prob-*

lem will have to be brought back into the foreground; it will be necessary to face in its entirety the unsolved problem left by the Risorgimento—the problem, that is, of the complete participation of the people in political life, which was raised, each in his own way, by Mazzini, by Cattaneo, and then successively by the Radicals, the Socialists, and the Christian Democrats, afterwards the Popular Party.

This problem the present dictatorship has to-day made more acute, but it is inherent in the Kingdom of Italy. The constitutional form of the new Kingdom was only a means for the conquest of independence and unity, and never achieved the true substance of liberty or a truly democratic *régime.* Hence, under the parliamentary formula, oligarchies and dictatorships have grown up, culminating in the last, which has trampled down even the outward forms of constitutionalism and openly set up an armed organization.

Now every party in disagreement with the present state of things, and conceiving of political life as the active participation of the people in the work of government, every party conscious of having survived the abrogation of the Albertine Constitution, and not having been identified with it, would do well to reconsider the problem of true democracy, such as it may be realized in Italy to-morrow, and to prepare for this event which cannot fail to come about.

But to do so, such parties must reconsider much of their own past and appraise it in relation to the events of Italian life from the Risorgimento till today. Then will it be seen that a fundamental error, of which the consequences are now graver than ever, was made in the system of State centralization, the subjection of all local life to political power and the suppression of all regional traditions and self-government. Citizens who are not free to govern themselves in their native place, who are not accustomed to direct responsibility in local life, who do not practice social self-control, who lack training in the exercise of power in their own region, are no longer capable of independent, free and responsible participation in national life. Vice versa, the men in the Government or the Civil Service, who are accustomed to govern and direct everything, concentrating local power in a few hands, controlling and encroaching upon the whole of provincial and regional life, not only believe that others are incapable of government but that the encroachments of the central power are indispensable. And the central power, once entered upon the road of State intervention, pursues it to the end, ever increasing in extent and intensity, and finally resulting in oligarchies and dictatorships.

Nor is this enough. The institutional question must be faced anew. The present writer has long upheld the extension of universal suffrage to women, Proportional Representation, an elective Senate. But it is necessary to reconsider even the question of the Monarchy–whether in Italy, the form most favourable to the advent of democracy is that of Monarchy or Republic. The question was never raised before the war; there were still too many Kings and Emperors in Europe, and it is only just to recognize that in the attainment of Italian unity, the Monarchy played its part. Since the war republican experiments in Europe have multiplied, and the democratic impulse has progressed, but on the other hand in the countries where the constitution is weak, reactionary oligarchies have been either created or strengthened. Is it a problem grown acute with Fascism, or was it in existence before? Is it to-day seen more clearly only because it has been thrown into greater relief?

Finally, the problem of the trade unions must be faced, for the attempt to solve it by the recognition of the monopolistic Fascist corporations in a setting of State paternalism, does not meet the requirements of modern economic life, either in Italy or elsewhere. At the same time the old type of free trade union, at the mercy of parties, with no other guarantee than the right to strike, cannot long suffice. All trade unions must have a legal personality, the right to representation, and responsibility for their actions. Economic arbitration should come as the result of direct organization rather than of State coercion and intervention. The unions, both of workers and employers, should share in the free play of economic forces with their own responsibilities and safeguards, but should have no privileges nor yet be reduced to dependence on the State.

On these three hinges–decentralization and local autonomy, the institutional problem, the freedom and responsibility of trade unions–may be hung, a new democracy, which, whenever a crisis makes its coming possible, will be able to face reaction.

In face of those who for three years have proclaimed the 'revolution' and armed themselves with the 'rights of revolution', we must repudiate all revolution based on violence and all revolutionary rights running counter to the moral law. Otherwise Italy would be dragged in a grievous chain of struggles and civil wars, with the sanguinary alternation of factions in place of the free alternation of parties.

But when the changing of the present Fascist order and the revision of institutions becomes possible, their revision will be a patriotic duty that not even force may hinder. For when a question enters into the consciousness of the people it cannot long remain without solution.

The Italian Popular Party has always opposed State centralization and raised the questions of local autonomy, trade unionism and the reform of the Senate. It has never considered the monarchical question. Yet even the first two questions which were raised in the teeth of the Democratic-Liberal–in substance, Conservative–tradition, were considered chiefly from their administrative and economic side and only secondarily from their political side. Now they appear purely political in relation to the question whether *and by what means the future of Italy can be made one of democracy.*

Fascism and the European Crisis of the Twentieth Century*

ANGELO TASCA

WHEN THE POST-WAR CRISIS began, Italian national unity had been established for barely fifty years, and the part played by the masses in winning it had been small. After 1870 the old oligarchies had only one aim in view: to suppress the fourth estate and deprive it of every means to direct action and power. On this point the conflicting forces of Vatican and monarchy were agreed. There were no democratic or revolutionary traditions, and the parliamentary system had remained an artificial improvisation grafted on to the life of the nation, whose growth had not been helped by the corrupt methods of Giolitti's reformism. The only really democratic force was the working-class and socialist movement, but this was handicapped by its narrow outlook and concentration on municipal affairs. Nevertheless the people —workers, artisans and peasants—with the traditions of their own independent institutions, were slowly making their weight felt in the state, when their progress was interrupted by the war. This was begun and carried on in Italy as a civil war, and coincided with a grave crisis in the ruling classes. The war

* From Angelo Tasca [A. Rossi], *The Rise of Italian Fascism*. Translated by Peter and Dorothy Wait, with a Preface by Herman Finer (London, 1938; New York: Howard Fertig, Inc., 1966), 323–24, 336–46, 347–52. Reprinted by permission.

was followed by depression and disorder: economic crisis in the country, which was exhausted and dislocated by the effort of victory; moral crisis among the people who, 'while being and feeling victorious, were suffering the humiliation and crisis of the vanquished'.

Within these wider causes there were other factors which helped to alter the course and the outcome of Italy's post-war history: the failure of the socialist movement; the reactionaries' and particularly the landowners' offensive in the form of military action and territorial conquest; the economic crisis of 1921; the help and complicity of the state and its dependent bodies; the discrediting of Parliament; the part played by Mussolini.

. . .

The Italy of 1919–1922 lacked political leaders. Giolitti's mentality was pre-war, and when he returned to power in 1920 he was in his seventy-eighth year. The others, Nitti, Bonomi, Orlando, Salandra, all suffered from the same handicap: they were good scholars, but too academic to be able to deal properly with the post-war situation. The socialists had a few first-rate men, mostly on the right, but they were hampered by the conflict of doctrines inside the party and the working-class movement. The personal qualities of some of the communist leaders, such as Gramsci and Bordiga, could not outweigh the damage done by hopelessly wrong-headed tactics, and sometimes aggravated it. The maximalist socialists were a body without a head. Lamartine's description of a Girondin chief applied to most of their leaders: 'One of those complaisant idols of which people make anything they wish except a man.'

Italian socialism had need of a man, several men, in order to win, or, which came to the same thing, to avoid being wiped out. This was why Mussolini was able to reduce Italy to his own size and fill the entire horizon. With his advent the rule of 'principle' came to an end, and his own personal adventure became that of Italy itself. For the better understanding of this crisis it is possible and indeed essential to trace back over centuries its remote and fundamental causes: the configuration of the land; the economic and social structure; the long enslavement of the people; the recent liberation, barely tolerated by some, barely assimilated by others. But these causes were not bound, inevitably, to lead to the events of the years 1919–1922 as they actually took place, with all their changes, their possibilities and their final result. New forces were growing up in Italy, alongside the prevalent lethargy, and for a certain space of time these balanced each other. In such cases momentary influences, including luck, may be decisive. The slightest variation may upset the balance and change the whole situation. Then it is that the actions of one man become of first importance, and history becomes a drama in which everything is linked up and nothing pre-determined, in which the epilogue may be changed up to the last minute, so long as the actors–individuals or groups–do not themselves rush towards the catastrophe. Contrary to a common belief, circumstances do not always of themselves create the men who are needed. Past history now provides a proof.

Fascism is a dictatorship; such is the starting-point of all definitions that have so far been attempted. Beyond that there is no agreement. Dictatorship of capitalism 'in the period of its decline', dictatorship of large-scale capitalism; dictatorship of finance-capitalism; 'openly terrorist' dictatorship 'of the most reactionary, chauvinist and imperialistic sections of finance-capitalism'; dictatorship of the 'two hundred families'; and so on, until sometimes one meets the definition of fascism narrowed down to the personal dictatorship of Mussolini or Hitler. Someone has said, 'Italian fascism is Mussolini'.

Each of these definitions contains some truth, but none can be accepted as it stands. Further, we shall take care not to produce a new one, which would of course be the right one, a pocket formula, which could be brought out at any moment to clear up our own and everybody else's doubts. Our way of defining fascism is to write its history. We have tried to do this for Italian fascism of the years 1919–1922. A theory of fascism can only be evolved through a study of all its forms, latent or open, modified or unrestrained. For there are many different fascisms, each one made up of numerous, sometimes contradictory tendencies, and capable of developing in such a way that its most characteristic features may be altered. To define fascism is to surprise it during this development, and, in a given country and at a given time, to seize upon its essential differences. It is not a subject with definite attributes which need merely be selected, but the product of a situation from which it cannot be considered separately. The mistakes of the workers' parties, for instance, are as much part of the definition of fascism as the use made of them by the proprietary classes.

The present study of fascism has not been carried beyond the march on Rome, but there is no reason why we should not glance further.[1] Although conditions in Italy ought to be comprehensively reviewed and compared with those in other countries during the years that followed, the present less enterprising method may at least enable us to point out a few common characteristics from which some conclusions can be drawn. For this purpose fascism must be considered in relation to the economic, social, political and psychological conditions from which it sprang; to its own social background and the class struggle; to its tactics, its organization; to its consequences and the regime that it set up; finally to its own programme and ideology.

Fascism is a post-war phenomenon and any attempt to define it by looking for an historical precedent, e.g. in Bonapartism, is fruitless and bound to lead to false conclusions. Foremost among the conditions that made fascism possible was the economic crisis. No crisis, no fascism; and this refers not to any economic crisis, but specifically to the one that settled permanently over the world after the war. The war left the world with industrial capacity beyond its immediate needs and a complete lack of co-ordination between the various branches of production, complicated by a reduced purchasing power in all countries. The result was over-production and

[1] Some use has here been made of research work undertaken for a more general history of the post-war world, which, given sufficient time, means and strength, I hope to complete and publish later on.

famine, inflation and paralysis. We are no longer faced by classical crises, which rise from a terrible slump to a still higher rate of production and consumption. The 'periodic' crises have been succeeded by 'chronic stagnation with slight fluctuations', the 'alternation of relatively short boom and relatively long depression', foretold by Engels more than fifty years ago. Even in the United States, where crises are more oscillatory owing to the possibilities of the home market, the existence of an irreducible mass of several million unemployed points to a new kind of depression. Fascism is bred in these depressions and forms part of the reaction to them. In countries without the large home market of the U.S.A., the British Empire, the U.S.S.R., depressions are more or less incurable. Economic discomfort fuses readily with nationalist aspirations and talk of 'a place in the sun'. This results on the one hand in isolation and the aggravation of the more artificial and parasitical aspects of the economic system, on the other in the illusion that the 'encirclement' can be broken by seeking some violent solution beyond the frontiers. The capitalist system, having to a great extent lost its resiliency, oscillates no longer between depression and boom, but between autarchy and war.[2]

[2] In this sense, therefore, it is true that fascism is the fruit of capitalism in decline and the expression of a retrograde economic system. It is also true, though inadequate, to say: 'to conquer fascism we must conquer the depression', and 'fascism must be fought in the world of economics'. Economic revival undoubtedly checks fascism, but by itself it cannot eliminate the danger altogether. In March 1937 the socialist minister Spaak, speaking of the Rexist movement, said: 'I used to think the eventual success of our steady campaign against the depression would be enough to stamp out this lawless, bold and dangerous propaganda. I frankly admit that I was wrong, and I realize to-day that a move-

In every country the end of the war and the beginning of the depression saw fairly considerable alterations in social status. The creation of a mass of *nouveaux riches,* and distinct changes in the traditional forms of capitalism resulted in the emergence of a new *bourgeoisie.* Practically all producers had become so used to exceptional war-time profits that they had lost sight of the notion of the rigidity of cost price, while the stimulus of competition had been entirely removed. Such considerations were always resurrected when workers' wages had to be discussed, but they had really ceased to operate, and almost everywhere capitalists were conscious that they could no longer manage without the direct help of the state. Its seizure by any possible means became for them a matter of life-and-death importance.

On the other hand, the war had set the popular masses in movement, and after the war this movement was accelerated. The organization of the workers' parties and the syndicates was breaking down under the pressure of the hundreds of thousands and millions of new members. They had no great stability, and the high tide was quickly followed by a rapid ebb. Moreover, in spite of the growth of the old organizations, there was a large body of waverers who remained outside, ready to rush in any direction. This

---

ment like Rex cannot be fought by a mere improvement of economic conditions. Although the work of improvement must go on, we have got to carry the struggle on to political and even sentimental ground.'

In addition, national boundaries to-day render the struggle against the depression hopeless. And a decisive victory against fascism can only be gained on the political plane by the reconstruction of Europe, after the deadly magic circle of autarchies has been broken and the way found once more to collaboration and unity.

body has been referred to as the 'middle classes'; but it must be emphasized that they were not the middle classes of the classical period of capitalism, absorbed after each crisis into the machinery of increased production and into a new proletariat. The post-war middle classes no longer had even the chance of joining the proletariat; the depression barred both their rise into the *bourgeoisie* and their descent into the proletariat. This petty and middle *bourgeoisie,* which found itself everywhere excluded, formed the backbone of fascism in Italy and everywhere else. But the expression 'middle class' must be given a wider meaning, to include the son of the family waiting for a job or for his inheritance to *declassés* of all kinds, temporary or permanent, from the half-pay officer to the *lumpenproletarier,* from the strike-breaker to the jobless intellectual. It includes workers who are more conscious of being ex-servicemen or unemployed than of their class, from which they break away in spirit to join the ranks of its enemies.

With the coming of peace the long pent-up demands of the masses were released, at a time when, as a result of the war, there was less than ever to satisfy them. A tendency to hoard available resources rather than find better ways of sharing them brought the problem of power into the foreground. Three factors combined to lead the way to fascism: the intensification of the class struggle, its increasingly political character, and the relative equality of the opposing forces. Given the first two, the third is of crucial importance. Such equality is paralysing to any form of government, whether it be a national coalition, a combination of left-wing parties, or a social democratic majority. So long as it continues and no better form of government is found, the state is at the mercy of blind upheavals caused by some instinct of self-preservation, by the defence of threatened privileges, and by the aspirations of classes that have been upset and thrown out of gear by the depression. By abandoning the attempt to gain a solution by legal methods, the working classes turn to the creation of a 'second power', within the state and opposed to it; the *bourgeoisie* then has recourse either to 'reactionary transformation of the state' or to fascist violence.

Amongst the general conditions of fascism that should be mentioned is the existence of a kind of 'climate', a special atmosphere of excitement and frenzy; this is so indispensable, both before and after victory, that the party leaders have to strain every nerve to keep it up. In this atmosphere all reactions are strained, all sense of proportion is distorted, and ordinary standards vanish. Psychological shock becomes as necessary as drugs to an addict. Delirium is exalted as normality. Fascism cannot be dismissed as mere war psychosis (any more than the Commune could be dismissed as a '*fièvre obsidionale*'); the history of fascism, however, is one of the most remarkable and disturbing chapters of social pathology.

Fascism finds its chief support in the post-war middle class, whose main characteristics we have just described. Must fascism, therefore, be defined as a middle-class movement taken up and exploited by reactionary capitalism? There is much truth in this definition, but it cannot be accepted without reservations. The social significance of a movement is not entirely decided by its social make-up. Although most of the supporters of fascism are recruited from the middle classes, its first historic role is that of the exterminator of working-class parties and syndicates. Afterwards, whatever its pretensions or its supporters, it takes a hand in the capitalist offensive. The suppression of the independent workers' organizations permanently alters the balance of social power. Fascists and capitalists can no longer behave as if these organizations had not been suppressed. Even when fascism pretends to play the part of arbitrator between capital and labour, it puts one of the parties in an inferior position–by destroying its independence–from which it can only free itself by throwing off fascism altogether.

It was chiefly the urban middle classes which were swept into fascism. In July 1919 Mussolini believed, not only that fascism was fated to remain 'a minority movement', but that it could not 'spread outside the towns'. And although Italian fascism was chiefly established, after 1921, through the influx of country-folk into its ranks,[3] its leaders were largely drawn from the middle classes in the towns, or were the sons of landowners–officers, students–town-dwellers with no desire to play the part of Cincinnatus, once they were back from the front. They were much more anxious to conquer the towns, the first step towards political power, than to be the leaders in their village. Further, fascism was never successful when confined to purely country districts, and the impulse to victory came less from the Po valley cam-

[3] Pp. 198–199.

paigns than from Rome and Milan. The big cities always played the leading part.

Fascism finds its chief support in those members of the middle class who either have or think they have no independent economic standing, and are thus easily 'liquidated' or absorbed into the new political framework provided by fascism. It is not pure chance which makes the French peasant oppose fascism so obstinately: he will obviously continue to do so as long as his economic basis–the patch of ground he owns and tills–and his more or less real independence are threatened. In the Balkans all the authoritarian regimes–bred in the great cities–were set up in face of the violent resistance of the peasants, who mostly supported opposition parties (National-Zaranist party in Romania, the Croat peasant party in Jugo-Slavia, the 'Agrarians' in Bulgaria).[4] In all these countries the land reform carried out after the war had created an important class of peasant proprietors, who remained anti-fascist even in subjection; while in contrast the absence of such reforms, or excessive slowness in carrying them out, have made of fascism a danger or a success in Italy, Germany and Spain.

Another theory that will not hold water represents fascism as a revolutionary movement turned reactionary under the influence of the ruling classes. Fascism is reactionary from the start. Its first steps are helped and guided by reactionary influence, and its intervention completely upsets the political and so-

[4] This also shows how difficult it is for the peasants to defend themselves against attacks from the towns and capitals, unless they have dependable allies. The alliance of the peasants with the urban proletariat is a necessity and a safeguard for both.

cial equilibrium.[5] The coincidence of fascist development and the political and economic offensive of the possessing classes is a common phenomenon. Italian fascism did not begin to be important until 1921, when 'agrarian slavery' appeared in the Po valley, Tuscany and Apulia, at the same time as the industrialists' attack on workmen's wages and collective labour agreements. National Socialism, in embryo in 1923, did not begin to get under way until after 1928–29, when wages were being cut and the policy of deflation had begun. After 1922 Mussolini's policy coincided with that of the 'liberals' of the *Corriere della Sera,* the conservatives of the *Giornale d'Italia,* the great landowners and the Vatican, namely, to keep the socialists from any share in power; just as Hitler, in 1930, insisted on the breaking up of the great coalition and the exclusion of the socialists from the Prussian government.

The middle classes had to some extent been caught up by the wave of popular feeling in the years 1919–20, but the inability of the socialist movement to find any solution had cooled them off. Tactless insistence on the 'dictatorship of the proletariat', although this was nothing but a form of words, had helped them to change their minds. Feeling that their pockets and their beliefs were threatened by the socialist movement, they turned towards fascism. All their latent hatred of the man in cap and blouse now came to the surface, finding expression on the one

[5] The importance of this intervention and of its effects depends on the balance held between the two great opposite forces, a balance which may be upset by the appearance of marginal or 'interstitial' forces. It is therefore impossible to judge the influence of the middle classes simply from a numerical point of view.

hand in savage attacks on the workers,[6] on the other in a vague desire for independence, and even a kind of idealism. This idealism and the new language it created made its own contribution to the victory of the possessing classes, winning over for them a section of the masses with which they had entirely lost touch.

The relations between middle-class fascism and the capitalist offensive were very close at the start, and have remained so for a long time. Does this mean that they are incapable of development and change? Only a very detailed analysis of these relations in the different countries at different times could lead one to any conclusion on this question; while it must be remembered that, whatever the relations may be, they are always affected and distorted by the absence of a third power, that of a freely organized labour group.

Fascism is not reaction pure and simple, but reaction employing mass effects, which alone are of any use in the post-war world.[7] Hence the use of demagogic slogans and even of socialist terminology: for a long time Mussolini called his paper a 'socialist daily', and the *Führer's* party still styles itself Na-

[6] A Tuscan squad chief, U. Banchelli, in his *Memoirs of a Fascist,* explains that those who carried out these attacks acted, 'not as fascists, but as sons of lawyers, doctors, tradesmen . . .', and, he adds: 'for long these gangs had only to meet people who looked like workers to attack them without pity.'

[7] Even the Vatican during this period was aiming at strengthening or creating mass Catholic parties nearly everywhere (the *Centrum* in Germany, the *Popolare* party in Italy, *Acción Popular* in Spain).

tional-Socialist. As a result the old political parties often find themselves left high and dry.

But the real originality of fascism lies not so much in its mass tactics or its demagogic programme, as in the all-important and independent part played by tactics at the expense of programme.[8] Giolitti used to say, 'Mussolini has taught me that it is not the programme but the tactics of a revolution against which we must defend ourselves.' The fascist method is tactical rather than doctrinal. Its supreme resort is the *fait accompli,* which is of no effect unless it finally leads to the seizure of power. Absolute power alone enables fascism to overcome its inherent inconsistencies and to maintain its advance, for the spoils can be used to satisfy the most varied appetites, the prestige of victory to attract supporters, and the power of the state to crush its enemies into submission for a long while. This is how the fascist writer Curzio Malaparte, in his *Technique of the Coup d'Etat,* describes the political crisis which preceded the march on Rome: 'These same liberals, democrats, conservatives, while they were summoning the fascists to join the National Bloc, were eager to install Mussolini in the Pantheon of the "saviours of the country" . . . but they were not so ready to resign themselves to the fact that Mussolini's aim was not to save Italy in accordance with the official tradition, but to seize the state, a much more sincere programme than the one he had proclaimed in 1919.'

Hence the importance to fascism of organization, especially armed organization. Every fascist move-

[8] The fascist myth of the 'leader' leads to the same result and necessarily involves the claim to absolute power.

ment has its armed organization, without which it is powerless. This does not mean that every fascist goes about armed, or that the movement has immediate access to arms dumps and arsenals. But its organization is military, with its cadre of officers, discipline, meetings, training, and the firm belief of every member, from top to bottom, that this organization is a necessary and effective instrument for the conquest of power. Fascism always begins by declaring itself 'anti-party' and ends by turning itself into a political party; in all the great countries, however, its military organization remains its chief characteristic. Mussolini was able to enrol the entire party in the squads in December 1921, and in 1936 de la Rocque could convert his squads into a party, with the same aim of saving the military organization by disguising it. This organization lies at the heart of fascism and determines its very nature.

Must fascism be resisted by military means? The question of force is undoubtedly involved. But the force behind a sound policy must come as a natural consequence of that policy. Military organization may be very extensively developed, but if it is out of touch with the country its position becomes desperate; this was the case with the fascist squads in the middle of 1921 and the socialist *Schutzbund* in Austria in February 1934. Both Mussolini and Hitler, on the other hand, won their chief victories on the political field (the Facta crisis in October 1922, and the von Schleicher crisis in January 1933).

. . .

To complete this analysis of the nature of fascism we must study the fruit it bears: its consequences, not only inside each country, but also on an international scale, which are closely inter-connected.

Wherever fascism is established the most important consequence, on which all the others depend, is the elimination of the people from all share in political activity. 'Constitutional reform', the suppression of parliament, and the totalitarian character of the regime cannot be judged by themselves, but only in relation to their aims and their results. Fascism is not merely the substitution of one political regime for another; it is the disappearance of political life itself, since this becomes a state function and monopoly. Political doctrines circulate, are abandoned or modified, but the people have nothing to do with their adoption or their fluctuations. Even when syndicates, or even a party, continue to exist, they are mere instruments, subordinate branches of the state. By becoming part of the machinery of state their nature does not undergo any change; they merely become instruments in the second degree, the instruments of instruments. With the removal of all freedom and independence from their institutions the people are reduced to a malleable raw material whose properties of resistance and yield can be calculated and controlled. They still take part in parades and demonstrations, and may be kept in a constant state of alertness and tension; but this is simply part of the drill and never approaches the level of political consciousness.

In this system there is no room for the fatal illusion, long held by the communists, that fascism might do some good by destroying 'democratic illusions'. The Italian communists actually announced in May 1921 that: 'It is true that White reaction is celebrating a few ephemeral victories over an enemy which is paying dear for its unpreparedness, but it is destroying the democratic and liberal illusion and breaking down the influence of social democracy among the masses.' And in the resolution of the Presidium of the Communist International, published in January 1934, the following statement concerning Germany may be read: 'The establishment of an undisguised fascist dictatorship, by dispelling the democratic illusions of the masses and liberating them from the influence of social democracy, is accelerating Germany's advance towards the proletarian revolution.' This is not the place for a detailed criticism of this conception, which the Communist International has never abandoned in spite of all its changes of front, and we need only record that fascism suppresses not only 'democratic illusions', but the workers' and socialist movement which is subject to them. Fascism is like a completely successful operation: the patient dies and all his illusions are removed.

By reducing the people to a mere instrument, fascism destroys the nation. This aspect of the system tends to pass unnoticed, disguised by the violent nationalist frenzy that fascism cultivates. National conscience as conceived in the nineteenth century by Mazzini, the prophet of the nation state, is ousted by state expediency. For him nations could not exist without free peoples, any more than humanity could exist without free nations. The winning of political liberty and the winning of national independence spring from the same instinctive urge, and in the best Jacobin and romantic tradition, 'patriot' and 'democrat' are identical. For Mazzini the awakening of national consciousness was no more than an essential step towards the formation of European consciousness: 'Young Italy' could only fulfil itself in 'Young Europe'.

Such conceptions take us far from fascism, while at the same time explaining why the fascists mean to destroy the working-class and socialist movement. Since the end of the nineteenth century socialism has almost everywhere taken the place of democracy in initiating the masses into national life. They have taken their place in the nation and state on social grounds. This has brought difficulties in its train and sometimes confusion and crisis, but it remains a great historical fact that the masses brought the whole weight of their needs and hopes with them into national life, and thenceforward it was impossible for this life to be organized on any but a higher level of conscience, liberty and individual well-being. For the fascists, on the other hand, the people are only the tool of their 'will to power'. This is inspired by a furious nationalism, which takes over the socialists' demands only to adapt them to serve their own purposes. The slogans of the class struggle in its narrowest sense become the passwords of armed strife between nations: 'young' nations versus 'old', 'poor' nations versus 'satiated', 'proletarian' nations versus 'plutocratic'. Hence in all forms of national socialism the nationalism inevitably absorbs the socialism, and in every fascist 'armed nation' the army swallows up the nation.[9]

This leads equally to autarchy and war. The eco-

[9] In fascist jargon, the very expression 'armed nation' has become suspect and is being replaced by that of 'military nation', 'warrior nation', etc.

nomic difficulties and contradictions of the fascist regimes speed up the process,[10] but they are not the sole causes. The fascist systems are not only 'driven' into war, all their activities lead up to it, and it provides the opportunities and the atmosphere they need. Though choice there may be, they cannot do otherwise than choose war. Preparation for war at a given moment ceases to be a means, and becomes an end in itself, completely changing the economic, social and political structure of the country. Fascism is committed to this preparation and can only fight its way out. For fascism preparation for war does not mean leaving one of many doors open just in case war should unfortunately break out, but leaving only one open and shutting all the rest. War is not merely a possibility which the state must bear in mind, but a certainty and a necessity to which everything is subordinated. Speaking at the meeting of the Corporations on March 23, 1936, Mussolini explained his policy and his ideas for the future as follows:

> 'Italy can and must attain the maximum of economic independence for peace and war. The whole of the Italian economic system must be directed towards this supreme necessity, on which depends the future of the Italian people. I now come to the crux, to what I might call the plan of control for Italian economic policy in the coming fascist era. This plan is determined by one single consideration: that our nation will

[10] In his speech in the Chamber of May 26, 1934, Mussolini said: 'Three-quarters of the Italian economic system, industrial, and agricultural, is supported by the state. . . . We touched bottom some time ago: it would be difficult for us to fall any lower.' This situation must be considered one of the immediate causes of the Italian attack on Ethiopia.

be called to war. When? How? Nobody can say, but the wheel of fate is turning fast.'[11]

The fascist economy is a closed and planned economy with war as its objective. Cost price, competition and even profit are of no importance in the general scheme. The political aim of preparation for war is more important than any economic consideration, and equally the resulting economic organization can serve no other aim. In his speech of May 26, 1934 (quoted above), Mussolini said: 'If I wanted to introduce state capitalism or state socialism into Italy, I should now have all the necessary external and objective conditions for doing so.' Can it be said that fascist economy is state capitalism? In spite of several points of resemblance, we believe not. Under fascism the state does not simply take the place of private capitalists as the organizer of the economic system, but forces them to follow its own policy. Fascism is interested in power, not profit. Naturally profit may one day have to be added to power, but between the two there is a wide gulf which the capitalist class, as such, would refuse to cross unless it were forced.[12]

But it is being forced to do so by a new political class, which is a product of the economic evolution of fascism, and which in its turn reacts on this movement by forcing it towards its most extreme consequences. The proletariat, as such, is entirely excluded

[11] Those who thought or pretended to think that the conquest of Abyssinia would appease fascist Italy and turn Mussolini into an apostle of European peace can now see how arbitrary were their conjectures.

[12] The ideal of every Italian capitalist is that war should never come, because it is so risky, but that preparation for war should continue, if possible, for ever.

from this new class. Preparation for war may relatively reduce unemployment and improve the lot of some classes of workers, but under a system of autarchy it is only achieved by sacrificing the standard of living of the working class as a whole. And since it involves a great concentration of industry, trade and credit, and necessitates large-scale agriculture and mass production of cereals[13] a great proportion of the urban and the whole of the rural middle class is more or less ruined. The increasing concentration of industry, the monopoly of foreign trade, the fixing of prices and the many forms of state intervention all tend to the elimination of the lesser industrialists and the small traders and farmers. On the other hand those members of the urban middle class who have no direct share in production[14] benefit considerably from the regime and pocket a nice share of the profits. They are to be found everywhere, occupying numerous places on the executives of the party, militia, syndicates, state institutions new and old. They form part of the immense fascist bureaucracy which is now the country's ruling class. Generally speaking this new class is the result of a compromise between the capitalists and the middle and lower middle class in the towns. It is interspersed with army chiefs, and members of the aristocracy, but the *homines novi* are in a majority,

[13] In spite of poetic appeals for a 'return to the land', the fascist regimes, in which some people imagined they saw a revival of agricultural life, only tend to encourage town life by their zeal for industrial methods. One of the conditions and results of preparation for war under fascism is that the relations between the country section and the town section are always being modified to the advantage of the latter.

[14] It was this class which contributed most towards forming the fascist organizations.

and theirs is the prevailing mentality: a mixture of furious nationalism and state worship, in keeping with both their ideology and their interests.[15] This new ruling class battens on the state, indulging in shameless scrambles for gain, runs through fortunes with ease, exploits and fleeces others, but has no definite place in the economic life of the country. Even when he becomes a landed proprietor or a capitalist this new fascist ruler continues to draw the best part of his resources from the political monopoly of which he is assured, and from the perpetual expansion of the machinery of state, which he encourages with all his might.[16]

Autarchy and preparation for war make this expansion inevitable. The expansion of state machinery in its turn is bound to involve autarchy and war. Nothing inside the country can break this vicious circle. Fascism has successively wiped out the working-class movement, the people, the nation, every restraining influence. Such is the tragic balance sheet of the fascist attack of the years 1921–1922, whose effects stretch far beyond the boundaries of Italy. The flames which destroyed the Peoples' Houses were only the beginning of a greater blaze which threatens to set Europe alight. The blows that shat-

[15] The 'left-wing' fascists, to be found chiefly amongst syndical officials, are the greatest extremists in foreign policy and are always asking for state intervention in internal policy and in the economic sphere. In this connection there is, for example, a considerable distinction in tone and even in attitude between the syndical paper, *Il Lavoro Fascista,* and *Il Sole,* the 'organ of commerce, industry, finance and agriculture'.

[16] In its present phase Italian fascism may be defined as a 'triarchy', in which power is exercised by the big capitalists, the bureaucracy and Mussolini himself.

tered the headquarters of workers' syndicates, co-operatives and socialist sections have struck at the foundations of the new Europe: the Europe loathed by fascism, since it means the end of war and fascists alike.

PART THREE

PRE-FASCIST ITALY BETWEEN POLITICS AND HISTORY

VII. THE OLD GENERATION LOOKS BACK AT LIBERAL ITALY

"THERE IS NO *greater sorrow than to recall a happy time in misery"—thus Francesca da Rimini told Dante in one of the most famous and beautiful passages of the* Inferno (*Canto v, 121–23*). *Such, indeed, may be taken as the major theme of the old liberal and democratic generation that had to live and suffer through Italian Fascism. Three of the most eminent Italian figures of the twentieth century, exceptional men of exceptional minds, thinkers and historians from almost irreconcilable traditions and world-views are the philosopher Benedetto Croce, the moralist Gaetano Salvemini, and the liberal Catholic Arturo Carlo Jemolo. All three were historians and yet more. They are in agreement, for different reasons, that the pre-Fascist liberal State of the Giolittian era (1900–14) had been part not of "a happy time" but of a time without the misery of Fascism. A member of their generation and almost of their* professional *stature, Gioacchino Volpe was also an historian, but one who threw in his lot with the "march of Fascism." It is he who raises the discordant voice against the illustrious trio's historical counterpoint in their remembrances and reconstructions of things past in Italy before the Great War of 1914, the post-War crisis, and the triumph of Fascism.*

On Benedetto Croce (1866–1952), the greatest

and most influential Italian philosopher of the twentieth century, something has been said already in the Introduction to suggest his place and function as a moral leader of internal Italian anti-Fascism after 1925. That his history of Italy from the close of the Risorgimento to the outbreak of the First World War defied the historical and moral foundations of Fascist claims that Mussolini was fulfilling the ideals of the "prophets" of the Risorgimento became clear to all who read Croce's work. Within three years, Croce was to come back to the offensive, in much the same manner but on a vaster scale, with his History of Europe in the Nineteenth Century *(1931), which exalted the "religion of liberty" that had inspired the Risorgimento and the Cavourian "masterpiece" in making the Liberal State. Croce's reconstruction of the pre-1914 Giolittian era presented* it *as the quiet but fruitful fulfillment through the pursuit of liberal policy and cultural renovation and intellectual freedom–and, therefore, by implication, exposed Fascism as a reversion to tyranny and not the rejuvenation of Italian life it claimed to be.*

How effectively, if with subtle undertones, Croce had scored against Fascism was soon demonstrated by the officious rebuttal which the pro-Fascist historian Gioacchino Volpe attempted in his L'Italia in cammino *(3rd ed., 1931). Volpe, whose merits as a historian of the religious currents of the early medieval period had been widely recognized, slowly became an "official" historian of Fascism just as, contemporaneously if more precariously, one of Croce's closest philosophical friends during the first decade of the century, Giovanni Gentile, had become the "official" philosopher of Fascism. Thus Mussolini had found two worthy attackers to harass the historical and philosophical flanks of Benedetto Croce. However efficacious at the time, Volpe's critique of Croce can now almost be read as a tribute by the "enemy" to the philosopher's anti-Fascist stature.*

A. C. Jemolo's reappraisal of Croce and Giolitti as the secular heroes of the Liberal period was written in the second, post-war, era (1948). The selection is not only highly revealing in itself, but it also illuminates the rising wave of anti-Crocean criticism inspired by the neo-Marxist ideological attacks of the post-1945 milieu. Incredible but true, as is evident from a reading of the selection, the liberal Catholic historian Jemolo makes a subtle eulogy of Crocean philosophy and of Giolittian politics which is in almost direct contrast to both *the Fascist condemnations of and the Marxist-Communist attacks on liberalism and idealism. By the time that Jemolo was writing his great* Chiesa e Stato, *the Italian Communist Party had tactically joined forces with the Christian Democratic Party toward insuring the inclusion of the Lateran Pact of 1929 as Article 7 of the Constitution of the Italian Republic—thus helping to perpetuate the demise of the Cavourian formula ("a free Church in a free State") and the Giolittian variation ("Church and State are two parallels that should never meet") of pre-Fascist Italian religious policy. Jemolo was obviously conscious that, in praising Croce and Giolitti in such circumstances as existed in Italian religious and secular politics in 1948, he was striking a blow against* raison d'état *and for the liberal Risorgimento.*

The short piece by Gaetano Salvemini (1873–1957) is evidently journalistic and occasional—it was written as a reply to emigré *republican criticism of the pre-Fascist liberal-democratic regime. Nevertheless, the article bears the stamp, at so early a date (1927), of a consistent position he was to maintain, despite differences of emphasis, for more than a quarter century on pre-Fascist democracy in Italy.*

Liberalism and Idealism in the Giolittian Era*

BENEDETTO CROCE

IN 1871, AFTER THE establishment of the capital of the kingdom in Rome, Italy was conscious that a whole series of aims, which had long been pursued, were now fully realized, and that she had reached the close of a period of history. Italy at last possessed independence, unity, and liberty: that is to say, the way lay open to her for the free development both of the people and of the nation, of individual personalities and the national personality. This had been the true significance of the romantic national movements of the nineteenth century, which were closely connected with the winning of civil and political liberty. Now there was nothing left to ask in this respect, and, for the time being at any rate, Italy could rest content.

But every close of a period of history brings with

* From Benedetto Croce, *A History of Italy, 1871–1915.* Translated by Cecilia M. Ady (Oxford: The Clarendon Press, 1929), 1–3, 214–20, 237–50, 252–55. Reprinted by permission of the Clarendon Press, Oxford.

it the death of something, however much the end may have been sought and desired, however essential it may be to the work which was so clearly envisaged and so energetically brought to completion; and, like all death, it is encompassed by an atmosphere of regret and melancholy. There were now no more youthful strivings and heartburnings after an ideal that was new, lofty, and far removed from realization; no more dreams, boundless as the ocean, shining with beauty and fascination; no more bittersweet torment of thwarted love; no more trembling hopes, as in 1848 and 1859; no more generous rivalries and renunciation of individual ideas in order to unite in a common purpose; no more understandings, whether tacit or avowed, between republicans and monarchists, Catholics and free-thinkers, ministers and revolutionaries, king and conspirators, all alike being dominated and inspired by devotion to the patriotic cause; no more outbursts of rejoicing from one end of Italy to the other, as in 1870, when the oppressed breathed again and exiles returned, and the inhabitants of the various provinces, who were at last all Italians, met as brothers. Men even went so far as to regret the dangers, labours, sufferings which they had endured, the battles, the persecutions, the breathless escapes in which they had taken part, the trials, the condemnations, the imprisonments. Many felt that the best part of their life was ended, and all, including the King himself in a speech from the throne, said that the heroic age of the new Italy was over while the commonplace era of practical work had begun, that prose had succeeded to poetry. It would, at the time, have been inopportune and useless to reply that poetry, that is, the aroma which exhales from idealism and generosity of mind, springs not from outward events but from the heart of man, which clothes with it those things which it touches, and that the new prose could be turned into poetry, different from, indeed, but no less beautiful than, that which had preceded it. A proof of this can be seen in Nino Bixio, a sort of Homeric Achilles turned privateer, who tried to win a carrying trade for Italy, and, having come unscathed through earlier battles, gave his life in this last. It would have been no less useless and inopportune to deride the restlessness and impatience of those who complained of the 'emptiness', which in their opinion characterized the debates in the Italian Parliament, who asked whether Italy had been created in order to do nothing, and regarded her as old before she had had time to be young, and who drew a mournful contrast between the prevailing hesitation as to what course of action should be pursued and the clearness and certainty of the preceding period. Such persons would not have been satisfied with the replies suggested by reason: that it was a matter for rejoicing that the times no longer called for heroic rebels and fighters, and for mourners in a land of mourning, that it was no great misfortune if Parliament had little to do, and that the simple lines which had directed the action of the past led to the intricacies and complexities of the present as inevitably as the particular succeeds to the general. They represented a state of mind which was entirely natural, so much so that the lack of it would have been contrary to nature. Nevertheless, it is neither superfluous nor inopportune to remind ourselves that the state of mind which prevailed after 'the harvesting of the dream' was valueless as a standard of judgement, and that comparisons, either expressed or implied, between the Italy of the Risorgimento and the united Italy which succeeded it, have no foundation in reason, any more than have the opinions which inspired them, and which describe the period between 1871 and 1915, whose story we are about to tell, as trivial or inferior or even decadent, when viewed in the light of the preceding age.

. . .

Liberal Government and Economic Expansion (1901–1910)

Italian life after 1900 had overcome the chief obstacles in its course, and, confining itself within the channels imposed upon it, flowed on for the next ten years and more, rich both in achievement and in hope. It was not that Italy entered upon a period of felicity, or 'golden age', for such times are known neither to philosophy nor history, and perhaps not even to poetry. But, as in the life of the individual there are years when a man reaps the fruit of the pains which he has endured and the experiences which he has gathered and suffered, and is able to work easily and freely without attaining to what is called felicity, or even thinking that he has attained to it, so it is in the life of nations. He who has eyes for what is vital and characteristic, and is not led astray by details of merely general significance, he who has escaped from the melancholy ideal of an abstract perfection, and the perpetual vain regrets which that ideal imposes, will discern, in the course of history, certain definite times of refreshment and peace, cheerfulness and prosperity. Such were for Italy the years in which the idea of a liberal régime was most fully realized. Here again we must beware of abstract ideas; we must beware of imagining something so sublimely perfect that we cannot recognize it when we find it in concrete form, and, through failure to recognize it, being led to deny its reality and value. Such is the fate of those visionary, impatient, and hopeless ideas of liberty which ultimately turn and rend themselves. We have seen how hesitating and chequered was the course of liberalism in Italy after 1870, and never before had conditions been so favourable to its development as they were now. The reactionaries had failed, both in theory and practice, in their attempts to constrain social forces by violence and police methods. The socialists had failed to gain acceptance for their theory of revolution, and they had failed also in their practical policy of abstention and protest and prophecies of disaster, which although it did not deliberately foment rioting on the piazza, which was generally condemned, did not restrain or discourage it. The problem of order and government, which had been raised, had in fact been solved by the triumph of liberal methods, which alone could satisfy the legitimate demands put forward by the two extreme parties, neither of which possessed the power to carry them into effect. On the one hand, the liberals upheld social order and the authority of the Government; on the other hand they recognized the new needs by giving free play to the competition of economic forces among both employers and employed, and by directing their attention towards social organization. Nevertheless difficulties persisted, and especially at the start, when the forces of reaction were crushed but not extinguished, and the socialists were emboldened, even although they were not unmindful of the fact that they had been merely the allies of the liberals and had received from them authority and support far exceeding any help which they on their part had been able to contribute. The King's speech pointed out the way of the future, and Saracco's ministry provided a breathing-space, although it did not mark a complete change of policy, as it sometimes showed leanings toward reaction and, for the rest, oscillated between attempts at energy and exhibitions of weakness. After its fall, Zanardelli, an old liberal by tradition and temper, strong in the faith of his youth to which he had steadily borne witness during recent events, set himself to bring about a liberal restoration in conformity with the spirit of the times. Giolitti, also a consistent liberal in his beliefs and practices, was associated with him as Minister of Home Affairs. After Zanardelli's death, save for the brief intervals afforded by the ministries of Fortis, Sonnino, and Luzzati, Giolitti held the reins of power for nearly eight years (1903–5, 1906–9, 1911–14). He was universally recognized as a man of much perception and wide parliamentary experience. He was no less conspicuous for his wholehearted devotion to his country, his strong political sense, his great administrative ability, and his clear-cut ideas; or, to be more exact, both in his thought and in his speech he reduced his ideas to their simplest and most essential form, so that he overcame opposition by the impression which he gave of his practical wisdom. To a man of his democratic views it was natural to feel sympathy with the sufferings and needs of the poorer classes, and hatred of the selfishness of the wealthy and well-to-do, who usually ask one thing only of the Government, namely that their own property and comfort shall be secured to them. One other problem troubled him, and this was his belief that the Italian political class was too small in numbers and in danger of becoming exhausted, and that it was therefore necessary to draw fresh ranks of society into public life. He showed greater concern for his favourite theory than he did for his own interests, and he laboured unceasingly to select and train politicians and administrators from among the younger men to succeed him, associating them with him in the Government and preparing them to assume its control. His efforts in this direction were not always seconded by fortune; for some of the men on whom he relied most died in their prime, while others were led away into less considered political ideas and methods.

Those who are fond of giving old names to new things—a habit we have observed before—might well say that under Giolitti there began a new phase of 'transformism'. To this we readily agree, both because we have freed the word from the evil meaning which at first attached to it, and also because whenever the antinomy between conservatism and revolution is transcended and weakened and seems for the moment to vanish, there follows a drawing together of extremes and a reshaping of their ideals in the direction of unity. Those who were reactionaries by temperament, or from narrowness of outlook, persisted in their opinions, whether openly or secretly. Those who like Sonnino had, sincerely, disinterestedly and out of pure and devoted public spirit, demanded constitutional reform and checks of various kinds, accepted the teaching of events and worked with the same sincerity, disinterestedness, and devotion, under conditions which had developed otherwise than they had anticipated. In September 1900 Sonnino wrote an article in the *Nuova Antologia,* of which the title 'Quid agendum?' showed signs of his perplexity. He expressed his continued fear lest Italy should fall victim to a false Left or a false Right, to socialist or clerical revolutionaries, and advocated the formation of a 'union of national parties', rising above the one-sided interests of classes or groups, dedicated to 'the higher ends of the nation as a whole' and to the State as a 'complex organism' which should turn its attention, not to visions of imperial power, but to a sort of political housekeeping, and to tasks which lay near at hand, such as the better organization of the administration, the negotiation of commercial treaties, emigration laws, educational reforms, railways, the mercantile marine, the control of Government employés and the like. He was, however, rightly met with the answer that the 'union' which he had conceived was artificial, that his idea of the State was too static, that he had not perceived the social development which had taken place in Italy, owing to the growth of industry and commerce, and that he had not grasped the true significance of the events of the last few years, which aroused forebodings in him, but were in truth a series of shocks enabling new currents of thought and action to penetrate into Italian politics, and foreshadowed not a double flight towards two extremes but a union such as had been effected forty years earlier between the Garibaldians and the Savoyard monarchy. Sonnino did not insist upon his programme, although he continued his opposition in the Chamber for some time, with, however, only a small following. A few years later he acknowledged to Giolitti that Italy could only be governed by liberal and parliamentary methods, and to this he held when, on two occasions, he was called for a few months to the Presidency of the Council.

To such a frank confession the socialists did not rise, but nevertheless during these years they wholly divested themselves of revolutionary socialistic theory, or in other words of Marxism, throwing away one by one all the weapons in its armoury, even to its classical idea of the State; for they had come to see that, above and beyond all class interests, there was a 'general interest' represented by the State. But they could not adapt themselves to work on these lines, not so much because they were imprisoned by their own past, or because they felt that to admit such a conclusion would be to destroy their individual chances of a political career, which on the contrary would have been facilitated by such a change of front, but rather owing to the necessities of the situation in which they found themselves. Openly to proclaim their conversion would have been to declare the dissolution of the socialist party, its tenets being no longer distinguishable from those of liberalism. Yet a declaration of this kind would not have destroyed the faith of the working-class masses nor of those who came forward, through conviction or self-interest, as their leaders, in the socialist ideal, which rested upon logic of a kind—a crude and oversimplified kind—and was fostered by the economic struggles between employers and employed, and other aspects of modern industrialism. The effect would have been to abandon the masses to revolutionary agitators, with grave danger and injury to society as a whole and to the working classes themselves. It was essential, therefore, that the men who had emancipated themselves from abstract and fanatical ideas, and were clear-sighted and moderate, should remain among the masses and guide them, at the cost of showing some indulgence to their illusions. To one whose work it is to seek out the truth and proclaim it, and to simple and honest minds, such a position may seem not merely painful but untenable. Yet practically-minded politicians actually do maintain themselves in such positions, and it is therefore unjust to judge and condemn them by standards applicable to other cases. The socialist leaders secretly favoured the new liberal Government; they welcomed the freedom to strike without interference on the part of the military and without soldiers being put on to agricultural work to replace peasants on strike, and the various other provisions and reforms of a social character which had been effected; they approved, moreover, all that promoted the growing industry and wealth of the country. Nevertheless it was a matter of necessity that they should force themselves to believe, for the quieting of their consciences, or should at least announce for the satisfaction of the masses, that all this was a preparation for the communist State of the future, because only by the gradual wearing down of the bourgeois régime in the sphere of politics and economics, and the maximum advance in the production of wealth, could the capture of the organs of government and the nationalization of capital be rendered possible.

Turati was asked by Giolitti to join the Government in 1904, and Bissolati received a similar invitation from him in 1911; both were obliged to decline, because if they had become ministers they would have lost all influence with the masses and would have been looked upon as traitors and deserters; they personally might have thrown in their lot with the Government, but socialism would not have done so. So again, when the maintenance of public order, during strikes and other disturbances, led to conflicts with the troops and the shedding of blood, even if the socialists felt that not only the Government but they themselves, if they had been in power under a socialist régime, could not have done otherwise, they were forced always to blame the Government, to demand that the representatives of the police, or the officers who had given the order to fire should be punished, and to propose legislation which should unconditionally prohibit the use of armed force against the crowd. They were obliged to remain permanently, or all but permanently, in an attitude of opposition, and to vote against every measure of every ministry, above all against military expenditure, although they were far from being unmoved by sentiments of patriotism, and an Austrian march on Milan would have been no matter of indifference to them. In acting thus, however, they were well aware that the measures would be passed and the supplies voted by large majorities. Their positive support of liberalism can be traced in other directions and in other ways: for instance in their restraint of the fanatics and hotheads who were their colleagues or rather opponents within the socialist party. These men took their stand upon the pure principles of Marxism, and admitted none but revolutionary methods, or to put it plainly, they remained uncompromising socialists and were not, like their associates, practical converts to liberalism. Intellectuals for the most part, they had fortified their Marxian principles with the syndicalism of Sorel (who, as has been said, obtained a better reception in Italy than he did in France) with its theory of the sharp division between the proletariat and the political world, its belief in the saving power of violence, and its myth of a general strike. As intellectuals they were able to stir up the masses, and the dangerous elements which existed among them, but they could not interpret their real and legitimate needs or their true psychology in the way that the more experienced and moderate socialists were able to do.

. . .

The Advance of Culture and Spiritual Unrest (1901–1914)

The general quickening of rhythm which we have described in internal and foreign politics, in the economic world, and in Italian national consciousness as a whole, might be expected in the field of culture also; and its occurrence here is shown by a review of the facts. But the information which might be put together as to the number of books printed, the reviews and daily papers in circulation, and the publishing houses and literary and scientific institutions which were founded or brought into prominence at this time, mainly a matter of statistics, can tell us very little. Such details belong to the domain of industry and commerce, not to that of culture, whose importance can only be estimated by its quality. To gauge in this respect the character of the period which we are considering, we must go back to the fountain-head of all culture, or to put it plainly, to contemporary philosophy, which alone makes it possible to understand and criticize any special manifestation of culture with sureness and precision.

During the early years of the twentieth century, both in Italy and elsewhere, a reaction set in against the cult of science, or positivism. In so far as it expressed legitimate needs and laid down true principles, it had created a sense of weariness by insisting on points no longer disputed; in so far as it had given promise of a philosophy, it had failed miserably and covered itself with discredit; by preaching the duty of accepting the discoveries of science and resigning oneself in all else to an attitude of agnosticism, it had ended in disappointment and dissatisfaction. Nothing could arrest the inward decay of this doctrine, which, forty years earlier, had been received with so much favour and had engendered so many hopes. In Italy, as we have seen, it had suffered severely from the dialectic of historical materialism, but many other causes combined later to hasten its end. Among these were the gradual reawakening of national traditions of thought, and the desire to get to the bottom of problems which had been passed over or inadequately treated by positivism and historical antiquarianism; the influence of foreign thinkers, Germans who were once more speculating over the conception of 'values', Frenchmen and Englishmen trained in classical German philosophy or affected by it; the scientists who were introducing a theory of scientific knowledge akin to that already expounded by idealism in its conception of the 'abstract intellect', and therefore denying the omnipotence of purely naturalistic methods; above all, a certain widely diffused spirit, half romantic and half mystical, to which the crude simplifications of positivism, particularly in delicate matters of art, religion, and the moral consciousness, were intolerable, and hardly less intolerable its peculiar style or jargon.

The result of this reaction was a widening of the spiritual horizon. Great ideas which had been obscured shone once more with their former brightness, fertile lines of thought were again pursued, courage and zeal for speculation was reborn, the books of the great philosophers both ancient and modern were reopened, including even such special objects of detestation as Fichte and Hegel. Philosophy was no longer obliged to make excuses for itself or to conceal itself. Its name no longer met with the derision and contempt to which it had grown accustomed, but was pronounced with honour. Both the word and the subject became fashionable. To those who remembered the stifling sense of oppression which marked the age of positivism, it seemed as if they had emerged into the fresh air beneath a clear sky and amid green fields. They had escaped also from the confines of the universities, where philosophy, treated merely as material for an antiquated educational programme, had languished during the last decades. For philosophy, like poetry, is nourished by the emotions and experiences of daily life, such as are unknown, or known only partially and intermittently, among places and individuals devoted to scholastic routine and academic rivalries. The reviews and books written by laymen threw the products of the universities into the shade by the novelty of their material, the variety of their intellectual interests, the liveliness of their style, and the acuteness of their criticisms; the improvement affected academic students, who tried to maintain their position by modelling themselves upon more successful examples. Several collections of philosophical authors were published by non-academic efforts, of which the chief was the series entitled 'Classics of Modern Philosophy', which rivalled and in some respects outstripped the only collection which existed outside Italy, the 'Philosophical Library' published at Leipzig. Reviews of philosophical books, discussions on their theories, and philosophical interpretations of the political, religious, and social questions of the day, were to be found in the literary pages of political papers. Their success was such that even the disciples of scholasticism saw that the time had come to look beyond seminarist schools and universities controlled by the Church; they founded a review of their own, which was careful neither to ignore the work of unfettered thinkers, nor to abuse it in the manner customary to priests and monks, but expounded, discussed, and often accepted the new theories, endeavouring to weld them into a more liberal system of scholastic philosophy. Nor was philosophy confined within its own limits; it gave a new impetus to many different interests–historical, literary, scientific, political, and economic–which were alike inspired by a longing for deeper understanding, alike sparkling with the fire of youth.

Into this luxuriant revival of speculative enthusiasm, which was in itself undoubtedly good, or productive of good, there crept a dangerous and morbid element. One condition of vigorous and fruitful philosophic activity is a vigorous and sensitive moral consciousness, conditioned in its turn by speculative thought, the two growing side by side in a vital interdependence. But the moral consciousness of Europe had been enfeebled when first the old religious faith and then that of the rationalists and illuminists had been overthrown, and when even the more philosophical religion, liberal in outlook and historical in basis, although not overthrown, had suffered challenge and opposition. Industrialism and Bismarckianism, with their repercussions and internal struggles, were unable to create a new and satisfying religion; but they had produced an uneasy condition of mind, a combination of lust for enjoyment, the spirit of adventure and of joy in conquest, frantic craving after power, restlessness and withal lack of enthusiasm and indifference, a state of mind that must be looked for in a life lived divorced from its centre, that centre being for man his moral and religious consciousness. Even in unsentimental and practically-minded Italy, the enemy of all fanaticism, such tendencies had taken root. They had been grafted into literature by D'Annunzio, who moulded many young minds in accordance both with his first manner, that of Andrea Sperelli, and with his second, that of the *Re di Roma* and *Gloria,* finding among the younger generation plastic materials upon which to exercise his powers; and they now gained fresh scope and force as industrial civilization grew and flourished in our midst. It was in the atmosphere prepared by D'Annunzio and by the growth of a plutocratic psychology that delights in things outwardly dazzling and fundamentally gross, that the philosophy of reaction against positivism developed in Italy. The attitude which it adopted towards the superficial rationalism of the positivists developed to some extent, and especially among those who could create their own atmosphere, in the right way, towards a sounder and truer rationalism. For the most part, however, it tended, under various and often deceptive forms, towards an irrationalism which, although it was christened and accepted as 'idealism', was rather a mixture of 'idealistic irrationalism' and 'sensationalistic spiritualism'. Philosophies of this kind followed hard upon each other, and met and mingled together: the philosophy of intuition, pragmatism, mysticism–a mysticism now Franciscan or Russian or Buddhist, now modernist, now Catholic in tendency; erotic after the manner of D'Annunzio or erotic after the manner of Fogazzaro –theosophy, occultism, and the like, including even futurism, which, as an idea or interpretation of life, was in its way a philosophy. Any one who desires to get an impression of this kaleidoscope should read the reviews of the period, especially the newer reviews which were more sensitive to the fashion and therefore more typical. Among these were *Leonardo,* which came out in Florence from 1903 to 1907, *Prose, L'Anima,* and lastly *Lacerba,* written to some extent by the same authors and belonging to the years 1913–14. In spite of certain efforts to restrain or combat or modify these tendencies, there is clearly visible in them all the natural result of irrationalism, that is a weaker and less definite grasp of distinctions: the distinction in the domain of theory, between truth and falsehood; in the sphere of practice, between duty and pleasure, or morality and utility; in aesthetics, between contemplation and passion, poetry and emotion, artistic taste and sensual enjoyment; and in the life of culture, between spontaneity and lack of discipline, originality and extravagance. With logical restraints removed, the critical faculty enfeebled, the responsibility of rational assent brushed on one side, the play of fancy and of a new-found rhetoric presented itself as something easy and attractive. Examples were daily provided by artists of the convulsive school, especially in the figurative arts. Educated in the aestheticism already preached by D'Annunzio, inspired seers or rather unreal visionaries, priests of pure beauty, which they worshipped now under sensual forms, now under arid symbols, they did not know that beauty is the longings and strivings of humanity transfigured by the imagination, and is therefore a solemn thing, a thing for virile minds. The example of the artists was followed by a few archaeologists, diggers among tombs and ruins, high priests of mysteries, somewhat resembling D'Annunzio's figures in *La Città morta,* who, it will be remembered, felt themselves drunk with incestuous and murderous passions from the exhalations given out by the stones of Mycenae. No less popular were the jugglings with paradox which aped original thought and concealed an incapacity to say anything worth saying, and the invention of novel artistic formulas, or more correctly of a new kind of art wholly different from that of the past and denying the eternal nature of art itself. To read the reviews and books of the day was to come under an incessant fusillade of ideas, sometimes happy, at other times ill-conceived; some intelligent, others confused; but not one of which was stayed in its rapid flight for closer consideration and analysis, in order that it might be developed and made productive. They revealed more excitement than ardour, more initiative than persistence, more restlessness than movement, more curiosity and dilettantism than serious interest. All this was the moral effect of irrationalism, precisely as its logical effect is the failure to distinguish between the valuable and the worthless. To construct or reconstruct a theory of reality and life, to establish sound principles of judgement and by their help to penetrate and inform the matter which history ceaselessly and untiringly lays before the silent inquiry of the mind, and thus to prepare the way for constructive thought and clear-sighted practical activity, in short, to win from philosophy the results that we have a right to demand—all this requires labour: methodical, slow, arduous. Some traces of this labour were visible, but it was soon interrupted and forsaken, for false idealism, or irrationalism, is compatible with acrobatic feats and fitful outbursts of activity, but not with real work.

There was at this time a certain student who was fully alive to the dangers attendant upon the reaction against the cult of science. He was a native of Naples, where the tradition and practice of speculative thought was long established, which had always held out, not entirely without success, against the tyranny of positivism, and had of recent years produced the first Italians to examine and criticize historical materialism and the Marxian dialectic from a philosophical standpoint. In 1902, when he sketched the programme of a projected review—*La Critica*—this student described the diverse and opposing forces against which he was prepared to do battle. These included both old and young, positivists, empiricists, and 'philologists' on the one hand, and pseudo-geniuses, mystics, and dilettanti on the other. He had not grown up in the D'Annunzian atmosphere, in the grasping, pleasure-loving spirit of the new industrialism, but had lingered among the memories and examples of the men of the Risorgimento, and the thoughts of classical idealism. He had derived his intellectual sustenance in the first instance from the teaching of De Sanctis, of whom he was an attentive student though not actually a pupil, and on this study he concentrated all the powers of his mind and spirit with an enthusiasm unsurpassed by the pupils who enjoyed personal acquaintance with the master. Possessed of a highly unprejudiced turn of mind and little disposed to surrender his mind to any one teacher, he tried in his youth to think like Spencer and the positivists, but failed. He listened with greater profit to the lectures delivered by Labriola in the University of Rome, which were anti-evolutionist and based on the philosophy of Herbart. He had learnt the methods of critical scholarship and had long devoted himself to learned researches of the most detailed character. He had let his imagination feed upon contemporary literature, delighting in Carducci and giving due attention to his own contemporary D'Annunzio. He had experienced in his own person the mental processes of Marxian socialism, and had made a close study of economics. Ultimately, he had been led to the conviction that a new and fruitful philosophical development must restore contact with classical idealism, but must not be content to rest there, or to confine itself to introducing new material and certain modifications into the framework of the older system, as the Italian disciples of Hegel had endeavoured to do. The framework must be broken down, in order that the fertile seeds of truth which it contained might be released and transplanted to the new soil created by the course of intervening intellectual and moral history. All legitimate claims made outside and against classical idealism must be respected, especially the unique character of the positive or natural and mathematical sciences which could not be reduced to an abstract philosophy of nature, and the no less unique character of documentary historical research, which cannot be reduced to an abstract philosophy of history. Further, he clearly recognized that, with the passing of theology and its influence and the disappearance of conceptions based on transcendence, the day of 'closed' or 'final' systems was over. Thus philosophy could only mean the perpetual solving of the ever-recurring theoretical problems raised by historical experience; or, as he afterwards put it, philosophy must resolve itself in substance into a 'methodology of history', alive and continually renewing itself, while its claims as a coherent system of thought must be limited to asking that each succeeding system should be coherent in itself and consistent with the systems which had preceded it. He was thus opposed at once to the positivists and to the metaphysicians. He rejected a merely scholarly or antiquarian treatment of problems, but was at the same time determined to bring about a true 'union of philosophy and philology'. He rejected the rationalism of the mathematicians and the empiricism of the naturalists, and also the panlogism and abstract monism of popular Hegelianism, and insisted upon the variety of spiritual forms, and the fundamental importance of diversity or 'distinction' as an element in concrete unity. He rejected no less emphatically pragmatism, intuitionism, mysticism, and irrationalism of every kind, insisting that spiritual dialectic and the interpretation of reality should abide by the principles of logic, not indeed empirical and formal logic but speculative and dialectical logic. With all this he rejected, either expressly or by implication, the moral ideas of which irrationalism was at once the product and the cause, whether Nietzschean, authoritarian and reactionary, or the opposite ideologies of illuminism and freemasonry; and he clung to the ideal of liberty, not as a barren will to power, but as the power to will, or the moral consciousness. Although he urged greater attention to foreign thinkers, and particularly recommended the study of classical German philosophy, he was no less aware of the importance of the ground which had been prepared and the foundations which had been laid at home, and he set himself to restore the reputation of the Italian, Giambattista Vico, the father of modern European philosophy, who for the past forty years had been well-nigh forgotten, and now became once more the object of devoted study.

The work of *La Critica* and its contributors, and the books written by them, played a leading part in the development of philosophical studies. More especially, the principles set forth in the volume on *Aesthetic,* which was published in 1902 by the editor of the review, penetrated everywhere, affecting the minds of young men and students, and through them disturbing the professors and academics, and producing not merely echoes but results in the international world of thought and knowledge. The book gave rise to innumerable studies, discussions, and monographs; it may be said to have inspired everything of importance that was produced in Italy in the field of philosophical and historical study, criticism of poetry, music, and the fine arts, linguistic studies, legal and economic science, the history of thought and civilization, and religious and educational controversies; thus, after an interval of two centuries, it recovered for Italian thought an active part in the thought of Europe, and even a kind of primacy in certain branches of study. Nevertheless, it must be recognized that the spirit which inspired the author was unperceived save by a few; the unity of his thought was destroyed and it was treated piecemeal, even the pieces being often twisted into a sense foreign to them. This was the case with regard to his principles of aesthetic, where theories such as the conception of 'lyrical intuition' which he had formed to interpret the great poetry of Dante and Shakespeare, and the painting of Raphael and Rembrandt, were exploited to provide shibboleths for the disciples of modernism and to justify 'futurism', a romanticism of the most distorted and decadent type, which he not only condemned in accordance with his theory, but for which he personally felt a whole-hearted loathing. The cause of this misunderstanding was the tide of irrationalism, which penetrated from the life of the age into its philosophy and threw it into confusion. So irresistible was this tide, that the editor of *La Critica* saw a kind of irrationalistic idealism suddenly appear at his side; its champion was one of his collaborators, who had done good service in the promotion of philosophical studies, had fought gallantly against the modernists (who had claimed for their little heresy within the bosom of the Catholic Church the character of a great reformation in thought), had contributed greatly to the study of the history of philosophy, and, unlike himself, was a product of orthodox Hegelianism, and on this account, and owing to his professorial standing, might have been thought to be shielded from the wiles of the Circe of the day by formidable weapons of defence. When this new irrationalism made its appearance, and showed itself to be a mixture of antiquated theological speculation and modern decadentism, combining the style of the moderns with the language of the ancients under the name of 'actual idealism', he was very much surprised, but set himself at once to criticize it, both in principle and in detail, and to give warning of the dangers which lay in its path. To-day, after many vicissitudes, after many fashions have come and gone, when 'actual idealism' has shown itself with increasing clearness to be a mass of ambiguous generalizations and obscure practical counsels, the only part of it which remains standing is the 'methodology' which he created. It is this that continues to inspire the work of those who labour in the fields of philosophy, history, and criticism, helping them towards clear and distinct conceptions; and its author has, in the course of years, continued to apply it in details and to test it historically, in the hope that others will continue the work of criticism, which is vital to the continuance of sound learning.

The moral and political outlook of the younger generation ran parallel to their irrationalism in the domain of theory; and this in its turn was, as we have seen, encouraged by the spirit prevalent in Europe, a spirit marked by violence and cynicism, and lust for conquest and adventure. The socialist ideal, which had been popular twenty years before, no longer attracted the youth of the day, nor even those who had been young at the period of its ascendancy. This was partly due to the criticism which had undermined the Marxian apocalyptic, partly to the gradual absorption of socialism into liberalism, partly to the reforms which were rapidly bringing into effect the 'minimum programme' in its entirety. The imagination and the desires, both of the new generation and of those of the preceding generation whose hopes had failed them, turned, as they had already done in England, Germany, and France, to 'imperialism' or 'nationalism'. Of this development D'Annunzio, in his novels, plays, and lyrics, was the spiritual father. From his youth up he had prepared the way for it with his whole psychological equipment, culminating in his dream of the sensual and blood-stained Renaissance of the Borgias, and more definitely after 1892, when he became acquainted with some of Nietzsche's works. In 1908 D'Annunzio produced his play *La Nave,* with the ringing line, '*Arma la prora e salpa verso il mondo*' (Man the prow and sail out into the world); in 1910, in *Forse che sì, forse che no,* he hymned the glory of the aeroplane, and tried to rouse to exaggerated heights the already existing passion for sport and for gladiatorial contests, a very different matter from the old severe gymnastic exercises which had been invented by the Germans as a training of the will at the time of their reaction against Napoleonic oppression. The style originated by him, which was widely imitated and caused the sincerity and simplicity engendered among the Italians by Manzoni and De Sanctis to be all but lost, and certainly sullied, was an 'imperialistic' style, with vast and solemn movements of phrase, seeming to say great things but losing themselves in vagueness, as in the poem mentioned above. To the spirit of D'Annunzio, steeped in sensuality and sadism and a cold-blooded dilettantism, Italian nationalist men of letters brought intellectual elements taken first from the equally sensual and sadistic French nationalism of Barrès, then from the rationalistic nationalism of Maurras and the *Action française,* and finally from the syndicalism of Sorel, with its theory of 'violence'. They were far more opposed to liberalism than to socialism, for many nationalists had been drawn from the socialist ranks; and they approved of the ideas of war and dictatorship, only asking that what the socialists taught about the class war should be applied to war between nations. Like the French nationalists, they were ready to make mock of the Revolution, the declaration of the rights of man, and democracy; like them, too, they were inclined to support the Roman Church and to receive its support in exchange, seeking a basis of agreement in an 'atheistic Catholicism'; they sang the praises of the past, of absolute monarchy, and of classicism after the manner of Boileau; they even at times coquetted with Catholicism, at least in so far as to render it artistic appreciation, D'Annunzio, always the leader in these movements, being among the first to do so. Strangely enough, they afterwards set themselves to restore and re-gild the effigy of Francesco Crispi, depicting him as the pioneer and martyr of their imperialism or nationalism. He was singularly ill-adapted to serve as the symbol of their cause, not only because his foreign policy was barren and his colonial policy had culminated in a national disaster, but also because his views always remained those of a democrat, an anti-clerical, and a freemason. A few simple minds, unaccustomed to observe and to think, applauded and assented, believing that the nationalism, whose brave and eager words they heard, was merely a patriotic reawakening from the socialists' repudiation of love for their country, and from an overcautious and prosaic policy on the part of the Government. Nevertheless, some of the leading champions of nationalism revealed a different attitude of mind when they said plainly that 'patriotism' and 'nationalism' were 'opposites', the first being 'altruistic', the second 'egotistic', the first aiming at 'service of our country to the death', the second looking upon nations as 'instruments for promoting the interests of the citizens', or as 'the egotism of the citizens regarded from the national standpoint'. The one was, in short, a moral, or in Nietzschean language, a 'base' ideal, the other utilitarian and 'heroic'. Nor, in truth, was nationalism a reawakening or strengthening of Italian national feeling and the national tradition, for it was by its very origin careless and ignorant of Italian affairs; to it and to its spirit belongs the name 'Italietta' which was then given to Italy, not as a sign of affection and tenderness, but because she was despised and laughed at by those who should have understood and loved her with the paternal love that endeavours at the same time to correct its child and raise it to higher levels. There were also among the nationalists those who, recalling Prussian ideas of the State, or under the influence of Pan-Germanism, tried to introduce into Italy a 'religion of the State', a dark and terrible idol, fantastically remote from human life and seeking to challenge and override it, or a 'religion of the race', such as had for some time past boasted apostles and priests in various parts of Europe and the world. The writer who has been mentioned above as the leader of the Italian philosophical movement never wearied of holding up these nationalistic sentiments and ideas to criticism and ridicule. It was not merely that he perceived the extent to which they were tainted with irrationalism and greed, but, in rejecting much of the teaching of Hegel, he had rejected first of all the exaltation of the State above morality; instead, he had restored, deepened, and developed the Christian and Kantian definition of the State as a stern practical necessity, which the moral consciousness accepts, while at the same time it dominates, controls, and directs it. Moreover, as an historian he realized how arbitrary, fantastic, and inconclusive are theories of race, as are also those theories which hanker after the past and a return to the Counter-Reformation, absolute government, and the like. By means of his protests and attacks, philosophy and history redeemed their honour; but it needed more than the criticisms of philosophers and historians to combat a European, indeed a worldwide, movement, which rested on genuine motives and was not to be stayed by force of argument, nor by efforts of individual goodwill, nor by the feelings of a few exceptional people; it had to run its course full circle until it brought about its own refutation, not by arguments but by facts.

• • •

Amid democratic Utopias and nationalist cupidity, where, it may be asked, was the temper of mind, the political literature, corresponding to liberalism, which in this same period had triumphed in the sphere of practical government and in the political life of the country? The facts are simply these. Liberalism was not a deep and living faith, an ardently-cherished enthusiasm, an object of thought and care, a sacred thing to be guarded with jealousy at the first hint of danger: it was rather a practical expedient. The leaders of the liberal revival in Italy were two old men–Zanardelli, a man of the Risorgimento, and Giolitti, who belonged to the early days of unity when he worked at the side of Quintino Sella; with them, therefore, liberalism was instinctive. In other statesmen of the day, liberal principles were for the most part less deep-seated. They had come to them as a legacy and had been found useful, or at least there was nothing which could take their place; and nowhere were they seriously contested, for the socialists had been tamed and the nationalists were intellectuals who might safely be allowed to talk, and even be heard with pleasure owing to their aspirations after national greatness and their abuse of democracy, demagogy, and freemasonry. If any one raised the question of liberty, he was told that liberty existed in fact and was recognized by every one, and that, since it was in no danger, it was better to speak of what was practical and urgent, for instance the evils of too much liberty, or the liberty which spelt licence and disorder. This would have been true enough, if liberty in Italy had had behind it the tradition of centuries of struggle and conflict and victory, as was the case in England, or even a tradition of a century and more, as in France. But the tradition of liberty in Italy was of recent growth, as had been constantly pointed out by her patriots, and as we ourselves have shown in these pages. Because it was of recent growth, it had not struck deep roots; the interest which the country showed in politics was still slight, and the Government, of necessity, played too large a part in the elections. Attempts to found societies and reviews of a purely liberal character were feeble and transitory; the strongest champions of the cause were free traders rather than liberals, that is to say they emphasized the economic, not the moral, aspects of liberalism. In Italy, liberalism as an ideal lacked the support of a religious creed such as it had enjoyed at other times and in other countries; at the same time, owing first to positivism and then to irrationalism, it had been denied the intellectual and critical support which would have enabled it to meet any crisis which might arise. Its own recent tradition, as expressed in the mind of Cavour, had not been kept fresh, and it had not been made a practice to turn back from time to time to the origins of Italian liberalism as to a source of moral refreshment. The philosophical, historical, and critical movement, which had returned to the theories of the age of idealism and liberalism, and had defined and developed them, was for the most part not fashionable, and its influence upon political opinion was hampered not only by the existing fashions already described, theoretical and practical, but by other causes. Among these was the increasing impatience of politicians with everying 'unpractical'. Statesmen respected students as they respected poets, and laughed at them as men who ranged the heavens of theory and brought back nothing practical from their travels. It was true that the students had set themselves the task of going down to the foundations and first principles of civilization, a task which must needs proceed gradually, carefully, and slowly; and owing to this, and to the tranquillity secured to them by the liberal Government, they remained in their own circle, somewhat removed from the political world, acquiescing, since circumstances allowed them to do so without dishonour, in what practically amounted to a division of labour: it is for you to govern the country and provide for its interests, for us the charge of things intellectual and the spiritual life of the nation. At bottom the two tasks were not separate, and ultimately the same spirit must rule both; but the union of intellects and wills in the practical and immediate problems of political life could not be effected at the time without transforming scholars into amateurs, of whom there were already too many in politics, as elsewhere, and nothing would have been gained by adding to their number.

Amid the growing emphasis on things practical, and still more amid the enormous development of the speculative, critical, and argumentative faculties during these years, it is not surprising that poetry should have declined and grown silent. It has occurred in other ages and at other times, although the necessary equation between the growth of philosophy and the decline of poetry is not a fixed sociological law, if only for the reason that there are no fixed sociological laws. As we have already observed, the true age of poetry and of art in the new Italy ended with the close of the century, or even ten years earlier. Even the poets who had flourished between 1890 and 1900 had suffered a decline. D'Annunzio, after he had harvested the lyrics of *Alcione,* and from the heart of his native Abruzzi had committed to verse his dream of passion and death, the *Figlia di Jorio,* which owed its inspiration to Michetti, had entered upon a phase in which the artist leaves little to the critics because he himself analyses his own work into its separate parts, indulges in exaggeration and mannerism, and, in order to gain fresh life or to bring himself up to date, makes use of materials and subjects alien to his nature. Fogazzaro, in his later novels, emphasized the weaker aspects of his art, and devoted himself to the championship and propagation of ideas. Pascoli tried to swell himself into a larger bulk and became more and more the occasional poet, writing lyrics on the events of the day. Such was his reputation in this respect that when the American Lubin came to Italy, in order to lay before the King his scheme for an international institute of agriculture, knowing Pascoli and his work, he publicly asked him to compose a poem in honour of this venture in the cause of agricultural research. Of futurism and its works we will not speak, for it is something other than poetry, and for the most part, like futurist music, it is simply noise; but apart from this, there appeared a few plays and novels which claimed attention, but only rarely showed real inspiration or flashes of genius. The joy of life had been sung by D'Annunzio until its poetic resources were exhausted, and now its practical effects were becoming increasingly apparent. The inmost feeling of the age, the feeling which expresses itself freely and irresistibly, was chiefly made up of a sense of satiety and weariness, of passive scepticism and bitter mirth, of an inclination to tears, and of a tendency to take refuge in the past, and in simple and natural affections, without being able to find rest there. The voices of the poets, for all their seeming variety, united in expressing this state of mind. Among various minor singers and isolated fragments of art, two real poets made their appearance. One was the Piedmontese, Gozzano, who showed the quality of his art in a few perfect compositions such as *L'amica di nonna Speranza* and *Le due strade.* The other, more many-sided than he and possessed of a wider vision and a deeper culture, was the Neapolitan, Gaeta. Gozzano died young of consumption. Gaeta committed suicide, unable to overcome his grief at the loss of his mother, his love for whom belonged to the range of affections to which he clung desperately, because they enabled him to bear an otherwise unbearable existence. His life was unbearable because, as with so many others of his generation, it had no aim and no meaning that was not imaginary.

Giolitti and Croce as Heroes of Liberal Italy: A Fascist Critique*

GIOACCHINO VOLPE

. . . A FEW MONTHS AGO Italians had for a moment the hope that [a definitive] history [of modern Italy] had been offered them even if limited to the brief

* From Gioacchino Volpe, *L'Italia in cammino* (3rd ed. Milan: Fratelli Treves Editori, 1931), Preface, XI–XXIII. Reprinted by permission of the author. Editor's translation.

space of time between 1871 and 1915: that is, the *History of Italy* by Benedetto Croce. Few men in Italy could have been held to be more prepared to offer such a work than Benedetto Croce. His long reflection upon the theoretical problems of history; his happy attempt to reunite history and philosophy; his investigations and vast historiographical reconstructions; his many essays of erudition and large breadth; his *History of the Kingdom of Naples* are all certainly notable. Particularly after 1915, after he had liquidated his past and corrected it and put in order his preceding production, Benedetto Croce had dedicated himself completely to this new activity, different from that of the philosopher and yet connected with it. After he had undeniably revived the study of the history of philosophy, of religion, of art, of literature, and breathed a new spirit into them, he thought that the moment had come to revive historical studies which had themselves been weak, arid, and fragmentary . . . This *History of Italy* of his, who can deny it?, bears not a few signs of the vigorous mind which has created it. There is in it a good mixture of various matters, evidence of very extensive readings, pages that are excellent as narration or pages that are excellent as exposition and in content. Some aspects and moments of the Italian development are illumined as no one else could have done, differently or better: thus the formation after 1870 of a common national life which overcame the closed and alienated regional lives; the various positions of Italian socialism, around 1900; the rising of culture and the rebirth of a speculative spirit during the first decade of this century, etc.

And yet, let us say it immediately, the *History of*

Italy by Benedetto Croce has not satisfied the expectation perhaps of any one. It is not yet the history that Italians want, the one that may truly help them to understand Italy, to know themselves, their past and present. The historian had proposed to himself to seek, outside the various "idols" arbitrarily assumed as a criterion of judgment of Italian reality, the "simple history" of what Italy was and felt and imagined herself to be from 1871 to 1915; and he intended to examine this "simple history" objectively, without preconceptions, without the pretense of finding in it what it did not contain. Very well! But it does not follow that the act of living through a revolutionary epoch and having one's spirit projected toward a moral should lead one to lose his historical sense. But in the practical act, Croce has after all done something different: he has made the eulogy of that past, now with the accents of the *laudator temporis acti* [extoller of things past], and again with the argumentations of a clever lawyer. No one, for instance, has asked and asks for the historical decapitation of the men who around the year 1880 guided Italian foreign policy, certainly with much patriotism, with much fidelity to principles, with much legalitarian spirit, but also with little self-awareness, with much ingenuousness, with insufficient energy, with a mediocre consciousness of the new tasks of the Italian state, of the new exigencies of a nation at long last united, and of its European orientations. But, as far as Croce is concerned, nothing different or better could have or should have been attempted by them. "Wise" was their policy, that which was called "freedom from engagements" and of "the clean hands." Was Europe changing its face, was it putting

Bismarck in the place of Napoleon, armed imperialisms in the place of "the spirit of the liberal revolutions"? But all this, says the historian, was happening outside and even against the will of the Italians. They had other traditions and other tastes. Which amounts to lauding them for not having wanted or having known how to adjust themselves to this new era of European life, which began after the close of the era of revolutions, after the resolution of certain internal problems, after the systematization as best one could of the problem of nationality and the people's independence, after the formation of new great and middle-sized states.

And what a charming portrait the historian has made of this Italy! In it there reigns "the cult of gentle affections"; partisan divisions are mitigated and sweetened in their parliamentary usages; "a liberty fully guaranteed . . . prevented the violation of laws, and rendered the control of justice a public affair"; from one part of the Italian peninsula to the other as if "a grand conversation" were being held, between the nation and the politicians and publicists and orators who "went from one city to another for lectures and conferences." There were all kinds of political associations, meetings of every tendency in the cafes of the capital; the Italians had their eyes turned toward Montecitorio, and toward Palazzo Madama; and a fervid life was stirring in ministries and in newspapers! . . . Then revolutionary socialism appeared upon the scene. But again, this revolutionism was disarmed by the freedom given it after its first persecutions; it was disarmed by the sympathy of the bourgeois—whether they were civil or military—as persecuted ones. And here are socialist leaders who in order to quiet down the masses point to socialism, but meantime, they secretly support the government; and they inveigh against the powers of the state and of public force if some conflict should bring blood on the streets. But "in their intimate spirit" they believe that the government could not do otherwise; and they vote against military budgets, and yet "their heart is not hardened and foreclosed to patriotism." Radicals, socialists, Freemasons all shout and make noises but "they cooperate toward a kind of democratic liberalism much more conservative and cautious than anyone would have believed, anyone who would have given too much importance to the style of oratory. . . ."

This is a stereotype, an artificial and, on the whole, false picture; at any rate it is insufficient to give a genuine view of the Italy of that time. The writer has gone on stressing colors, his own colors. He has been pleased to present to his readers a certain kind of Italy, cut according to a model of his own political ideal and according to his own human temperament. In an Italy thus imagined, personages like Crispi appear to be disturbers and deviators. With them, the natural process of development of the Italian people is interrupted. Italy—that virtuous, balanced, tolerant Italy, good at heart even if at times she made a bad face, wise enough not to risk anything, careful not to let her reach exceed her grasp, judicious in not getting into bad company, fell sick —political Italy got into its head that it had fallen both internally and externally into some sort of illness. The advent of Crispi was therefore heralded with general applause. The country felt itself in good hands, strongly governed. Ended once and for all was the remissive and cowardly attitude toward other states and peoples! Crispi would deliver that government which Italians had for so long and vainly yearned for! Thus men of all parties—even the Right, so they said, and the Left—greeted him. But these people, Croce objects, asked of Crispi neither a reconstitution of parties nor reforms of the State in a reactionary sense, not even in a parliamentary or constitutional sense, nor did they expect a greater radicalism or liberalism, nor a religious struggle for the exaltation or repulsion of religious values and of Catholicism, nor a foreign policy which would have followed roads different from those indicated by Crispi, nor a belligerent policy, nor an economic direction in one sense or another. In other words, they sought not new experiences and life, but only the "so-called energy," which was in particular "the very expectation of supreme benefits and of national greatness, from an individual who would conceive those thoughts which the Italian people did not know how to conceive, who would discover those roads which the Italian people did not know, who would find in himself that strength which the Italian people did not possess, or who would awaken it under his command and under his guidance." In other words, what was wanted was a sort of dictator who would operate within the existing framework and yet who would achieve some miracle. For Italians the hopes reposed in Crispi were not a sign of vigor, not the beginning of new experiences and life. Rather those hopes arose as a positive manifestation of the disorientation and bewilderment and pessimism and discomfort that weighed upon an epoch and a generation dominated by a philosophy which was by then exhausted. Crispi–unable to express and synthesize what did not exist in the people, incapable of executing works for which the necessary conditions were lacking, not possessing the virtues of the precursor, since he was only a politician altogether enclosed within the society of his time–could not offer to those who were so expectant anything but that formal energy which they demanded: all he could offer was his inflamed imagination and credulousness and his passion-driven character, and his predisposition to suspicion and fear, instead of depth and logical solidity. . . .

Here, among other things, we must ask Croce to account for this hiatus between the Italy of Crispi and the Italy of the preceding and following era. We must ask how this Italy of Crispi, this Italy sick and addicted, maniacal, should have sprung up between two Italys so differently disposed; and what this represented and what, if we may so call it, this sickness in the organism of the nation represented. Perhaps a bad philosophical tendency could account for this phenomenon? But when in our country his philosophy so dominated and tyrannized, whether for good or ill, sentimental and practical life? Is it really beyond possibility that Crispi may have himself represented a certain tradition of the Risorgimento, of men on both the Right and on the Left? These men had perhaps foreseen the needs, expressed the consciousness, however morbid it may have been, of a nation which was beginning to catch its breath–after 1866, after 1878, after 1882–and was beginning again, as happens after all moments of growth or when men of greater stature give them a helping hand, to painfully notice the contrast between its past and its present.

Croce starts with a definitely fixed idea of a *History of Italy,* very modest, very recent, which does not permit Italians too much pride or too many pretensions: a history of Italy that begins with national unity and with the national state, and that can be begun only from that time, whereas before then there were only events and histories of particular States, of the Kingdom of Naples or of Sardinia, of the Venetian Republic or of the States of the Church. This is a bit true and a bit untrue. At any rate, our historiographical problem and the difficulty of writing a history of Italy is one thing, and the state of mind of the Italian people, the sense felt among cultured classes concerning its unity and its greatness through the centuries, is another. And how can one throw out of the heart of these people–grown upon the soil of Rome and of the papacy, of Dante and Machiavelli and of the Renaissance–how can one remove from it the ferment of all this past? The Risorgimento itself cannot be explained or would have been something else without the stimulus of a great history which pressed upon it from behind and aided, illumined, and spiritualized economic progress, the rise of new classes, the perfecting of the state machinery, etc. That a great poet like Carducci should have adhered to Crispi, does that not mean anything for the evaluation of Crispi himself?

In this manner, just as there is no adequate treatment of Crispi, there is no place, that is, there is no historical explanation, in Croce's *History of Italy from 1871 to 1915* for those movements and tendencies which in some manner were connected with him or, at least with the spiritual situation from which he had drawn not a little of his brief fortune. Even Italian nationalism is a sickness. It made its first appearance in Germany, with Bismarck, at a time, as we mentioned above, when European politics was changing its face and "the ideals that had guided it until then were dissolved and were to take a temporary but rather long rest." In its place there was instituted a reactionary policy, the policy of a government that was semi-absolute and bureaucratic, and yet was capable of acting upon the modern world with its industrialism, its banks, its science, its state socialism. Meanwhile, faith in treaties seemed to be uncertain as a result of the "understood clause," which stated that their validity would last as long as convenient (a novelty? and, altogether, an extravaganza?). Plebiscites were rejected in favor of a policy of annexations, even as problems of nationality were not yet resolved. . . . A sickness of moral conscience was bound to fester, says Croce. The first and most ancient religious faith having fallen, and, after that, faith in rationality and in the Enlightenment, new currents of thought and ideologies arose and fought even against the more mature religion, that of history and liberalism. Thus "Bismarckism and industrialism and their repercussions and internal contrasts were incapable of recomposing themselves into a new and serene religion, for they have molded a turgid state of mind, somewhere between lust for enjoyment, spirit of adventure and conquest, frenzied mania of power, restlessness and at the same time disaffection and indifference, as happens to whomever lives in the maelstrom, at the center of things, for only outside that center is the religious and ethical conscience of man." It was, in some, a "spirit of conquest and of adventure, violent and cynical." These predispositions of mind, which had their beginning in Germany, England, and France, then made progress even in that "simple and sane Italy." At this point D'Annunzian literature appeared.

At that time there matured in Italy, it is true, a philosophy of reaction against positivism and scientism. But unfortunately it was maturing in the environment that had been prepared by D'Annunzio and by a wave of plutocratic psychology, which was in quest of gaudy, shiny, and, at bottom, coarse things. True that there was "a more solid and truer rationalism": in most people, however, it amounted to irrationalism, however baptized as idealism–in a word, an extravagant "irrationalist idealism." And with all this irrationalism or false idealism there were other things: intuitionism, pragmatism, mysticism, theosophism, belief in magic, futurism, etc., which were the result of a confusion of concepts and characterized by the absence of logical breaks, depressions of the critical sense, games, and tricks of the imagination. And in the moral and political field there was something which corresponded to this theoretical irrationalism. No more socialist ideals. Rather the imagination and the desires of the new generation and of those who had been deluded by antecedents turned themselves toward "imperialism" or "nationalism," of which D'Annunzio was the spiritual father, with his psychology "culminating in the dream of a sanguinary and lustful Borgian Renaissance." Into this psychology the Italian literati of nationalism infused intellectual elements drawn from the literary nationalism of Barrès or from the rationalist nationalism of Maurras, and then from syndicalism and the theory of "violence" of Sorel . . . in other words, even here terrible things! But Benedetto Croce exaggerates. Personal tastes, dark ill humor, the spirit of contradiction and excessive importance given to mental habit, to the logical elements of life, and to *a priori* philosophical principles and assumptions, that is, to a predetermined philosophy rigidly assumed as a measure or touchstone of reality, indeed of reality on its way of being formed: all these have put the historian off the track. To me Croce seems to be scandalized—he condemns more than he evaluates. A defect exists in his sense of proportion and in his sense of orientation, moralism, and pedagogical inclination,—and that defect embroils him in condemnations and recriminations. Can one possibly reduce to those exotic philosophies the travail of a generation of Italians who, spurred by new problems, revealed a change of mind and thought, even while attempting to orient their spirit and systematize their thinking (blessed are those individuals and those people who proceed by the full light of logic alone! but do they exist then?). . . .

Benedetto Croce has conducted his work very far away from such a spiritual attitude [as Carducci possessed]. He had begun his work with the intention of putting to flight the "idols" which obscure the vision of the real Italy, of "not contaminating historical inquiry with political polemic." But alas! the "idols" are all there, even if they are different from those of a former day. And thus political polemic appears on every page, on every line. It did not seem enough to exclude from the treatment the more recent and problematical years! And in reality the polemic, the polemical spirit, is in us and in the very nature of things. This book, according to the judgment of all, of those who like it and all those who don't, is nothing but a polemic—implicit and explicit—both in its rapid allusions and its documentation, whether in the text or, even more, in the notes. Sometimes we lose sight of the history of Italy and we see before us only Benedetto Croce, armed with his critique from head to foot. At the end, there rises in the reader a sense almost of tedium and of dissatisfaction. Weary of correctors, of interpreters, of translators, he is assailed by a lively desire for simple material, for raw and clear material not too much handled or mixed or manufactured to serve the purposes of a thesis. He almost desires a chronicle of the good old days, a simple and live recital, not overwhelmed by the excess of conceptual elements with which the historian, interposing himself with too much insistence and petulance between the reader and the facts, takes away from these their clearest, most persuasive and emotive virtues.

The truth is that Croce is desperately fighting against today's [Fascist] Italy; and every one of his judgments upon the past, from 1871 to 1915, becomes colored by the reflections of this battle. Have not the Italians—and not only they after all!—subjected to discussion and division the doctrines and the practice of their liberalism? Here, then, is the progress of the history of Italy after 1871 seen almost theologically, as if it were the progressive realization of liberalism and of the liberal method, connected in its term with the renewal of philosophy in the idealistic sense. Have Italians absorbed something from the nationalist movement? Does the entire social life of the masses of workers and peasants, their socialism of a former day, their tendency toward internationalism and the class struggle–do these give evidence of their having become "nationalized"? And then appear [Croce's] sarcasms and completely negative judgments on the nationalism of fifteen or twenty years ago, which he identifies with hypocrisy and portrays as being nothing but utilitarian calculation or dismisses with the statement (and how can the two be reconciled?) that everything was "a tendency toward adventure of wars." Have the Italians once again excited themselves for Crispi, even admitting his weaknesses and deficiencies in his work in Government? And here is Croce, admonishing for thirty pages that Crispi was nothing, that he was sterile because, after his fall, "all the motives of Crispi's policy, colonial foreign and internal, were abandoned one after another, and new criteria were formed which effectively upheld Italian life until the Great War and in fact during the course of that War" –for, at any rate, even they were temporary! Do [present day] Italians, who have a high sense of their country, feel themselves carried, more than the two preceding generations, to conceive and to hope for great things? And here is Croce who recites once again the eulogy of the "mediocre," of the simple life. Have Italians left behind them, I will not say Rudinì, but Giolitti, without, regarding the latter, praising some of the merits he possessed as a statesman? And here is Croce to praise Rudinì, to place Giolitti on the altar.

Giolitti is the hero of this book. He towers in it as a political man just as Croce towers in it as a philosopher. Crocean idealism and Giolittian liberalism are seen and are placed before us as if they were animated by the same spirit and as if they tended, in different ways and without too many conscious contacts, toward the same goal. They have matured together, together they accompanied Italy in its laborious ascent, the one in the theoretical order, the other in the practical sphere. Last of all: Have the Italians cast behind them socialism, Freemasonry, the sacred principles [of the French Revolution]? And here is Croce, almost reconciled with all this, pointing, for the edification of his readers, to the idyll shared among socialists, radicals, and Freemasons during the Giolittian era. *A propos* of the socialists who had been persecuted during the Crispi era, he says that the "Utopia of today is the truth of tomorrow" (if any Utopia does remain!). Truly, the Italians have now heard from Croce words and judgments which to them sound different from those he expressed at that time [during the Giolittian era]. From him they learned, and they have been stimulated to think about, not a few of the things in which they now believe. He engaged in the critique of political democracy and of Freemasonry, with many counsels to guard against this Gallic germ. He placed in their hands the *Reflections on Violence* by Sorel. He derided in 1914–18 the mythology of the Entente and he exhorted them rather to hold in esteem the good teachings of the Italian political tradition, even if in the latest times it had returned to us through some sort of German disguise. He had pointed out to them a realistic conception of politics, which develops through struggles now open, now insidious, of individuals and peoples and states intent upon maintaining and developing their existence, even at the cost of others, if it is not otherwise possible . . . Has the philosopher changed his way? or have the Italians misunderstood and equivocated, having taken from Croce his words and not his spirit? Or rather did they, at a certain moment, abandon the philosopher by drawing for themselves logical consequences before which he himself had stopped?

But I do not seek the explanation of these enigmas: and even less do I seek an accounting from Benedetto Croce of his political convictions. I only seek to explain to myself how it has come about that a writer like him, who for an entire decade occupied a high post, exercised an efficacious propulsive action in our culture, and struggled with honor even in the historical field as such, should have given us now so mediocre a *History of Italy.* Croce the historian has remained at last much inferior to Croce the erudite, to Croce the philosopher, to Croce the theoretician of history. . . .

Croce and Giolitti as Protagonists of the Secular Tradition: A Catholic Appraisal*

ARTURO CARLO JEMOLO

IF A REFERENDUM were held among Italians to nominate the two greatest personalities of the last fifty years, without regard to the nature of their activities, I believe that most—with the exception of an inconsiderable number of Fascists—would put their crosses against the names of Benedetto Croce and Giovanni Giolitti. Of very different types—they had a wholesome respect for each other—Croce was a minister in Giolitti's last Government and as a historian of the twentieth century reassessed Giolitti's work: the one a thinker, a front-rank figure among European intellectuals, a man of vast culture, but who for the greater part of his life remained on the fringe of politics, and only in his old age played an active part in them, and even then only a minor part; the other a man whose culture, though considerable, was nevertheless limited, who devoted all his energies to political life and saw everything through the eyes of a parliamentarian, who in politics was not a theorist but an empiricist with a special

* From A. C. Jemolo, *Church and State in Italy, 1850–1950*. Translated by David Moore (Oxford: Basil Blackwell, 1960), 91–102. Reprinted by permission of Basil Blackwell, Publisher.

flair for dealing with problems of finance and administration.

Cultivated people outside Italy know of Benedetto Croce the idealistic philosopher and the historian; but it is impossible for those who have no direct experience of Italian life to realize what he has meant to Italians. It is not enough even to say that he was the philosopher and teacher of at least two generations, from the eighties onwards, for Croce, who never occupied a university chair, not only had a decisive influence on the intellectual development of those who knew him, who read his books and adhered to his philosophy, but, as happens to the very few who for a time completely dominate the intellectual life of a country, he made an essential, if indirect, contribution to the education of those who did not come under his immediate influence, did not read his works, or remained for ever hostile to his teaching.

Neither the Catholic anchored to the teaching of the Church, with its traditional philosophy founded on Thomism, nor the Communist intellectual enslaved by dialectical materialism, could ever claim to be a disciple of Croce. But among the exponents of Catholic culture it is necessary to distinguish between the many who have read Croce, absorbing his doctrines if only later to repudiate them, who have continually revised their traditional beliefs in the light of Crocean idealism, and who have constantly reconsidered and brought up to date almost all their literary and historical judgments in the light of what Croce wrote: and the few who, shut away in monasteries or languishing in remote villages, have remained in fact inaccessible to Croce, and in some cases have never even heard of him. Between them there is a great gulf fixed. The first are contemporaries with whom one can talk and argue; they differ from us in outlook, but their world is the same. The second belong to a different world, and with them no argument is possible; they exert no influence, nor are they amenable to any, because all the channels of communication between themselves and the outside world are blocked.

In the same way, one cannot adequately explain Italian Communism to-day, or the fact that it is still possible for intellectuals of opposite convictions to achieve a limited measure of agreement, unless one reflects that the Communist intellectual who has hitherto stolen most of the limelight is not the man who has been brought up exclusively on the standard texts of Communism, but the man who has matured in the grammar schools and universities of Italy and who, however much he likes to cite only those standard texts as his sources, is in reality also of Crocean derivation.

In this sense, I believe, Croce's influence was far greater than that of Gioberti and Rosmini, whose work covered a much narrower field and who, moreover, could not claim to have set a whole generation talking and arguing about their doctrines. It may be compared (although his work made a far less profound social impact, and–as the formative element of two generations, not as a contribution to European philosophy–it had a purely domestic significance) with that of the great precursors of the French Revolution, Voltaire and Rousseau, or with that exerted over a similar period by Goethe.

What was Croce's contribution to Italian thought about the relations between Church and State?

During the early years of Fascism there were some who accused Croce of having been one of its originators. This ridiculous accusation was prompted perhaps by the recollection that, at the beginning of the Fascist era and of the period of nationalism that preceded it, the Italian people had found themselves without the means of combating the anti-Risorgimental, anti-illuministic, anti-humanitarian doctrines which those movements proclaimed. For Croce had dispelled many of the animosities, exposed the baselessness of many of the ingenuous beliefs, and exploded many of the myths which, though they represented the dross of the thought of the Risorgimento, were nevertheless the medium through which it imposed itself on the humbler classes, on those who were no more than half educated.

In 1905 Croce published in his review, *La Critica,* his 'personal recollections' *A proposito del positivismo italiano,* in which he wrote: 'Among the imbecilities which the man who concerns himself with philosophy and with the pursuit of learning in general may commit in the course of his life, there is one which I can boast that I have always avoided, even in my earliest youth: I have never been a *positivist.*' And he describes the adherents of positivism–students, lawyers, doctors–who read nothing, repeat the usual parrot-cries, and quote at second and third hand without even bothering to check their facts. What depresses Croce is the vulgarity of the masses, of the half-educated people who crowd the universities and leave them with the regulation diplomas and degrees, and the sight of so much vulgar anti-clericalism, compounded of ignorance and incomprehension, nurtured on legends which no self-respecting historian would ever dream of discussing, and incapable of discriminating between the various branches of the Church's activity. What offends him is the average man's superstitious, fetishistic attachment—the fruit of mental laziness much more than of enlightened enthusiasm—not to the doctrines of the Risorgimento but to its dross, to its incomprehension of all that went before, of the centuries of history that preceded it (an attachment which, he feels, incidentally casts a slur on the traditions of his native province and of his family, on the judgments which he as a historian has passed on the Kingdom of Naples). What pains him is the puerile negation of the whole life of the spirit, the puerile belief that chemistry and physiology can take the place of philosophy.

But even the great positivists do not escape his censure. Herbert Spencer is described as 'one of the most jejune philosophers who ever lived'. 'The only philosophers recognized as legitimate and treated with respect [by the positivists] were those who promised, with the gestures of quack dentists haranguing the crowds from the top of their barrows laden with medicine bottles and tins, to pursue their philosophical researches in the laboratory, with the aid of scientific instruments and mechanical gadgets.'

Are we still in the realm of pure philosophy? Yes and no.

With his usual candour Croce continues: 'My horror of positivism . . . became so intense that for several years it stifled even the democratic sympathies which I have always possessed. . . . For some reason unknown (unless, perhaps, it was that blind adulation of popularity which is almost inevitable under this form of government), Italian democracy was positivistic in character; and my stomach refused to digest it until it had been seasoned with Marxian socialism, which, as everybody now knows, is impregnated with classical German philosophy. Even to-day the positivistic phraseology of certain Italian democrats gets on my nerves and makes me almost wish I were a conservative . . . and many more or less worthy democratic agitators would be well-advised to refrain from discoursing upon science and philosophy, of which they lack the expert knowledge with which one must credit them in other fields of human activity.' From this position he never retreated.

If we turn to *La filosofia della pratica* we read: 'This function of an idealistic ethical symbol, this affirmation that the moral act is an expression of the love and the will of the universal Spirit, is characteristic of the religious and Christian Ethic, the Ethic of love and of the anxious search for the divine presence, which, as a result of narrow partisanship or lack of insight, is spurned and vilified to-day by vulgar rationalists and intellectualists, by so-called free-thinkers and similar riff-raff who frequent masonic lodges. There is hardly any truth of Ethics that cannot be expressed in the words of traditional religion, which we learned as children and which rise spontaneously to our lips because they are the most sublime, the most appropriate, and the most beautiful of all: words that are, to be sure, still redolent of mythology, yet at the same time instinct with philosophy. Between the idealistic philosopher and the religious man there is undoubtedly a deep rift; but it is no different from that which appears in ourselves on the eve of a crisis, when we are mentally divided, and yet very close to inner unity and harmony. If the religious man cannot help regarding the philosopher as his adversary, indeed as his mortal enemy, the philosopher for his part sees in the religious man his younger brother, himself as he was but a moment before. Hence, he will always feel more strongly attracted to an austere, compassionate, allegorical religious ethic than to one that is superficially rationalistic.'

This page forms a prelude to the better-known essay published in 1942, *Perché non possiamo non dirci 'cristiani'*.[1]

Even before Croce we can discern, in the cultured bourgeoisie of liberal traditions—we need not here attempt to define the sentiments of the Catholic middle class—an impatience both with the exponents of positivistic pseudo-philosophy, who actually believed that physiology and the other positive sciences could dispel all shadows, leaving no further room for speculation, and with the pseudo-history which sought to substantiate slanderous tales about Popes or kings, devoid of any documentary foundation, as well as with those who evinced an intense and unqualified admiration for all the personalities and events of the Risorgimento.

[1] Anyone who wishes to obtain an idea of the vehement reaction on the part of convinced positivists to Croce's writings should read the little-known posthumous essay by the economist Achille Loria, *Una crociera eccezionale* (Milan, 1947), in which it is asserted (p. 72) that it was Croce's 'undisguised intention to rebuild religion on the ruins of positivism. In spite of everything, he is still no more than an archpriest of the *Scuole Pie*. . . .'

Croce used his influence to encourage these still half-hearted and sporadic tendencies.

The old anti-clericals, who saw the hand of the 'Jesuit' in every disaster, and regarded the great saints merely as impostors or eccentrics or even as madmen, gradually degenerated into figures of fun; and the old patriotic rhetoric, based on invective and on evocations of Italian glories, became equally insupportable.

All this helped in no small measure to increase the seriousness of our outlook, to purify our culture; it had a powerful educational effect on the Italian middle class and on university students. But it is none the less true that a first defensive barrier against a revival of anti-illuministic doctrines–the weakest of all, but the one that protected the least-cultured classes–had now fallen. When men of fervent piety and lofty sentiments take up the axe and proceed to demolish legends and superstitions, truly religious spirits take heart of grace and breathe more freely: they cleave to their Church, which becomes stronger than ever; but men of smaller minds, who are more numerous, the mentally lazy, incapable of abandoning their routine or of reasoning, quickly lose their bearings; beneath the outer crust of superstition and legend that has fallen away they fail to discern the vibrant pulse of faith. So it was that those who taught men to regard the Risorgimento with a dispassionate eye, to venerate it for its truly good qualities, for the currents of thought which had inspired it and run through it, for the virtues of its most illustrious figures, contrived in the process to educate a certain number of enlightened spirits, inveterate anti-totalitarians whom Fascism could never have deflected from their course. At the same time, however, they imbued the minds of ordinary men with the idea that it was permissible to criticize the followers of Garibaldi, that one need not be a Jesuit to maintain that there had been some good in the world before the Risorgimento, that the latter had even destroyed a number of excellent institutions. And so for many mediocre intelligences, for certain indolent minds, the Risorgimento, ceasing to be above criticism, ceased also to constitute a safeguard against the temptation to return to the cult of the despot which relieves the individual man of the necessity of thinking for himself, to the cult of blind obedience to the ruler, in which the voice of conscience is silenced.

There was, moreover, running through the whole of Croce's work, a vein of anti-illuminism, which certainly represented an intellectual achievement on the part of the philosopher, and which influenced even minds more acute than those whose judgment might have been warped by a too-realistic vision of the Risorgimento.

Croce's philosophy is a-religious, and there is no place in it for the infinite. It lays due emphasis on the ethical and social values of Christianity, but all meditation and speculation on a possible supernatural world are held to be outside its province. It is not concerned with effecting compromises, with tracing out lines of demarcation, with allocating spheres of influence. The worlds of thought and reason, all the possible achievements of the human intellect—these are the province of philosophy, which is sovereign and independent in its own field. Beyond is the realm of poetry, the realm of mythology; beyond, too, in accordance with a poetic convention, is the realm of religion. But the compromise which other philosophies have attempted, the consideration of an aspect of reality which cannot be explored by reason and which represents the special province of religion, the legitimate domain of a faith not subject to rational controls, remains extraneous to the philosophy of Croce.

It is well known that certain thinkers, following in the wake of this philosophy, have believed in the possibility of reaching a compromise with Catholicism: a compromise which, however, in the best-known attempt, that of Giovanni Gentile, entails the complete subordination of the traditional Catholic doctrine, which is left with only a nominal independence, to the idealistic philosophy, which appropriates its substance.[2]

Personally, through *La Critica,* Croce was always a champion of lay culture and of the secular State. His writing was frequently anti-clerical in tone, and he deprecated the way in which Catholic writers falsified history and the tendency of men with religious prejudices to reassess and disparage literary epochs and periods. This anti-religious strain is even more pronounced in the man who, after the dismissal of Gentile, collaborated with Croce in the work of editing *La Critica:* Adolfo Omodeo.

However, among the ways in which the political world might have exploited Croce's thought was the

[2] See also the last published writing of G. Gentile, a lecture entitled *La mia religione* (Florence, 1943), where there is an echo of Lambruschini in the references to the negativity of religious dogmas and the restrictive character of the authority responsible for their maintenance as also for their formulation.

possibility that, basing itself on the clear-cut distinction between religion, which belongs to the realm of poetry, and the Church, which represents social power, with aims that are realized in every sphere of practical life, it might have discerned no inconsistency of conduct in a State which described itself as secular and claimed to preserve the autonomy of its own ethical life, but which at the same time made all sorts of concessions to the Church in the juridical field—which, no less than the economic field, is a sphere of practical life—and bound itself to the Holy See through concordats giving the latter a privileged position.

Giovanni Giolitti was a minister during Italy's years of prosperity (1900–15)—the era of her industrial development, of the conquest of Libya, of the paper lira which more than held its own against the gold currency.

He belonged to a generation which in its adolescence, when it was too young to participate in military or political events, had seen the unification of Italy completed as if by a miracle within the space of two years; a generation which could not recall the conspiracies, the political trials, the Mazzinianism of the heroic period, even though its members must have been fully conversant with the history of such recent events and in their early childhood may even have heard them described by their parents. This generation had grown up in the years following 1861. It may therefore be said (speaking generally) that it had not experienced the dissatisfaction and indignation which so many of the pre-1860 liberal middle class had felt at the corruption and the inadequacy of the infant State and at its failure to reflect the renewed national consciousness. It had, however, been considerably influenced in its most formative years by that feeling of disappointment which always follows the realization of plans long prepared and contemplated—of designs hitherto regarded as the key to a substantial betterment of conditions—and in particular the institution of new political régimes: a feeling which was in fact widespread in Italy during the years that followed the country's unification.

Giolitti belonged to the Piedmontese middle class—which, although it had furnished the extreme parties with supporters, for the most part had continued to regard the conflicts of parties with suspicion and had remained hostile to and contemptuous of platform orators and extremists. This class was convinced of the necessity for the State (but for its horror of strong words it might, even have spoken of its 'sanctity'), convinced that it was every man's duty to see that the country was well governed. It did not share that distrust of all forms of State control and intervention which was apparent in other provinces; but its confidence in the State was fixed upon the administration, and did not extend to the various political organizations. Those who have known Piedmontese of Giolitti's generation are aware that in most cases—especially when they talked freely—they revealed an extreme bitterness towards the Garibaldini and the old radicals and an intense dislike and distrust of priests who dabbled in politics. For the most part they pursued moderate political ideals. Thus, they envisaged a separation of Church and State free from all rancour and unmarred by legalistic quibbling, together with a just administration, an irreproachable civil service, and a prudent financial policy, designed to keep taxes low and the market value of consolidated stock high. They were, accordingly, opposed to all adventures in the realm of foreign policy and, later on, to all colonial enterprises.

The middle class of that generation had one dominating characteristic (shared, incidentally, by all North Italians): a profound horror of advertising their feelings, which they felt should in no circumstances be exposed to public view.

Italians younger than himself who came from other provinces often disliked Giolitti for those characteristics which he shared with his fellow Piedmontese and with the rest of his generation of the provincial middle class. They disliked his persuasive but restrained oratory, sometimes witty and challenging but unrhetorical, never appealing to sentiment, yet, when the necessity arose, he did not hesitate to invoke the great moral principles, making frequent references to the importance of a sense of duty and to the sanctity of the plighted word. They disliked the roughness of his style, which in his speeches was masked by a certain persuasiveness, a certain liveliness in debate, as well as by occasional flashes of wit, but which was fully apparent in his infrequent writings, and which in a literary sense placed him on a lower plane than such of his contemporaries as Crispi, Luzzatti, Sonnino, and even the modest Boselli. They disliked his seeming disregard for culture. In office, however, he strove to satisfy the educational needs of the people at all levels, formed a complete and accurate picture of the leading figures in every branch of Italian art and science and honoured in the most fitting ways those of his countrymen who had distinguished themselves in the literary, scientific and artistic fields. But it was completely foreign to his nature to adorn his conversation with literary quotations or in any way to reveal the extent of his knowledge and of his interests outside the sphere of politics and government. Again, even in the years of his greatest triumphs the majority of Italians were displeased by his ostentatious preference for internal politics, particularly for questions relating to finance, public works and departmental administration. But his apparent indifference to foreign affairs did not prevent him from bringing Italy's most auspicious colonial enterprise to a triumphant conclusion and from clearly defining in 1913 the limits of his country's obligations under the Triple Alliance, thereby nipping in the bud Austria's plans for a Serbian adventure. They disliked his way of considering every question from the point of view of Parliament, his profound conviction that the only 'country' of which it was necessary to take account was the legislative body. Finally, they disapproved of what was in fact his supreme virtue—his great sense of proportion, which led him to discourage excessive hopes and over-bold aspirations.

Was Giolitti a religious man? Did he believe in God? The Piedmontese of his generation had a great horror of displaying their feelings, particularly in the matter of religion. They did not flaunt their beliefs, however fervently held; their religion, in fact, was devoid of any lyrical quality. On the question whether or not they were practising Christians they always maintained a discreet silence. (For that matter, history does not record whether Cavour himself was in the habit of attending Mass and partaking of the sacraments: all we know is that he received the consolations of religion on his death-bed.)

To the best of our knowledge, even in conversation within Giolitti's family circle the subject of religion was never mentioned. He had the deepest respect for the beliefs of others. He considered it natural that the great events of life–birth, marriage, death–should be signalized by a religious ceremony. But he took no intellectual part in religious discussions, even in those which concerned the external life of the Church, its basic policies. On his death-bed he found it natural to receive the consolations of religion, and to no one did it seem that his attitude represented the return of one who had strayed from the fold. But certainly he had remained in a corner of the fold, showing little curiosity about what took place elsewhere within it.

If there is one conviction which seems clearly to underlie the whole of Giolitti's work–alike as Minister, as President of the Council, and as leader of the party in power–in so far as it concerns the relations between Church and State, it is this: that the past is dead and buried; that Italy, united as never before, has nothing to fear from the by now platonic demands of the Holy See–whether propounded by Leo XIII, who, clearly, still cherished territorial ambitions, or by Pius X, who merely deplored the conditions imposed on the Papacy. That the possibility of a formal reconciliation did not exist was the opinion of all clear-sighted Italians, at any rate after the disappointment of 1887 and until 1918. But Giolitti considered that such a reconciliation was not even desirable. In character he was the antithesis of Crispi and—to compare him with a more recent figure—of Mussolini. By no means inclined to underrate the importance of personal success and prestige, he was attracted not by their superficial glitter but by their value as a means to an end. Thus, he loved to dominate the Chamber, but every so often he himself provoked crises which enabled him to retire for a period from the direction of public affairs. In his eyes they were to be measured in terms of concrete results achieved, not of interminable parliamentary ovations in which deputies joined with the spectators in the public galleries, and still less of popular acclamation, which would merely have irritated him. Like all the parliamentarians of his generation he tended to identify the country with the legislature, and so was inclined to underrate the significance of any manifestations of opinion which did not culminate in parliamentary divisions and in alterations of parliamentary majorities and minorities. (What view, incidentally, did the politicians of the early 1900s take of irredentist feeling, which counted for nothing in Parliament?) Because of this he considered that his great achievement in the matter of the relations between Church and State lay in the fact that he had succeeded in inducing Catholics to participate in political life without constituting a party of their own, which would have provoked reactions and revived controversies that might have proved embarrassing. In this way he had strengthened what he regarded as the *pars sanior* of the country, that which favoured enlightened and moderate progress. Unwittingly, too, he had realized the ideal of the statesman who makes the most effective contribution to reconciliation by never speaking of it, never setting a term for it—knowing that it will come about after he has descended into the peace of the grave, yet creating the spiritual atmosphere necessary to ensure that the work of time, which heals all wounds, shall not be impeded by controversies or by incidents that may inflame wounds not yet healed. But in truth we do not know whether in his heart of hearts he ever envisaged a formal reconciliation, however long delayed, whether he thought fit to work for it, if only in the interests of his own generation's children and grandchildren. He was, we must remember, always a man of the Left, and he was always the bureaucrat of the Piedmontese provincial middle class, with their characteristic horror of any manifestation of feeling, particularly religious feeling, and their aversion to any form of theatricality. I think he would have been not a little shocked to be shown the scenes so often depicted in popular oleographs, of the Pope arm-in-arm with the King, or of cheering crowds lining the route between St. Peter's and the Quirinal. His formula, almost certainly not premeditated, and not intended to be an amendment of Cavour's famous dictum, of the State and the Church advancing along two parallel lines, and hence never destined to meet, certainly expressed his true sentiments. And well did it epitomize the liberal creed, which a well-known German publicist had expressed many years before when he asserted that never in the course of his journey from the cradle to the grave should the citizen be asked by the State to expound his religious beliefs. Nor did his formula make it necessary for the State to adopt the dangerous procedure of blinding itself to facts, to remain in ignorance of the ways in which religious feeling found expression, of what the Faithful expected from the State in the way of moral leadership, and above all of the nature of the political forces that were arrayed on the side of the Church. Instead, it signified—and in this respect Giolitti's policy conformed to it—that legislation, which represents only a small part of a Government's activity, should never concern itself with religious matters, nor seek to give statutory effect to decrees or interdicts or sanctions designed to weaken the authority of the Church.

Pre-Fascist Democracy and the Tasks of Anti-Fascism*

GAETANO SALVEMINI

YOU HAVE WRITTEN that an "Italian democracy has never existed." This statement of yours that "Italian democracy has never existed" is repeated in England and America by all the propagandists of Fascism. One of the chief battle forces of their propaganda is precisely the following: "The Italian is very different from the people of England and from that of the United States; the Italian people is incapable of governing itself; it can only be governed by dictatorial means; in fact in Italy there has never been a democ-

* From Gaetano Salvemini, "Che cosa è stata la democrazia in Italia," a letter to *L'Italia del Popolo* [Paris: Organ of the Partito Repubblicano Italiano], May 31, 1927; reprinted in *La Resistenza: Giustizia e Libertà* (Turin), Anno XVI, September 9, 1962, p. 4. Reprinted by permission of *La Resistenza: Giustizia e Libertà*. Editor's translation.

racy. The Italian people has always been governed by dictators, whether they were called Cavour, Depretis, Crispi, Giolitti, etc.; the difference between Mussolini and his predecessors is only this: that while his predecessors used to mask their dictatorship under the fiction of democracy, Mussolini has demolished this fiction; he has not suppressed any democracy because in Italy there never was a democracy; he has committed an act of sincerity by putting an end to the democratic comedy, an act which has interpreted the deepest instincts and needs of the Italian people that has never had a democracy and that would not know what to do with democracy."

If it were true that in Italy there never has been democracy, the Fascists would be in a strong position in maintaining that the Italian people is not made for democracy; to the historical experience, which would be in favor of the Fascists, we could only oppose an act of faith which no one would be obliged to share, if that experience were true. Furthermore, no one would succeed any more in understanding what the Fascists have done in Italy, if they have not destroyed democracy; no one would any more understand what kind of responsibility we anti-Fascists attribute to the Fascists.

But is it really true that in Italy there never was democracy?

If by democracy we mean "all democratic institutions, none barred," then it is certain that we did not have democracy. In fact, we did not have a republic; the separation between church and state was not perfect; the press was largely corrupted by capitalistic influences; universal suffrage was all too often perverted through governmental interferences; the control of Parliament over the executive powers of the government was very imperfect, etc., etc.

But what people in this world has ever had or will ever have perfect democracy, if this word means "all the democratic institutions, none barred"?

We did not have *all* of democracy, but we had a number of institutions from whose sum democracy results. There *were* universal suffrage, freedom of speech, freedom of the press, freedom of association, freedom of conscience, freedom of worship, freedom to strike, freedom to live. No democracy in Italy?

Perhaps you say that "in Italy there never was democracy" because in Italy there was no republic. If this is your thought, allow me to say that it is wrong. The republic is one among the institutions of a democracy: it is not all of democracy. France between 1870 and 1877 was a republic, but it did not have many of those other democratic institutions which she has attained from 1877 to 1905. If Mussolini after the march on Rome had proclaimed a republic–as some Republicans, and not the least among them, hoped–we would have had in Italy this democratic institution but we would have lost at the same time all the other institutions of democracy. The "republic and nothing more" is not *all* of democracy.

In Italy we did not have *all* of democracy. We had less democracy than there was in Switzerland, England, the United States, even France; but we were continually enlarging the area of democracy. We were on our way to construct an Italy always less oligarchical and always more democratic. We had more democracy between 1901 and 1914 than we had had between 1876 and 1901. We had had more democracy between 1876 and 1900 than we had had between 1860 and 1870. From 1860 to 1882 the deputies and the members of the town councils were elected by 250,000 persons; in 1921, 6,500,000 persons took part in the national elections. In 1860 there were only the most undeveloped and rudimentary working-class organizations in Italy; in 1920 there were 4,000,000 organized workers and peasants. Having started on the road later than other peoples we were still behind them in comparison. But they, too, had not yet reached the ideal goal. And we were marching toward their own ideal goal, behind them as we were. We were not England; but we had come a long way along the road which during the first half of the nineteenth century separated, say, Turkey from England. Today we have been brought back to the condition of Turkey; the entire work of seventy years will have to start all over again.

If we say this, we only tell no more and no less than the truth. Let us not furnish our enemies arguments with which to make their apologia. Thus we shall prepare for ourselves a concrete basis, without equivocations, upon which we can discuss the tactical and programmatic problems of anti-Fascism.

If we assert that "in Italy there never was democracy" then we commit a factual blunder, or at least we engage ourselves in an equivocal paradox. In so doing we would place ourselves in a position of not being able to define what responsibilities the Fascists have for the crisis which today troubles the moral and political conscience of our country. We would thereby abandon exactly that concrete and unequivocal ground outside of which any search for new anti-Fascist methods and programs would become lost in vague generalities or in oblique maneuvers.

VIII. UNDER FASCISM: THE NEW GENERATION FIGHTS BACK

LONG BEFORE *Sir Lewis Namier popularized the term in connection with the European revolutions of 1848, a number of historical critics in Italy had characterized the Risorgimento as a "revolution of the intellectuals." However accurate or not the expression may be regarded (perhaps, as some claimed, a "revolution of liberal social elites" would have been closer to the truth), it may be tentatively adopted for an understanding of the origins and early character of the leadership of the anti-Fascist opposition in Italy. Between the atrocious assassination by the Fascists of the socialist leader Giacomo Matteotti (June 10, 1924) and the full-fledged explosion of the Armed Resistance against Fascism in 1943–45, whatever the attitudes and reactions of the masses of Italians, organized anti-Fascism had almost of necessity to be a revolution in the making led by social, cultural, and ideological elites and, essentially, libertarian intellectuals dangerously working at home in Italy or more openly agitating abroad against the totalitarian regime. That anti-Fascist liberals, democrats, Catholics, socialists, Communists, and anarchists were divided in their programs and finalities goes without saying; but it is indisputable that, with all their difficulties in creating or maintaining a cohesive anti-Fascist movement under single-minded leadership, they all visualized Fascism as a negation of Italian historic continuity or potentialities. Those individuals among them who, either by choice or by force, were impelled upon a lonely anti-Fascist road, fought the dictatorship as the incarnation of the anti-Risorgimento and projected their political and spiritual passions toward the achievement in Italy of a "second" or "new Risorgimento." The fight against Fascism and the overthrow of the dictatorship was thus envisaged as containing the potentialities for the fulfillment of the ideals and motives of the "first Risorgimento" of the nineteenth century. Therefore, despite their essentially activist motivations the anti-Fascist intelligentsia had, at some moment or another, in one way or another, to engage first or contemporaneously during the moment of action, indeed as a form of action, in meditations upon Italian history and in reappraisals of the past, the more clearly to give their present and future efforts meaning and effectiveness.*

Whatever separated the radical social and spiritual liberalism of Piero Gobetti from the Marxist-Communist ideology of Antonio Gramsci and both from the democratic socialism of Carlo Rosselli, and, again, all three of them from the constitutional-monarchical liberalism of Lauro de Bosis and particularly from the "unpolitical" libertarianism of young Giaime Pintor—all of them would for one reason or another have agreed with the phrase in Pintor's spiritual testament that the fall of Fascism would "re-open all the possibilities of the Risorgimento." This, perhaps, is the most significant thing to note as the assumption common to all five members of the younger anti-Fascist generation whose words appear in this section. There are also two other aspects worthy of some consideration. The dates of the birth and death of all five of these men are revealing: the oldest among them was born in 1891 (Gramsci) before the great "times of trouble" in *Liberal Italy began in the Crispi period, and the youngest (Pintor) was born the year Mussolini was founding the first Fascio: 1919. The average age of this entire extraordinary group of activist intellectuals when they died as victims of Fascism was thirty-two. The second point is also quite illuminating. With the exception of young Pintor, all of these men had been personally or intellectually close to or had felt the direct influence of both "great masters" of the anti-Fascist generation—Benedetto Croce and Gaetano Salvemini. Temperamentally and ideologically, however, Gobetti, Rosselli, and De Bosis directly and Gramsci indirectly had been closer to the democratic inspiration of Salvemini than to the liberal philosophy of Croce.*

The selections from the writings of these five younger Italians of the Fascist era are offered here on their merits, as contrasting expressions of historical consciousness engendered by meditations upon Italy's Risorgimento, post-Risorgimento, and Liberal past in the light of a tragic present for them. The historical judgments they contain may be admired or criticized, accepted or rejected, but they must all be seen as spiritual documents of exceptional value toward understanding the passage from thought to action, from passive contemplation of the Italian past to active visions of the future, from history to life—or death. It is perhaps more for the new dimensions they all suggest toward appraisals of the past than for the objectivity of judgment, that their message may contain a relevance in terms of human dignity itself rather than for purely contingent values.

Fascism as Nemesis of the Liberal Revolution that Failed*

PIERO GOBETTI

PIERO GOBETTI *(1901–26) was the* enfant-prodige *of post-war Italian intellectual life. Before he died in France as a result of a fantastically cruel Fascist assault, Gobetti had managed to create around himself and his famous periodical* Rivoluzione Liberale *(1922–26) a cultural group of immense significance. As student of the Risorgimento Gobetti had always felt intellectually closer to its nonconformist defeated "leaders" and spokesmen (particularly Carlo Cattaneo, the democratic federalist) than to the Cavourian victors. In Turin, in and out of the university, he had studied Croce, had been close to the liberal economist Luigi Einaudi (the future President of the Italian Republic after 1948) and to Gaetano Salvemini, and had actively associated but never officially joined Gramsci's Marxist circles. Gobetti's anti-Fascism was almost indigenous to his intellectual formation and moral personality. He kept himself in an intransigent opposition that made him*

* From Piero Gobetti, *La Rivoluzione liberale* [1924] (new ed. Turin: Giulio Einaudi Editore, 1948), 42–49. Reprinted by permission of Franz J. Horch Associates. Editor's translation.

personally, politically, and ideologically hated by Mussolini himself—and that hatred cost Gobetti his life. In essence, Gobetti tended to see Fascism as a function of "the biography of the Nation," of the historical and moral defects of Risorgimento liberalism and pre-Fascist democracy.

CAVOUR WAS THE only statesman of his time to have had a complete consciousness of the liberal results achieved by the [Italian] unitary revolution. After his death, a historical situation remained, but the revolution found itself without either a content or a guide. The problem posed by Cattaneo became dominant once again.

New adventures of foreign policy imposed themselves upon the nation without any correspondence to the economic life of the nation.

The middle classes had conquered the government without instituting bonds of communication with the other classes. After 1870, from 27,000,000 inhabitants, the number of voters inscribed for political elections was half a million. The poverty of the general economy generated a situation of parasitism: the dominant regime could be considered like a caste of employees interested in conserving their privileges and in impeding every kind of popular participation [in the government]. The heritage of the Kingdom of Naples weighed heavily upon the new state and thus led to increased corruption and the creation of a superstructure of bureaucratic and electoral parasitism against the natural life of the peasants. We should not be surprised that the political struggle resembled a hunt for jobs.

Upon such premises the Italian government naturally had to be a state socialism. But while Lassalle, through the calculation of realistic contingencies, led to Marx, in Italy the terms of the process proved to be Rattazzi and Mazzini. Mazzini and Marx—when one transcends the sentimental expressions and myths which posited an antithesis of style and psychology between them: Mazzini, romantic, vague, imprecise; Marx, clear, inexorable, realistic—posed in two different environments the revolutionary premises of the new society and, through concepts of national mission and of the class struggle, they asserted a voluntaristic principle which harkened back to the function of the state as a liberator of popular activities through a process of individual differentiation. In this sense Mazzini and Marx were liberals. Nevertheless Marx spoke to the people in a language which could be understood because it was founded upon the basic exigencies that characterize life; Mazzini, on the other hand, remained in a generic and rhetorical apostolate, suspended in the vacuum of his ideology, because, finding it impossible to turn to the men in industry or in the factory, he spoke to a people made up of displaced persons, of unemployed, of public employees.

Such objective conditions could not promote a liberal movement, but they generated an almost instinctive utilitarian exploitation of socialist and solidaristic ethics. That is the reason why from 1850 to 1914 the Catholic heritage and the social disaggregation, terrible in the South, obliged the new state organism in Italy to assert itself according to an abstract function of morality which corrupted liberal principles into a democratic conception of mere weary utilitarian pettiness. Italian reformism was not invented by our socialists. Rather it arose naturally with the first discussions concerning popular schools in order to give some sense to the struggle against the Jesuits. Vincenzo Gioberti and Domenico Berti were its legitimate fathers.

After 1860 in the social evolution of Italy, since a new element of economic reorganization had been introduced into the life of the new nation, a much more open economic reformism began to be substituted for the state socialism which had promoted the educational reforms.

School reform, which had been attempted as a moral revolution, might have created the nucleus of a ruling class, but it revealed itself incapable of effective political expression to give proper value to individual forces. The first moment in the development of a popular consciousness had, as a matter of fact, to be a moment essentially economic, the elementary assertion of autonomy and liberty.

Unfortunately, in the customs of Italian life this tenuous economic awakening became confused with a hunt for privilege; the first working class "aristocracies," rather than maintaining themselves in a position of intransigence, invoked, as the bourgeoisie had done, the protection derived from social legislation, just as the small beginnings of industrialization sought the support of tariff protectionism and of government subsidies.

The work of the Left as an economic reformist movement was therefore a logical crowning of our revolutionary impotence. It was the dialectical result of two undeveloped forces incapable of expression; the theocracy was to continue in democracy and reformism while the diplomatic traditions were reduced to the opportunism of administrators. The attitude of conciliation transformed the initial equivocation between Church and State into an equivocation between government and people.

The ideal of government became an eternal monarchy which dispensed privileges. The heritage of a revolution that had not succeeded was such that the Italian reformist movement (like that of a later socialist party) could not grow within the framework of a state the people did not believe in because it had not created it with its blood. Prussian socialism coincided in its ethical value of popular liberation with the significance of the state; it represented the continuation of the spirit of solidarity of the Reformation, it was the heir of a religious sentiment, and it measured itself against the realization of the idea of the state within the conscience of citizens. The practical struggle reduced itself to the terms of economy because a common principle lived within the spirit [of citizens], and it derived meaning from a common development; the unitary revolution in Germany was popular and moral.

In Italy a tradition which was not consciously liberal, but rather instinctively individualistic, was opposed to the vitality of every system which ignored free initiative and attributed to the state an activity distinct from the activity of the citizens.

Thus [in Italy] state socialism renewed itself as an ephemeral moment, as a transaction that had to be surpassed. Once one arrived upon the ground of social legislation, politics became a perpetual transaction in which continuous concessions were followed by continuous requests, without the introduction into the political struggle of a principle of responsibility.

The state was worn out by dissension between

government and people: a government without authority and without autonomy because it was out of touch with and removed from the defective economic conditions—a government founded upon compromise; a people educated in materialism, in a perennial anarchic attitude when confronted with the problem of the social organization.

Neither the Right nor the Left was successful in escaping this necessity of demagogic protectionism; Sella, who followed in a minor style Cavourian practices, was the most unpopular man in the country.

The new [unitary] state, engaged since 1870 in a foreign policy that had been pre-established, found itself without financial resources, with a generation of patriots to compensate through public beneficence and through jobs, prey to and faced by an inconclusive spirit of Garibaldian restlessness. It seemed as if all future success would be compromised if one did not keep alive the state of tension and of expectation in which there was prolonged the enthusiasm of the preceding years; and the truth concerning financial policy was hidden, a show was made of engaging in public works, necessary as some of them may have been. As demagogic and anti-conservative as the Left, even the Right participated in the same radical illusions, and became a *consorteria.* The transformism of Depretis was the most evident expression of an Italy that killed itself in conciliations and shows of unanimity but could not succeed in confronting the terrible duties of founding a state. The Left was also the expression of a characteristically southern situation: for it the problem of unity was posed from the start in the disconcerting terms of a tax policy and of public works.

Only a quick resolution of the electoral problem and of the bureaucratic problem could have resolved this parasitic situation. But one did not dare speak of regional autonomies, in order not to compromise unity, and it seemed necessary to maintain a restrictive electoral Right within an oligarchical circle, as if to recompense the minority that had prepared unification, and in order not to complicate that problem of the state through the intervention of new popular masses, which until now had been neglected and ignored. Thus one did not succeed in consolidating a real or intelligently conservative situation that might have given a tone to national life and disciplined the upsurge of new revolutionary ideologies and forced them to face future responsibilities. Sonnino and Franchetti invoked in vain an enlargement of the suffrage; Stefano Jacini, who represented the most lucid mind in Italian politics after Cavour and Sella, was accused of clericalism when he proclaimed the exigency of creating a new conservative party and traced out a program for it with exemplary critical precision.

When Italians became tired of the tricks and blandishments of Depretis, they abandoned themselves to the facile seductions of Crispi's megalomania, and in the African defeat the entire nation became compromised. Whatever may be said in belated rehabilitations, [the defeat at] Adowa [1896] marked the supreme condemnation of a facile romantic mentality. Adowa, moreover, represented a preventive critique against all nationalist ideologies, destined to arise in Italy through the mentality of adventurers, and with the help of the parasitic spiritual preparation of the lower middle class. Imperialism was ingenuous when there were elementary problems of existence to be resolved.

At the beginning of the twentieth century Italian politics necessarily culminated in *giolittismo,* after a reactionary parenthesis which was sufficient to corrupt the program and the spirit of the emerging socialist party and to demonstrate the danger to which liberty in Italy is always exposed. With Giolitti, the return to the methods of government of Depretis reveals a new kind of seriousness. The historical intuition with which the political action of the Piedmontese statesman began was absolutely genial in its response to the precise situation of the country: the statesman Giolitti recognized his duty by creating an atmosphere of toleration amidst the emergent social conflicts. Thus he did not compromise the slow formation of wealth and of a modern economic mentality, through which the Italian people attempted to repair their historical inferiority. To Giolitti Italy owes ten years of social peace and honest administration. Even if he erred in the measure of his indulgence to demagogy, in his dictatorial poses and in his inconstancy in parliamentary skirmishes, even if he was inferior to himself in the Libyan adventure and in the face of the European War [1914], he remains the most characteristic man of the situation.

The European War found the nation in a full unitary crisis and interrupted the progress of the ordinary administration and of the economic sobriety with which Giolitti had begun his work. It was the test of maturity which Italy had to pass before coming in contact as an equal with the rest of Europe. This period of the war was in fact popular and severe: it marked for the first time the participation of the South in national life, a meeting of the first challenge to the unity of the nation. The sacrifice proved the more heroic the humbler and more anonymous it was. However, during the war there arose the spirit of interventionism which resuscitated Garibaldian rhetoric without its original generosity, and thus limited and deformed whatever lessons might have been derived from the war. The nationalist war—fought with the spirit of the leagues for anti-German action and with the spirit of committees of public safety—was the "unpopular," the oligarchical war which returned to divide Italy once more between a plutocratic, adventuresome minority and a mass of workers not yet well differentiated. The subsequent economic crisis and the psychological disparities generated by privilege appear to the historians in the guise of a preventive explanation of Fascism, which they say represented the last victory of the patriotic oligarchy—courtly and petit bourgeois—that had governed Italy for many centuries and had thus arrested every popular initiative.

The history of post-war Italy appears to the serene observer as the recognition of the political struggle, as the prelude to an effective exercise of freedom. The civil war put to the test all parties and all the forces which constituted the most intense expression of new wills.

Nevertheless, these ferments and these hopes lacked the directing energies, the aristocracies capable of interpreting and reïnforcing them. The old elites survived and the new ones added to the lack of preparation by giving themselves over to the war-mentality and to messianic restlessness. Two groups,

Unità and *Volontà,* were deprived of influence by their non-militant attitude toward politics, and they proved insufficient to redeem the politics of those who had served in the war.

The old parties were not able to understand or to give expression to the new needs since they were dried up by an insuperable cleft between interpretation of reality and practice. For four years [1918–22] the political struggle did not succeed in giving the true measure of the social struggle.

Liberalism lost its efficacy because it showed itself incapable of understanding the problem of unity. Clericalism, after having sung the obsequies of the liberal idea, lost itself in a party which adopted democratic practice for conservative ends. Socialism, which had within it elements that might have succeeded in the future, proved the poverty of its attitudes at the crucial moment of realization, and it expressed in Turati its impotence as a party of government. Thus socialism accepted the heritage of a corrupt democracy rather than maintain its revolutionary logic.

In Italy, the only revolutionaries were those Communists who by calling up the myth of Lenin saw in the revolution the test of the political capacity of the working classes and of their capacity to create a state. But not even Marxism, which had stimulated the masses, was able to create leaders.

The working-class movement was nevertheless after the war the first lay movement in Italy capable of carrying through to its ultimate logic the revolutionary significance of the modern state, and of encompassing in a new ethic and in a new religiosity the struggle against dead faiths. It lacked a comprehension of the national value it represented. It lacked leaders to carry on its functions, leaders who through fear or vanity refused to govern. The unitary politics of Serrati, upon whom at a certain point the fate of the revolution depended, turned out to be a bad kind of *giolittismo*. Serrati lacked the ability of Giolitti and showed himself unprepared to dominate the situation with serene faith in his work. Only struggle can lead to cohesion and discipline. The unitary function was at any rate taken up by the government: for it, abstention became the essence of morality.

In the thought of Serrati there were confused the opposing aspirations of peasants and workers before they in fact knew one another's aspirations. In order that the political struggle might have a reasonable responsibility, it needed to proceed autonomously from below as if following its own law of separatism. Conciliation is always a result of the struggle: to demand it *a priori* means to annihilate free efforts while they are arising. Thus the revolutionaries initiated in fact a reactionary practice.

Modern Italian History as the "Work of Minorities"*

CARLO ROSSELLI

CARLO ROSSELLI (*1899–1937*) *was an anti-Fascist of the first hour, a revolutionary activist of Mazzinian temper and attitudes, and of Salveminian education. He came from an upper-middle-class professional family of democratic tendencies* (*in 1872, Mazzini had found refuge and died in the Rosselli family house at Pisa*). *Rosselli had collaborated with Gobetti on* Rivoluzione Liberale, *but, after the murder of Matteotti in 1924, he joined the Socialist Party. Together with his brother Nello, who was a historian of the Risorgimento, Carlo came under the influence of Salvemini and remained spiritually close to the old historian to the very end. Continually on the move to help imprisoned or threatened anti-Fascists, Rosselli was instrumental in bringing to safety in France the old socialist leader Filippo Turati. Rosselli was arrested, tried, and condemned to "internal exile"* (*the* confino) *on the Lipari island prison. It was while confined at Lipari that he wrote* Socialismo liberale (*1930*), *first published in French. After his escape he emigrated to France and there organized the anti-Fascist revolutionary movement of* Giustizia e Libertà (*GL*) *which, eventually, formed the cadres*

* From Carlo Rosselli, *Socialismo liberale* (Rome-Florence-Milan: Edizioni U, 1945), 168–70, 172–73, 174–76. Reprinted by permission of John Rosselli. Editor's translation.

of the new "Party of Action" of which Ferruccio Parri was to be the leader during the period of the Armed Resistance against Fascism (1943–45). At the outbreak of the Spanish Civil War, Rosselli became the Commander of the "Italian Column" fighting against Franco's Fascist-Falangist insurrection against the Republic. Early in June 1937 he took a leave from the Spanish front (where he had been wounded) and was joined by his wife and his brother Nello at Bagnolle de l'Orne in France. On the evening of June 9, 1937, while Carlo and Nello were returning by car to their hotel, after having seen Carlo's wife off to Paris, they were blocked on the lonely road they had taken and literally massacred on the spot by assassins hired by the French Fascist organization of the Cagoulards, themselves in touch with and secretly in the pay of Mussolini's son-in-law, Count Galeazzo Ciano. The selection from Rosselli's book Liberal Socialism *may suggest the fusion of historical and ideological elements that constituted both the strength and weakness of the successor of the GL movement, Parri's Party of Action* (Partito d'Azione) *which made a significant contribution to the Armed Resistance and to the immediate postwar period in Italy.*

For centuries we have lived in the reflected light of the world of politics. The great waves of European life have reached us in attenuated forms. There was nothing, not even through our struggle for independence, which was not the work of a minority rather than the passion of a people. Only a certain number of urban centers of the North participated actively in the revolt against the foreigner. In the Center and in the South of Italy, after a first moment of enthusiasm, the Savoy monarchy became the equivalent of the House of Lorraine and of the Bourbons. The Piedmontese bureaucracy locked in its coils all of Italy and thus paralyzed the last movements for autonomy. The triumph of the monarchical and diplomatic current succeeded, as in Germany, in violently separating the unitary myth from the libertarian myth. Mazzini and Cattaneo were the great defeated of the Risorgimento political liberty which was to be slowly won in the course of the following decades, and which was actually the result of compromises and of tacit concessions.

The conquest of liberty was not bound in Italy with any mass movement capable of playing its role as myth and precursor. The masses were absent. The proletariat was not able to conquer its special freedoms of organization, the right to strike, the right to vote at the price of efforts and long-range sacrifices. Its apprenticeship around 1900 proved too brief. As far as universal suffrage was concerned, it appeared that what it actually was was merely a calculated expansion granted by higher spheres. The rule according to which one loves and defends only that for which he has much struggled and sacrificed himself has had its most typical proof in the Fascist experience.

The liberal state collapsed helplessly under the first blows of its enemies, and the working classes were forced to assist impotently at the destruction of liberal values which were alien to their political consciousness.

When today Mussolini enumerates the numbers of his followers and his flocks and brags of the unanimity he has obtained, of the single party, of the disappearance of every kind of substantial opposition and of every free initiative on the part of fighting minorities—all this in the name of a pretended revolution which is carnival-like—he does nothing else but celebrate the annals of the Bourbons.

He does not even give us the consolation of seeing in him a foreigner, the master of armed forces from outside encamped in our midst.

As a matter of fact his spirit of turbulent Romagnole would easily dispose him for battle: but he is not capable of conceiving a battle except in terms of brutal force. His despotic pride as dictator compels him to repress systematically every outburst of opposition and struggle. Despite everything, his sectarian intransigence does serve the cause of freedom. With the cudgel and handcuffs, with his refined persecutions, Mussolini is creating out of tens of thousands of modern Italians the volunteers of a battle for freedom. The formidable logic of the instruments of furious repression, of which he is actually the prisoner, is becoming our best ally.

For the first time in the history of Italy, the vindication of the inalienable rights of human beings and of self-government poses itself as a problem for an entire people, not merely for a sect of initiates. There is not a single Italian, however uneducated and poor he may be, who can ignore Fascism and the problems of life and death which it has raised. The last of the workers in the heart of Calabria today suffers and hopes in behalf of the same cause that makes the most refined intellectual and the most modern industrialist of the North of Italy suffer and hope. Through so many miseries and humiliations the consciousness of the value of freedom is emerging in a dramatic way among vast numbers of the Italian people.

One could almost say that the Italians are psychologically freer today in the course of this desperate struggle for the conquest of essential autonomies than they were in the past under the self-styled constitutional state of Giolitti and of the thousands of independent associations. Rightly, therefore, everyone sees the problem through the eyes of his own interest and of his party; but the flame is about to envelop everything, and that flame is freedom. The Communists themselves, despite all their facile irony, see themselves forced to explain the dictatorship through the idea of freedom; Fascist oppression is preparing the moral unity of the Italian people.

What is the position of Socialists in regard to the problem of freedom? . . . The impotence of Marxist socialism in the face of problems of freedom and morality may be understood from its evident incapacity to understand the Fascist phenomenon. It sees in Fascism only a brutal phenomenon of class reaction; it sees the modern and typical form of a capitalist reaction. In brief, Fascism is the bourgeoisie which has recourse to violence in order to oppose the rise of the proletariat: everything else, say the Marxists, is nothing but an ideological screen. With a facile simplification which seeks to appear as realism, it forgets completely the moral side of the question, that is, all that the Fascist phenomenon reveals as an Italian affair. But the mistake is very gross: Fascism cannot be explained away as a simple class reaction. The action squads were not born of the simple blind rage of reactionary and subversive people. Factions, a spirit of adventure, romantic inclinations, a petit-bourgeois idealism, nationalist rhetoric, sentimental reaction against the war, a restless desire for anything new: Fascism would not have arisen without such motives as these. Stimulated by class interests, obviously and profoundly influenced by class interests, the Fascist phenomenon was born like an explosion caused by fermentation hidden within the people, through the experience of generations. During that Bolshevik period of 1919 a great number of aspects not nearly Fascist in exterior may be espied fully. Fascism had its roots in the Italian subsoil, it expressed profound vices, latent weaknesses, the miseries of our people, of a whole people. . . .

To struggle against Fascism therefore does not mean to struggle only against a blind and ferocious class reaction but also against a certain mentality and a certain sensibility within Italian traditions which have unfortunately found responses among vast popular currents. For this reason the struggle is difficult and it cannot consist simply in the problem of mechanically overturning a regime. Above all, the struggle is a problem concerning the political and moral education of ourselves and others, independent of all class divisions. Constructive problems, far from being resolved the day in which Fascism will fall, will then really be posed. This is the reason why the struggle is worthwhile, this is the reason why it is vital and truly worthy of all sacrifices.

Now it is not uncommon to find socialists who, with their eyes fixed upon the economic structure, would like to ignore out of hand all of these problems. In their eyes what does the struggle for freedom become? An instrumental struggle, a struggle for the conquest of institutions and of practical positions that possess merely a value of transition and convenience insofar as they will be denied with the advent of a socialist society.

The habit of considering the economic problem as the master key and the determining phenomenon by which to measure all values in the light of utilitarian ends causes profound and permanent values which only a regime of freedom would be capable of arousing to escape them. What interests them is solely the form of the political struggle and not the substance of a liberal climate. When Marxists vindicate or claim freedom they do so not for its own value but only because they assume that it will favor the awakening of the proletariat and even of capitalist development. Thus placed in contradiction with themselves by the liberalism of method and the antiliberalism of goal, they find themselves fatally ill at ease in the struggle for freedom, and participate in it with an infinite number of reservations, of attenuations, of subtle interpretations: this takes away from their utilitarian and transient claims every kind of suggestive force or proselytizing meaning. Indeed how can one spur the working class toward a revolutionary struggle in the name of freedom when at the same time one tells it that freedom does not exist, that today democratic methods are useful but that they may be denied tomorrow, and that the struggle which we are waging is a socialist struggle only at long range? It is the squaring of the circle.

Since history began, revolutions have not been made by means of relative values; tactics and calculation may nourish an academic discussion, but not a street battle. Without the light of a supreme ideal which illumines profoundly the substance and the aims of the actual struggle, without a very strong consciousness of the values of the good for which one struggles, one cannot create a revolutionary temper. As long as socialists shall not have affirmed the absolute value intrinsic to the liberal climate, of democratic institutions, of concrete freedoms of the press, of thought, of association, they will be impotent in victoriously facing the struggle for freedom.

Paralyzed as it was by a thousand disquietudes related to its underrating of the ethic of freedom, Italian socialism has not yet succeeded in arousing an anti-Fascist insurrection among the masses. It lacks a profound faith in freedom and it consumes itself in the contradiction between ends and means.

The superiority of the position of liberal socialism that we have sought to sketch is this: that thanks to it we feel perfectly in our place in this struggle for freedom; that we need not renounce anything or compromise our program by borrowing motives or ideas from bourgeois ideologies. For us the myth of freedom illumines our entire program: we demand the most advanced social transformations and we justify our demands in the name of the principle of liberty—of a full, effective, positive liberty for all human beings, in all aspects of their existence.

Today we demand political and spiritual freedom in order that it may constitute the premise, the instrument, the indispensable atmosphere for our battle, and tomorrow we shall demand freedom and autonomy for the economy and for the state. Thus we shall attain freedom both as a means and as an end. We fight for the means, for the democratic method insofar as it is entirely penetrated by the end. Our position is nothing but the logical development of the principles of freedom carried to its final consequences.

The liberal socialist does not have a program to suspend, he does not have doctrines in reserve or vindications to keep silent because they are in contrast with the actual orientation of the struggle. It seems to me that in this one may espy a marvelous harmony, a perfect correspondence between ends and means, between thought and action, between today's struggle and the struggle of tomorrow.

The Conflict Between City and Countryside in Modern Italy*

ANTONIO GRAMSCI

ANTONIO GRAMSCI (*1891–1937*), *the son of an impoverished Sardinian family, studied through his winning of a state scholarship at the University of Turin. During his youth he was a militant in the ranks of Italian socialism, but it was the Leninist Revolution in Russia 1917 that acted as a catalyst in his thought and action. In 1919 he founded at Turin the Marxist organ* Ordine Nuovo *and, in 1921, at the Livorno Congress of the Italian Socialist*

* From Antonio Gramsci, *Il Risorgimento,* to be published in three volumes by Lawrence & Wishart Ltd. in the United Kingdom and by International Publishers in the U.S. Reprinted by permission of Lawrence & Wishart Ltd. Editor's translation.

Party, Gramsci inspired the separation of the "Leninist" group from the Socialist Party and created the Italian Communist Party (PCI), which was officially a member of the Third International. Gramsci's uniqueness of ideological education and preparation (there was perhaps always in him a sort of fusion of voluntaristic and reflective tendencies that, in a sense, never fully made him into an "orthodox" Marxist-Communist) and the exceptional intellectual resources that he possessed made him the undisputed leader of Italian Marxism. Only for a time was his leadership "threatened" by the ultra-activistic positions assumed by Amadeo Bordiga. Gramsci's opposition to Fascism was personally profound, but from 1922 to 1926, chiefly in deference to the official position taken by the Third International vis-à-vis *Fascism in Italy, Gramsci did not join the "underground" resistance but chose rather to work openly, under the aegis of the Chamber of Deputies, to which he was elected and of which he was a member when he was arrested. For eleven years, from 1926 to 1937, Gramsci was one of the most carefully watched prisoners of the Fascist regime. Under the most difficult conditions imaginable for a man of his weak physical constitution and uniquely strong character and caliber of mind, Gramsci managed to turn his imprisonment into an "opportunity" to meditate, study, and write a series of fantastically rich and suggestive* Prison Notebooks (Quaderni del Carcere) *which, upon publication after 1945, became the basis for a neo-Marxist cultural, philosophical, ideological, and historiographical "revolution" in Italy. Gramsci had died almost immediately after his release from prison in 1937. The impress of his moral figure, of his internal resistance, and of his historical meditations upon modern Italian intellectual and cultural history has been equaled only by that of Benedetto Croce.*

The Relation Between City and Countryside During the Risorgimento and Within the National Structure.

THE RELATION BETWEEN an urban population and a rural population is not only of a schematic type, especially in Italy. It is necessary, in the meantime, to establish what is meant by "urban" and "rural" in modern civilization and what combinations may result in the permanence of antiquated and backward forms within the general composition of a population, studied from the point of view of its tendency more or less to agglomerate. Sometimes the paradox results that a rural type may be more progressive than a self-styled urban type.

An "industrial" city is always more progressive than the countryside that depends upon it organically. But in Italy not all cities are "industrial" and even fewer are typically industrial cities. The "hundred" Italian cities are industrial cities as agglomerations of population in non-rural centers, which represent almost double those of the French: but does this prove that there is in Italy an industrialization that is double that of France? In Italy urbanism is not only, and not even "especially," a phenomenon of capitalistic development and of big industry. Naples, which for a long time was the largest Italian city and which continues to be one of the largest, is not an industrial city: not even Rome, which at present is the largest, is industrialized. Nevertheless, even in these cities, of medieval type as they are, there exist centers of typically modern type: but what is their relative position? They are submerged, squeezed, crushed by the other side which is not of modern type and that constitutes the bulk of the population. The paradox of the "cities of silence."

In this type of city there exists, among all social groups, an urban ideological unity against the countryside—a unity that not even those among those groups that are most modern through their civil function can escape. There is the hatred and contempt for the "peasant," a united front against the vindication of rights by the countryside, a vindication which, were it to be realized, would render impossible the existence of this type of city. Contrariwise, there exists a "generic" but nonetheless deep-rooted and passionate hostility of the countryside against the city, against the entire city, against all groups that make it up. This general relationship, which in reality is very complex and manifests itself in apparently contradictory forms, has been of primordial importance in the development of the struggles of the Risorgimento, during which that relationship was even more absolute and active.

. . . During the Risorgimento, moreover, there was already manifested, in embryonic form, the historical relationship between North and South, a relationship similar to that between a large city and a large countryside—and, since this relationship was not of that normal organic kind that holds between the province and an industrial capital, but was rather the result of the separation between two vast territories with very different civil and cultural traditions, it accentuated aspects and elements of a conflict between "nationalities." What is especially remarkable during the period of the Risorgimento is the fact that in political crises the South [the Mezzogiorno] takes the initiative for action: 1799, Naples; 1820–21, Palermo; 1847, Messina and Sicily; 1847–48, Sicily and Naples. Another noteworthy fact lies in the particular aspect that every movement assumes in Central Italy, as a middle way between North and South; the period of the (relatively) popular initiatives that runs from 1815 to 1849 and that culminates in Tuscany and in the States of the Pope (Romagna and the Lunigiana must always be considered as belonging to the Center). These peculiarities find counterparts even subsequently: the events of June 1814 culminated in some regions of the Center (Romagna and the Marches); the crisis which began in 1893 in Sicily had repercussions in the Mezzogiorno and in Lunigiana and then culminated in Milan in 1898 ["Fatti di Maggio"]; in 1919, the seizures of the land [by the peasants] in the Mezzogiorno and in Sicily had their counterpart in 1920 in the occupation of the factories in the North. This relative synchronism and simultaneity reveal the existence after 1815 of an economic-political structure [throughout Italy] that was relatively homogeneous on one side, while, on the other, they show how during periods of crisis it is the weakest and most peripheral part that takes the initiative for action.

The relation between city and countryside can also be studied in diverse cultural conceptions and mental attitudes. As we have already suggested, at the beginning of this century, B. Croce and G. Fortunato were the leaders of a cultural movement that, in one way or another, was contraposed to the cultural movement of the North (i.e., idealism versus positivism, classicism or the classic style versus Futurism). It is noteworthy that Sicily separates itself from the Mezzogiorno even in respect to culture: if Crispi is the man of northern industrialism, Pirandello, in his general attitudes, is closer to Futurism, and Gentile and his Actualism are themselves closer to the Futurist movement (viewing this in a large sense as opposition to traditional classicism, as a form of contemporary romanticism). The structure and origin of the intellectual classes [of North and South] are also different: in the Mezzogiorno, the type of the *paglietta*-intellectual predominates, and it is he who puts the masses of the peasantry in contact with the landowners and the state apparatus; while in the North there predominates the type of the factory "technician," who acts as the link between the masses of the workers and the entrepreneurs. [In the North] the link with the state was a function of the trade-union organizations as well as of the political parties, directed as they were by a completely new intellectual class (the present [Fascist] state syndicalism, with its resulting systematic spread over a national scale of this social type in a manner that is more consistent and consequential than was possible under the old trade-union system is, up to a point and in a certain sense, an instrument of moral and political unification).

This complex relation between city and countryside can be studied in the general political programs which tried to assert themselves before Fascism's advent to power. The program of Giolitti and the liberal democrats tended to create in the North an "urban" bloc (of industrialists and workers) that would be the basis of a protectionist system and that would re-enforce the northern economy and hegemony. The South was reduced to a semi-colonial market, to a source of savings and taxes, and it was "kept in line" through two kinds of measures: police-measures requiring merciless repression of every mass-movement through periodic killing of peasants, and through political policing measures, that is, through "personal favors" granted to the *paglietta*-intellectual class in the form of employment in public administrations, of permits to loot with impunity local administrative offices, of an ecclesiastical legislation applied less rigidly than elsewhere, leaving in the hands of the clergy notable [public] patrimonies, etc.—that is, the incorporation of this class into the ruling state apparatus through "personal contacts" with the most active southern elements who enjoyed special "judicial," financial, and other kinds of privileges. Thus, the social class that might have organized the endemic southern unrest became instead an instrument of northern policy, its accessory as a private police-force. Because of lack of direction [southern] unrest did not succeed in attaining a normal political form and its manifestations—since it took only chaotic and disorderly channels, which fell within the judiciary "police sphere." In reality, through their fetishistic conception of unity, men like Croce and Fortunato, even passively and indirectly, adhered to this form of corruption. . . .

. . . From an examination of the relation between city and countryside one must proceed to the examination of the fundamental moving forces of Italian history and to a consideration of the programmatic points of the Partito d'Azione [the Party of Action] from which one must judge its function during the Risorgimento. Schematically, one may obtain the following picture: (1) the northern urban force; (2) the southern rural force; (3) the north-central rural force; (4) the rural force of Sicily; and (5) that of Sardinia. Assuming the first to have acted as the "locomotive," it is necessary to examine the various "more useful" combinations apt to construct a "train" that might proceed as expeditiously as possible through history. In the meantime, the first force starts by having problems of its own, internal problems of organization, of structuring in quest of homogeneity, of political-military leadership (Piedmontese hegemony, the relations between Milan and Turin, etc.). However, an acquired datum can be depended upon, at least "mechanically," since, once such force had achieved a certain level of unity and of fighting capacity, it already exercised an "indirect" directing function over the other forces. During various periods of the Risorgimento it appears that once the [northern urban] force had assumed a position of intransigence and of struggle against foreign domination [the Austrians], this fact determined a rousing of the progressive southern forces—and from this resulted the relative synchronism but not the simultaneity of the movements of 1820–21, of 1831, of 1848. In 1859–60 this historical-political "mechanism" brought about the most fruitful consequences possible; since the North initiated the struggle, the Center joined in more or less freely, and in the South the Bourbon state collapsed under the thrust of the Garibaldians [*garibaldini*], a thrust which was relatively weak. This happened because the Party of Action (Garibaldi) intervened at the right moment, after the Moderates (Cavour) had organized the North and the Center: that is, it was not the political-military direction (of the Moderates or the Party of Action) that accounted for the relative simultaneity but rather the (mechanical) collaboration between two directions that were happily joined.

The first force should, therefore, have faced the problem of organizing around itself the urban forces of the national sections, particularly those of the South. This was the most difficult of problems, bristling with contradictions and complicated by those whose motives were to unleash waves of passion (a farcical solution of this contradiction was the so-called parliamentary revolution of 1876). But its solution was exactly on this account one of the most crucial points of national development. Urban forces are socially homogeneous and they must therefore find themselves in a position of perfect equality. This was theoretically true, but historically the question was quite different: the urban forces of the North were unquestionably at the head of their national section, while this was not true of the urban forces of the South, at least not quite to the same extent. The urban forces of the North had, therefore, to secure from those of the South acquiescence that their directing function should limit itself to insuring the leadership of the North over the South within the city-countryside relation, that is, that the directing function of the urban forces of the South could be nothing but a subordinate element in the vaster directing function of the North. The most glaring contradiction arose from this order of things: the urban force of the South could not be considered as something apart, independent from that of the North. To set the question in its proper terms would have meant a preventive acknowledgment of an unbridgeable "national" dissension, a dissension so grave that not even the federalist solution [Cattaneo's ideas] could have resolved it. One would thus have acknowledged the existence of different "nations," between which only a diplomatic-military alliance could be made against the common enemy, Austria (the only element making for common action and solidarity would, in a word, have been the "common" enemy). In reality, these were only some of the "aspects" of the national question, not "all" of the aspects, not even the most essential. The gravest aspect was the weak position of the southern urban forces compared to the [southern] rural forces, an unfavorable balance that sometimes expressed itself as a veritable subjection of the [southern] city to the countryside. A strict linking between the urban forces of the North with those of the South, by giving the latter the representative prestige-power of the former, should have helped them to become autonomous, to acquire a consciousness of their directing historical function in a "concrete" manner, not in a purely theoretical and abstract way, by suggesting to them the solution for their vast [southern] regional problems. It was natural that there should be in the South strong currents of opposition to unity: the greatest task toward the solution of the problem devolved at any rate upon the North, which not only had to convince their "brothers" in the South but had to start to convince themselves concerning the complexity of this political system. In practice, therefore, the question was how to organize a strong center of political direction in which a number of strong popular southern personalities and those from Sicily would by necessity have had to co-operate. The problem of creating a North-South unity was strictly bound with and in large part identical to the problem of creating a cohesion and solidarity among all the national urban forces.

The north central rural forces, by expelling interferences and influences alien to the development of the new state, raised in their turn a series of problems that the urban force of the North had to face in order to establish a normal city-countryside relation. In these [north-central] rural forces it was necessary to distinguish between two currents: the laic and the pro-Austrian-clerical forces. The clerical force exerted its greatest weight in Lombardy and Venetia, as well as in Tuscany and in a part of the Papal State; the laic force was strong in Piedmont, with more or less vast influences throughout the rest of Italy, down to the Mezzogiorno and the islands [Sicily and Sardinia]. Through an effective resolution of these immediate [regional] problems the northern urban forces would have given a rhythm to the tackling of similar questions on a national scale. On this entire range of complex problems the Party of Action failed completely. Indeed, it limited itself by turning into questions of principles and essential programs what was simply a question of political ground upon which such problems could be concentrated and receive a legal solution: that is, the question of a constituent assembly. It cannot be said that the Moderate Party failed, since it had as its aim the organic expansion of Piedmont; it wanted soldiers for the Piedmontese army, not insurrections or large-scale Garibaldian troops.

Why did the Party of Action not raise the agrarian question in its full extent? That the Moderates did not raise it was obvious: the way the Moderates framed the national problem required a bloc of all the forces of the Right, including the big landowners, around Piedmont as a state and as an army. The threat by Austria to resolve the agrarian question in favor of the peasants—a threat that was made good in Galicia against the Polish nobility in behalf of the Ruthenian peasants—not only played havoc among all interested parties in Italy and thus precipitated all the oscillations of the aristocracy (the revolutionary attempts in Milan in 1853 led the most illustrious Milanese families to pay homage to Franz Joseph right on the eve of the gallows of Belfiore), but it also polarized the Party of Action itself, which, on this question, had the same views as the Moderates and held the aristocracy and the landowning classes to be "national," but not millions of peasants. Only after February, 1853, did Mazzini have a substantially democratic moment (see *Epistolario* for that period), but he was unable to bring about a decisive radicalization of his abstract program. What should also be studied is the political conduct of the *garibaldini* in Sicily in 1860, a political conduct that was dictated by Crispi: the movements of insurrection undertaken by the peasants against the barons were pitilessly crushed and an anti-peasant national guard was created. Typical was the repressive expedition of Nino Bixio in the region of Catania, where the insurrections were most violent. And yet even in the *Noterelle* of G. C. Abba there are elements to show that the agrarian question was the mainspring by which to set the large masses in motion: be it sufficient to recall the talks that Abba had with the friar who came to meet the *garibaldini* after their landing at Marsala. In some short stories by Verga there are picturesque elements concerning these peasant uprisings which the national guard put down with terror and mass executions. This aspect of the Expedition of the Thousand has never been studied and analyzed.

The failure to raise the agrarian question led to the almost impossible situation of not being able to resolve the question of clericalism and of the anti-Unitary attitude of Pope Pius IX. In this respect, the Moderates were much bolder than the Party of Action. It is true that they [the Moderates] did not distribute the land among the peasants, but they did use it to create a new class of big and medium-sized landowners who became beholden to the new political situation. Nor did they hesitate to manumit landed property, if only that belonging to the religious congregations. The Party of Action, furthermore, was paralyzed in its action in behalf of the peasants by Mazzinian velleities toward a religious reform, which not only did not interest the large peasant masses but, on the contrary, rendered them indifferent toward any incitement to rebellion against the new heretics. The example of the French Revolution very clearly demonstrated that the Jacobins—who had succeeded in crushing all parties on the Right, including the Girondins, on the very ground of the agrarian question, and had thus not only stopped a coalition of rural forces aimed against Paris but had also multiplied their adherents in the provinces–were injured by Robespierre's attempt to institute a religious reform which, at that time, did have, in a real historical sense, significance and immediate concreteness. . . .

Moments of Intensely Collective and Unitary Life in the Development of the Italian People.

One needs to examine in the development of national life from 1800 on all those moments during which the Italian people faced the at least potentially common task through which an action or a movement of collective and unitary character (whether in depth or in breadth) might have been realized. During various historical phases these moments may have been of diverse nature or of different national-popular importance. What is required is research into the potential character (and therefore into the extent to which the potentialities were translated into action) of collectivity and unity, meaning the extent of the territory encompassed (the region, if not quite the province itself, would satisfy the requirement) and the mass-intensity (that is, the greater or lesser numbers of participants involved, the larger or lesser positive repercussions, even if they were actively negative, which the movement aroused among different strata of the population).

These moments may have been of different character and nature, that is, they may have been wars, revolutions, plebiscites, general elections of special significance. The wars to be studied are those of 1848–49, 1859, 1860, 1870, the African wars (Eritrea, Libya), the World War; the revolutions, those of 1820–21, 1831, 1848–49, 1860, the Fasci Siciliani

[1893–94], 1898, 1904, 1914; 1919–20, and 1924–25; the plebiscites for the formation of the Kingdom, those of 1859–60, 1860, 1870; and finally, the general elections under different extensions of the suffrage. Typical elections were that which brought the Left to power in 1876, that which was held after the enlargement of the suffrage after 1880, and that which followed 1898. The elections of 1913 were the first that had a distinct popular character due to the very extensive participation of the peasants; those of 1919 were the most important of all because of the use of proportional representation and because of the provincial representative character of the votes which obliged parties to regroup, and also because through the entire national territory all parties had to enter the lists under more or less national programs.

In a measure which was larger and more organic than in 1913 (when the single-list constituencies restricted possibility and falsified the political choices of the masses due to the artificial delimitation of the constituencies themselves), in 1919 throughout the whole national territory, in a single day, the entire active part of the Italian people faced the same questions and sought to resolve them in its political-historical conscience. The significance of the elections of 1919 resulted from a gamut of "unifying" elements, both positive and negative, that flowed into them; the war had been a unifying element of the first order in so far as it had given the large masses a consciousness of the importance that the construction of the government apparatus has for every single individual. The war besides raised a series of concrete problems, both general and particular, that reflected the popular-national unity.

One cannot assert that the elections of 1919 assumed for the people the character of a constituent [assembly], even if that was not true of "every" party of the period: in this contradiction of and separation between the people and the parties lay the drama of 1919, which was understood only by a few among the most self-aware and intelligent ruling groups (those, that is, who had most to fear concerning the future). It is noteworthy that the very party which in Italy had traditionally stood for the call for a constituent assembly, that is, the Republican Party, showed the least historical sensibility and a minimum of political capacity by letting itself accept the program and aims (an abstract and retrospective defense of intervention in the war) of the ruling classes of the Right. The people, in its fashion, looked to the future (even in reference to the question of war-intervention) and in this lay the implicit character of a constituent assembly that the people gave to the elections of 1919. The parties looked back to the past (only to the past) concretely, while they looked at the future "abstractly," "generically," as if to say "have faith in your party," and not as a constructive historical-political conception.

Among the differences to note between 1913 and 1919 it is important to remember the active participation of Catholics, with their own men, their own Party [Partito Popolare Italiano led by Don Luigi Sturzo], and their own program. In 1913 Catholics had taken part in national elections, but through the Gentilone Pact, in a kind of sly manner which falsified the meaning of the political alignments and of the influence exerted by traditional political forces. For in 1919 it is significant to recall the speech of Giolitti [at Dronero, October 12, 1919], with its (retrospective) constituent-intonation, and the attitude of the Giolittians *vis-à-vis* the Catholics, such as became evident in the articles of Luigi Ambrosini on the *Stampa* [of Turin]. In reality the Giolittians were the victors of the elections, in the sense that they imposed upon the elections the character of a constituent without the actual constituent, and succeeded in distracting attention from the future to the past.

Fascism as Anti-Risorgimento: The Intellectual as Rebel Against Fascism*

LAURO DE BOSIS

LAURO DE BOSIS (*1901–31*) *was a poet and dramatist and a translator of Aeschylus and Sophocles. During the early years of Fascism, like some other members of his young intellectual generation, he had believed in its "rejuvenation" myths. Indeed, as he himself tells us in his spiritual testament, he had never ceased to believe that the Savoy Monarchy, which had been the channel and symbol of the unitary movement during the Risorgimento, constituted a strong liberal protective shield against the excesses of Fascism. In due time he came to realize that Fascism and "excess" were synonymous. De Bosis' fam-*

* From Lauro de Bosis, *The Story of My Death*. With the original Text in French and a Biographical Note [by Ruth Draper] (New York: Oxford University Press, 1933), 9–16. Reprinted by permission of Arturo Vivante.

ily background—his father Adolfo was a famous poet and his mother was American from New England—his linguistic facility, his cultural and poetic talents, and the charm of his personality had led him to retain a semi-official position under the category of "cultural relations," as Directing Secretary of the Italy-America Society. From 1924 to 1926, Lauro made several trips to the United States and later lectured at Harvard University. In 1927 his lyrical drama Icaro *received the Olympic Prize for poetry at Amsterdam. By 1930 his complete disenchantment with the early "promise" of Fascism had occurred simultaneously with the realization that his role as an artist did not exempt him from vital engagement in the freedom of his people. He stayed abroad, in France, and founded the Alleanza Nazionale, a liberal-monarchical movement dedicated to arousing a new Italian national solidarity between his countrymen and the monarchy. In his own words, the rest was to be "the story of his death." At 3:15 on the afternoon of October 3, 1931, Lauro de Bosis took off in his plane from Marseilles, his destination: Rome. He reached the skies of the Eternal City at 8* P.M. *and, as Ruth Draper reported, Lauro "flew very low over the streets, and in places it seemed as if snow had fallen, so thickly were the leaflets strewn." In the leaflets, he exhorted the people and the monarchy to make common cause against Fascism—for the sake of the ideas and ideals of the Risorgimento. When at last he flew away it was into the unknown: "whether he was shot down by pursuing planes or fell into the sea for lack of fuel will probably never be known."*

The Story of My Death

TOMORROW AT THREE o'clock, in a meadow on the Côte d'Azur, I have a rendezvous with Pegasus.

Pegasus is the name of my aeroplane. It has a russet body and white wings; and though it is as strong as eighty horses, it is as slim as a swallow. Drunk with petrol, it leaps through the sky like its brother of old, but in the night it can glide at will through the air like a phantom. I found it in the Hercynian forest, and its old master will bring it to me on the shores of the Tyrrhenian Sea, believing in perfect sincerity that it will serve the pleasures of an idle young Englishman. My bad accent has not awakened his suspicions; I hope he will pardon my subterfuge.

And yet we are not going in search of chimeras, but to bear a message of liberty across the sea to a people that is in chains. To drop figures of speech (which I had to use in order to leave the origins of my aeroplane discreetly vague) we are going to Rome to scatter from the air these words of liberty which, for seven years, have been forbidden like a crime. And with reason, for if they had been allowed they would have shaken the Fascist tyranny to its foundation within a few hours.

Every régime in the world, even the Afghan and the Turkish, allows its subjects a certain amount of liberty. Fascism alone, in self-defence, is obliged to annihilate thought. It cannot be blamed for punishing faith in liberty, and fidelity to the Italian Constitution more severely than parricide: that is its only chance of existence. It cannot be blamed for deporting thousands of citizens without trial, or for meting out several thousand years of imprisonment in the space of four years. How could it dominate a free people if it did not terrorize them with its garrison of three hundred thousand mercenaries? Fascism has no choice. If one shares its point of view, one is obliged to declare with its apostle Mussolini: 'Liberty is a rotten carcass'. If one merely wishes it to last, one must approve the murder of Matteotti and the rewards meted out to his murderers, the destruction of all the newspapers of Italy, the sacking of the house of Croce, the millions spent on espionage and on *agents provocateurs,* in short, the sword of Damocles suspended over the head of every citizen.

I know that the Austrians in 1850, the Bourbons and the other tyrants of Italy never went thus far; they never deported people without trial; the total number of their condemnations never reached the figure of seven thousand years' imprisonment in four years. Above all, they never enrolled in their army of mercenaries the very sons of Liberals as Fascism does. It takes the children from all families (even if they be Liberal or Socialist) at the age of eight, imposing on them the uniform of executioners and giving them a barbarous and warlike education. 'Love the rifle, worship the machine-gun, and do not forget the dagger', wrote Mussolini in an article for children.

One cannot both admire Fascism and deplore its excesses. It can only exist because of its excesses. Its excesses are its logic. For Fascism, the logic of its existence is to exalt violence and to strike Toscanini in the face. They say that the murder of Matteotti was a mistake; from the Fascist point of view, it was a stroke of genius. They say that Fascism is wrong to use torture to extort confessions from its prisoners; but if it wants to live it cannot do otherwise. The foreign press must understand this. One cannot expect Fascism to become peaceful and human without desiring its complete annihilation. Fascism has grasped this, and for several years Italy has been turned into a great prison where children are taught to adore their chains and to pity those who are free. The young people of twenty can remember no other atmosphere. The name of Matteotti is almost unknown to them. Since the age of thirteen, they have been taught that men have no rights except those which the State has the goodness to grant them, according to its whim. Many believe it. The myth that Mussolini has saved Italy from Bolshevism is accepted without discussion. But it must not be thought that Italy is deceived. The proof that she is by a very great majority profoundly anti-Fascist is given to us by the régime itself, through the fear it shows of all whispering, and the ferocity with which it punishes the slightest expression of free thought. A régime that knows its own strength does not need to resort to such measures.

In June 1930 I started to put in circulation bimonthly letters, of a strictly constitutional character, explaining the necessity that all men of law and order should be in accord in preparation for the day when Fascism should fall. Since Fascism seems to have adopted the motto 'after us the deluge', the initiative was most opportune, and as a matter of fact, the letters, according to the principle of the snowball, began to circulate by thousands. For five months I carried on the work alone, sending every fortnight six hundred letters signed 'National Alliance', with the request that each recipient should send on six copies. Unfortunately, in December, during a short voyage which I was obliged to make abroad, the police arrested the two friends who had agreed to post the letters during my absence. They were subjected to torture and condemned to fifteen years' imprisonment. One of them, Mario Vinciguerra, one of the best-known writers of Italy, literary and art critic, although he was not well at the time, was left all night entirely naked (a night in December) on the roof of police head-quarters in Rome. As a result of repeated blows on the head he has remained completely deaf in one ear. He was thrown into a cell six feet square, where there was not even a chair to sit on, and from which every morning his bed was removed. After the protest of foreign papers and of eminent political personages, both English and American, his conditions were bettered. Mussolini even went so far as to offer their liberty to both men if they would write a letter of submission, but this they refused to do.

The day on which I read of the arrest of my friends, I was on the point of crossing the frontier to return to Italy. My first instinct, naturally, was to go to Rome to share their fate, but I realized that the duty of a soldier is not to surrender, but to fight to the end. I decided immediately to go to Rome, not in order to surrender, but to carry on the work of the National Alliance by throwing four hundred thousand letters from the air, and then, either to fall in fighting or return to my base to make other plans. The sky of Rome had never been flown by enemy aeroplanes. I shall be the first–I said to myself–and

I began at once to prepare the expedition. The venture was not an easy one, because for a poet it is always difficult even to earn his daily bread, and if he is exiled besides, and to cap the climax in a year of crisis, it is not surprising if he quickly descends to the lowest degrees of a Bohemian life. And then, I did not even know how to drive a motor-cycle, not to mention an aeroplane! I began by finding employment as a *concierge* at the Hotel Victor Emmanuel III, rue de Ponthieu. My Republican friends said that I was rightly punished there where I had sinned! To tell the truth I was not only *concierge* but also book-keeper and telephone operator. Often three or four bells would ring at the same time, and I would cry up the stairs in a stentorian voice, 'Irma, two portions of butter for number 35!' As a preparation for my raid over Rome it was not very effective. However, between the baker's bills and the clients' receipts, I was writing a message to the King of Italy and studying the map of the Tyrrhenian Sea. The rest of my preparation is the most interesting part of the story, but unfortunately it must remain secret.

In May I made my first solo flight in a Farman machine near Versailles. Then, having heard that my secret had reached the ears of the Fascists, I disappeared, and appeared again under another name in England. On July 13th I left Cannes in an English biplane, carrying with me eighty kilos of tracts. As I had only done five hours of solo flying I went alone so as not to risk the life of a friend. Unfortunately an accident on the coast of Corsica ended my venture, and I had to escape, leaving my aeroplane in a field. My secret was now revealed. In Italy they had no difficulty in realizing who the mysterious pilot was. The English and French police began a search for me with a diligence that flattered me; they even disputed my portrait. I ask their pardon for the trouble that I have caused them.

The worst of it was that I could now no more rely on the surprise, my greatest chance for success. None the less, Rome became for me as Cape Horn to the Flying Dutchman: dead or alive I swore to get there. My death—however undesired by me personally, who have so many things to achieve—could not but add to the success of my flight. As all the dangers lie on the return flight, I shall not die until after I have delivered my four hundred thousand letters, which will only be the better *recommandées!* After all, it is the question of giving a small example of civic spirit, and to draw the attention of my fellow citizens to their real situation. I am convinced that Fascism will not end until some twenty young people sacrifice their lives in order to awaken the spirit of the Italians. While during the Risorgimento there were thousands of young men who were ready to give their lives, to-day there are very few. Why? It is not that their courage and their faith are less than that of their fathers. It is because no one takes Fascism seriously. Beginning with its leaders, every one counts on its speedy fall, and it seems out of proportion to give one's life to end something that will collapse by itself. That is a mistake. It is necessary to die. I hope that many others will follow me and will at last succeed in rousing public opinion.

It only remains for me to give the text of my three messages. In the first, to the King, I have sought to interpret the sentiment of the mass of my people in making a summary of my sentiment. I think that a Republican as well as a Monarchist can subscribe to it. We only put the question: for Liberty or against it? The King's grandfather, after the most terrible defeat in the history of Italy, resisted the Austrian marshal who wished to force him to abrogate the Constitution. Does the King after the greatest victory of Italian history (a victory of Liberals) really wish to let the last remnant of this Constitution perish without a single gesture?

Besides my letters, I shall throw down several copies of a splendid book by Bolton King, *Fascism in Italy*. As one throws bread on a starving city, one must throw history books on Rome.

After having flown over Corsica and the Island of Monte Cristo at a height of twelve thousand feet, I shall reach Rome about eight o'clock, having done the last twenty kilometres gliding. Though I have only done seven and a half hours of solo flying, if I fall it will not be through fault of pilotage. My aeroplane only flies at 150 kilometres an hour, whereas those of Mussolini can do 300. There are nine hundred of them, and they have all received the order to bring down at any cost, with machine-gun fire, any suspicious aeroplane. However little they may know me, they must realize that after my first attempt I have not given up. If my friend Balbo has done his duty, they are there waiting for me. So much the better; I shall be worth more dead than alive.

L. DE B.

The "Shock of Recognition": An Unpolitical Youth on the Road to a New Risorgimento*

GIAIME PINTOR

GIAIME PINTOR *(1919–43) was one of the most extraordinarily gifted intellectuals of modern Italy. Ironically, his life coincided exactly with the rise and fall of Fascism in Italy. Pintor's letter to his brother, which we reproduce in its entirety below, was written three days before his death resulting from the explosion of a mine planted by the German-Nazi forces in the Volturno zone of war. Pintor was just about to cross the line to join the anti-Fascist partisan group known as Volunteers of Freedom. In Giaime Pintor, a magnificent intelligence had been fused with an exceptional capacity for literary and linguistic expression that rendered him close to an artistic and critical genius prematurely blasted by Fascism and war. Ironically, too, he had been one of the most refined Italian cultural "Germanists" of his generation. With the combined talents of translator, critic, and artist, Pintor had rendered into Italian the poetry of Rainer Maria Rilke and Heinrich von Kleist and the works of Hugo von Hoffmansthal and Ernst Jünger. The posthumously collected es-*

* From Giaime Pintor, *Il Sangue d'Europa* (*1939–1943*), ed. by Valentino Giarratana (Turin: Giulio Einaudi Editore, 1950), 245–48. Reprinted by permission of Franz J. Horch Associates. Editor's translation.

says of Pintor, in a volume significantly entitled Il Sangue d'Europa (The Blood of Europe), *reveal both the depth and span of his unique sensitivity, culture, and intelligence. Pintor's letter to his brother speaks for itself. Ferruccio Parri, the leader of the Italian anti-Fascist Resistance, was to accurately call that letter "perhaps the most beautiful and highest expression" of the ideal motives of the fight against Nazi-Fascism in Italy.*

Naples, November 28, 1943

MY DEAR,

I leave these days for a mission of uncertain result: I am on my way to groups of refugees in the vicinity of Rome to bring them arms and instructions. I leave you this letter in order to salute you in case I should not return and to explain to you the state of mind with which I undertake this mission. The particular antecedents that lie behind it are of a certain biographical interest, but they are too complicated for me to speak of them here. Some of our friends who have been in these parts will tell you about my flight from Rome and how I arrived in the territory controlled by Badoglio, how I spent ten awful days in Brindisi with the Supreme Command, and how, after having convinced myself that nothing had changed among the military, I succeeded through a new flight in reaching Naples. Here it has been easy to find a congenial environment among political friends and returnees from the emigration, and I have contributed toward the creation of an Italian center of propaganda which might have a useful function and which has temporarily brought me back to my normal activities and to a peaceful rhythm of life. But during this period there has remained in suspense the necessity of participating at closer range in an order of things which does not justify the comfortable methods of psychological warfare; and the present static condition of the military situation, the preview of the misery in which the majority of Italians will live and which must worsen, has rendered more urgent my decision. Thus, after the failure, for reasons independent of our will, of other projects more ambitious but not unreasonable, I have agreed to organize an expedition with a group of friends. It is the natural conclusion of this last adventure, but above all the point of arrival at an experience which coinvolves our entire youth.

In reality the war, the last phase of triumphant Fascism, has acted upon us more profoundly than appears at first sight. The war has considerably distracted men from their daily habits, it has forced them to take cognizance with their hands and with their eyes of the dangers which threatened the presuppositions of every individual life, it has persuaded them that there is no possibility of salvation in neutrality and in isolation. For the weakest, this violence has acted as a break of the exterior framework within which they lived: it will be "the lost generation" which has seen its "careers" shattered; for the strongest, it has brought a mass of raw materials, of new data upon which will grow a new experience. Without the war I would have remained an intellectual with predominantly literary interests: I would have discussed problems of political significance, but above all I would have pursued the history of man alone as my deepest interest, and a date with a girl or any sort of fanciful impulse would have counted for me more than any party or doctrine. Other friends, better disposed to feel immediately the political fact, had dedicated themselves for years to the struggle against Fascism. Although I always felt close to them, I do not know if I would have decided to engage myself totally on that road: there was in me too strong a foundation of individual tastes, of indifference, and of critical spirit for me to sacrifice all of it to a collective faith. Only the war has resolved the situation—overturning certain obstacles, clearing the ground of many comfortable shelters, and brutally putting me in contact with an irreconcilable world.

I believe that for the majority of men of my age this passage has been natural: the race toward politics is a phenomenon which I have encountered [in my studies] in many of the best, in a situation similar to that which occurred in Germany when the last romantic generation was exhausted. Phenomena of this kind reproduce themselves every time politics ceases being ordinary administration and engages all the forces of a society in response to an extreme danger in order to save it from a grave sickness. A modern society is based on a great variety of specifications, but it can only subsist if it retains the capacity to abolish them at a certain moment in order to sacrifice everything to a single revolutionary necessity. This is the moral meaning not the technical sense of the mobilization: a youth that does not maintain itself "disposable," that loses itself completely in various techniques, is compromised. At a certain moment, intellectuals must be capable of transferring their experience to the ground of common utility. Everyone must know how to take his place in a fighting organization.

This is above all true for Italy. The Italians are a weary people, profoundly corrupted by their recent history, always at the point of giving in to a cowardice or to a weakness. But they continue to produce revolutionary minorities of the first order: Italian philosophers and workers are in the vanguard of Europe. But today in no civil nation is the separation between vital possibilities and the actual condition as great: it is up to us to fill this separation and to declare a state of emergency.

Musicians and writers, we must renounce our privileges in order to contribute to the liberation of all. Contrary to what is affirmed by a famous phrase, revolutions succeed when they are prepared by poets and painters, as long as poets and painters know what their part must be. Twenty years ago the dominant confusion might have allowed someone to take the adventure in Fiume seriously. Today all the possibilities of the Risorgimento have been reopened for Italians: no gesture is useless if it is not an end in itself. As for myself, I assure you that the thought that I am going to become a partisan during this season amuses me very little: I have never appreciated as much as now the attractions of civil life, and I have the consciousness of being a fine translator and a good diplomat, but I am in all probability a mediocre partisan. Nevertheless it is the only possibility open and I accept it.

If I should not return, do not show yourselves inconsolable. One of the few certainties which I have acquired through my experience is that there are no indispensable individuals and irreparable losses. A live man always finds sufficient reasons for joy in other live men, and you who are young and healthy have the duty of leaving the dead to bury the dead. For this very reason I am writing to you and have spoken of things that perhaps may seem less obvious but that ultimately count more than others. It would have been difficult for me to address the same exhortation to Mother and to our uncles, and the thought of their anguish is the gravest preoccupation I have at this moment. I cannot stop on a difficult sentimental matter, but I would like them to know of my gratitude: their affection and their thoughtfulness have been one of the principal positive factors in my life. Another great reason for happiness has been friendship, the possibility of conquering loneliness by establishing sincere relations among men. Friends who have been close to me, Kamenetzki, Balbo, some of the girls I have loved, share with you these serene thoughts of mine, and they assure me that I have not spent these years of youth uselessly.

GIAIME

IX. AFTER THE FALL: REAPPRAISALS AND DEBATES ON PRE-FASCIST DEMOCRACY

IN THE INTRODUCTION *to this collection of readings, the larger context within which the post-Fascist reappraisals and historical debates on the pre-Fascist era took place has been described. Here it must suffice to call attention to some major factors that may help toward the understanding of the forms of expression assumed by the post-1945 reviews of the Italian past. In the first place, the "debates" were at the same time paradoxically more theoretical and practical than ever before. When they occurred, Fascism had fallen, a world war was over. It now seemed possible to take a more dispassionate, if not more objective, look backward at pre-Fascist democracy and the prehistory of Fascism. Yet, both the apparent possibility of being able at long last to grapple with history, with the problems that Italian history before and during Fascism had left behind, and the urgency of having to deal with those problems in such circumstances as had arisen in Italy by 1945, conspired to make discussions of the past less than purely abstract and inconsequential. For, it was rightly assumed in the most serious quarters, Fascism and the war had not disappeared into the thin air of metaphysics but had rather compounded the historic problems that could be ascribed to or associated with the pre-Fascist period. In facing the questions of reconstruction of a state, of a nation, of a so-*

ciety, no one in his right mind could assume that the heavy burden of previous Italian history could be shrugged off and discarded like ragged old clothes. The question therefore was: What was one to do with that history now that much of it was no longer directly oppressive? Did one want an Italy that, after the historical "parenthesis" of Fascism, would or could pick up the broken strands of the liberal and democratic tradition, or had Fascism represented a rupture so great that only an absolutely revolutionary new start was desirable? What, in fine, was the substantive connection between historical continuity and political, social, or moral innovation? These were the fundamental questions with which the "great debate" on pre-Fascist Italy was indissolubly connected after 1945.

Reconstruction and Reassessment

The Italian Consulta Nazionale was, as its name implies, a consultative national body established in the summer of 1945 to hear expert opinion on "what to do" with post-Fascist Italy, how to begin reorganizing it on an institutional, political, and social basis. The members of the Consulta were representatives of Italian political parties, not popularly elected constituents, and it was their task to clear the ground for the reconstruction of Italy. During its meetings, the atmosphere throughout Italy was tense and uncertain at the same time, free and yet pregnant with catastrophe in the wake of the physical ruin and moral shambles left by Fascism and war. In the Consulta, profound repercussions were felt and found new expression in the political strug-

gle between conservatives and revolutionaries, democrats and liberals, socialists, Communists, and Catholics. On June 19, 1945, Ferruccio Parri, the radical leader of the Partito d'Azione and former commander of the Italian Resistance forces, was chosen as Prime Minister, even as he was a member of the Consulta. Given the mood, expectations, and ambitions of other political leaders, Parri's position was precarious from the start, and it was made even more so by his famous aside in a speech at the Consulta on September 26, 1945, in which the Prime Minister made the apparently casual remark on pre-Fascist democracy which we quote below. The following day, the venerable philosopher and now spokesman for the reconstituted Liberal Party, Benedetto Croce, replied to Parri in what amounted to the Italian thinker's swan song on Liberal Italy.

A Resistance Leader Judges Pre-Fascist Democracy*

FERRUCCIO PARRI

Prime Minister Ferruccio Parri's Famous Aside at a Meeting of the Italian Consulta, September 26, 1945:

PARRI: . . . Keep this in mind: with us democracy is practically just at its beginnings. I am not sure,

* From Ferruccio Parri's speech in the *Atti della Consulta Nazionale. Discussioni dal 25 settembre 1945 al 9 marzo 1946* (Rome: Libreria dello Stato, 1946), p. 6. Editor's translation.

but I do not believe that one can define those regimes which we had before Fascism as having been democratic. (*Interruptions–exchange of apostrophes–comments–noises*)

With my words I would not want to offend those regimes. (*Comments–interruptions–noises*)

I regret that my definition should be unacceptable. I meant to say this: "democratic" has a precise meaning, I would say a technical [meaning]. Those were regimes that we can define and believe to have been liberal. (*Interruptions–comments–shouts of: "Viva Orlando"–very enthusiastic, prolonged applause in the direciion of the Honourable Orlando–shouts of "Viva Vittorio Veneto!"*)

. . .

PARRI: No one more than I associates himself with the salute and applause tendered to the Honourable Orlando.

PRESIDENT: I remind the Consulta to consider that the entire country expects from it an example of work, of concord and of discipline. (*Enthusiastic approbation*)

PARRI: These incidents demonstrate how difficult it is to think about a democratic regime and how long a road we must still travel (*approbation*) before there is achieved a real democratic sensibility in our national life.

. . .

A Philosopher Defends Pre-Fascist Liberalism*

BENEDETTO CROCE

MY ADMIRATION, MY gratitude as an Italian for the work of Parri in the tenaciously heroic struggle against Fascists and Germans is so great and so sincere that it not only does not prevent me, indeed it compels me to speak a word of clear rebuttal against an historical judgment which he made yesterday and which has aroused not really scandal but astonishment. He said that before Fascism Italy had not had democratic governments. Such an assertion is in evident contrast to the fact that Italy, from 1860 to 1922, was one of the most democratic countries of Europe, and that her development was an uninterrupted and often an accelerated ascendancy toward democracy. Patent evidence demonstrated that the people, or rather the masses [of Italians], which the old governments had left in misery and illiteracy and, even in external conduct, shamelessly servile, progressed not only in their physical health—as was proved year after year by the decreasing statistics of those who were rejected for the [army] drafts, as well as the continuous diminution of illiteracy, achieved through public compulsory education—but also through the acquisition of the character and

* From Benedetto Croce's speech of September 27, 1945, in the *Atti della Consulta Nazionale. Discussioni dal 25 settembre 1945 al 9 marzo 1946* (Rome: Libreria dello Stato, 1946), pp. 37–38. Reprinted by permission of Alda Croce. Editor's translation.

semblance of free citizens. Those masses were able to organize themselves in their own associations and labor unions, to defend their rights, to gain their right to strike. They gained laws for the protection of labor, and, through the successive expansion made possible by new electoral laws, they achieved universal suffrage. Thus political parties arose which formulated and advanced the rights of workers and expressed their ideals. The Socialists who at first had only one or two members [in Parliament] went in numbers to the Chamber of Deputies, so much so that, during the last [pre-Fascist] legislature they were, if I remember correctly, more than a hundred fifty; and among them were Giacomo Matteotti and, together with him, Amendola and Gramsci, who died for democratic Italy. That "democracy" was, undoubtedly, "liberal," as every true democracy must be, since if liberalism without democracy must perforce languish through lack of substance and stimulus, democracy, in its turn, without the observance of the liberal system and method, becomes perverted and corrupted and opens the way to dictatorships and despotism. This is indeed what happened to the democracy of the [Italian] medieval communes in giving way to the tyrannies of the Renaissance and the First and Second French republics in leading, respectively to the First and Second empires.

Anyone who, like myself, was born during the first years of the new Italy, united and free, saw some relics of those picturesque aspects of the old life which in my city of Naples were called *lazzari;* but he also witnessed their rapid disappearance, so that they remained merely in the memory of old descriptions and anecdotes of history. And whoever, like myself, was educated in that period of fruition of a liberal and democratic Italy will never forget that he owes the best in himself to that way of life and rhythm which made it possible for him, as had not happened to preceding generations, to be formed without any sort of restraint, to soar truly in the vast world of universal culture, to learn from everyone, be they Italian or foreign, from whatever and however diverse a tradition, to speak and uphold the truth as he saw it, to test his mettle with anyone in civil contests, to bring to this kind of competition that sense of honor which previously had been possible only in the rarest fields. And one cannot but wish that Italy may return, certainly not to the state and condition of that time—since such stupendous and terrible things have happened since then and actual conditions are different and new and other kinds of problems press upon our spirit—but rather to return to the mode of that other time, since it corresponded to the eternal mode of a high level of human life: to be, as Faust said, free among a free people. And it is this very profound consciousness of the debt which all in today's Italy owe to that past wherein lies the reason for this defense of ours today, just as we formerly defended against the "Italietta" ["Little Italy"] invented and scorned by Fascism, the real Italy, the Italy created by our fathers of the Risorgimento, which should always be venerated—that Italy in which we had as masters of our intellectual and moral and aesthetic rules of life such men as Francesco de Sanctis and Giosuè Carducci.

From Politics to History

The publication late in 1945 of a work by an American student of modern Italian history entitled Italian Democracy in the Making *bore an introduction by one of the most illustrious historians of the twentieth century, the irrepressible anti-Fascist democratic exile, Gaetano Salvemini. Whether on its own merits or as a function of the post-Fascist political situation in Italy, the book itself received almost instant attention in Italy and Croce recommended it to the "meditation of Italians." Salvemini's introduction aroused even more sensational attention exactly because, incorrigible anti-Giolittian that he had been before 1914, he now courageously acknowledged that he may have exaggerated his censures of the old liberal and by his critique of Giolittian policy had contributed less toward the consolidation of Italian democracy in the making than toward furnishing arms to those militarist, nationalist, and reactionary groups who were the common enemies of both Giolittian liberalism and Salveminian democracy. Salvemini's introduction is reproduced in full in order to afford a direct estimate of an historical reappraisal of the pre-Fascist past by an extraordinary man whose entire life had been a crusade for justice and liberty.*

An Historian Revisits Italian Democracy in the Making*

GAETANO SALVEMINI

ITALIAN POLITICAL literature from 1861 to 1922 is drenched with a flood of bitter criticism about everything and everybody. To the turn of the century the Clericals regarded newborn Italy as a creation of the Evil One, and everything which was done or not done was wrong to them. After 1876, the Conservatives, who had been turned out of power and were no longer able to have their own way, found that Italy, deprived of their light, was going to rack and ruin. The Republicans, the Socialists, the Anarchists criticized men who were in power owing to the fact that they were neither Republican nor Socialist nor Anarchist. The non-party men who desired honest and efficient administration and more rapid social progress complained that the men in power were not efficient enough and not progressive enough and not honest enough or were downright dishonest. Even the politicians who were in control were disheartened by the gap which divided their everyday inconspicuous job from the alluring expectations of the men who had carried out the Italian Risorgimento.

* From A. William Salomone, *Italian Democracy in the Making. The Political Scene in the Giolittian Era, 1900–1914* (Philadelphia: University of Pennsylvania Press, 1945; new ed., 1960), Introductory Essay by Gaetano Salvemini, XIII–XXII. Reprinted by permission of University of Pennsylvania Press.

In his *Goliath* Borgese describes with a master hand the disease which gnawed at the Italian soul after 1870: the memory of, and the nostalgia for, the grandeur of the Roman Empire, coupled with a restless urge for impossible achievements and, as a consequence, disappointment and self-vilification. Italy was crushed by her past. Instead of comparing their present with their immediate past and realizing the strides the people were making, Italians contrasted present conditions with the memories of past greatness or with dreams of impossible primacies. No measurable degree of progress could satisfy them. They had words only to lament the mediocrity, incapacity, dishonesty, failures of their politicians. A certain amount of self-criticism is a useful corrective to national smugness: it is a factor of that "divine discontent" which leads to improvements. But absurd ambitions are poisonous drugs. They create persecution-mania and make for blunders.

After Mussolini came to power Fascist propaganda overturned the procedure. Everything now became a monument of wisdom, of efficiency, of moral integrity, while everything, before the Dictator began to perform his miracles, had been wrong.

One has to take into account these two floods of misrepresentation, coming from two opposite angles, if one wants to understand the history of Italy from 1870 to 1922. Only a man endowed with a sharp critical sense can avoid the risk of misreading that history completely. Nobody would write the history of the Roosevelt Administration using only the evidence furnished by Republican or isolationist sources. Most people write recent Italian history by a method that is no more sensible.

To be sure, pre-Fascist politicians were responsible for all sorts of mistakes and misdeeds, ill-advised undertakings, unused opportunities, waste, and extravagance. Not all the problems that confronted the country were solved. Not always were the solutions reached the best nor the methods employed the most efficient. But could all problems have been solved at a moment's notice? Has there ever been in history any country which solved all its problems at one stroke and without blunders and whose politicians were monsters of untainted intelligence and moral integrity? If one judges the handiwork of Italian pre-Fascist politicians by the standards of some flawless ideal—the method of the political crusader—there is no politician who would not be sent to hell. But if one adopts the method of the historian, that is if one compares, as far as Italy is concerned, the starting point in 1861 with the point of arrival, the First World War, and the poverty of national resources with the wealth of other countries, one cannot fail to conclude that no country in Europe had made such strides in so short a time.

The author of the present book [*Italian Democracy in the Making*] knew how to avoid the pitfalls of pre-Fascist self-vilification and Fascist propaganda. At the same time he knew how to avoid the opposite pitfalls of "idealistic" historiography, according to which (with Dr. Pangloss) everything which is real is rational and everything which is rational is good. Where most people concern themselves with passing unwarranted judgment, Mr. Salomone first endeavored to understand and then passed cautious and balanced judgment. I do not know of any book which gives a better informed and more objective account of one of the most elusive periods of Italian history, the so-called "Giolittian" years. When one learns that this is the work of a young man, one realizes that there are in this book the beginnings of an exceptionally well-gifted historian.

Mr. Salomone's book is entitled *Italian Democracy in the Making*. What does he mean by these words?

If one understands by "democracy" a political regime in which all personal and political rights are granted equally to all citizens without social, religious, or racial discrimination, and those rights are granted not only by the written law but in actual daily practice, and in addition all citizens, to the last one, intelligently and honestly share in community life, one has to admit that before the First World War Italy possessed a very low form of democracy. But does perfect democracy exist anywhere? Is not democracy in the making everywhere?

The Italian Risorgimento between 1859 and 1870 was the work of an oligarchy of upper and middle classes. The right to vote was granted only to males over twenty-five who paid a minimum of eight dollars in direct taxation and knew how to read and write. In 1871, 72.96 per cent of the population was illiterate. As a consequence, no more than 530,000 citizens were enfranchised out of a population of about 27 million, i.e., 1.98 per cent. By 1880, the enfranchised citizens had risen to 620,000, i.e., 2.18 per cent of the population. All agricultural day laborers, almost all small-holders, almost all city artisans and workers and a good many of the lower middle classes had no right to vote.

This oligarchic system was not an exception in Europe eighty years ago. Between the Reform of

1832 and that of 1867, Great Britain had no more than 700,000 citizens on the electoral list out of a population of 32 million. She remained an oligarchy after the Reform Acts of 1867 and 1884. France had a restricted franchise before 1848; and universal suffrage, enacted in 1848, brought about Napoleon III's dictatorship in 1851. In Germany universal suffrage for the Reichstag from 1867 onward acted as a façade hiding an oligarchic social and political structure. Austria got universal suffrage only in 1908.

In Italy the Reform Act of 1882 extended the franchise to males over twenty-one who could read and write, even if they did not pay any direct taxation. At the same time, 62.80 per cent of the population, that is, almost all of the peasantry and the great majority of artisans and workmen, were still illiterate. It was only in the most progressive cities of northern Italy that workmen had begun to send their children to school. Thus in 1882, no more than two million were registered. The fact, however, remains that the electorate rose from 2.18 per cent to 6.97 per cent of the population. The urban had more electors than the rural sections of the constituencies since those who could read and write were chiefly concentrated in the cities. As a consequence, the political influence of the industrial, commercial, and intellectual classes outweighed that of the landowning class. In the cities themselves the Reform gave great influence to the lower middle classes.

In 1912 a new Reform Act added, to those who had a right to vote, all men under thirty who had served in the armed forces and all others who were over thirty. In neither of these classifications was literacy required. This was almost universal suffrage.

The number of enfranchised citizens rose from three to eight and one-half million. Five and one-half million workmen and peasants submerged the old privileged body of three million.

In order to understand this reform one has to take stock of the fact that by 1911 the percentage of illiteracy had dropped to 38 per cent. Illiteracy had practically disappeared among the rising generations of northern Italy and had been sharply reduced among the youth of southern Italy. Of the young people who attained their twentieth year in 1927, and therefore had gone to school before or during the war, 87 per cent knew how to read and write. Moreover, peace-time conscription had for half a century forced men from peasant stock into the army, removing them from their villages to faraway regions, bringing them in touch with communities which followed different ways, returning them to their homes with a new outlook on life. In addition, emigration–especially emigration to North America–had brought about an upheaval of immense importance among the peasantry of southern Italy. The southern Italian peasant who emigrated not only found work but was made aware of different civilizations. When he returned home he was a new man. Last but not least it was no longer possible to leave disfranchised the majority of the Italian male population who were serving in the war for the conquest of Libya and might at any moment be expected to fight in a European war and all this at a time when even Austria was endowed with universal suffrage.

When the franchise was extended to those who did not know how to read and write, it was thought in Italy–and rightly, in my opinion–that experience of life is more important than mere literacy. A peasant might be unable to read and write but, if he had been to America and returned home with not inconsiderable savings, he possessed a greater knowledge of practical affairs than, for instance, the young gentleman who read French novels and had never faced greater difficulties than that of arranging his necktie in front of his looking-glass.

In Italy, under any voting system, no more than fifty to sixty per cent of the electorate went to the polls. This, by observers readier to pass judgment than to understand, was branded as an evidence of political inertia and hopelessness. The fact is that the same percentage prevails in the United States today. To appreciate the Italian percentage, however, one has to take stock of the fact that millions of Italian workers were far away in Central Europe or along distant Mediterranean shores or in North and South America. They naturally were not in a position to go to the polls, but their numbers were generally included in the population figures. Those men also who were under the colors—Italy had peace-time compulsory military service—were not allowed to vote. Lastly, the citizen was registered as a voter in the city where he was born; therefore, those who were away on business or as government officials had no opportunity to vote. Thus analyzed the Italian percentage compares very favorably with the American.

Parliamentary Italy did not possess the two-party system. During the eighties the traditional division between Conservatives and Democrats had vanished. The transformation of parties (*trasformismo*) had brought about in Italy the splitting up of those parties into small groups, kept together, as Mr. Salomone points out, by personal rather than ideological loyalties. According to Anglo-Saxon doctrine the two-party system is indispensable to a rightful working of a parliamentary regime. Italy lacked that blessing. Was she alone? Did she follow a universal rule or was she a scandalous exception?

During the nineteenth century in England people spoke of only two political parties: the Conservative party and the Liberal party. But the Liberal party was not a party; it was the coalition of two parties, that is, the English Liberal party and the Irish party. When the Irish party refused to coöperate with the English Liberal party and was numerically sufficiently strong to hamper the working of the House of Commons, a political paralysis resulted. But that was not the end of the world. Nobody proclaimed that the English people were incapable of living under a free regime. "We must be patient, the crisis will be solved," it was said. In the present century another party came upon the scene: the Labor party. In 1921 the Irish members went home. Thus three parties remained in England: the Conservative, the Liberal, and the Labor parties. Soon a fourth party appeared: the Communist party. Lately a fifth party has asserted itself in England: the Commonwealth party. If to all of these is added the Independent Labor party, which according to circumstance aligns itself or breaks with the Labor party, we actually see six parties performing upon the political stage. The Communist party, it is true, sends one lone member to Parliament. Presently it has no weight, but it may have more in the future. The Commonwealth party as well will certainly exert a noticeable influence. But even if the political parties should be reduced to only three, the legend of the two-party system would be seen for what it is—a legend.

Moreover, the so-called English parties are not homogeneous and compact political monoliths, as is often thought when the sacred word "party" is pronounced. During the nineteenth century the English Liberal party always had a Cobdenist Right which strenuously advocated laissez-faire doctrines, and a radical Left which demanded social reforms. Scottish Liberals, Welsh Liberals, and English Liberals are not at all the brotherly associates they often appear from afar. Within the Conservative party also there is a Left and a Right. The same thing is true of the Labor party. One of the greatest difficulties faced by party leaders is that of holding together the various groups whose ideas and interests are often in bitter conflict. The English parties are in reality coalitions of local groups which often disagree on essential points, but which are nevertheless held together by the necessity of making compromises in order to gain or to remain in power as against opposite coalitions.

In Canada there are six parties.

As for the United States, the attractive fairy-tale of sharply outlined and opposed political parties is even more imaginary than that of the two English parties. It is true that in the United States one speaks only of the Republican and the Democratic parties. But the United States are really forty-eight sections spreading over a vast continent. In each of these forty-eight sections there are two local parties, one of which is called the Democratic party and the other the Republican party. But the Republican party of

California does not have a single idea in common with, for example, the Republican party of Massachusetts, while at the same time the Democratic party of Texas is as much in agreement with the Democratic party of Wisconsin as the devil with holy water. In the United States there are not two parties. There are ninety-six local parties, with many differences among them, but which come together as two large national "coalitions" for the purpose of electing the President of the Republic. Once elected the President must deal, both in the House of Representatives and in the Senate, with a hodgepodge of heterogeneous and fluctuating groups in comparison to which the groups in the pre-Fascist Italian Chamber of Deputies were a heavenly chorus. A President of the United States must shrewdly bring about among the many local groups an almost infinite number of "combinations of fortune" whose life span may be only one day and for one particular purpose, after which they disband. In this parliamentary strategy he must be prepared to utilize a subtlety and often a lack of scruples in contrast to which Giolitti's maneuvers in Italy were child's play.

In short, those political entities which in Italy one calls "parties" are known as "groups" in England and America, while those which in Italy would be coalitions of "groups" are called "parties" in England and America.

During the fifteen years preceding the First World War there was in Italy a coalition of "parties," or "groups," the Giolittian coalition. It enjoyed an almost permanent stay in power. There certainly was stability then in Italy. As a matter of fact there was even too much stability, despite the fact that Italy did not enjoy the blessing of having only two parties, a blessing which, for that matter, was also unknown to Belgium, France, Switzerland, Germany, and Austria-Hungary. Whether the Giolittian coalition's long stay in power was for Italy's good or evil is an altogether different question.

A voting system would be meaningless if it were not buttressed by freedom of the press and freedom of association.

During the nineteenth century, freedom of the press was limited in Italy by the faculty given to the Attorney General in each province to confiscate any issue of a newspaper which contained illegal material. The Government also was entitled to declare illegal such associations as it could expect to cause disturbances in public peace and could indict their members before the judiciary as "associates for the purpose of crime" (*associazione a delinquere*). But after 1900 no associations were any longer declared illegal. Trade union rights became unrestricted. And in 1906 the Attorney General was deprived of the power to confiscate newspapers. Italian democracy was in the making.

Town councils were elected by the citizens. But they were not autonomous bodies as in Switzerland, in England, or in the United States. There was in each one of the Italian districts (*provincie*) a permanent agent of the central government, the *Prefetto,* who was sent by the Home Secretary (*Ministro degli interni*) to supervise local government. This agent could annul all decisions of municipal councils. He could even remove mayors and councillors and send his own agents (*commissari*) to run the municipality. In 1896, A. Lawrence Lowell, in his classic work on

Governments and Parties in Continental Europe, remarked that Italian administration was modeled on the French and not on the Anglo-Saxon pattern. The Italian prefect, like his French prototype, used his influence more or less openly at elections. This was the gnawing cancer of Italian democracy in the making.

The prefect was always in a position to bring pressure to bear upon the mayors and town councillors. The mayors and councillors who, during an electioneering campaign, used their influence in favor of the governmental candidate remained in office even if they were the worst scoundrels. Those who supported opposition candidates, even if they were the best possible administrators, were replaced by government commissioners. Against eventual injustice there was no redress.

Under Giolitti's rule, the interference of the prefects with local government and elections reached unprecedented heights of brutality. Where the electorate was refractory to pressure and the elected mayors and town councillors refused to bow, the prefect not only dismissed them, but "managed" local and national elections. If an election had to be carried out, the police, in league with the Government supporters, enrolled the scum of the constituencies and the underworld of the neighboring districts. In the last weeks before the polls, the opponents were threatened, bludgeoned, besieged in their homes. Their leaders were debarred from addressing meetings, or even thrown into prison until election day was over. Voters suspected of upholding the opposition were refused polling cards. Those favoring governmental candidates were given not only their own polling cards, but also those of opponents, emigrants, deceased voters, and were allowed to vote three, five, ten, twenty times. The Government candidates were always the winners. Any deputy who dared Giolitti had to confront a bad time at his next election. In Italy people used to say that Giolitti sold prefects in order to buy deputies. Giolitti was not the first Home Secretary to "manage" elections. But he "managed" one after another three national elections (1904, 1909, 1913) and he surpassed all in clarity of purpose and lack of scruples.

But Giolitti did not strangle local government or "manage" elections all over Italy. In those sections of Italy where public opinion was alive and opposition hard to quell, he let things go their own way. It was only in backward southern Italy that Giolitti strangled local government and "managed" elections. Northern Italy was left free to run its local business as best it pleased. Not a few city governments in northern Italy were models of intelligent, honest, and efficient administration. And the worst city governments in the South were no worse than many of those of the United States. Southern Italy gave Giolitti about two hundred representatives ready to obey him under any conditions.

Northern Italy sent to the Chamber of Deputies about three hundred representatives who were split into those who favored the "boss" and those who were against him. Giolitti's majority consisted of a "solid block" from the South and those among the Northerners who were interested in playing ball with him and who, on the whole, had been freely elected. The opponents coming mostly from the North were free to protest in the Chamber of Deputies or in the press as much as they wanted. They were helpless —and hopeless. And little by little hopelessness brought "wisdom." One by one, sooner or later, they came to terms with the boss, and either they joined his flock or they carried on a mock opposition which was more useful to him than open submission.

Yet before terming Giolitti a "parliamentary dictator" one should be careful to qualify those words. A dictator is a man who suppresses freedom of speech, freedom of the press, freedom of association, and sends his opponents to jail or to the next world. Giolitti never did this. He circumvented opposition by reducing the Chamber of Deputies to the position of his maid-servant. There was in the Chamber a majority which blindly obeyed him and an opposition which was sure of always remaining in the minority and was steadily invited to come to some compromise with the master of the circus. If being a dictator means being supported by a huge parliamentary majority and therefore being able to do much as one thinks fit and necessary, Roosevelt was also a dictator in America from 1933 to 1940 and Churchill was a dictator in England from 1940 to 1945. But let us say "powerful leaders" and not "dictators." As soon as his parliamentary majority wavered Giolitti used to resign in order to allow his opponents to try their luck, keeping alert to return to the foreground as soon as his followers reorganized themselves.

Giolitti was an extraordinarily able and skilful parliamentarian. He grasped with extreme shrewdness and lightning rapidity the slightest current of opinion among the five hundred men who formed the Chamber of Deputies. But he had little sensitivity for what was going on in the country at large. Here dissatisfaction with the "managing" of elections was steadily growing among non-party citizens. He thought that he could control the electorate under universal suffrage as easily as he used to when the franchise was restricted. He never realized that the peasantry of southern Italy was no longer that of the eighties. When, in 1913, he was confronted not with a mere two or three thousand voters, but with ten thousand or more voters in a constituency to be "managed," he was forced to increase the dose of violence to insure success. He won another of his overwhelming electoral victories. But the scandals of that campaign provoked bitter indignation everywhere. On the eve of the war of 1914–18, Giolitti was the most powerful man in Parliament, but the most unpopular man in the country. Italian democracy was in the making.

Italian democracy would have needed still another generation of trial and error before becoming not a "perfect democracy" but a "less imperfect democracy."

The crisis that followed the First World War, however, was fatal to that democratic process. So long as the Italian masses had remained indifferent toward public life and had been deprived of the right of suffrage, the Royal House, the professional militarists who headed the armed forces, the big industrialists and land-owners, the chief editors of the large dailies had all been satisfied that parliamentary institutions, whether they functioned well or badly, furthered their purposes. But during the first twenty years of the present century the Italian working classes came forward demanding their place in the sun and after the war of 1914–18 they became "unruly." More than half of the members of the Italian Chamber of Deputies were now the representatives of these masses and they did not lend themselves to the traditional game of the old masters. That was the reason why the coup d'état of October 1922 (the so-called "March on Rome") was contrived by politicians blinded by class interests and by personal ambitions as well as by the leaders of the armed forces. The Giolittian method of stifling local government and of curtailing the personal and political liberties of citizens in southern Italy at election time —and only in those constituencies where the victory of the governmental candidate was necessary—was now extended and practised by the Fascists all over Italy and became permanent. And worse yet, systematic assassination was added. Now, Italy truly had a dictatorship, Mussolini's dictatorship, and not "parliamentary dictatorship." The coup d'état of October 1922 would not have taken place if a greater acquaintance with, and a more extensive practice of, democracy on the part of the people had not threatened the very roots of the conservative interests.

In the course of his researches Mr. Salomone has come upon my name and he has devoted some space in his book [*Italian Democracy in the Making*] to my activities in Italy during the years of Giolitti. It is not up to me to comment on what he has written about me. But to one point I feel duty-bound to call the reader's attention. While during those years I practised, as well as I could, my profession of historian (which has always been my true profession), I devoted my spare time to a political crusade. The reader will find in this book the crusader and not the historian.

Looking back at the work of the crusader after thirty years, I find that I have nothing to regret. I must acknowledge, however, that I would have been wiser had I been more moderate in my criticism of the Giolittian system. My knowledge of the men who came after Giolitti in Italy as well as of countries in which I have lived during the last twenty years has convinced me that if Giolitti was not better, neither was he worse than many non-Italian politicians, and he was certainly less reprehensible than the Italian politicians who followed him. For while we Italian crusaders attacked him from the Left accusing him of being–and he was–a corrupter of Italian democracy in the making, others assailed him from the Right because he was even too democratic for their taste. Our criticism thus did not help to direct the evolution of Italian public life toward less imperfect forms of democracy, but rather toward the victory of those militarist, nationalist, and reactionary groups who had found even Giolitti's democracy too perfect. It often happens that he who seeks only the best not only fails to get it but also plunges into the worst. It is said that in the next world we shall be assigned either to hell, or purgatory, or paradise. In this world, however, there is no paradise. If, in seeking an impossible paradise, we scorn purgatory, we will surely end in hell. If it were possible for me to live again in Italy between 1900 and 1914 with that modicum of experience which I have gained during these successive thirty years, I would not omit any of my censures of the Giolittian system, but I would be more indulgent and I would regard with greater suspicion those who found pleasure in my criticism because they wanted to lead Italy in the opposite direction from that which I envisaged for her.

Perhaps I may be allowed to excuse my error with the example of a man who possessed an intelligence much greater than mine: Gaetano Mosca. The reader of this book [*Italian Democracy in the Making*] will find in it an account of the criticism of the Italian parliamentary regime made by Gaetano Mosca when he was still very young–a young man of exceptional intelligence and moral integrity, but still quite young. It might be well to remember, however, that speaking on the bill which was to institute Mussolini's dictatorship, at the sitting of December 16, 1925 of the Italian Senate, Gaetano Mosca, by then ripe of age and experience, closed his address with the following words:

> I who have always sharply criticized parliamentary government must now almost lament over its downfall. In order to judge a form of government there is one possible method, that is, to compare it with both that which has preceded it and that which has followed it. It would be premature, at this time, to speak of the latter. As to the former, the forms of government immediately preceding the parliamentary regime were such that it can be frankly asserted that this system was better than they. . . . Let us consider the road traveled from 1848 to 1914, eve of the war. Let us see what Italy was in 1848 and what she had become by 1914. We must then acknowledge that the progress made by the country during this period was immense. . . .

> Certainly representative parliamentary government must not and can not be immutable. As the conditions of society change political organizations are changed. But should the change have been rapid and radical, or should it have been slow and wary? This is the very grave question which vexes my soul. As an old adversary of the parliamentary regime, I believe that this problem must be solved in the most moderate and prudent manner.

Mosca too discovered that, with his criticism of the parliamentary system, he had not encouraged a moderate and prudent reform but rather the total abolition of the system. As for the results of the Fascist dictatorship in contrast with those of Italian democracy in the making, they are here before our very eyes. Let us hope that the Italians will not be the only ones to learn from that frightful experience.

From History to Ideology

The work on Italian Democracy in the Making, *first published in the United States in 1945, was translated and published in Italy in 1949. Between the two dates a huge wave of new* giolittiana *had spread over Italy through memoires, books, articles, radio commentaries, and discussions that, among other things, reveal the extent of the Italian interest in the pre-Fascist past. Giolitti had seemingly come back to haunt the historical consciousness of the post-Fascist generation. The problems concerning how he had governed Italy before 1914 and what progress Italy may have made during his rule toward a liberal way of life and a democratic regime became "topical" and inescapable in practically all Italian intellectual, cultural, and ideological quarters. Indeed, the wave of* giolittiana *seemed now so overwhelmingly pressing that none other than the leader of the Italian Communist Party, Palmiro Togliatti (1893–1964), attempted to stem it or turn it into a "cultural force" in favor of his Party's doctrinal-historical attitudes toward the pre-Fascist past. At the end of April 1950, Togliatti delivered in Turin a "Discourse on Giolitti," which established a kind of new Italian Marxist "line" of interpretation that had not received* that *kind of ideological attention even in Gramsci's* Prison Notebooks. *Not too surprisingly, Togliatti practically appropriated Giolitti as a "good" progressive liberal statesman and repudiated "Italian democracy in the making" during the Giolittian era as a spurious bourgeois progress that had necessarily led to an imperialist prologue to Fascism in Italy. No one who was less than completely ingenuous in matters of Marxist dialectics could miss the major point that Togliatti had sought to make against the Salveminian democratic interpretation of Giolitti and "democracy in the making" before 1914. Within two years, the old fighter Gaetano Salvemini returned in full force to the polemical fray against Togliatti and his new "idol" Giolitti, but* not *against his consistently held view that on the eve of the Great War of 1914 Italian democracy had been "in the making." The two readings that follow offer the core of Togliatti's 1950 "Discourse on Giolitti" and Salvemini's 1952 article on pre-Fascist democracy.*

A Communist Leader as Historian: "Giolitti, Yes–Democracy, No"*

PALMIRO TOGLIATTI

THE THEME WHICH has been proposed to me for this lecture and which is "Giolitti and Italian Democracy," seen, it is true, by a socialist, might at first sight appear to be if not easy of treatment at least simple of resolution by me, since I must give a general judgment upon the Italian and Piedmontese political figure whose life and activity dominated Italian political history during the first decade of this century and even afterwards. The speaker indeed not only belongs to the socialist camp, but he is a Communist, that is, he belongs to the most advanced rank in that camp. It would therefore seem for this reason an easy task, since from me there might be expected the repetition or reasoned illustration of a pure and simple negative judgment of Giovanni Giolitti, of condemnation such as was given in the past, precisely by those socialist currents which were most advanced, revolutionary, or intransigent, as it used to be said during those days.

It is perhaps even superfluous to document this negative judgment of the past. I believe that it is still alive in the minds of all those who have had direct experience with the political struggles of the first

* From Palmiro Togliatti, *Discorso su Giolitti* (Rome: Rinascita, 1950), 9–18, 23–24, 27–28, 57–59, 61–62, 63–64, 66–67, 69–70, 74–75, 76–78, 94–96. Reprinted by permission of Editori Riuniti. Editor's translation.

decades of this century. True, there was a moment, around 1900, during which in working-class meetings in the north of Italy one would shout "Viva Giolitti," and it is not difficult to understand why. With that shout one was applauding the proposed concession of freedom to organize and to strike which Giolitti had made to the workers, and which was realized during the first years of the century as a general criterion of government. That moment, however, was very brief, since not only criticism but bitter polemics and violent attacks as well began immediately after to prevail, arising from zones clearly beyond the range of the socialist movement, and not just in the camps of those so-called extremists, but even among men of different tendencies, such as Gaetano Salvemini, for instance. It was the latter who created the epithet *Ministro della Malavita* [Minister of the Underworld], which was the title of a pamphlet published for the first time in 1910 as a commentary on certain electoral episodes that had occurred in Puglie and in Sicily. The epithet, admittedly, was successful, not so much, I believe, because of its somewhat demagogic violence as because it recalled the language of the lower worlds of our southern cities, and tended to bind the subversive socialists' attack upon the representative exponent of the bourgois ruling classes to that more reasoned and profound criticism which was aimed against his system of government by a considerable part of the intellectual middle class, indeed that part which was not socialist.

Thus it happened then that while from one side socialists were protesting with vehemence–particularly against the killing of workers in conflicts with carabineers and soldiers, or against the war in Libya, or against electoral corruption–from the other side an entire political school composed of democrats, liberals, and even conservatives bitterly criticized the system of Giolittian government as being unadapted to the real situation of our country, so that instead of helping it overcome its weaknesses and of healing the contrasts in its structure, this group tended instead to aggravate and accentuate both. Thus it happened that even before the last and most ferocious attack by nationalists and Fascists of "the first hour" was loosened upon Giolitti as a result of his so-called neutralism of 1914 and 1915, the very term "*giolittismo*" had come to be associated in the Italian political vocabulary then current with a deprecating meaning, as if it meant the corruption of men and things, an art of government favored for the purpose of rendering power more illicitly solid, less controlled and less controllable at the same time. Satire, caricature, popular songs, the entire folklore of politics contributed powerfully to diffuse this judgment in which seems to be summed up–thereby adding new shadows to an already dark picture–the word of those who, even if they approved the substance of the governmental action of Giolitti, found, on the other hand, that action prosaic and Giolitti himself capable of living only day by day, like an ordinary bureaucrat who had been denied the true qualities of a statesman.

Everyone can understand how such a criticism was destined to be attractive above all to those young students and inexpert intellectuals who during the first decade of this century, having broken their earlier sympathies with the working-class movement and socialism, were now in search of new "genial" guides; and found them in the dilettantish philosophical systems and vulgarised general ideas of Hegelians who wrote for the ladies, poets of the superman, "Seers of the Nation," and similar things. No, that good man from Cuneo [Giolitti], who had been cured of philosophy after reading [Gioberti's] *Teorica del soprannaturale,* and who, when he had finished what he really wanted to say, could not find a word to add and would sit down, was not endowed with such kind of "genius" and in the "genial" gentlemen of the kind mentioned above, who boasted the possession of "inspiration and faith," he inspired indifference and repulsion.

True that these searchers for the "genial" and these other so severe judges of Giovanni Giolitti ended by admiring the "genius" and bowing before it, exalting it, even adoring it, when at long last they discovered it under the semblance of Benito Mussolini. This lamentable and rather empty search for great men and this pretended anxiety for great things has in a very clear sense not given them special qualifications. We all have come to realize by now what they were and what they were looking for. . . .

This state of affairs is recognized today even by Gaetano Salvemini who was himself in contact with, indeed I would say in concert with, those "genials" during the period of interventionism. "Our criticism [of Giovanni Giolitti]," Salvemini writes today, "thus did not help to direct the evolution of Italian public life toward less imperfect forms of democracy, but rather toward the victory of those militarist, nationalist, and reactionary groups who had found even Giolitti's democracy too perfect." What can one say of such criticism, which favors not a betterment but a worsening of things? At least one can say that those who made criticism of this sort had good intentions, but despite good intentions, they failed to take into account all the elements of the situation, and they neglected the preparation of those forces which have the task of inhibiting the victory of worse ones.

And then? Are we here today in order to achieve a general revision of judgments which I have so briefly recalled, ready to pass from the condemnation and negation [of Giolitti] formerly made by that same Gaetano Salvemini, to what in evident irritation, as revealed by a letter published a few days ago by a daily paper in Rome, Salvemini calls "Giolittian hagiography," that is, to the sanctification of the old statesman? I do not believe that we have reached such a point, and if the question is so posed it is not correct.

The tendency to revise judgments on the past has arisen during recent times principally for two motives, which reduce themselves to a single one, that is, to the contrasting of the government of Giolitti with those which follow later: the government of Fascism first, and then that of the clericals. Under the shameful tyranny of Mussolini it was inevitable that the minds of honest Italians should turn back with nostalgia to the first decade of this century, which could only appear to everyone as the vanishing of a distant oasis of a happy life. And even today when it is said that a parliamentary regime has been restored, the comparison with the Giolittian period is not always favorable to the latter: indeed, to the contrary! But the question immediately arises: How did it happen that those ten years of tranquil government were followed by the hurricane of the First World War, then by the convulsion of the post-war, and finally, that from the very bosom of Italian society the Fascist catastrophe should have arisen? And why didn't the liberal and democratic Giolitti find successors and followers and why did those whom he had, inferior to him as they were from many points of view, become so rapidly overwhelmed, almost without resistance, by the [Fascist] tyranny. And that tyranny having fallen, why was there no one who succeeded in restoring the tradition established by him? Had his more than ten-year long government [1904–14], therefore, not served to create a solid foundation upon which one might have solidly built for an entire historical epoch? Was there a rupture which overwhelmed that tranquil regime, or was there instead a consequential development of elements and contrasts which had already been present and profound within that regime, even if superficial observation did not reveal it and a vain optimism wishes to deny it?

The First World War was certainly a rupture and it provoked profound ruptures. The internal events [in Italy] of May 1915, on the other hand, had nothing revolutionary about them and indeed they merely served to place into relief a situation that had already matured within its own elements. At any rate, here is an historical problem that it is necessary to resolve. . . .

I must say that the recently published books dedicated to the study of the political man from Dronero [Giolitti] and his time do not make a contribution worthy of note toward the solution of these historical problems and that, in substance, they do not escape from the framework of the old discussions of it. I will call to your attention three [of these works], that by a young Italian in America, A. William Salomone, entitled the *Giolittian Era;* that by Giovanni Ansaldo, which introduces a new epithet, *ministro della buona vita,* thus counterposing a new one to the old coined by Salvemini; and that by Gaetano Natale, whose title is larger since it deals with *Giolitti and the Italians.* The first two are prevalently, indeed almost exclusively descriptive. They offer facts and judgments, they narrate, but they do not reveal contrasts, they do not resolve problems. Of the two, Ansaldo's is without doubt inferior since it does not surpass the level of a mediocre journalistic feat and it tends to give a picture of the Giolittian epoch as a period of quiet living and well-ordered labor in which all of Italy was supposedly engaged in a kind of shabby provincial sense. Such a picture is false, stereotyped, founded upon that superficial journalistic method that isolates and underscores secondary aspects by neglecting essentials. The book by Gaetano Natale is certainly the most interesting and useful due to the copiousness of documents it gathers, the episodes of which it speaks and the information it furnishes; but it suffers from vagueness inevitable in anyone who occupies himself with so many things and places everything on the same level in a tone of continuous rectification, of continuous defense, of continuous corrections and computations of inexactness [in others], of petty and great malices, and of calumnies, whether well founded or not. . . .

But it now becomes necessary to detach oneself from the polemics of the past, since to continue to engage in them from such a distance, during the present moment, is not conducive to much progress. We are in need of a research which starting from the characteristics of the political man, of his programmatic affirmations and of his activities, will lead us to a better understanding of the structure of the civil and political society of his time, of the contrasts in which it was immersed, of the transformations it was undergoing. It is in fact true, as Friedrich Engels admonished, that men make their own history; but they make history above all upon premises and in conditions that are well determined. The task of the historian lies in re-establishing an exact relationship between these premises and these conditions, on one side, and the person who affirms himself among them, who seeks to understand them, who seeks to adjust himself to them or to transform them through his own action, on the other; for it is only in this relationship that the value of men is placed in its proper light. Thus the "demiurges" disappear and one acquires a consciousness of the difficulties of one's actions, of the limits of our liberty in the midst of the clash and of the inexorable process of real forces. . . .

Among the many stupid things said about us Marxists and Communists is the statement that we would be incapable not only of understanding but even of narrating history because our conception would reduce all that happens and has happened in the world to a struggle between the good and the bad and vice versa, and that all humanity would be divided by us into two camps, in one of which would be all the good and in the other all the evil, judged according to a rigid scheme of values. This is a bizarre Manichean falsification of that vision of history and of that [philosophical] world which indeed foresaw the end of capitalistic bourgeois domination, but which also knew how to offer an objectively grandiose picture of what the advent of that same bourgeoisie has signified in the development of humanity! No one knows better than we that history is not a series of quarrels among gossiping women nor a civil trial in which the task of the historian is to apportion equally right and wrong. Often one must conclude that both contending parts are wrong, if we may so put it. This is what happened in the struggle between Giolitti and the Italian socialists during the first decade of this century, because neither the one nor the other understood in an adequate manner the necessity of that moment nor how to let it express all the forces which were in motion within it. "Right" is he who finds himself attuned to the development of the objective forces and of the masses who tend to give life to an advanced social regime; "wrong" is he who does not take notice of this development, who does not understand it, who does not succeed in helping with his action the creation of a new social regime, or who opposes it cautiously, thus rendering more painful the march of men, of nations, of classes.

It is absurd to pretend that Giovanni Giolitti, who came out of the old bourgeois and conservative ruling class, should have been the herald of a renewal of Italian society. However, it cannot be denied that among the politicians of his epoch he appears today the one who more than others understood the direction in which Italian society should have moved in order to overcome the contrasts of that time. Italy was no longer that of 1848 or of 1860. Under the old shell new social groups had formed themselves, and the formation and consolidation of the unitary state had rendered their development even more rapid. From among the artisans, from among the undifferentiated masses of city and countryside, had come the salaried classes in industry and agriculture, a new class, whose numerical growth had been made necessary by the very progress of the Italian economy and of civil life, and these social classes presented themselves upon the scene with a homogeneity until then unknown among popular strata, demanding the urgent vindication of a higher way of life, possessed as they were of a consciousness first of being a group and a new social category, then of being a class, and finally of being a political and social entity, from which springs the capacity to give life to an organization and to engage it in the struggle against the old constituted order, the old ruling groups. How could this new and vigorous push be tolerated by the old structures of society? It cannot be denied that Giolitti possessed at least an intuition of the problem, as being not a problem of policing but rather one of economic and political direction. He saw, therefore, that it was not enough for the traditional ruling groups to resist and maintain their old positions, but that it was necessary to change something in the old way of living and of governing. . . .

But we come to one of the central points of our inquiry. In order to extend the internal market it was not enough to increase industrial salaries; it was necessary to raise the conditions of labor and the level of existence of the masses of peasants. Even for the peasants Giolitti demanded economic betterment; concretely, however, this meant only the salaries of the *braccianti* [farm hands] of Sicily and the Po Valley. He ignored the central question: that of the land and of its possession by those who worked upon it. He missed, therefore, the entire vision of Italy that had resulted from the compromises of the Risorgimento and from the socially egotistical administration of the Right and of the transformists [*trasformisti*]. Italy was weighed down by an underdeveloped agrarian economy and by a revolution that had not taken place, by ancient questions to be resolved, by flagrant injustices to be redressed, with millions of peasants whose aspiration, always disappointed, had been the direct possession and cultivation of the land, that is, who desired a profound transformation of all their relationships, and of the relations between class and power. Thus his economic and social action was limited, unilateral. To the workers of the North he conceded, besides the freedom to organize and to strike, other no less significant advantages, such as the granting of contracts for public works to workingman's cooperatives, and some good protective legislation, concerning night work, work done by women and children, Sunday rest, etc. In the agrarian regions which were more underdeveloped, and which Giolitti himself had reproached the Right for having neglected, one finds only a few insignificant laws devoid of practical consequences, and the policy of public works. He did not understand the profound economic and social significance of the spontaneous movements of the Southern masses, which were substantially analogous to the strikes in the North. To him they appeared as pure and simple revolts, and against them he utilized the armed force of the state as his sole weapon.

The conflicts with the public force and the repeated killings of workers bespoke in a flagrant way the vice of the system, which was the organic vice of all liberalism and of all Italian democracy. . . .

As we have seen, we have had to add many qualifications to the affirmation that the political inspiration and the fundamental points of the program of Giolittian government were directly related to a democratic regime. We must, however, recognize that even for the realization of a program of democracy so limited, it was not easy to find in the Italy of the end of the last century a political basis that was large, secure, and permanent enough. What were the parties? Despite the fact that in his *Memoires* Giolitti speaks continually of a "liberal party" of whose program Giolittian policy was supposedly the realization, a national political organization that could have been so-called did not exist. The liberalism of which Benedetto Croce speaks is an historical and philosophical construction of ten years later. . . .

The fact is that Giolitti himself was forced to take note that the ruling conservative class which sat in the Italian national parliament was not very different from that of the little states which Italian unification had caused to disappear. Profound transformations had not occurred. Directing groups organized themselves locally on the basis of restricted interests. They would take the shape of clienteles not of political parties, and as clienteles they were disposed to absorb new men coming from the camp of forces of the "Left" so long as the substance did not change. The formula of government adapted to this situation was *trasformismo* [transformism]: not a government by parties, not a coalition of parties, but rather contacts, collaborations, compromises among groups of clients, achieved through the prevalence of those who were not always the best or the most capable. To continue to govern through this formula became a difficult thing in the first decade of this century, when economic life developed in such a manner that it brought about the dispersion of the old formations. Only at the extreme Left, in the socialist party, can one see evidence of a modern political transformation, both democratic and national. The old conservative Italy was on its way to becoming the new imperialist Italy; capital and industry became concentrated, economic monopolies began rising; from the wearing down of the old political structures however, no great new things emerged. . . .

With this system, it is said, Italy was ruled for more than ten years and there was well-being and relative tranquillity, indicating that underneath there must have been a stable balance of forces. Here, however, we must judge otherwise if we do not wish to fall into that banal superficiality through which the history of Italy up to 1915 is reduced to the history of a progressive realization of the liberal idea and, then, suddenly we find ourselves, without apparent reason, face to face with the end of all political and civil liberties. It is necessary to concentrate our attention upon the profound contrasts that were smoldering under the Giolittian system, contrasts that did not permit it to consolidate itself as a democratic ordering [of society], that rendered it feeble and not coherent as a real democracy, incapable of dominating the contrasting forces that were maturing in its bosom, destined to succumb to their clash. In the system itself, what strikes one after all—and we have pointed it out a number of times—is the contradictoriness of the positions which is revealing of those latent or open contrasts. . . .

The result which at this point we may see shows [in Giolitti] a figure not always simple and unilateral, such as the prevalent historiographical tradition presents him to us, but an extremely contradictory figure such as had not existed before during the last decades—a man of profound contradictions which do not derive from uncertainty or hesitation, at least during the period preceding the First World War, but which spring out of the nature of things, from the real conflicts already matured or in the process of maturation within the web of society. For the old cautious statesmen, it had seemed impossible in this society which was rapidly evolving to continue on the same road; but the new road led to new difficulties even graver than the old; the forces which he had not succeeded in holding at bay now advanced with such an impetus that every day a pacific proceeding was impeded, and the danger that all would be overturned had to be considered as being real. The bell of alarm was to be sounded full blast by the Libyan War and by Red Week of 1914. On both sides the crash resounded. . . .

. . . It is vain historically to discuss what Giovanni Giolitti would have done if, in 1914–15, he, rather than two such men of inferior capacities as Salandra and Sonnino—of whom one was incompetent—had been in the government. One might say that it would have resulted in a much more wary diplomacy; one must, however, add that the documents induce us to conclude that Giolitti's opposition to the war was essentially inspired by preoccupations about internal order, about the consequences of any violent upturning that might put in disarray all of Italian society. His intuition was correct, although it is only right to observe that the shock of war only rendered more rapid the processes [of decay] already set in motion. . . .

It is said that after the war Giovanni Giolitti was no longer himself. It is true, if with such a judgment one wishes to underline the by now evident inadequacies of the system, but it is not true insofar as the man and his programs were concerned. The words that he pronounced at the provincial Council of Cuneo before Caporetto, and his successive political manifestations–among which was the famous discourse of Dronero [October 12, 1919]–are products of the same inspiration that had determined his liberal conduct toward the working class movement around 1900 and his concession on enlarged suffrage after the Libyan War. Now it was necessary to concede in order to avoid the worst, and since the waves that came from below looked this time to be more potent than ever, concessions to the very last possible limit had to be made. In the public order, that limit was a constituent assembly that might have radically reformed the system, thus insuring its popular basis. Giovanni Giolitti does not speak of it directly, but in his programmatic declarations there is in substance mention of a constituent [assembly], which may be logically deduced from his proposal of a limitation of the powers of the Crown. In the economic and social order, we find the same old tendency to annoy the plutocratic class through the proposal of a revision of war contracts and the confiscation of profits made from them, by means of the introduction of personal registration of investments. There is the same search for friends in that camp which by now has become practically untouchable, the socialist party. There is the same cautious tolerance toward working class movements and some comprehension, a new element, of the present movement. But there are also the same contradictory elements of a previous time: the incapacity to see through to the very bottom the [national] problems, the confidence that police pressures might succeed in modifying the course of things, the tragic error of maintaining a belief that the vigilante-like violence of Fascists, together with police action and its accompanying pressures, might serve as an instrument of restraint. The position he assumed during the occupation of the factories [August-September 1920] contained all the elements of Giolittian policy, and culminated in the most advanced and threatening of the anti-plutocratic legislations, that is, his proposal of a working class control over production. . . .

When everything is taken together, among the political men of the bourgeoisie Giolitti had thrust himself forward more than others, whether in the comprehension of the needs of the popular masses, in the attempt to give life to a political ordering of democracy, or in the formulation of a program in which one can espy, even if only as a beginning, the hope of a renewal. We must add that the inspiration and the push to move himself in this direction derived less from a rigorous political analysis than from a sense, a vision, and a comprehension of the misery of the people, the majority of whom had been denied a human level of existence. The way he speaks repeatedly of the conditions of life of the worker and of the peasant, whether in his speeches or in his *Memoires,* should lead one to give greater attention to the question of whether this should not be considered as the salient feature of his person as well as the source of the contradictions which we have seen, exactly because he was burdened with and in the course of action overwhelmed by superstructures, by the practice of the parliamentary game, by the rigidity and coldness involved in administering in behalf of the bourgeois ruling class.

I remember that after the Libyan War, in 1913 and 1914, there was undertaken here in Piedmont a collection of signatures to render him homage and that in the message which accompanied it, he was hailed for his "faith in progressive democracy." A curious prefiguring, in different terms, of today. But that democracy, as we now know, could not progress, and when it is impossible to progress one must go back or be overwhelmed. History has given us proof of this, and the study of the man and of his time reveals the reason to us. No progress is possible for democracy in the modern world until the working class shall have asserted itself as a participant in the direction of the life of the country and a protagonist in it. The question which was maturing at the time of Giolitti today is posed in an ineluctable manner. History has, however, at the same time created the forces to which the task of resolving it belongs, and they will resolve it.

Turin, April 30, 1950

The Historian as Polemicist: "Giolitti, No–Democracy, Yes"*

GAETANO SALVEMINI

THE DOMINATING FIGURE of Italian public life from 1901 to 1914 was Giovanni Giolitti, Minister of the Interior from 1901 to 1903 and almost perennial president of the Council from the fall of 1903 on. This permanence in power is itself a proof that the man possessed qualities superior to those of his contemporaries. If in addition one compares Giolitti with those who came after him, for instance with the "Man of Providence" [Mussolini] who was always right, we cannot but recognize that the first was better than the second; and it can be well understood why Giolitti was preferable to Mussolini, even by those who at the time of Giolitti did not feel any great transports of love for him.

We should not at any rate forget that even the "Man of Providence" was followed by someone who was worse than he, Hitler. . . .

In a speech held in Turin in May [*sic, but read* April] 1950 on Giolitti, Togliatti attributed to Giolitti "the concession of the freedom to organize and to strike to the workers."

* From Gaetano Salvemini, "Fu l'Italia prefascista una democrazia," [*Il Ponte,* Florence, 1952], reprinted in Gaetano Salvemini, *Il Ministro della mala vita ed altri scritti sull'Italia giolittiana,* ed. by Elio Apih (Milan: Feltrinelli Editore, 1962), 544, 545–50, 554–55, 565–67. Reprinted by permission of Giangiacomo Feltrinelli Editore. Editor's translation.

"Concession"? Even for this word everything depends upon the meaning we give it. If "to concede" means to stop a resistance which has become very dangerous, we can say that Giolitti "conceded" freedom to organize and to strike to the workers. In fact, that "concession" came after a relentless parliamentary obstructionism which in 1900 had obliged the President of the Council, Pelloux, a man close to King Umberto, to dissolve the Chamber [of Deputies] with the aim of eliminating those deputies who had been the authors of the obstructionism. The elections of June 1900 not only had not eliminated the obstructionist deputies from the Chamber, they had also increased their number to almost fifty, and the sum of the votes cast for ministerial candidates in all of Italy had not been above a few tens of thousands over those of the opposition of all colors. Therefore the King had to choose: either to dismiss Pelloux or to carry out a coup d'état; and he had not dared to carry out a coup d'état. Furthermore Giolitti's "concession" came after July 1900 when the anarchist Bresci had killed Umberto, that is, after it had been demonstrated that a reactionary policy, too much disguised as the personal policy of the king, offered risks of a personal character. Finally that "concession" came after December 1900 when a lightning-like general strike in Genoa—the first of such a kind in Italy—had demonstrated that certain *coups de main* against working-class organizations could not be undertaken with a light heart.

Giolitti had the good sense to understand that it was necessary to change ways or to change route and not to continue—given the new social and psychological conditions of the Italian people—the policy of the blindered mule. It would be foolish to deny him that good sense. But it should be made clear that when Giolitti undertook to make that "concession," the Italian workers had already taken that concession for themselves, thanks to their sacrifices and to their determination.

In order to give him all the credit he deserves it is necessary to remember that as soon as Giolitti became Minister of the Interior in 1901 and abandoned the policy of repression of the workers' organizations, there broke out for two years in Italy, especially in the countryside, a cyclone of strikes without precedent. Face to face with that storm a man who might have been endowed with a nervous system less solid than his would have lost his head and would have returned to the use of terroristic methods of the past years, thus provoking who knows what kind of violent complications. Giolitti did not lose his head. He stood firm. This was his personal contribution—and it was great—toward the overcoming of the crisis. During those years the "poor devils" in Italy were lucky—reason prevailed. To have placed himself against those "poor devils" would have meant for Giolitti not only to go against his own personal convictions but also to have adopted the policy of the conservatives whose hatred he had experienced during the preceding years and was still experiencing. Either the man passed the test or his political career would be ended forever. The coincidence between the pressure of the working-class movement and his personal predispositions and political interests turned Giolitti at that moment into a statesman.

But when we have given Giolitti all the merit he deserved for having accepted and not diverted the new beneficent currents of Italian life, let us be very careful not to lose our own heads in the way in which he did not lose his in 1901 and 1902 by attributing to him merits which he did not possess, and —even worse—engage in a conspiracy of silence on the good which he did not realize and on the evil which he did. Bookkeeping consists of comparing the columns of assets and liabilities, and not of a single column.

What was the good that Giolitti did not do?

I do not believe that one can reasonably reproach him for not having resolved that which, as Togliatti says, "was and is still the central problem of Italian economic social and political" life—the problem "of an underdeveloped agrarian economy and of a revolution that did not take place, of age old questions to be resolved and of flagrant injustices to be redressed, of millions of peasants whose aspirations, always unrealized, had been the direct possession and cultivation of the land, that is, a profound transformation of all the relations of class and power." (Togliatti, *Giolitti,* pp. 57–58.) It would be reproaching Giolitti for not having done the business of Togliatti forty years ago, thus leaving Togliatti unemployed today. Giolitti was what in the eighteenth century would have been defined as an upholder of enlightened despotism: that is, a paternalistic conservative, who recognized for the "poor devils" the right to eat a little more, to dress a little better, to do their best in order to achieve these results. But he never realized that the "poor devils" might change the basis of society in which they were born or that they should be bold enough to change them.

After all, the socialists themselves, who, had they

been able to, would have changed those bases, never asked Giolitti himself to change them. Since they were revolutionaries, they were certain that capitalistic society had by then arrived at such a boiling point as to make the outbreak of a revolution necessary, and therefore they did not ask Giolitti for anything, just as they did not ask the good Lord to let summer and winter arrive. And those [among the socialists] who were reformists, that is those who recognized that the boiling point was still far off, were satisfied with those crumbs which, thanks to the Giolittian non-resistance, the "poor devils" succeeded as best they could in recovering from the table of the rich. Giolitti was neither a socialist nor a reformist, nor a revolutionary socialist—least of all was he a Communist "1951-style." That is the reason why he did not do what no one asked him to and which, as far as he was concerned, he would never have done.

It has been recently stated that such free traders as Vito de Marco, Giretti, and Einaudi accused Giolitti for his not having instituted a "free trade policy," that is for not having demolished the tariff system which hurt agrarian Italy and particularly the South of Italy. If Giolitti had proceeded to bring about such a demolition "he would have been in trouble with the Northern industry and encountered such a strong social movement in the North as to compromise perhaps that same unity which after all was the advantage and the defense of the southern masses" (G. Ansaldo, *Il ministro della buona vita,* p. 150). This kind of argument is false in its premise. No one ever expected Giolitti to demolish the industrial protectionism which had arisen during the preceding twenty years; no one asked him to bring about a crisis in northern Italy (which had never been avoided when southern Italy had to be hit through the introduction of industrial protectionism). What the critics of Giolitti's tariff-policy deplored was that Giolitti aggravated through new provisions the protectionism which already existed, that is, that he sharpened the evil already done before him by accentuating the iniquitous inequalities between North and South. The protectionism granted to the sugar magnates, the protectionism granted to the steel magnates, the favors granted to shipbuilders reached unhoped-for heights exactly during the Giolittian era.

One must go and search for the good which Giolitti did not do where one is sure of finding it.

Giolitti had, as a deputy, invoked a "large" measure [of administrative] decentralization. But under him centralization became ever more sturdy and rigid, and it reached a definitive juridical systematization with the Law of 1908 on the status of public functionaries, a law which left citizens defenseless before the despotism of functionaries and functionaries defenseless before the despotism of general directors.

When he was not in the government, Giolitti had always deplored that the Italian tax system was progressive backward. But during that decade when he was in the government, when the economic and financial conditions in Italy would have been favorable for a reform from the bottom, and when he had at his command a vast and definite parliamentary majority and a solid bureaucracy, he never found the willpower to undertake some minor retouching of the tax structure, toward which he was often dragged through his parliamentary opponents' initiative.

Today one glorifies the man as a great reformer because during the decade when he governed Italy he passed laws, some of which were undoubtedly good. It would have been quite a surprise if during so many years he had not passed any laws or if he had passed only bad laws!

The man came to political life after twenty-five years of experience in the central state administration. He therefore had a direct and intimate knowledge of the wheels that made for inertia in the bureaucratic machine. In addition, he had learned under the ministries of the Right and of the Left to understand the utility of the parliamentary machinery. This, exposed as it was to the public eye, attracted the attention and the accusations of the public, while the bureaucratic machine, sheltered as it was from the public eye, ground its daily bread or wheat in discreet obscurity. Naturally, the bureaucratic machine every once in a while had to concede something to the parliamentary machine without letting itself go to pieces. Those concessions used to be praised at the time, and today the hagiographers of Giolitti glorify them as grandiose reforms. In reality, after the second crisis of 1901–2, Giolitti lived as an excellent bureaucrat, day by day doing nothing, since he could do nothing, and plugging holes where they needed to be plugged.

The Giolittian system—after, I repeat, the not easy "settlement crisis" of 1901–2—revealed itself efficient during the years of economic progress and during those of not-too-stormy political crises. When, however, difficult times came, the man who had in the meantime aged was incapable of controlling the machine.

Up to now we have spoken of the good that Giolitti did not do. What about the evil he did?

The Italian Chamber of Deputies was at that time composed of 508 deputies, among whom three fifths were elected in northern and central Italy and two fifths in southern Italy and the islands.

In the North there existed by then a rather robust and well-organized public opinion which prevented the Minister of the Interior from engaging in any whims during electoral periods. Therefore in the North elections were freely held except for those influences, more or less legitimate, which find their way into elections in all the countries of this world. And the three hundred deputies who, on the whole, had been freely elected, would divide themselves according to their interests and their ideologies either in favor of or against the policy of the Ministry.

Not finding in the North a solid and permanent majority Giolitti would go and build one for himself in the land of the peasants [*terroni*]. There "he would sell the prefect in order to buy the deputy," that is, he would place the prefect at the service of that deputy who in Rome would place himself at the service of Giolitti.

What does all this mean?

Those who lived in southern Italy during the first decade of this century—and they are still alive—already know. Those who at that time were children or not yet born must make a certain effort of imagination in order to understand it.

Where the electoral body was faithful to the ministerial deputy there was unlimited administrative autonomy for the mayors and the well-to-do councilmen, even if they were the worst rascals in the world

–and there was absolute freedom for their electors. Where, on the other hand, the electoral body was refractory and the mayors and the town councilmen were reluctant to bend to the "good advice" of the prefect, the latter would institute inquiry after inquiry to discover irregularities that might serve as pretexts to fire mayors, assessors, and councilmen. If irregularities were not found, then there was recourse to so-called "grave reasons of public order"; that is, the opposition party, in league with the local delegate of public security, would concoct a demonstration against the communal administration,–they would throw some stones and break some windows. Then the prefect would intervene for "grave reasons of public order," and would propose to the Minister of the Interior the dissolution of the communal council. Naturally the Minister of the Interior would accept such a proposal. And then a Royal Commissary would take the place of the mayor, of the assessors, and of the elected councilors. The Commissary was a government functionary who, naturally, was paid at the expense of the municipality: a method to help out his meager stipend. The Commissary would receive from the prefect, who in his turn received it from the deputy, the notice of the chiefs of the party that they must win the election. Installing himself in the town hall he would render life impossible for suspected functionaries, and he might even give them their walking papers under a futile pretext of putting in their place friendly electoral agents: he would frighten those who were doubtful and oblige them to march with him; he would multiply summons against the enemies and would annul those which existed against friends; he would invent the most extravagant charges against certain poor harmless individuals in order to revoke their permits, or else he would retire and concede permits to the public domain and thereby secure other votes; he would spend funds for public charity for electoral purposes; he would spend in one month the appropriations for public works which should have been sufficient for an entire year, and naturally the contractors would take the money and not perform the work. The master blow consisted in denouncing to the judiciary authorities mayors' and assessors' nonexistent misdemeanors and thus render them ineligible in the next administrative elections; the magistrates in their good time would absolve the accused "for not having committed any crime," but in the meantime the aim of putting them out of action had succeeded.

When the day of [electoral] decision approached, the police would grant permission to carry arms to the *malavita* [hoodlums] of the city and of the nearby towns. The *mazzieri* [club-wielders] would concentrate upon the city to be conquered, having, as used to be said, carte blanche. Opponents could not hold their meetings in public; they were besieged in their homes; if they came out they would be hustled and rounded up without too much fuss and put in prison until the day after the elections. Voters who were suspected of supporting the opposition did not receive electoral certificates and therefore were not able to vote. Those, on the other hand, who militated in the government ranks would not only receive their own certificates but even those of their opponents and of the emigrants. In the voting halls, since the representatives of the opposition were missing—either because they were sequestered at home or had been temporarily put in jail—those who were footloose would vote as many times as they pleased; even the dead voted: "The tombs are opened, the dead arise" (today [1952] they use for the same end cloistered nuns). One of the most common methods of victory was that known as the *coppino:* the *coppino* was the little ladle with which water is added to the pot; the water consisted of the votes which were added to the voting urns.

What occurred in the administrative elections was repeated, when necessary, in the national elections. A southern deputy, who in the Chamber might have challenged Giolitti, was sure to lose the battle during the next elections, except for some "rare chap" whose clientele was so solidly consolidated that there was no hope of breaking it up without utilizing too much violence: that "rare chap" anyhow served to demonstrate that even some southern deputy who might not wish to vote against the Prime Minister was completely free to do so.

Among the deputies who arrived in Rome from the Mezzogiorno [the South] there were not lacking, naturally, some men of stature or of value. But the bulk of them were contemptible persons for whom a knight's cross [Royal decoration] was more important than a commercial treaty. One of the most typical representatives of that intellectual and moral rot, the Pugliese called Vito De Bellis, used to say: "We are a cooperative of fools [*fessi*] and I am the king of fools." He was not stupid. Indeed he had a kind of talent all his own.

Thus the Giolittian parliamentary majority was constituted by a solid block of southern "fools" and by those from the North who had economic or ideological reasons for following the President of the Council.

Opponents and independents, who came largely from the North, were free to debate as much as they desired, but the unshakable Giolittian majority had the last word. Little by little their impotence caused opponents to use better wisdom. One by one, sooner or later, they would come to terms and, "like doves recalled by desire they would fly into the sweet nest to which their will carried them." Or—and this was the case for the bulk of the northern socialists—placated by personal blandishments or local favors, they would turn indifferent to all that happened "down there" in the country of the "zulus" and would end by conducting a spiritless opposition: more useful for Giolitti than their open friendship since it kept alive the fiction of a hostility behind which there was nothing. . . .

Giolitti did not invent the electoral customs of southern Italy, just as he did not invent economic prosperity and the surplus in the [national] budget. But while for economic prosperity and for the surplus in the budget he let "nature herself do her work" [*vis medicatrix naturae*], the same thing cannot be said for the electoral customs of southern Italy. He took advantage of them with a cold calculation, with a total lack of scruples, and with a profound scorn for those who lent themselves to his game. To such heights none of his predecessors had aspired or reached. And, after he was gone, those heights were surpassed both for the Mezzogiorno and for all of Italy through the totalitarian plebiscites of the Fascist period.

It is clear that we would be outside of reality if we should speak of Giolitti as a dictator.

A dictator is one who suppresses the freedom of speech, the freedom of the press, the freedom of association, and who sends his opponents to jail or to the other world. Giolitti did not do this. If to be a dictator means to receive the support of a solid majority which lets the minority "sing" as much as it desires but always votes for everything that the government wants, the history of all free countries has been full of "dictators," that is, of political men who have been supported by solid electoral majorities and have therefore been omnipotent. Even Roosevelt, Churchill, Attlee, De Gasperi, would be "dictators" in such a case. As a matter of fact, it might be said that while De Gasperi waits for the parliamentary majority to be given him by the electorate, which has been sweetly solicited, Giolitti would manufacture [those majorities] by himself, through the work of the *mazzieri* [club-wielders]! In a word he was dictator only for a day, the day of the elections, only when necessary, and within the limits of necessity. . . .

On March 16, 1928, the last time that Giolitti spoke in the Chamber of Deputies and gave his reasons for voting against the electoral proposal of Mussolini, the latter interrupted him: "Of course, we should come to you to learn how to 'make' elections." Giolitti retorted: "You are too modest. I have never dreamed of having a Chamber like yours." He was right: he had never aspired to have unanimity; he had been content to "manufacture" only majorities. The difference between Mussolini and Giolitti was one of quantity and not of quality. Giolitti was for

Mussolini what John the Baptist was for Christ: he paved his way. Gobetti rightly said that Mussolini did nothing but extend to all of Italy the *mazzieri* of Giolitti. . . .

Now we can risk an answer to the question whether during the period 1901–14 Italy was a democracy.

In September 1945, Ferruccio Parri asserted that democracy had never existed in Italy. Countering, Benedetto Croce asserted that Italy had possessed a first-rate democratic regime.

Who was right?

Croce had always poked fun at the "illuministic" ideal of democracy: in this world, as far as he was concerned there was even too much democracy; therefore there had been more than enough even in Italy. It was a question, as always, of understanding the meaning of words. The trouble began when Croce began to explain to what extent Italy from 1860 to 1922 had been "one of the most democratic countries of Europe" and that the history of Italy had been "an interrupted and often accelerated ascendancy toward democracy." "That people," Croce said disputing with Parri, "or rather those masses, which the old governments had left miserable and illiterate and shamelessly servile progressed in their physical health, learned to read and write in the public schools, gathered in associations and chambers of labor, obtained protected labor laws, achieved universal suffrage. Socialist deputies who had at first been one or two rose to more than one hundred fifty in 1919." For whom did Matteotti, the socialist, Amendola, the liberal, and Gramsci, the Communist die? They died for a democratic Italy. How can one then say that pre-Fascist Italy was not democratic?

In this outburst of democratic historiography, Croce forgot that the Italian "masses" in order to be able to associate, to found Chambers of Labor, to win the right to strike, to elect socialist deputies, had had to face states of siege, trials, prison, enormous difficulties raised by a parliamentary oligarchy —an oligarchy to which no one has the right to attribute the merit for progress which it attempted, as long as possible, to impede and which it accepted only when it was no longer possible to oppose it. If one draws the logical conclusions from Croce's opinions one would have to think that the Leagues of Resistance and the Chambers of Labor were established by police agents, that socialist deputies were elected by the Minister of the Interior, and that the struggle against illiteracy was fought by the big landowners of southern Italy—indeed, especially by those deputies and senators who depended upon those Sicilian proprietors who in 1894 held a meeting in Palermo and demanded that the compulsory appropriations for elementary schools should be abolished from communal budgets.

It might be well to ask whether Croce has not equivocated between a "democratic" regime and a "parliamentary" regime.

Parri, instead, had in mind an ideal of democracy nobler than that of Croce, and not recognizing it in a former Italian democracy, defective, incoherent, and limping as it was, denied that Italy had ever had a democracy. Furthermore, he looked with suspicion upon that pre-Fascist regime that had generated the Fascist regime of which Croce until 1925 had been a *fiancheggiatore* [flanker] and to which Parri had no intention of returning.

It is certain that if by "democracy" is meant a political regime in which all personal and political rights are assured for all citizens–not only by the written law but also in daily effective practice–and, moreover that all citizens without exception participate with intelligence and probity in political life, always having close at heart only the general welfare–if this is "democracy," we must admit that Italy never had a "democracy."

But a perfect "democracy" has never existed in any country of this world. Democracy has been and will be everywhere and always something imperfect, something that must be perfected.

If one compares the Italy of 1860 with the Italy of 1914, it is not possible not to recognize the immense progress, not merely economic but also political and moral, that had been achieved in that half century. In 1914 the Italy of the North and of the Center were still far from that level of democracy which had been achieved in Switzerland, in the Scandinavian countries, in England, in the United States, even in France. But it was on the way. Italy did not have a "perfect" democracy but a "democracy in the making." Even southern Italy–despite its backward conditions, despite the shame of the "governmental" elections–had had its share of progress, and that was not to be scorned. The South's democracy was so imperfect that it would not have been easy to define it even as a "democracy in the making." But there are grades even in imperfection, and the imperfection of 1914 was less than that of half a century before, even of fifteen years before, thanks to the improvement which the general progress of the world had brought even there.

Universal suffrage, granted in Italy from above and not conquered from below, could not produce an immediate rebirth, not even in southern Italy. The old equilibrium of forces was upset from top to bottom and one of the immediate results was attained even if fortified by violence and by local and governmental frauds. Universal suffrage pitted new and overwhelming masses of workers against the oligarchies which until 1912 had dominated without obstacle both in the municipalities and in parliament. It would no longer do to shoot down those southern masses when they rose in protest in the streets and then go back to the same old ways. It was now necessary to worry about what those chaotic multitudes might do on the day of elections, even if the thought of deceiving them or beating them might linger somewhere. The old *mazzieri* would no longer be sufficient. It was necessary to adopt other methods of government and of electoral campaigns. With time, with experience, and thanks to the competition among the political parties, the last to arrive would have gradually acquired their political education for themselves and would have learned to make themselves worthy of respect.

If Italy had had another thirty years of economic, intellectual, and political progress, even southern Italy would have made its entrance into what was then the zone of "civilization." Those thirty years did not come. The First World War came.

But that is another story.

X. CONCLUSION: THE CLOSING OF A CYCLE—FROM POLITICS TO HISTORY

THAT HISTORIOGRAPHICAL ENDEAVOR *can neither avoid nor refuse the vitalizing spur that almost continually comes from outside forces, elements, and motivations has become an assumption of all realistic practitioners of the historian's craft. In this sense, Benedetto Croce's famous dictum that "all history is contemporary history" seems relevant and indisputable. On the other hand,* all *interpretations of history would be capriciously relativistic and anarchically presentist if they were not or could not be subjected to critical analysis that might lead to the recognition of the distinction between purely contingent elements and more universally acceptable factors of judgments on history. History is not an exact science but neither is it a completely individualistic art. Up to a certain point, every man can believe that he is "his own historian," but beyond that point he can only be believed to be "his own" theoretician, philosopher, ideologue, or system-builder—a great inventor, perhaps, but not a discoverer of history. No one can know for certain when that certain point is reached that may constitute the great divide between history as past reality and history as idea, as the stuff but not the essence of history. That perhaps by 1950–52 such a point had been reached at least in reappraisals of Italian pre-Fascist democracy is the suggestive contention of Professor Nino Valeri*

(1897–), the successor of Federico Chabod to the Chair of Modern History at the University of Rome. As an acute student of the politics of the Italian Renaissance and of modern Italian ideologies, particularly nationalism, Valeri envisages a new, pacific historiographical day after the mid-twentieth century, that will perhaps see the political and ideological battles waged over interpretations of pre-Fascist Italy transmuted into fertile experiments at "pure" reconstructions of Italian history from the Risorgimento to the hegemony of Fascism.

The Waning of Ideological History*

NINO VALERI

. . . ALL THE VARIETIES of criticism that have been launched, in one form or another, against the Crocean interpretation [of pre-Fascist Italian history], are predicated upon two real difficulties.

The first consists of the doubt whether the line of development and progress of the history of Italy to the coming of Fascism was, in essence, represented only by the work of the exponents of the "liberal" ruling class. On this score the researches conducted by historians of the [anti-Crocean revisionist] opposition have thrown new light upon the importance of the proletarian movement as an expression not of

* From Nino Valeri, "Premessa ad una storia dell'Italia nel Postrisorgimento," in G. Pepe, F. Chabod, N. Valeri, D. Demarco, and G. Luzzatto, *Orientamenti per la storia d'Italia nel Risorgimento*. Quaderno No. 1 (Bari: "Amici della Cultura," 1952), 81–85. Reprinted by permission of the author. Editor's translation.

the good will of the optimates, or at least not of theirs alone (since those optimates at any rate limited themselves to sanctioning the proletariat's own conquests). That movement was also an expression of the will power of a political class ever more self-aware and courageous, indeed capable of making obscure but no less historically effective sacrifices. The political class appeared almost in the guise of a revitalized mass society open to substantially new forms of social life as against those which had bound Italian society together during the nineteenth century, based as that old society had been upon the free play of rich bourgeois and big landowners who were economically independent and politically individualistic. The presentation of the history of Italy from 1870 to 1925 as a sequence of inevitable evils connected with the structure of a society that was fast aging does not, therefore, exclude a positive consideration of the youthful world that was emerging from the crisis of the old. Light thrown upon the road that leads to the dust of death serves also to illumine the new life that arises.

The second objection (closely bound with the first) might be formulated as follows: Croce—and together with him other renowned historians and political men, both Italian and foreign, such as, for instance, Hermann Rauschning and Friedrich Meinecke, who, in connection with pre-Hitler Germany, viewed the advent of totalitarianism as a fracture, a "revolution," vis-à-vis the preceding noble liberal tradition—insists upon founding his judgment upon two different standards: one for the period from 1870 to 1915 and another for the years that followed and culminated in Fascism. In his approach to the first period, Croce is guided by a warm sympathy for the recent past which was dear to our fathers, and which even in our day some people would like to resurrect by relinking our arid and avid present with the tender affections that the Risorgimento had preserved together with its human ideal of freedom. For the second period, Croce's standard of judgment is an exclusively political and practical one of condemnation, and it is bound to present action, in accordance with the passions and requirements of a party. The distinction was not only legitimate but also fruitful during the time when constitutional freedoms had perished, when it was necessary to address words of faith and hope to Italians who had been reduced to slavery, and, by so doing, to demonstrate to them that Fascism had not come—as its improvised historians claimed—to act as the executioner of a cowardly and rotten ruling class but, on the contrary, that it had come as the interrupter of an ascending phase of our history, a phase in which the entire nation as well as its ruling class had co-operated. In that tense climate of battle, the wrath against the servants of the Fascist regime—men who, in their joy to be of service to it, disfigured the image of that modest post-Risorgimento Italy and of its most representative men, with the aim of justifying, almost of sanctifying, the iron fist of the new victorious masters—united in a common cause historians and men of politics of every tendency who felt that, however few and dispersed they might be, they were the defenders of a free Italy. Salvemini himself, from his American exile, softened the harsh lines of his old interpretation of Giolittian Italy in order to demonstrate how much better (or less bad) it had been than Fascist Italy.

Now, however, after twenty-five years [1925–50], in the new climate in which that past has been swept away by a more complex and radically different reality, Fascism has shown its mettle by ruining itself as well as Italy. True that in our day the old parties and the old controversies and Fascism itself have reappeared with their old ideological labels, but they do so with an altogether different impact and significance within both the national and the international spheres. Now, therefore, even Croce's polemic, together with that of the anti-Fascists of every political color who had been momentarily united against a common danger, belongs to the past. It is part of a closed cycle, and as such it does not seem any longer an effective or live motive for a present battle. It, too, has become an object of history.

Of what history? Of a history that evidently still needs to be written since none of the interpretations we have rapidly reviewed transcends the burning climate of passions from which it arose; each of them remains still as if enveloped and suspended in that climate, lacking that serenity which is necessary for a free and independent comprehension that seeks to understand every fact within the logic of its internal necessity. These brief notes have sought to constitute, therefore, a preface or a start toward the historicizing of that era: they have sought to place the rise of Fascism up to 1925 outside the living fabric of today's political battles and thus to draw it within the framework of the history of the post-Risorgimento, as its epilogue.

A CENTURY OF ITALIAN HISTORY: AN ANALYTICAL CHRONOLOGICAL SUMMARY

The Early Risorgimento: From the Restoration to the Revolutions of 1848–49

1814–15: The fall of the Napoleonic Empire in Italy; restoration of most of the older and some of the newer dynasties in the ten states of Italy, chief among them the Bourbon in the Kingdom of the Two Sicilies, the Pope in Central Italy, the House of Lorraine in Tuscany, the House of Savoy in Piedmont-Sardinia, and the Austrian Hapsburg Monarchy in Lombardy-Venetia. Metternichian Austria was the predominant foreign power in Italy and it was upon her political-military hegemony and protection that the other states of Italy depended. The rise of the secret societies, particularly the Carbonari, threatened the re-established "old order" in Italy, but with unclear programs, inadequate methods, and undefined objectives.

1820–21: Outbreaks of liberal-aristocratic revolts in North and South Italy, particularly in the kingdoms of Piedmont and Naples, put down with the aid of Austria's military force; widespread arrests of Italian revolutionary elites; ferocious countermeasures instituted, ranging from executions to long-term imprisonments.

1831–32: Following upon hopes aroused in European and Italian national-revolutionary quarters by the "liberating" pretenses of the July Monarchy in France, the last flareups of secret revolutionary movements, led by the Carbonari and other political sects, occurred–particularly in Central Italy and the Papal states; the ineffectuality of undercover direct action was demonstrated by failures, and new means and aims of changing Italy were formulated. The founding of Giuseppe Mazzini's Giovane Italia (Young Italy) movement was the most important revolutionary innovation. Young Italy was unitary, republican, and democratic in program and objectives and constituted a wide-ranging challenge to the Metternichian scheme of Italian affairs and to the conservative Europe of the Great Powers through its efforts to create a Young Europe movement having as its goal a United Europe of Free Peoples. During the next three decades the early Mazzinian movement "trained" the cadres for the Italian Party of Action that stood against moderate-liberal solutions of the national question in Italy.

1832–46: Mazzinian revolutionary republicanism was challenged by alternative movements and "parties" whose programs, with one exception–Carlo Cattaneo's Italian and European federalist ideology–were liberal-moderate (Cesare Balbo, Massimo d'Azeglio, Gino Capponi, and, eventually, Count Camillo di Cavour) rather than democratic, and whose methods were reformist-evolutionary rather than actionist-revolutionary. After 1843, with the publication of Abbé Vincenzo Gioberti's sensational work on *The Civil and Moral Primacy of the Italians* (*Il Primato*), a neo-Guelph movement gained strength. His aims were to resolve the Italian "national question" through the creation of a "Confederation of Italian States" under the presidency of the Pope. Neither the moderates nor the neo-Guelphs had as yet a clear program of action concerning the presence of Austrian domination in Italy.

1846–48: The election of Pius IX (Pio Nono) to the Papal throne in June 1846 aroused great enthusiasm among all sectors of Italian liberal classes and eventually constituted a unique outburst of messianic expectation among the larger masses of the Italian people. Giobertian neo-Guelphism now had a "leader" as well as a program and a cause. The contradictions implicit within this strange chiliastic moment of the Risorgimento—and they touched upon profound religious, political, social, and personal problems—were temporarily submerged in the acclamations tendered all over Italy to a "liberal pope" who would peacefully fulfill the hopes and dreams of an Italian "national war of liberation."

1848–49: The "springtide" of revolutions in Europe and in Italy. Throughout all of Italy—from Palermo to Naples, from Rome to Florence, from Genoa to Turin, from Milan to Venice —a series of constitutional acts by the rulers of the Italian states quickly led to demands for wider reforms and radical measures and finally directly to revolutionary outbreaks. The radicalization of the revolution, which mobilized the emotions, actions, and expectations of relatively large masses of urban and rural Italians (who were not concordant in their aims and interests), merged with the problem of war against Austria, and eventually led to a fragmentation of the

Italian "unitary" moment and movement of the preceding neo-Guelph phase. The collapse of the initial collective impetus toward a "total" revolution was almost "predetermined" by the complexity and contradictions inherent in the historic condition of Italy on the eve of the revolutions. By the spring of 1849 only the Venetian Republic under Daniele Manin and the Roman Republic under Mazzini and Garibaldi were surviving and resisting the onslaughts of two "interventionist" powers in Italy: that of "reactionary" Austria in Venice and that of "revolutionary" France in Rome. But not for long, for this was the moment of despair and agony in the Italian national revolutions. By July–August 1849 both the Venetian Republic and the Roman Republic had been tragically destroyed by foreign powers. "Peace" had returned, and with it all the unresolved national problems: disunity, foreign domination, political reaction (except in Piedmont), and social injustice. The year 1848–49 indeed marked a great "revolution that failed" in Italy. The revolutionary debacle led to a sense of defeat and disenchantment in its victims, but it also led to "realistic" reappraisals with a view toward future success among some of the Italian liberal-national elites.

The Culmination of the Risorgimento: The Cavourian Decade and the Making of Italian Political Unity, 1850–61—The Occupation of Rome, 1870

1850–52: The "second Restoration" in Italy. By 1850, with the exception of the Kingdom of Piedmont-Sardinia which, under its new ruler, Victor Emmanuel II, retained the

Constitution of 1848,[1] the territorial, political, and social *status quo* ante–1848 was fully re-established throughout Italy.

1852–61: The Cavourian decade. The failures of the revolutions of 1848–49 had almost totally eliminated both wings of the Italian "federalist" movement: Carlo Cattaneo's democratic-republican idea of a United States of Italy within a United States of Europe and Vincenzo Gioberti's neo-Guelph design for an Italian Confederation of States under the leadership of the Pope. Now the two major antagonists left in the field with alternative programs for the resolution of the "Italian Question" were the Mazzinian Party of Action (Partito d'Azione) and the complex Cavourian liberal-Moderate initiative under the auspices of the Piedmontese Monarchy. In due time, Giuseppe Garibaldi, a Mazzinian by origin, became the truly "active" leader of the Partito d'Azione. But also, ironically through his unique action of the liberation of the South in 1860, he became the unwitting link and at times the unwilling instrument of Cavourian liberal-Moderate politics. Cavour's approach to the Italian Question was multiple, complicated, and subtle. Though he was not "converted" until very late to the idea of realizing a full-fledged political-territorial unification of Italy, Cavour was flexible enough in his political approach to accommodate within it the most diverse forces in Italian revolutionary activism and European liberal international diplomacy. Internally,

[1] The Statuto was the basic juridical and institutional Charter which, after the unification of Italy in 1861, remained in force until after the fall of Fascism. In 1948, it was officially abolished by the Constitution of the Italian Republic.

he pitted the "respectable" and moderate middle-class liberals of the National Society (*Società Nazionale*) against the revolutionary democrats of the Party of Action and used them toward his own and the Piedmontese Monarchy's political interests. On the international European level, he won over liberal England to a pro-Italian benevolent neutrality in the War of 1859 and persuaded Bonapartist France to intervene directly on his side. Whenever he found it necessary or expedient, Cavour frightened European conservatism by raising the specter of Italian revolutionism, at the same time holding at bay Mazzinian republicanism and Garibaldian insurrectionism by threatening to invoke European interventionism to "shield" Italy against subversion. Thus toward the full victory of the Cavourian "alternative" in 1860–61 a vast array of concordant and discordant elements and complementary or conflicting forces had paradoxically co-operated.

1860: Chief among those forces was the great liberation movement of the South (Sicily and the Neapolitan Kingdom) achieved from May to November 1860 by Garibaldi's Expedition of the Thousand. One of the most exquisitely ironical facts of Risorgimento history was that the fruits of Garibaldi's decisive contribution to the making of united Italy were reaped neither by his own populist sympathies for the masses of Italian peasants and artisans nor by the democratic program of the "Party of Action" which Giuseppe Mazzini had so strenuously labored to realize through a whole generation of efforts and self-sacrifice. Whether in 1860 the Party of Action was helplessly obliged or willingly self-victimized in not realizing its aspirations for an Italian "Jacobin" or democratic political and social revolution has been one of the most passionately debated questions of modern Italian history.

1861: In the Subalpine Parliament at Turin, in March 1861, Cavour proclaimed the existence of a Kingdom of Italy extending from the Alps to Sicily and united under the rule of Victor Emmanuel II and the aegis of the Statuto. This was the supreme moment of Cavour's unique political career as maker of a state. Although Venice was still Austrian, Rome was still Papal and under the protection of French troops, and still more "remote irredentas" (Trent and Trieste) loomed on the national horizons, this territorial "unfinished business" was, in a sense, less important than the complex of unresolved Italian problems—political, administrative, economic, religious, social, and, perhaps above all, "moral"—that Cavour bequeathed to his successors. His death in June 1861 prematurely removed the unique protagonist of an Italian historic drama before the denouement was fully in sight. The post-Cavourian phase of the Risorgimento was bound to prove an anticlimax and, in a fundamental sense, the whole post-Risorgimento found itself returning again and again to the gigantic new questions of national life opened when Cavour's work was done. For fifteen years after his death a group of his "heirs," the Destra Storica (the Historical Right), formed a kind of restricted collective leadership drawn from the liberal-Moderate classes that found itself strenuously struggling to give new substance and structure to the vision of national life that Cavour alone had seemed to fulfill.

1866: Austro-Prussian-Italian War: Italy's acquisition of Venice. In September, a large-scale popular revolt against the old social and the new political rulers occurred at Palermo, Sicily. The revolt was repressed by harsh military measures which left a profound sense of disenchantment over the character of the "new Italy" among masses of artisans and peasants in the South. In a dramatic, tragic way, the Palermo revolt of 1866 officially opened the frightfully grave Problem of the South (Questione del Mezzogiorno) in all its complex political, social, and moral aspects.

1870: On September 20, in the midst of the Franco-Prussian War, the troops of the new Kingdom of Italy assaulted and occupied Rome, thereby putting an end to the thousand-year-long temporal power of the Popes in Italy. The Roman Question was now opened in all its erosive aspects: the Roman Catholic Church in Italy was now an official "enemy" of all the Italian Risorgimento had striven to attain and the liberal state would seek to consolidate. Vast masses of Italian Catholics, already alienated from the new liberal state through disillusionment over its political and social finalities, now found their estrangement, indifference, or antagonism reinforced by the opening of a question of conscience. From 1870 to 1929 the Cavourian formula of "A free Church in a free State" guaranteed the basis of religious freedom in Italy, but it also led to bitter relations between the Vatican and the Quirinal, the government of the Church and the governments of Italy. Italian Catholicism and Italian liberalism never really found a fundamental ground of reconciliation, despite momentary empirical adjustments they managed to make when they feared common political, social, or ideological enemies, chief among them the rising forces of Italian socialism. At times of critical local or nationwide elections, particuarly during the Giolittian period (1904, 1909, and 1913, through the notorious Gentiloni Pact between Catholic conservatives and Giolittian liberals), the Cavourian formula of separation of Church and State was not honored in full observance. Though from 1870 to 1922 opportunities for an organic resolution of the "Roman Question" were not lacking, Italian liberalism and Catholicism did not take advantage of them. Ironically, therefore, the Roman Question was "solved" only in 1929, in a manner and at a time when Fascism reaped the full credit for much work toward reconciliation between Church and State that had been done during the liberal era. When it was consummated, the Lateran Pact of 1929, however much it gained for the Church in Italy, proved of even more immediate value to the self-justifying claims of Fascist "morality."

The Post-Risorgimento: Reconstruction, National Problems, and Rebellion, 1871–1900

1871–76: The rule of the Cavourian party of the Historical Right continued. Enormous administrative, financial, and political problems were tackled by the Cavourian successors with probity and self-dedication, and a number of those problems were partly "resolved" toward the laying of the institutional foundations of the new Italian unitary liberal state. Because of the essentially elitist character and gradualist conservative liberalism of the Destra Storica, its rigidity of outlook toward national questions, and the combination of its fears over the explosive social question (fomented as it appeared to be by the forces of an international "socialist" revolution under the auspices of the First International established in 1864), the acute religious problem precipitated by the Roman Question, and the new European situation created by the hegemonic victory of Bismarckism in Germany, the leaders of the Cavourian party found themselves progressively isolated both from the country at large and the other political currents in Italy. When it fell from power the Historical Right left to its opponents on the Historical Left a precious legacy of solidly achieved institutional work, but its fall caused no regrets in the masses of the Italian people.

1876: On March 18, a successful parliamentary revolution ably conducted by members of the Sinistra Storica (Historical Left), whose outstanding chief was Agostino Depretis, dispossessed the Right of all political power.

1876–87: The period of the rule of the Sinistra Storica was consolidated under the semi-permanent "parliamentary dictatorship" of Depretis. Under the guise of promoting a "great change" in Italian political life, the Left, whose leaders included Francesco Crispi and other former members of the Garibaldian and Mazzinian Party of Action, continued along lines in essence set down by the Destra. The real innovations of the Sinistra may be summarized as follows: (1) the diplomatic alignment of Italy, from 1882 on, with the Germanic Powers of the Triple Alliance: the fact that the Italian Left sought international security in the camp of the European conservative powers (among which was the Hapsburg Empire, the secular enemy of the Risorgimento) was remarkable in itself and in its consequences —the Alliance lasted practically till the outbreak of the Great War in August 1914 and was not "denounced" juridically by Italy until May 1915; (2) the institutionalization of *trasformismo* (transformism) as a new mode of parliamentary, political, and electoral compromises which, for purposes of partisan expediency, tended to reconcile the most openly divergent currents and interests of the Italian political and social struggle; *trasformismo* may be said to have marked the official end of Risorgimento ideologies in Italy; (3) the encouragement and official aid given to the rise in Italy of an industrial-capitalistic regime, which slowly transformed the North into an area of advanced economy and therefore separated it still further from the underdeveloped agrarian South; this phenomenon, which was to be repeated in different ways throughout the nineteenth and into the twentieth century, enlarged the historic gap that lay at the heart of the Questione del Mezzogiorno and, while it paradoxically gave common cause to big northern industrial elements and large South Italian agrarian interests, it further separated the emerging industrial workers from the peasant masses. Thus, during the period of *trasformismo* and after, while the real forces of the Italian neo-capitalistic classes and neofeudalistic elements tended to merge, the *potential* forces of workers and peasants which, later in the liberal period, socialism sought to fuse, were hopelessly divided. These developments, however differently interpreted in the twentieth century by the southern democrat Gaetano Salvemini, the northern socialist and, in due time, Fascist Benito Mussolini, or by the Marxist Antonio Gramsci, gave a special character to Italian economic and social history until the mid-twentieth century.

1887–96: The Crispi period. Though not continuous —indeed, in 1892–93, it was interrupted by the first Ministry of Crispi's arch-enemy, Giovanni Giolitti—the political rule of Francesco Crispi characterized this near-decade of Italian history. Crispi was a Sicilian by origin and a former Mazzinian and Garibaldian "actionist" whose activity during the "Liberation of the South" in 1860 had been very important. Though converted to the conservative monarchist cause, Crispi claimed to be above partisan and ideological factions. Again and again, when pressed to reveal his political allegiances and programmatic position, the old Sicilian conspirator would proudly answer: *"Sono Crispi* [I am Crispi]!" The epithet "The Bismarck of Italy," which has occasionally been urged to describe him, was as wrong for Crispi as it was for Cavour, if for different reasons. Aside from the fascinating particulars of his person and the exasperating details of his politics, three principal aspects of the Crispi period seem noteworthy: (1) the continuing and soon truly hopeless alienation of the peasant masses of the South from much of "civil Italy," chiefly brought about through the Draconian political and military repression of the "Fasci Siciliani" (1893–94), a social protest movement and explosion that had risen out of the misery and injustices that victimized Sicily: Crispi's use of measures of "blood and iron" to resolve social questions acted as a kind of catalyst in precipitating the mass emigration of the Sicilian and South Italian peasantry through the following decade and a half; (2) the confusion, which Crispi himself compounded, and the almost complete disarray of Italian economic and international policy, the outstanding examples of which were the "tariff war" with France and the Crispi "international conspiracy" delusions, which saw the Vatican as the principal intriguer and socialism as the chief fomenter; and (3) the unnecessary ignominy that Crispi, the ultra-nationalist, almost singlehandedly brought to Italian "national pride" through his senseless colonial war against Ethiopia and the tragic Italian defeat at Adowa in 1896. Although this marked his downfall in Italy, Crispi left his country a legacy of troubles that lasted to the bitter end of the nineteenth century.

1896–99: The "caretaker" governments of Di Rudinì, General Pelloux, and finally Saracco marked the stages of a "dark age" in Italian national life. After Crispi, Italian politics definitely turned "to the right," though not again in his fashion: in a basic sense, however, Crispi's imprint lasted until 1900, and it was to mean that the Italian state would seek to resolve profound parliamentary, social, and moral problems not by peace but by the sword. This was the day of the Italian generals, of an experiment at a collective military rule, of reactionary repression—and popular revolution. The outbreak of "famine" tumults in the South led to the bloody Fatti di Maggio (May Days) of 1898 in which numbers of peasants in the South and workers in the North were killed for openly protesting official outrages to elementary human, civil, political, and constitutional rights. But while in the North the coalition of democratic-liberal forces was achieved through the creation of a "common front" (Estrema Sinistra) among the parties of the new Extreme Left (socialists, radicals, and republicans), in the South, political and social forces of protest remained dispersed and helpless before the assault of the reactionary-military Establishment. The Italian Socialist Party (PSI), which had been founded at Genoa in 1892, courageously led the Estrema in and out of Parliament in forcing a return to a constitutional regime in Italy. Through legal and "illegal" protest, demonstrations, obstructionist tactics in the Chamber of Deputies, and stoic acceptance of arrests and long prison-terms, by the end of 1899 the Estrema had won the day toward restoring Italy to civil existence. The reactionaries and the generals fell: the dawn of a new era was about to break with the new century in Italy.

1900: At the end of July, the "final" nemesis of post-Crispian reaction took its toll in Italy: an anarchist named Gaetano Bresci returned from Paterson, New Jersey, and killed the King of Italy, Umberto I. This supreme act of violence marked the great divide in Italy between a dark period of reactionary government and an emergent era of liberal policy. At the beginning of the twentieth century the Italian ruling and political classes had to make a fateful choice between the perpetuation of government by force or beginning a government by liberty. Fortunately for the masses of the Italian people they chose the latter.

The Giolittian Era: The Turn Against the Old Order, Liberalism Triumphant, Democracy in the Making, and Tremors of a New Rebellion, 1900–14

1901–4: These years signaled the prelude to a full-fledged return to constitutional liberal government under the leadership of Giuseppe Zanardelli as Prime Minister, with Giovanni Giolitti as his Minister of the Interior.

1904–14: The "classic" Giolittian decade. Having become Prime Minister in his own right Giovanni Giolitti implemented and extended the "liberal promise" of the Zanardelli government. The legalization of restored constitutional measures was fully brought about; civil liberties were guaranteed; political rights insured; the recognition of the right of workers to organize, peaceably protest, agitate, and strike was achieved. Over and above the details of one of the most complex and fruitful eras of modern Italian history, the Giolittian decade may be subsumed under five "primordial" developments: (1) the beginning of a clear detachment of Italy from the ironlike diplomatic "embrace" of the Germanic powers of the Triple Alliance: Italy was "the smallest of the big powers and the biggest of the small powers," torn between the duality of European-continental and Mediterraneanmaritime interests; Giolitti realized that *his* Italy needed greater flexibility of international action than his predecessors had been able to obtain; dangerous as a policy of pragmatic reconciliation with the Entente powers, particularly France and Russia (England was assumed all along to be Italy's international "friend"), might be, Giolitti consummated it over the protestation of Italy's Germanic allies. Like all nations and states, Giolittian Italy sought additional security on the international level, through a policy dictated by the recognized unofficial rules governing the pursuit of "national interest"; (2) the Italian liberal state's making of tentative, unofficial reconciliatory "moves" toward the leadership of conservative Catholic social and political circles—leading to their temporary electoral "alliance" against "subversive" (that is, socialist) forces in 1904, 1909, and 1913; (3) the adoption of "gradualist" policy toward the Question of the South, which led successive Giolittian governments to go from direct interest to neutralism to indifference to passivity and, finally, to negative intervention in South Italian political life; during the Giolittian decade the masses of the southern peasants undertook their own unorganized but truly massive "solution" to the Questione del Mezzogiorno—by emigrating to North and South America in large numbers; (4) the pursuit of the dual policy of winning the practical parliamentary support of Italian socialism, particularly through concessions to North Italian labor-union organizations, and of curbing the consolidation of independent socialist influence through functional use of anti-socialist conservative forces (conservative Catholicism and capitalistic elements in the North, big landowners and "freebooting" political and professional personages in the South): in a real political sense, Giolitti was one of the stanchest friends and most destructive liberal "enemies" that Italian socialism had during his decade of rule; (5) the giving by the State of direct or indirect incentives toward the further development of Italian capitalism (industrial, commercial, and financial) which, during the Giolittian era, made a new "great leap forward," particularly in the North, and brought Italy as a whole within the outer circles of the European economically advanced nations.

1910–13: These years marked the apex of the Giolittian system which, by its very success, began revealing signs of a subtle internal transformation and decline. Practically all five major characteristics of Giolittian policy slowly turned, precisely through their implementation, into forces erosive of the Giolittian "system." Thus it was that by 1913–14 five related but contrasting developments had begun to undermine the principles and procedures of Giolittian policy: (1) relations with political Catholicism led in 1913 to the Gentiloni Pact between Giolittian liberals and Catholic conservatives for purely electoral purposes, without contributing toward the resolution of the "Roman Question" or of the persistent antagonism between liberal secularism and political clericalism in Italy; (2) from its position of "ally" of Giolittian policy, socialism detached itself from the complex of supporting political and social elements of the Giolittian "system"; the growth of socialist radicalism, particularly during the Libyan War (1911–12), led to the dispossession from the leadership of the Italian Socialist Party of such "reliable" reformists as Filippo Turati and Leonida Bissolati and to their replacement by such extremist-activistic revolutionaries as Benito Mussolini who, from 1912 to 1914, was the almost undisputed *duce* of Italian socialism; (3) during its early phases, the Libyan War which Giolitti undertook against the Ottoman Empire for the conquest of Italy's "fourth shore" in the Mediterranean, acted as a cementing force of national consensus, but, by its end, it had not merely disturbed the uneasy balance of European international power but also the internal Italian equilibrium of forces between the "internationalist" liberal and socialist elements and the nationalistic-imperialistic currents which had their spokesmen in the irrepressible anti-Giolittian and renowned novelist and poet, Gabriele D'Annunzio, and the founder of the Italian Nationalist Party (1910), Enrico Corradini: through the Libyan War, Giolitti, himself an "anti-nationalist" by temperament and policy, had unwittingly unleashed nationalistic passions and imperialistic ideologies in Italy that proved to be exquisitely anti-Giolittian in 1914–15, in 1919–22, and after the triumph of Fascism; (4) the passage of the "great reform bill" of 1912, which had been initiated by Giolitti himself as a sort of "compensatory measure" for the sacrifices imposed by the Libyan War and as a democratic act that would balance out the nationalistic forces that war had aroused, brought practical male-universal suffrage to Italy; the Electoral Reform Act of 1912 was first put to the test in the elections of 1913 and, for the first time since the achievement of national unity, made possible the participation of vast masses of Italians, particularly from among the peasants of the South, in active political life; in 1913, there was no question that the conservative expectations which the great liberal, Giovanni Giolitti, had reposed in the Electoral Law were not disappointed; Giolitti's democratic opponents, chief among them Gaetano Salvemini, felt that there was potentially "revolutionary" stuff in the Act of 1912 and that, given time and opportunity, "on some other occasion" the masses of the Italian electorate would turn this democratic measure against its liberal sponsor: that opportunity did not arise until after a Great War had swept over Europe and Italy–in 1919–when the Italian political struggle had acquired exasperating elements that had not existed before 1914; and (5) the fusion of liberalism and empiricism, of economic progress and gradualist political action, of internal and foreign policy with limited objectives, and of bureaucratic efficiency and non-ideological attitudes had spelled what some characterized as the "deadly prose" of bourgeois moderation of the Giolittian era; by its very nature that "prose" created and maintained the atmosphere of liberty in which the "poetry" of rebellion against it was able to thrive; by 1913–14 a vast and noisy cult of revolt, not so much against Giolitti the man but Giolitti the symbol of an "unadventurous" cultural period, had sprung up in a number of literary, intellectual, artistic, and philosophical quarters in Italy, the essence of whose "message" was that a "great change" was needed toward the "renovation" of Italian life, culture, or society; there is hardly any question that this cultural revolt was part and expression of a European phenomenon on the eve of the War of 1914, but in Italy its "negative" aspects tended to predominate over the positive and potentially constructive elements it undoubtedly contained; by the eve of the War, nationalist ideologies, Futurist doctrines, neo-Nietzschean creeds, pragmatist theories, syndicalist ideas, and Idealistic philosophy promiscuously merged to spell a strange revolt of the Italian intellectuals against "the way of life" secured during the Giolittian era.

1914: In the spring, Giolitti resigned from the government and gave over the reins to a southern conservative, Antonio Salandra, in the expectation of "returning" to power after another of his not uncommon resignations "for reasons of health." Giolitti did not return officially on the national scene until after the War, in 1919. Early in June, "Red Week" broke out in central Italy and it found such different personalities as the revolutionary socialist Benito Mussolini, editor-in-chief of the Party paper *Avanti!*, the young republican Pietro Nenni, and the old anarchist Errico Malatesta strangely cooperating toward social revolution in the Romagna and the Marches. After a brief euphoric period during which "social republics" were festively proclaimed in some towns of central Italy, the Salandra government put an end to the dangerous experiment through the use of military force. Three weeks later came news of the Sarajevo assassinations, followed by the great European July 1914 crisis, the declarations of War between the Germanic and the

Entente powers, and, early in August, the proclamation of Italian neutrality.

Italy in Peace and War: The Post-War Crisis and the Coming of Fascism, 1914–22

1914–15: From August 1914 to May 1915 Italy was a neutral in the Great War that swept over Europe. This period of "peace" turned into one of the most acute and, in a sense, decisive times of crisis in the history of modern Italy. In origin, form, and expression the crisis was political, in so far as it divided Italians over the issues of war and peace or of neutrality and intervention. In spirit, substance, and consequences the crisis was "vital," organic, truly historic in so far as it engaged Italians of practically all currents of thought and feeling, all parties and political currents, and all secular and spiritual leaders in a crucial confrontation with the fundamental problems of the past and present and with alternative visions of the future of Italy. On whatever side they stood and however they formulated it, all participants in this agonizing crisis knew that Italy's choice between continued neutrality or intervention, between peace or war while the rest of Europe was locked in mortal conflict, spelled a stupendous "to be or not to be" for the Italian nation. The fact that, for the most part, the socialists (minus Mussolini who, in November 1914 was expelled from the Italian Socialist Party for war-mongering activities), the Catholics, and the Giolittian liberals found themselves on the same neutralist side (which, undoubtedly, was that of the majority of Italians) or that nationalists, conservatives, futurists, syndicalists, and democrats were on the same interventionist (pro-Entente) side is, in a deeper sense, less important than the larger fact that the arduously acquired "moral unity" of Italians was shattered almost irreparably by a political and ideological dissension which was merely the visible (and audible) part of a profound crisis of the national conscience. When in May 1915, through a kind of parliamentary coup d'état, the Salandra government, with the full connivance of the Monarchy, cut the Gordian knot by denouncing the Triple Alliance and declaring war on Austria, the great Italian crisis seemed momentarily "resolved"—by a kind of political-international "surgical" operation that basically "killed" the "patient": liberal Italy. It is interesting to note that, among others on either side, Giolitti, the old reformist socialist Turati, and Pope Benedict XV had been against that "operation" while the "renegade" revolutionary socialist Mussolini, the nationalist poet D'Annunzio, the editor-in-chief of the great Milanese newspaper *Il Corriere della Sera,* Luigi Albertini, the liberal socialist Bissolati, and the Mazzinian democrat Gaetano Salvemini had, each for his own reason, applauded Salandra's "surgical" act of interventionism. The masses of Italians were now launched on the dark road of a World War.

1915–18: Italian participation in the First World War. For Italians, no less than for other Europeans, the war proved an atrociously long and destructive affair whose ultimate consequences no one could predict. In its ideological aspects, for Italians the War was contradictorily presented as "the last war of the Risorgimento" and "the first war of social revolution," as a "historical necessity" for national survival and as "an act of liberation" from the "evils" of liberal-bourgeois Giolittian society, as an "ugly job" to be done for the sake of material existence and as "an ideal struggle for justice," and finally as a "Garibaldian" campaign to free the "enslaved Italian brothers" in the *irredentas* of Trento and Trieste and as a D'Annunzian adventure to give Italy "a place in the sun" of world powers. Six hundred thousand Italians died in the Great War and even greater numbers were wounded, disabled, lost, or reduced to shadows of their former selves. When, on November 4, 1918, the war was ended for Italy, a new kind of desperate "civil war" broke out among Italians over the questions of "war guilt" and "war profits," of "return to normalcy" and revolution, of economic readjustment and social subversion, and over socialism, bolshevism, Catholicism, liberalism, and democracy. The new crisis raged furiously for a biennium (1919–20) and then began to subside and give way to a fruitful national truce when it was suddenly, violently reopened by the upsurge of Mussolini's newly created Fascist movement.

1919: The Paris Peace Conference had compounded the sentiment that the War had been a kind of "useless massacre," as Benedict XV had referred to it in 1917. Wilson's great expectations of achieving a "peace without victory" for all sides was blasted for Italians by the frustrations of peacemaking at Versailles and soon they became converted into the D'Annunzian cry about "the mutilated peace." The irreconcilable conflict of war aims among the Great Powers themselves found their counterpart in the explosion of the contradictory formulas that had variously and often irresponsibly accompanied the Italian participation in the war. Versailles proved the nemesis of those contradictions. It was tragic that Wilson, who, in early 1919, had been an Italian "hero," chose Italy's territorial claims as the testing ground for the reassertion of his moral principles already shattered by the lethal blows of Anglo-French diplomatic "realism" at Versailles. Relatively "petty" as it may have appeared to internationalists and *rinunciatari* ("renunciators" were men like Salvemini and Bissolati who would have given up Fiume toward a pacification that might have insured fruitful co-operation between Italy and the "successor states" of the disintegrated Hapsburg Empire, chief among them Yugoslavia), the "Fiume Question" exasperated Italian national feeling and remained an open international problem until after 1922.

1919–20: Gabriele D'Annunzio's "March on Fiume" in September 1919 was an act of defiance against both the internal Italian and the international European "order." Important as it was in itself, it became a prefiguring, if not a model, for Mussolini's "March on Rome" three years later. Between those two "marches" lay a full cycle of Italy's post-War crisis. Italian nationalism had its first activistic demiurge in the warrior-poet D'Annunzio. It was only after December 1920, when D'Annunzio's *bête noire,* Giovanni Giolitti—now once again returned to power—forcibly dislodged him from Fiume, that the "star" of Mussolini began truly rising on the nationalist horizon in Italy. In the meantime, obscurely but strenuously, great efforts were being made to resolve the larger Italian national crisis by other means. The elections of 1919 had brought to the fore a powerful new mass party—Don Luigi Sturzo's Partito Popolare Italiano (PPI): Italian Catholics now appeared on the political scene in full autonomous force, with a Christian democratic program and an able leadership. Hereafter they were a real force to be reckoned with. Italian socialism had undergone its own internal crisis which had been exacerbated by the impact of the Bolshevik Revolution in Russia. Already splintered between Maximalists, reformists, and centralists, Italian socialism began to feel the impact of Lenin's Marxism and of the Russian revolution itself. In August-September 1920, through a combination of spontaneous action and the inspiration of a small but energetic group of Marxist intellectuals led by Antonio Gramsci, the workers in the giant industrial plants of North Italy, particularly the Fiat factories in Turin, attempted their own brand of "revolution": a sort of active sitdown strike through which they occupied the factories and attempted to run them on an independent basis, minus "management" and highly placed technicians. While Giolitti took a "neutralist" view of the occupation of the factories, all the conservative classes in North and South Italy saw the specter of Communism looming over Italy. The strike ended not by "bombardment," as some reactionaries would have wished (provided their own factories and property were not involved), but by exhaustion and negotiation. But the powerful North Italian industrial and middle classes and the large South Italian agrarian *notables* (some of whom had seen their lands occupied by the peasants) never forgot or forgave the experience of September 1920. And they swore "vengeance" on Giolitti who, they felt by the end of 1920, had dared leave the "Communist" workers alone and had given orders to fire upon Fiume if the patriot-poet did not obey the ultimatum to abandon it. Thus a "great fear" was engendered among conservative, patriotic, and nationalistic bourgeois classes in Italy, and with it, messianic expectations for a "deliverer." Mussolini was as if waiting in the wings for just such a mood of "collective" frustration in order to step once again upon the stage of Italian history.

1921–22: Mussolini had founded his Fascio in the spring of 1919, but for practically two years his band of followers had had neither a clear-cut program nor effective leadership. Mussolini himself had been as eclectic during this period as ever: he had spoken of revolution and republic in the same breath that he had invoked "law and order"; he called himself both socialist and a nationalist; he had supported with equal conviction D'Annunzio's occupation of Fiume and the Turin workers' occupation of the Fiat factories; he had spoken admiringly of Lenin while continuing to use the language of Bakunin; he hated the middle classes and wanted to save them. Few had taken him seriously—until after the turn of 1921. And then his day and that of his movement arrived, bringing not peace, when national pacification seemed on its way, but the sword of violent action. Knowing and even asserting that, despite the fact that an Italian Communist Party was founded at Livorno in January 1921 by Antonio Gramsci, Palmiro Togliatti, Angelo Tasca and their friends, the danger of Communism in Italy had vanished after the fall of 1920, Mussolini continued to "fight" against it for agitational purposes, to keep the conservative and nationalist classes in "fear and trembling" and at his "disposal." In 1921, under the auspices of Giolittian elections, thirty-five Fascist deputies entered the Italian parliament, but with obstructionist intentions that not even the Communists dared entertain. Through the governments of Giolitti and then of his successors, Ivanoe Bonomi and Luigi Facta, Mussolini's Fascist squads succeeded, in and out of Parliament, by verbal violence and direct action, by intrigue and threats, in keeping Italy in a state of tension and new crisis. While liberals, democrats, socialists, and Catholics stood in wonder and suspense, incapable or unwilling to create a united opposition, Fascism gained strategic mastery over North and Central Italy and large urban centers of the South.

1922: By the summer and fall of this fateful year the great new "Italian question" was *not whether but when and how* Mussolini would come to "official" power in Italy. Machiavellian "fox" that he was, Mussolini knew quite well that he had neutralized most of his irreconcilable opponents in the liberal, socialist, and Catholic camps, even as he had won over to his "flanks," if not to his ranks, the bulk of the conservative, reactionary, and militaristic elements of Italian society. The various strata of the middle classes were gripped by a combination of anachronistic fears of "bolshevism" and secret expectations of the re-establishment of social peace and "law and order" through the "strong hand" (*la mano forte*) of a central national "power," be it the monarchy or a new charismatic personality. In 1922, therefore, while he still had many complex tactical problems to solve—including that of retaining leadership of the Fascist Party against the ambitious maneuvers of the "total extremists" and "hotheads" in the movement—Mussolini faced one last and decisive question of strategy: Would King Victor Emmanuel III, the constitutional monarch of Italy and commander-in-chief of all armed forces of the state, be with or against Mussolini and Fascism when the supreme moment of the assumption of power arose? For a while this, for Mussolini, was the riddle of the Sphinx, but by October 1922, he had unraveled it almost beyond any question. Under the threat of a Fascist "revolution," the King would have to be faced with the dilemma of losing either his head or his throne—or of keeping both. Mussolini, therefore, somehow managed to impress upon the King the "fact" that an open "civil war" that might result in Italy from royal armed opposition to a Fascist "March on Rome" might have consequences for his security, if not for his life, while even a purely political resistance on his part might lead Fascism to sponsor a dynastic *coup de main* that would place the Duke of Aosta on the throne, the consequences of which would be much the same—facilitation of the success of the Fascist "revolution." As the Fascist legions began to take the road to Rome, on the fateful night of October 27–28, 1922, Victor Emmanuel III chose to lose nothing, refusing to sign the order for a state of siege presented to him by the last, insignificant Liberal Prime Minister of Italy, Luigi Facta. In the morning, the Fascist troops, minus their Duce, who still warily stayed on in Milan until the official telegraphic "invitation" should arrive, marched on Rome. The royal "invitation to form a Government" came to Mussolini more or less "on schedule," and the following day the Duce of Fascism took a sleeping-car compartment on a train from Milan to Rome. The former anarchistic-revolutionary socialist leader wore a bourgeois top-hat to his first act of official acceptance and of formal obeisance to a King whose attempted assassination he had defined in 1912 as the calculated risk of "royal business." For the masses of the Italian people, astonished, angry, or resigned as they may have been, the first open evidence of Mussolini's conquest of power was a Fascist parade through the streets of the Eternal City in which the black-shirted legions were led by the Duce and his Quadrumvirs. Until confronted with this show of force, the freely elected representatives of the people in the Italian parliament had been in the dark as to the royal-Fascist maneuver that had destroyed their mandate, and the masses of workers and peasants who constituted the bulk of the Italian people had been ignorant of the *coup de main* that had brought to power this new "master" of their lives. The Fascist "counterrevolution against a revolution that had never occurred" had succeeded. It was thus that on a sordid October day of 1922 Liberal Italy died. Within slightly more than two years, somewhere between the assassination of the leader of the Socialist parliamentary resistance, Giacomo Matteotti, on June 10, 1924, and Mussolini's pronunciamento of total victory over all opposition in his speech of January 3, 1925, Italy was obscurely converted into a Fascist totalitarian State.

SUGGESTIONS FOR ADDITIONAL READING

NOTE: This is not a bibliography on the five periods or phases of modern Italian history—the Risorgimento, the post-Risorgimento, the Liberal era, the Fascist period, and post-Fascism—which, in one way or another, are all historical points of reference or are touched upon in the selections of readings in the text. A minimum of suggestions is offered in the hope that they may lead to further individual exploration of problems in modern Italian history not fully or adequately treated in the Introduction, the analytical chronology, and the readings themselves. Whenever possible, the references proceed from general works to special studies in English first, if they are deemed of sufficient value, then, of course, in Italian, French, or German, unless a strict adherence to a formal order would violate substantive importance or relevance.

General Works on Nineteenth- and Twentieth-century Italian History:

Luigi Salvatorelli, *A Concise History of Italy,* tr. Bernard Miall (New York, 1939), Chapters XVIII–XIX, gives a schematic but useful compendium which, incidentally, reads much better in the Italian original: *Sommario della storia d'Italia* (1938; 11th ed. Turin, 1965). A "running" summary for a very general first orientation is in H. Hearder and D. P. Waley, eds., *A Short History of Italy* (Cambridge, England, 1963), Chapter VI–VII. In Italian, two "standard" works on the period from the French Revolution to the establishment of the Italian Republic after the fall of Fascism are: Franco Catalano, Ruggiero Moscati, and Franco Valsecchi, *L'Italia nel Risorgimento, 1789–1870* (Milan, 1964), and Giacomo Perticone, *L'Italia contemporanea,*

1871–1948 (Milan, 1964). For a wise and brilliantly written "epilogue" on Italian history, following a profound analysis of its medieval and Renaissance developments, see Leonardo Olschki, *The Genius of Italy* (New York, 1949), pp. 430–65. In approach, style, and substance, Olschki's work ought to be compared to G. A. Borgese, *Goliath: The March of Fascism* (New York, 1938), which revisits the long-range historical, cultural, and "moral" foundations of Italian Fascism. A piece of journalistic *bravura* by Luigi Barzini, *The Italians* (New York, 1964), has gained more notoriety than it deserves: with its sensation-mongering impressionistic historical exaggerations and distortions it is almost a caricature of Borgese's moralistic but *engagé* reconstruction and amounts to an attempt to reduce Italian history to an abstract portrait of the fixed "eternal character" of "Italians" through the complementary techniques of the bedroom- and public square-views of their "manners and morals." After glancing at Barzini, it might be well to restore some historical balance by reading, analyzing, and meditating upon the reflections of a modern democratic aristocrat, Carlo Sforza, *Contemporary Italy: Its Intellectual and Moral Origins,* tr. Drake and Denise De Kay (New York, 1944): Count Sforza had a vast cultural preparation and long diplomatic experience first under Giolitti in 1920–21, then as an anti-Fascist exile, and, finally, as a diplomat in the service of the Italian Republic.

Three works in Italian and one in French deserve to be read by serious students of 19th and 20th century Italian history: Adolfo Omodeo, *L'Età del Risorgimento* (Naples, 1931; new ed., 1960), the work of a "Crocean" liberal historian who attempted to present the whole "age of the Risorgimento" on lines analogous to those in Benedetto Croce's *A History of Italy from 1871 to 1915,* tr. Cecilia M. Ady (Oxford, 1929) and *History of Europe in the Nineteenth Century,* tr. Henry Furst (New York, 1933; new ed., 1963); Egidio Reale, *Le origini dell'Italia moderna* (Zürich, 1944), a democratic neo-Mazzinian interpretation reflecting the anti-Fascist

Resistance in exile and its review of the pre-Fascist past in the light of the national problems of the emerging post-Fascist period; Luigi Salvatorelli, *Pensiero e azione del Risorgimento* (new ed., Turin, 1963), a concise reconstruction of the Risorgimento as thought and action; Georges Bourgin, *La formation de l'Unité italienne* (Paris, 1929) [Italian translation, *La formazione dell'Unità italiana* (Perugia-Venice, 1930)], with a preface by Robert Michels, is a much ignored but very valuable work by one of the few and best among French historians of modern Italy: in his work, Bourgin adumbrates some of the "revisionist" themes of the post-Fascist period.

For contrasting examples of Anglo-American historical writing on modern Italy, see the slim but well meditated volume by Elizabeth Wiskemann, *Italy* (New York, 1947); Cecil J. S. Sprigge, *The Development of Modern Italy* (New Haven, 1944), a serious historical appraisal, chiefly of Giolitti, the First World War and post-war crisis, and the rise and decline of Fascism; A. J. Whyte, *The Evolution of Modern Italy* (Oxford, 1950), is chiefly political history from 1715 to 1920 more or less conventionally treated; René Albrecht-Carrié, *Italy from Napoleon to Mussolini* (New York, 1950), a critique, as much as political-diplomatic history, in which, in quasi-revisionist fashion, the negative elements of nineteenth- and twentieth-century Italian history are so highlighted as to constitute almost predetermined links in a chain of Italian developments that runs from one to the other of the two "high personages" in the title of the work; Maurice F. Neufeld, *Italy: School for Awakening Countries. The Italian Labor Movement in Its Political, Social, and Economic Setting from 1800 to 1960* (Ithaca, N.Y., 1961), a rich and challenging contribution to modern Italian social history studied within the poles of Italian national questions and of the problems faced by the emerging nations, African and Asian, of the post-Colonial period of world history. The best single-volume introduction to modern and contemporary Italian problems is by H.

Stuart Hughes, *The United States and Italy* (rev. ed. Cambridge, Massachusetts, 1965), which, despite its title, deals infinitely less with political-diplomatic "relations" between the United States and Italy than with social, economic, and political problems of the Fascist and post-Fascist periods. Ernesto Ragionieri, ed., *L'Italia giudicata, 1861–1945, ovvero la storia degli italiani scritta dagli altri* (Bari, 1969) is an illuminating collection of writings and judgments on modern Italy by non-Italian "outsiders," European and American, from the Risorgimento to the fall of Fascism. For selections dealing chiefly with political history, see Shepard B. Clough and Salvatore Saladino, eds., *A History of Modern Italy: Documents, Readings, and Commentary* (New York, 1968).

The Age of the Risorgimento:

The historical literature on the Risorgimento as an Italian cultural epoch and as a political phenomenon is vast and complex and therefore beyond any brief biblio-historiographical summation. For preliminary bibliographical orientation to works which, on the whole, are not referred to below, see: G. M. Dutcher *et al.*, eds., *A Guide to Historical Literature* (New York, 1937), pp. 675–80; G. F. Howe, *et al.*, eds., *The American Historical Association's Guide to Historical Literature* (New York, 1961), pp. 533–36; Kent Roberts Greenfield, "The Historiography of the Risorgimento since 1920," *Journal of Modern History,* VII, No. 1 (March 1935), 49–67; Walter Maturi, *Interpretazioni del Risorgimento* (Turin, 1962), an almost exhaustive, authoritative, and critical compendium on practically all aspects of the Risorgimento. In English, for the problems connected with post-1945 reinterpretations of the Risorgimento, see the documentation in the following two articles: A. William Salomone, "The Risorgimento between Ideology and History: The Political Myth of *Rivoluzione mancata,*" *American Historical Review,* LXVIII, No. 1 (October 1962), 38–56; John Cammett,

"Gramsci and the Risorgimento," Appendix to *Antonio Gramsci and the Rise of Italian Communism* (Stanford, 1967), pp. 313–22. In Italian, the impact of the neo-Marxist historiography on the Risorgimento is critically analyzed in the following: Rosario Romeo, *Risorgimento e capitalismo* (Bari, 1959); Umberto Marcelli, *Interpretazioni del Risorgimento* (2nd ed. Bologna, 1962); Vittorio Frosini, *Breve storia della critica al marxismo in Italia* (Catania, 1965).

The better to appreciate what has occurred in the post-Fascist, Italian and non-Italian, reinterpretations of the Risorgimento in so far as approach, emphases, and the quest for meaning are concerned, it might be well to read or re-read some of the old "classic" works first, among which the best and most accessible are the following: Bolton King, *History of Italian Unity* (2 vols. London, 1912); William Roscoe Thayer, *The Life and Times of Cavour* (2 vols. Boston and New York, 1911); George Macaulay Trevelyan, *Garibaldi and the Making of Italy* (London, 1911); Kent Roberts Greenfield, *Economics and Liberalism in the Risorgimento. A Study of Nationalism in Lombardy* (Baltimore, 1934; new ed., 1965); G. F. H. and J. Berkeley, *Italy in the Making, 1815–1848* (3 vols. Cambridge, England, 1932–40); Gaetano Salvemini, *Mazzini* [1905; 1925], tr. I. M. Rawson (Stanford, 1957). For a preliminary orientation to the post-1945 "new history" of the Risorgimento period, see the article "Italy" in *The New Cambridge Modern History* (1960), X, 552–76, written by Denis Mack Smith, the most outstanding contemporary British historian of modern Italy, whose brilliant, if in part controversial, monographic analysis of *Cavour and Garibaldi: 1860. A Study in Political Conflict* (Cambridge, England, 1954) is a truly original piece of historical writing quite in contrast with the portraits of Cavour and Garibaldi penned by Thayer and Trevelyan and a number of other modern biographers of the two heroes of the Risorgimento at its culminating moment in 1860. For two newer studies that approach Cavour and Garibaldi, respectively, from different angles of biohistorical vision and are, at the same time, in some contrast to Mack Smith's interpretation, see Ettore Passerin d'Entrèves, *L'ultima battaglia politica di Cavour. I problemi dell'unificazione italiana* (Turin, 1956); Christopher Hibbert, *Garibaldi and His Enemies* (Boston-Toronto, 1966). Noteworthy for the elaboration on his thesis that "success spoiled the Risorgimento" even before the fateful encounter between Cavour and Garibaldi in 1860, see Raymond Grew, *A Sterner Plan for Italian Unity. The Italian National Society in the Risorgimento* (Princeton, 1963). For readings on the politics of the Risorgimento period, see Denis Mack Smith, ed., *The Making of Italy, 1796–1870* (New York, 1968).

In Italian, two differently conceived but equally excellent multivolume histories of the Risorgimento are: Cesare Spellanzon, *Storia del Risorgimento e dell'Unità d'Italia* (7 vols. Milan, 1933–60), a huge, uniquely documented and beautifully illustrated "classic" which had reached only 1848–49 when its author died: Giorgio Candeloro, *Storia dell'Italia moderna* (5 vols., Milan, 1956–68), a progressively moderate neo-Marxist reconstruction of modern Italian history from 1700 to 1871, sophisticated in approach, rich in data, and challenging in analysis of social and ideological currents. Among the most recent and useful collections of contemporary documents on the Risorgimento are: Cesare Giardini, ed., *Il Risorgimento italiano* (*1796–1861*) (Milan, 1958); Paolo Alatri, ed., *L'Unità d'Italia* (2 vols. Rome, 1959). For two studies that attempt, each in its special fashion and for its special historical-empirical purpose, to view the Risorgimento and the making of Italian unity not merely in their European context but in "world dimensions," see Maurice F. Neufeld, *Poor Countries and Authoritarian Rule* (Ithaca, New York, 1965); Alberto Caracciolo, *Le istituzioni del nuovo Stato nelle dimensioni mondiali* (Milan, 1966).

The Post-Risorgimento and the Liberal Era:

On the post-Risorgimento considered as the "long period" from the completion of political unity to the outbreak of the First World War, see the appropriate sections or chapters in the volumes cited under "General Works." The most original and brilliant single piece of historical writing—truly a masterpiece—on the post-Risorgimento is the work of Federico Chabod, *Storia della politica estera italiana dal 1870 al 1896. Le premesse* (Bari, 1951). In this study, which was to be only the first volume of a vast reconstruction of Italian foreign policy from the occupation of Rome in 1870 to the fall of Crispi in 1896, Chabod succeeded in attaining, if (due to his premature death in 1960) only for the immediate aftermath of the Risorgimento, that rare fusion of political and cultural history that seems to be the ideal-model for all serious students of modern Italian history. An excellent collection of documents through which most of the post-Risorgimento period can be intelligently studied is by Nino Valeri, ed., *La lotta politica in Italia dell'Unità al 1925* (2nd ed. Florence, 1958).

Varying in treatment and substance, each of the following works in English will be found helpful toward clarification of aspects of post-Risorgimento history: Denis Mack Smith, *Italy. A Modern History* (Ann Arbor, 1959; new ed. rev., 1969), fascinating and exasperating at the same time, this book, like other works by its author on modern Italy, is a *sine qua non* for those who want to grapple with the problems of late nineteenth- and twentieth-century Italian history; Christopher Seton-Watson, *Italy from Liberalism to Fascism, 1870–1925* (London, 1967), neo-liberal, well-documented, essentially political history; John A. Thayer, *Italy and the Great War. Politics and Culture, 1870–1915* (Madison-Milwaukee, 1964), anti-revisionistic, detailed, thoughtful, neo-Crocean, it ought to be read, at least in part, as a sort of counterpart to Mack Smith's book; A. William Salomone, *Italy in the Giolittian Era. Italian Democracy in the Making, 1900–1914* (Philadelphia, 1960). Covering more or less the same periods of time are the following: Maurice Vaussard, *Histoire de l'Italie contemporaine, 1870–1946* (Paris, 1950), a French liberal Catholic view of the period; Ivanoe Bonomi, *La politica italiana da Porta Pia a Vittorio Veneto, 1870–1918* (Turin, 1946), the work of a former reformist socialist who, in 1912, was expelled from the Italian Socialist Party at the instigation of Mussolini, was Italian Prime Minister in 1921–22, and again an important political figure after the fall of Fascism in Italy; Alberto Carocci, *L'Età giolittiana* (Turin, 1961), a neo-Marxist interpretation of the Giolittian era.

The following four contrasting views on the character of post-Risorgimento liberalism, the working of the parliamentary regime, and the vicissitudes of the political struggle in post-Risorgimento Italy ought to constitute a challenging exercise in comparative history: Guido De Ruggiero, *The History of European Liberalism,* tr. R. G. Collingwood (London, 1927; new ed. Boston, 1964), Chapter IV on Italian liberalism; Gaetano Mosca, *The Ruling Class,* tr. Hannah D. Kahn (New York, 1939), a work of theorization on a European historical level of the author's empirical observations of the Italian parliamentary regime first ennunciated in his *Teorica* (1884); Vilfredo Pareto, *The Ruling Class in Italy before 1900,* ed. Giuseppe Prezzolini (New York, 1950), two articles and two "political letters" in Italian and French castigating the Italian parliamentary regime, in which the author, the future organic theorist of elitism, who was later claimed as one of his "teachers" by Mussolini, foreshadows some of the principles of his famous *Trattato di sociologia generale* (1916); Guglielmo Ferrero, *Principles of Power,* tr. Theodore R. Jaekel (New York, 1942), advanced the curious "legitimacy" theory as the sustaining principle of power and that, therefore, "Philippism" (derived from the strange status of Louis Philippe in France) represented, in its Italian variety, a hybrid between constitutional and royal, dynastic and popular, system of government that could not last—and, in a sense, led to Fascism.

For treatments of economic, social, and ideological history of the pre-Fascist period, see particularly the following: Shepard B. Clough, *The Economic History of Modern Italy* (New York, 1964), basic for an understanding of the economic development of post-Risorgimento Italy; Gino Luzzatto, *L'economia italiana dal 1861 al 1914.* Vol. I: *1861–1894* (Milan, 1963), the work of the master economic historian of modern Italy; Amintore Fanfani, ed., *L'economia italiana dal 1861 al 1961. Studi nel primo centenario dell'Unità d'Italia* (Milan, 1961), a collection of authoritative studies in Italian economic history through the first centenary of unity. Two very interesting documentary collections on North and South are: Rosario Villari, ed., *Il Sud nella storia d'Italia* (Bari, 1961); Luciano Cafagna, ed., *Il Nord nella storia d'Italia* (Bari, 1962). The most authoritative study of the Questione del Mezzogiorno (Problem of the South) is available in the original German and in an Italian translation: Friedrich Vöchting, *Die italienische Südfrage* (Berlin, 1951) [*La questione meridionale* (Naples, 1955)]. The old work by Robert F. Foerster, *The Italian Emigration in Our Time* (Cambridge, Massachusetts, 1919) is possibly still the best on a vast and complex mass-movement of Italians before the coming of Fascism. On Italian socialism, the best short general history is now that by Gaetano Arfè, *Storia del socialismo italiano, 1892–1926* (Turin, 1965), and it ought to be made available in English; W. Hilton-Young, *The Italian Left* (London, 1949) is readable but perhaps a bit too generic in parts; Richard Hostetter, *The Italian Socialist Movement. Origins, 1860–1882* (Princeton, 1958), upon completion, through at least to 1914, should become "standard" in English; Salomone, *Italy in the Giolittian Era, cit.,* Chapter V–VII, contains a history of Italian socialism during the Giolittian era. Gastone Manacorda, ed., *Il socialismo nella storia d'Italia*

(Bari, 1966) is a useful anthology on Italian socialism from the Risorgimento to 1948.

On the problems of Church and State in Italy: Arturo Carlo Jemolo, *Church and State in Italy, 1850–1950,* tr. David Moore (Oxford, 1960); the two works by Luigi Sturzo, *Italy and Fascism,* tr. Barbara B. Carter (new ed. New York, 1966), and *Italy and the Coming World* (New York, 1945). Among the best older studies are the two works by S. William Halperin, *The Separation of Church and State in Italian Thought from Cavour to Mussolini* (Chicago, 1937), and *Italy and the Vatican at War* (Chicago, 1939). On Catholicism and socialism in the latter part of the 19th century, see Lillian Parker Wallace, *Leo XIII and the Rise of Socialism* (Durham, 1966). For some special monographs that carry the history of political Catholicism through the Fascist regime, see: D. A. Binchy, *Church and State in Fascist Italy* (London, 1941), a "classic" in its own right by a liberal Catholic; Leicester C. Webb, *Church and State in Italy, 1947–1957* (London-New York, 1957), a sort of sequel to Binchy's work, but neither in dimensions nor in substance really close to the work of the "master"; Richard A. Webster, *The Cross and the Fasces: Christian Democracy and Fascism in Italy* (Stanford, 1960), very able fusion of fruits of new research in problems of political Catholicism and the religious policy of Fascism; Elisa A. Carrillo, *Alcide De Gasperi. The Long Apprenticeship* (South Bend, Indiana, 1965), a promising first volume of a biography of the Christian Democratic leader of the post-Fascist period. Pietro Scoppola, ed. *Chiesa e Stato nella storia d'Italia* (Bari, 1967) is a fine collection of materials on Church and State in Italy from Cavour to De Gasperi.

On the role of Italian culture and the varieties of intellectual life during the liberal era and the early twentieth century, see: H. Stuart Hughes, *Consciousness and Society. The Reorientation of European Social Thought, 1890–1930* (New York, 1958), which contains enlightening sections dealing with the European contexts of

Crocean Idealism, the elitist critiques of Mosca and Pareto, and the foundations of Gramsci's Marxism; James Joll, *Three Intellectuals in Politics* (New York, 1960), devotes Chapter III to F. T. Marinetti, Futurism, and Fascism; Salomone, *Italy in the Giolittian Era,* Chapter VIII deals with the rise of nationalist ideologies and the soil of the anti-Giolittian cultural rebellion; Mario Praz, *The Romantic Agony,* tr. Angus Davidson (Cleveland-New York, 1965), on *fin de siècle* decadentism and Gabriele D'Annunzio. Among the best post-1945 critical works issued in Italy dealing with intellectual and cultural history, literary movements and philosophy, are: Eugenio Garin, *Cronache di filosofia italiana* (new ed. 2 vols. Bari, 1966); Carlo Salinari, *Miti e coscienza del decadentismo italiano* (Milan, 1962); Michele Abbate, *La filosofia di Benedetto Croce e la crisi della società italiana* (new ed. Bari, 1966), a Marxist critique on Croce's influence during the Giolittian era.

On the crisis of 1914–15 and the Italian participation in the First World War: for diplomatic history, see the "classic" work by Luigi Albertini, *The Origins of the War of 1914,* tr. Isabella M. Massey (3 vols. Oxford, 1952–57), Vol. II, Chapter VI; Vol. III, Chapters VI–VII. New archival materials have been utilized in the article by Leo Valiani, "Italian-Austro-Hungarian Negotiation, 1914–1915," *Journal of Contemporary History,* I, No. 3 (1966), 113–36. On the grave internal crisis of the Italian national conscience during the period of neutrality, the work of Brunello Vigezzi, *L'Italia di fronte alla prima Guerra mondiale.* Vol. I. *L'Italia neutrale* (Milan-Naples, 1966), gives every promise of becoming "definitive." For a fascinating collection of materials on the vast-ranging material and moral repercussions of the Great War in Italy, see the work by Mario Schettini, ed., *La prima Guerra mondiale. Storia e letteratura* (Florence, 1965). Giovanna Procacci, "Italy from Interventionism to Fascism, 1917–19," in *Journal of Contemporary History,* III, No. 4 (1968), 153–76, deals with the critical passage from war to peace. The most sustained, and perhaps the best, reconstruction of the immediate post-War years and the series of diplomatic, political, and moral elements involved in the great Italian crisis that nurtured the rise of Fascism is in Roberto Vivarelli, *Il Dopoguerra in Italia e l'avvento del Fascismo* (1918–22). Vol. I: *Dalla fine della guerra all'impresa di Fiume* (Naples, 1967). On the fearful transmutation of the literary-poetic expressions of the pre-1914 Italian cultural rebellion into the ideological-political rhetoric of the myth of the "great war" as a function of hallucinatory visions of an organic and "totalitarian" metamorphosis of Italian life and society, see Mario Isnenghi, *Il mito della grande guerra da Marinetti a Malaparte* (Bari, 1970).

Italy in the Fascist Period:

No attempt will be made here to treat bibliographically the rise of Fascism, the evolution of the dictatorship, and the institutionalization of the totalitarian regime; for some of the latest and most significant references, see the bibliographies following my articles on "Mussolini" and "Fascism" in *The New Catholic Encyclopedia* (Washington, D.C., 1966), Vol. V, 843–47; Vol. X, 141–43. The best brief history of Italian Fascism is, of course, that by Federico Chabod, *A History of Italian Fascism,* tr. Muriel Grindrod (London, 1961), which contains an exhaustive bibliographical survey. The work by Ernst Nolte, *Three Faces of Fascism. Action Française-Italian Fascism-National Socialism* (New York-San Francisco, 1965), studies Italian Fascism in a European context. In Italian, the best work on the Fascist period as a whole is by Luigi Salvatorelli and Giovanni Mira, *Storia d'Italia nel periodo fascista* (Turin, 1957). A new approach, with emphasis on social and ideological history of the Fascist era, is contained in Enzo Santarelli, *Storia del movimento e del regime fascista* (2 vols., Rome, 1967). For a brilliant, though as yet not fully appreciated, reconstruction of events, personalities, and intrigues connected with the "March on Rome," see Antonino Répaci, *Marcia su Roma. Miti e realtà* (2 vols. Rome, 1963), the second volume of which reproduces extensive documentary materials drawn from the official and private papers of Luigi Facta, the last prime minister of the pre-Fascist liberal regime. Alberto Acquarone, *L'organizzazione dello Stato totalitario* (Turin, 1965) is the best work to date on the structure and organization of the Italian Fascist totalitarian state. A useful anthology on Fascism, particularly for the reproduction of literary self-images by both exponents and opponents of the regime, in Costanzo Casucci, ed., *Il Fascismo* (Bologna, 1961). In English, Herman Finer, *Mussolini's Italy* (London, 1935) is still useful if, in some crucial parts, no longer as "authoritative" as it once was. The following works in English, all more or less of recent vintage, testify to a new, lively historical interest in the study of Fascism both as a world phenomenon and as an Italian "invention" of the interwar period: Eugen Weber, *Varieties of Fascism* (Princeton, N.J., 1964), a brilliant little work of reinterpretation between social structures and the politics of dissension; Walter Laqueur and George L. Mosse, eds., *Journal of Contemporary History,* Vol. 1, No. 1 (1966), a symposium dedicated to "International Fascism, 1920–1945," contains illuminating essays by G. L. Mosse, Adrian Lyttleton, and Hugh Seton-Watson directly bearing on the genesis, development, and nature of Italian Fascism; John Weiss, *The Fascist Tradition* (New York, 1967), a partly controversial but wholly stimulating interpretation with emphasis on the function of social struggles and with an inner theme that "to Mussolini goes the credit for inventing the totalitarian state." Alan Cassels, *Fascist Italy* (New York, 1968) is a slim but carefully conceived interpretation of the historical and innovative elements in the Fascist movement. The following three works are all anthological-interpretative, each in its way reflecting newer, more "sophisticated," approaches to European and Italian Fascism: Nathaniel Green, ed., *Fas-*

cism: An Anthology (New York, 1968), contains a special section dedicated to "The Italian Example" (pp. 36–112); S. J. Woolf, ed., *European Fascism* (New York, 1968) and *The Nature of Fascism* (New York, 1968), both of which reflect some of the latest international-historical preoccupations with the phenomenon of Fascism as a "total" as well as totalitarian movement of the twentieth century. On Fascist foreign policy, see the following three works: Gaetano Salvemini, *Prelude to World War II* (Garden City, N.Y., 1953); Elizabeth Wiskemann, *The Rome-Berlin Axis. A History of the Relations between Mussolini and Hitler* (New York-London, 1949); H. Stuart Hughes, "The Early Diplomacy of Italian Fascism: 1922–1932," in Gordon A. Craig and Felix Gilbert, eds., *The Diplomats, 1919–1939* (Princeton, 1953). The best biography of Mussolini is now that by Ivone Kirkpatrick, *Mussolini. A Study in Power* (New York, 1964). Renzo De Felice is now working on a five-volume biography of Mussolini; to date (1970), De Felice has published the first three volumes: *Mussolini il rivoluzionario, 1883–1920* (Turin, 1965), *Mussolini il fascista, 1921–1925* (Turin, 1966), *Mussolini il fascista, 1925–1929* (Turin, 1968). The best work on the waning and the end of Mussolini's career is that by F. W. Deakin, *The Brutal Friendship. Mussolini, Hitler, and the Fall of Fascism* (London, 1962), of which there is now available a brief version entitled *The Six Hundred Days of Mussolini* (Garden City, N.Y., 1966).

Anti-Fascism, the Resistance, and Reappraisals:

The documentation on Italian anti-Fascism now available in Italian centers and elsewhere in Europe promises to render the movement, particularly in its culminating aspects and phases of the armed Resistance, a new "unit" for the study of modern Italian history. The best work in English is now that by Charles F. Delzell, *Mussolini's Enemies. The Italian Anti-Fascist Resistance* (Princeton, 1961). One of the few rare collections in English, still superbly rich and useful, for an understanding of anti-Fascist activities and writings to the eve of the Second World War, is that by Frances Keene, ed., *Neither Liberty nor Bread. The Meaning and Tragedy of Fascism* (New York-London, 1940). For reappraisals of the Italian Resistance movement after the first decade of its victory over Fascism, see Aldo Garosci *et al., Il secondo Risorgimento* (Rome, 1955). See also Luciano Pasqualini and Mario Saccenti, eds., *Due Risorgimenti: Pagine di storia italiana, 1796–1947* (Bologna, 1965), which, through an anthological approach, seeks to demonstrate the historical and spiritual continuity between the classic, "first" Risorgimento and the "second" subsumed under the anti-Fascist Resistance movement. Frank Rosengarten, *The Italian Anti-Fascist Press, 1919–1945* (Cleveland, 1968) is an excellent study on one of the chief instruments–the underground press–in the fight against Fascism. Paolo Alatri, ed., *L'antifascismo italiano* (Rome, 1965), an anthology of anti-Fascist writings. Luigi Cortesi, ed., *Lettere di antifascisti dal carcere* (2 vols. Rome, 1962), a collection of letters written from prison by a large and varied number of opponents of Fascism. A unique documentary collection of last letters, writings, messages, and intimate confessions that, together, spell a collective moral history of the values immanent in the Italian anti-Fascist Resistance is to be found in Piero Malvezzi and Giovanni Pirelli, eds., *Lettere di condannati a morte della Resistenza italiana (8 settembre 1943–25 aprile 1945)*, with a preface by Enzo Enriques Agnoletti (Turin, 1952). For a European and world perspective on the generation that saw the rise and fall of Fascism in Italy, see Armando Saitta, ed., *Storia e miti del '900. Antologia di critica storica* (2nd ed. Bari, 1961).

Three critical bibliographical essays in English might be found useful toward further exploration of historical literature relating to the recent Italian past: Charles F. Delzell, "Italian Historical Scholarship: A Decade of Recovery and Development, 1945–1955," *Journal of*

Modern History, XXVIII (1956), 374–88; Emiliana P. Noether, "Italy Reviews Its Fascist Past," *American Historical Review,* LXI (1956), 877–99; Claudio Pavone, "Italy: Trends and Problems," *Journal of Contemporary History,* II (1967), 49–77.

INDEX